Climate Change

Climate Change

IMPACTS AND ADAPTATION AT REGIONAL AND LOCAL SCALES

ANDREW **STURMAN,** HERVÉ **QUÉNOL**

OXFORD
UNIVERSITY PRESS

OXFORD
UNIVERSITY PRESS

Great Clarendon Street, Oxford, OX2 6DP,
United Kingdom

Oxford University Press is a department of the University of Oxford.
It furthers the University's objective of excellence in research, scholarship,
and education by publishing worldwide. Oxford is a registered trade mark of
Oxford University Press in the UK and in certain other countries

© Andrew Sturman and Hervé Quénol 2024

Published in the United States of America by Oxford University Press
198 Madison Avenue, New York, NY 10016, United States of America

British Library Cataloguing in Publication Data
Data available

Library of Congress Control Number: 2023937655

ISBN 978–0–19–880750–6

Printed in the UK by
Bell & Bain Ltd., Glasgow

How to Use This Book

HELPING YOU TO LEARN ABOUT CLIMATE CHANGE

Climate Change: Impacts and Adaptation at Regional and Local Scales provides a rich learning experience in which issues and concepts are brought to life and examined globally, regionally, and locally, and in which you are guided and supported to become active, critical thinkers. We've included a number of key features to make this book as effective a learning tool as possible. The features and digital resources are included in the book to ensure that you understand each topic and, importantly, that you can use this knowledge to form your own ideas and strategies. These features include the following:

TO HELP YOU MASTER THE ESSENTIALS

CHAPTER OUTLINES

An outline at the beginning of each chapter serves as a mini table of contents, indicating each issue and topic to be discussed. Use this feature to navigate your way through each chapter and find your way to important discussions.

LEARNING OUTCOMES

Learning outcomes posted at the beginning of each chapter provide a framework of what you will learn by the end of reading the chapter.

TO MAKE THE STUDY OF CLIMATE CHANGE RELEVANT TO YOU

CASE STUDY BOXES

Case study boxes throughout the book provide practical illustrations of the impacts of climate change on both the human and the natural environment, as well as development of adaptation strategies at the local and regional scales, reinforcing concepts introduced in each chapter and inviting you to think critically about current events.

If you're reading the main text and find yourself thinking 'How does this relate to real-world events?', read some of these case studies to see how climate change strategies are being applied around the globe.

TO REINFORCE YOUR LEARNING

BOLDED KEY CONCEPTS

Each chapter includes bolded key concepts, which correspond to glossary definitions. Use these concepts as an easy way of checking whether you understand main definitions, and as a prompt for going back to reread any sections or ideas you're not quite clear on.

SUMMARIES

End-of-chapter summaries offer an overview of the key takeaways of each chapter for your review and revision. Use these bulleted lists to ensure you have a solid understanding of the main points of each chapter.

TO TAKE YOUR LEARNING FURTHER

ADDITIONAL CASE STUDIES

Additional case studies, complete with discussion questions, are available as a further resource to support your understanding of the text. These case studies will give you a chance to dig into even more climate change topics, providing you with further real-life scenarios of the impacts of climate change. We encourage you to read these cases and consider the adaptation techniques that may be applied to each scenario.

BLOG-STYLE CLIMATE UPDATES

Because climate change events, issues, and strategies move so quickly, the authors of this book will highlight new and evolving climate issues as they occur in blog-style digital updates. Review these posts if you are looking for the most up-to-date examples of climate change occurring around the world today, and use these posts to think critically about how to adapt to current climate events at the global, regional, and local scales.

Contents

Detailed Contents

Preface

Many previous texts on climate change impacts and adaptation are focused on the global or hemispheric scale, tend to be generalized in their approach, and often concentrate on single areas of human activity such as agriculture, forestry, and tourism, and yet responses to the effects of climate change will by necessity be addressed in an integrated way at much smaller scales by communities and individuals in different parts of the world. Recent research has made it increasingly apparent that there is significant regional variability in the impacts of global climate change, so that broad generalizations of the effect of climate change on human activities are often not valid at the regional and local scales. This text therefore aims to fill an important gap in the literature that must inevitably become increasingly important over coming decades as the world attempts to respond to climate change.

Global climate models (GCMs) that form the basis of future climate scenarios are still of insufficient resolution to account for the spatial variability of the climate generated by the varying nature of the Earth's surface. The influence of factors such as topography, land use, and proximity to the sea can create strong spatial variability of climate over relatively small areas. In this text, it is argued that GCM-based future climate scenarios merely provide a broad generalized framework of future climate conditions, and that assessing impacts and developing practical solutions for adaptation need to be based on good scientific understanding of climate variability at regional and local scales. Climate analysis at such finer scales can be used to reduce the uncertainties related to GCMs and thus to develop pragmatic approaches to adaptation to climate change that are appropriate to the scale at which community decision-making takes place. The originality of this book is in describing ways in which scenarios of climate change at the global scale can be integrated with simulations of the spatial variability of the climate at fine scales in order to develop pragmatic adaptation strategies. Examples are used to illustrate the nature of impacts of climate change at the community level, as well as to propose practical approaches to adaptation based on both analytical and modelling techniques.

This text therefore provides a contemporary understanding of impacts of climate change at regional and local scales, including the problems of identifying and quantifying those impacts. It also describes approaches to the development of adaptation strategies at regional and local scales based on a scientific understanding of the natural and human processes involved. Throughout the book, data and research results from different countries and environments are used to illustrate the wide range of impacts of climate change on human activity and the environment, as well as possible approaches to developing adaptation strategies to ensure the future sustainability of rural and urban communities. Tertiary students and local government officials and regional planners from a range of backgrounds should therefore be able to relate their own experiences to the concepts and examples provided in the book.

Andrew Sturman

Hervé Quénol

CHAPTER **ONE**

Setting the Scene
Why Do We Need to Downscale Climate Change to Regional and Local Scales?

LEARNING OUTCOMES

Having read this chapter, you should be able to:

- describe why it is important to take a regional- and local-scale approach to developing effective climate change adaptation strategies

- outline the key sources of evidence and main causes of global climate change

- understand the different time frames of climate change

- explain the nature and significance of time lags and feedback within the climate system

- recognize the complexity of assessing the impacts of climate change at a range of scales

- comprehend the problems and uncertainty encountered when investigating climate change

1.1 Introduction: climate change and the importance of scale

The world appears to be increasingly beset by environmental crises that have a significant impact on humanity, and many of these are said to be associated with the current global warming trend. Some recent examples include more intense storms such as tornadoes and tropical cyclones, wildfires, heatwaves, floods, and drought, which typically have regional and local impacts. As an example, wildfires have affected many countries in different parts of the world (e.g. California, Canada, Portugal, Russia, and Australia), causing significant damage to housing and **infrastructure**, as well as loss of life and impacts on wildlife. The majority of these fires are started by human activity, but the fact that they are becoming so prevalent appears to be due to changing climatic conditions that provide copious quantities of fuel that is available to be burnt and **weather** conditions that increase the frequency and intensity of the resulting fires. It is clear from Figure 1.1 that these fires traverse a range of different **climate** regions from the tropics to the mid-latitudes, supporting the hypothesis that global warming is a major cause. However, it is also evident that the environmental processes that lead to the increasing frequency and intensity of fires in these diverse parts of the world must vary significantly, from the hot and moist tropical regions of Southeast Asia and the hot and dry semi-desert of eastern Australia, to the warm temperate mid-latitude regions of the western United States and Europe. This example therefore illustrates the underlying rationale that is the focus of this book—which is, although we have an environmental impact that results from global-scale **climate change**, to understand its impact on local communities and to develop appropriate strategic responses, we need to downscale the problem to the **regional and local scales**.

Most publications describing the impacts of and adaptation to climate change tend to focus on **scenarios** of future climate (2050–2100) at the large (global/hemispheric) scale, and to be generalized in their approach (e.g. IPCC 2014a; Metz 2009). However, responses to the effects of climate change need to be addressed, by necessity, at much smaller scales by communities and individuals throughout the world. Decision-making at these smaller scales relies on an improved understanding of the processes that link the global and hemispheric atmospheric circulation with regional- and local-scale weather and climate. This new knowledge will become increasingly important over coming decades as the world attempts to respond to the growing effects of climate change.

There is also a tendency for recent literature to focus on specific areas of human activity impacted by climate change, such as agriculture, forestry, or tourism (e.g. Fuhrer and Gregory 2014; Nelson et al. 2009; Simpson et al. 2008; van Noordwijk et al. 2011), or specifically in a region or a continent (Leal Filho 2017; Leal Filho and Keenan 2017; Leal Filho et al. 2017). Such studies provide useful information for particular sectors seeking to understand the impact of climate change on their activities, as well as help them develop **adaptation strategies** specific to their needs. However, their focus is mostly generalized and wide-ranging, rather than providing guidance concerning impacts and adaptation that can be used at the community level. In contrast, we will examine impacts of and adaptation to climate change at regional and local scales across a range of important areas of significance to human activity, including urban environments, agriculture and forestry, energy and infrastructure, natural **ecosystems**, and **environmental hazards**.

Recent research has made it increasingly apparent that there is significant regional and local variability in the impacts of global climate change (e.g. Sturman and Quénol 2013), and that broad generalizations of the effects of climate change on human activities are often not valid at these smaller scales. **Global climate models (GCMs)** are complex computer programs containing **algorithms**

FIGURE 1.1 Global map of fire occurrence observed by the NASA Terra and Aqua satellites over a 10-day period
Source: https://www.climatesignals.org/data/global-fire-map

that aim to represent the range of physical, chemical, and biological processes that affect the climate of planet Earth. They form the basis of future climate scenarios (e.g. IPCC 2021), but are still of insufficient resolution to account for the spatial variability of the climate caused by the varying nature of the Earth's surface. The influence of factors such as topography, land use, and proximity to the sea can create significant spatial variability of climate over relatively small areas. It can be argued that GCM-based future climate scenarios merely provide a broad generalized framework of possible future climate conditions, and that assessing impacts and developing practical solutions for adaptation in response to these impacts need to be more finely tuned to the regional and local scales. Climate analysis at such fine scales can be used to reduce the uncertainties associated with global climate models and thus to provide pragmatic approaches to climate change adaptation that are appropriate to the scale at which community decision-making takes place. It is therefore important to integrate scenarios of climate change at the global scale with analysis and simulation of the spatial variability of the climate at much finer scales

in order to develop appropriate adaptation strategies. In the following chapters, we will use examples to illustrate the nature of impacts of climate change at the regional and local scales, as well as the development of practical approaches to adaptation based on both **analytical** and modelling techniques.

Throughout the book, we will provide a reasonably detailed but selective introduction to contemporary understanding of the impacts of climate change at regional and local scales, including problems of identifying and quantifying those impacts. The development of adaptation strategies at the regional and local scales is also elaborated, based on a scientific understanding of the natural and human processes involved. We will use data and research results from different countries and environments in the following chapters to illustrate the wide range of impacts of climate change on human activity and the environment, as well as possible approaches to developing adaptation strategies that ensure the future **sustainability** of both rural and urban communities. Readers from a range of backgrounds should therefore be able to relate their own experiences to the examples provided.

The overall structure of the book is designed, first, to establish the rationale for exploring climate change impacts and adaptation at regional and local scales. The following section in this chapter provides a short overview of the contemporary understanding of the nature and causes of climate change in order to set the wider context for the rest of the book. This section includes a brief discussion of interpretation of available evidence of change, as well as what is known of the causes and time frames of climate change, links between cause and effect, time lags, and **feedback**. Other sections in this chapter provide a general overview of current knowledge of climate change impacts, problems and uncertainty, possible responses, and the importance of scale in both understanding the issues and developing appropriate solutions.

Chapter 2 provides an introduction to the methodological approaches to **downscaling** global climate models to the regional and local scales, and evaluation of the uncertainty involved. It also examines analytical techniques used to support development of sound adaptation strategies and decision-making at the regional and local scales. In the following five substantive chapters, we investigate climate change impacts at the regional and local scales in several key areas of our environment in order to provide the basic knowledge needed to develop effective adaptation strategies. In the final chapter, we will summarize recent approaches to developing regional- and local-scale adaptation strategies based on understanding the natural and human processes that operate at these smaller scales.

Selected scientific studies are included in the text in order to develop understanding of the key issues underlying assessment of climate change impacts and development of adaptation strategies, and to inform decision-making at regional and local scales. Case studies are also embedded within the text to provide practical illustrations of the impacts of climate change on both the human and the natural environment, as well as development of adaptation strategies at the regional and local scales.

1.2 What are the nature and causes of climate change?

Climate change is a normal phenomenon, but there is significant concern that the atmosphere is warming at an unprecedented rate and that this is largely due to the effect of human activity, particularly through the widespread burning of **fossil fuels**. Evidence from a range of independent sources indicates that global temperatures have changed significantly over many hundreds and thousands of years (Figure 1.2). Although most of the temperature variation observed over the past 800,000 years is clearly the result of natural processes, there is significant concern that the recent increase in temperature over the past 100 years is the result of human activity.

Long-term indicators of temperature change over recent decades/centuries show the effects of both cyclical and random processes. For example, Figure 1.2(a) shows the occurrence of peaks in the temperature **anomaly** time series that are approximately 100,000 years apart, while much more random peaks and troughs are common in both Figures 1.2(a) and 1.2(b). Clearly, the processes behind these two types of change are quite different, as discussed below. A clear message from Figure 1.2 is that the main causes of climate change prior to 1,000 years ago would have been natural, as the human population of planet Earth was insufficient to have had large-scale effects on climate.

A range of different climate variables exist (e.g. temperature, humidity, rainfall, wind, and **solar radiation**), but the main focus in the analysis of climate change has been on temperature. The temperature variations shown in Figure 1.2 are based on **proxy data** alongside the more recent instrumental record, in an attempt to reflect trends in global temperatures. In particular, as indicated by the **temperature anomaly** graph shown in Figure 1.3, it has been noted that global average air temperature has

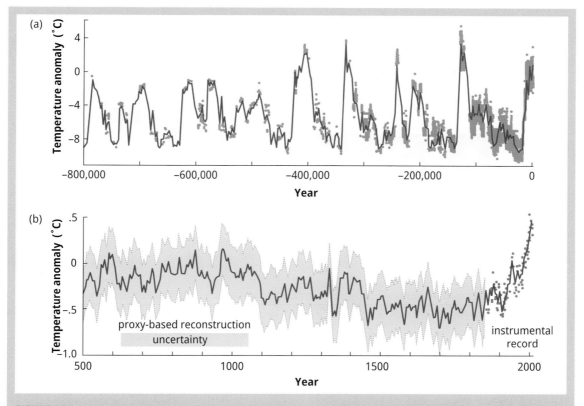

FIGURE 1.2 Variation of mean global temperature anomaly derived from: (a) air bubbles trapped in Antarctic ice (departure from present day temperatures), and (b) other proxy data (departure from 1961–1990 reference period), such as boreholes, caves, corals and tree rings from various parts of the globe

Source: NASA graph by Robert Simmon, based on data from Jouzel et al. (2007). Orbital and Millennial Antarctic Climate Variability over the Past 800,000 Years. *Science* 317, 793–796

risen by more than 0.6 °C over the last 100 years. The temperature anomalies shown in Figure 1.3 are deviations from a long-term average, in this case calculated over the period 1910–2000. The annual anomalies are calculated using data collected at sites across the world, although there is significant regional variation in the magnitude of observed temperature changes. To put this warming trend in context, a further rise in global temperature by 1 °C would take us close to a 1-million-year record high (see Figure 1.2), and predictions suggest that a rise of 4 °C by 2100 is possible (IPCC 2014b).

It should be noted that although most interest has been focused on long-term trends in mean annual temperature, changes in extreme values associated with both seasonal and daily cycles may also be significant, particularly in relation to their impact on human activity.

There is significant evidence to suggest that the warming trend over the past two centuries has been largely due to human impacts on the **Earth–atmosphere system** (IPCC 2021). Fundamentally, the current global warming trend is the result of an imbalance in the **Earth's energy budget**, which is the balance between incoming and outgoing energy for the Earth–atmosphere system (as shown in Figure 1.4). The '**greenhouse effect**' is a natural process that has an important role in this energy budget, and which helps to maintain temperatures on Earth suitable for life to exist. It does this by acting as a selective filter of radiation emitted by the Sun and Earth

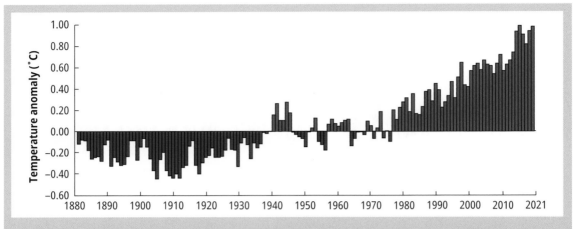

FIGURE 1.3 Trend in global mean temperature anomalies 1880–2021, with respect to the 1910–2000 average

Source: https://www.ncdc.noaa.gov/cag/global/time-series/globe/land_ocean/ytd/12/1880-2021

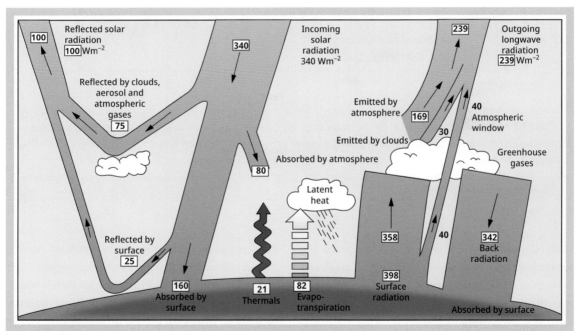

FIGURE 1.4 Schematic representation of the Earth's energy budget

Source: modified after IPCC (2021). Summary for policymakers. In: Masson-Delmotte, V., Zhai, P., Pirani, A., Connors, S. L., Péan, C., Berger, S., Caud, N., Chen, Y., Goldfarb, L., Gomis, M. I., Huang, M., Leitzell, K., Lonnoy, E., Matthews, J. B. R., Maycock, T. K., Waterfield, T., Yelekçi, O., Yu, R., and Zhou, B. (eds), *Climate Change 2021: The Physical Science Basis*. Contribution of Working Group I to the Sixth Assessment Report of the Intergovernmental Panel on Climate Change. Cambridge University Press, Cambridge and New York and IPCC (2013). *Climate Change 2013: The Physical Science Basis*. Contribution of Working Group I to the Fifth Assessment Report of the Intergovernmental Panel on Climate Change [Stocker, T. F., D. Qin, G.-K. Plattner, M. Tignor, S. K. Allen, J. Boschung, A. Nauels, Y. Xia, V. Bex and P. M. Midgley (eds)]. Cambridge University Press, Cambridge, United Kingdom and New York, NY, USA, 1535 pp

as it passes through the atmosphere. **Trace gases** such as carbon dioxide (CO_2) and methane allow most of the incoming solar radiation to reach the Earth's surface, but act to block large amounts of **terrestrial radiation** from escaping from the Earth–atmosphere system. Increased **greenhouse gases** resulting from human activity are considered to be the primary cause of the observed warming through greater absorption of outgoing terrestrial radiation, so that more heat is retained within the Earth–atmosphere system. However, there are other factors that can affect the Earth's energy budget, such as changes in the reflectivity (**albedo**) of different surfaces and the amount and type of cloud. Figure 1.4 provides a schematic representation of the transfer of energy (mostly via radiation) within the Earth–atmosphere system. The interaction of natural and human processes within this system is complex and improved knowledge of both the causes and consequences of climate change is required to be able to decide on appropriate responses.

EVIDENCE OF CLIMATE CHANGE

There are many forms of evidence of climate change over the past several decades, as indicated in Figure 1.5. Given the main focus on near-surface temperature variations, a number of direct and indirect (or proxy) forms of evidence exist. For example, the instrumental record of air temperature comprises both *in situ* sensors (climate stations, ocean buoys, weather balloons, and aircraft) and

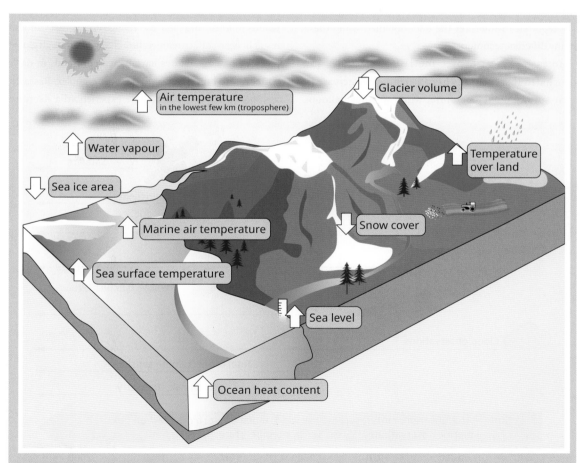

FIGURE 1.5 The main forms of evidence for climate change

Source: IPCC (2013). *Climate Change 2013: The Physical Science Basis.* Contribution of Working Group I to the Fifth Assessment Report of the Intergovernmental Panel on Climate Change [Stocker, T. F., D. Qin, G.-K. Plattner, M. Tignor, S. K. Allen, J. Boschung, A. Nauels, Y. Xia, V. Bex and P. M. Midgley (eds)]. Cambridge University Press, Cambridge, United Kingdom and New York, NY, USA, 1535 pp

remote sensing using weather satellites, while proxy data are often used to infer environmental conditions in the past. As shown by the blue part of the plot in Figure 1.2(b), the instrumental record only covers the past 150 years or so, so that various proxy data are useful in providing estimates of temperature changes over much longer periods of time. These temperature proxy data have been obtained from such sources as **tree rings**, **speleotherms** (obtained from stratified cave deposits), coral layers, water **isotopes**, pollen analysis, boreholes, and lake and ocean sediment. Other indirect forms of evidence for climate change include glacier melt/retreat, sea ice melt, snow and ice distribution, **acidification of ocean water**, and various kinds of ecosystem impact (e.g. on corals, fauna, and flora). It is evident that researchers with wide-ranging backgrounds are required to interpret the data obtained using these many different techniques.

Intensive research over the last few decades has concluded that there has been a significant increase in near-surface air temperature, while weather balloons and satellite measurements indicate that, although warming has occurred in the **troposphere**, cooling has occurred in the stratosphere. The globally averaged near-surface land and ocean temperature data show a warming trend of 0.7–0.9 °C between the late 1800s and the present day based on a range of different sources (IPCC 2021). Changes in the technology used to obtain the measurements create some uncertainty (see Figure 1.6), as do changes in land use such as urbanization, but overwhelming evidence supports the conclusion that the warming trend observed over recent decades (especially since the 1970s) is real and increasing.

Internationally, significant effort has gone into trying to eliminate **bias** within the measurements, especially that generated by urban development, which can cause heat islands to form, and land-use change effects that can also result in near-surface temperature change. Although global mean daily temperatures have increased, trends in **daily temperature range** appear to be more complex. Research has shown that some areas have experienced a decrease

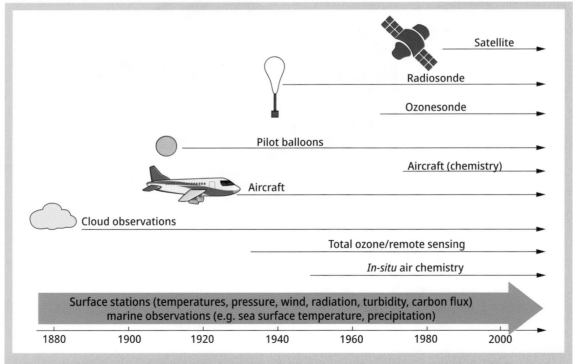

FIGURE 1.6 Changes in the number and type of observations used to monitor climate change since the late 1880s

Source: adapted from IPCC (2013). *Climate Change 2013: The Physical Science Basis.* Contribution of Working Group I to the Fifth Assessment Report of the Intergovernmental Panel on Climate Change [Stocker, T. F., D. Qin, G.-K. Plattner, M. Tignor, S. K. Allen, J. Boschung, A. Nauels, Y. Xia, V. Bex and P. M. Midgley (eds)]. Cambridge University Press, Cambridge, United Kingdom and New York, NY, USA, 1535 pp

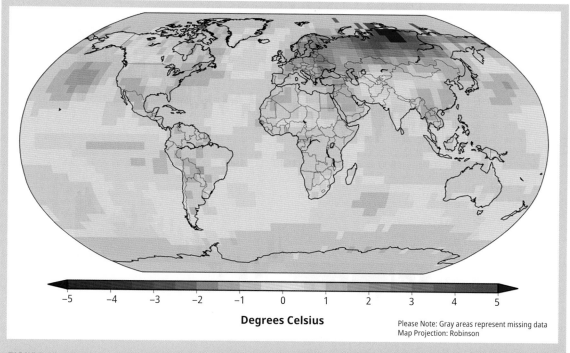

FIGURE 1.7 Mean annual temperature anomalies over land and ocean for January to December 2020, with reference to the 1981–2010 average

Source: https://www.ncdc.noaa.gov/monitoring-content/sotc/global/map-blended-mntp/map-blended-mntp-202001-202012.png

while others have recorded an increase, while a general trend towards a reduction in daily temperature range occurred between the 1960s and the 1980s, but since the 1980s there has been little consistent change (Thorne et al. 2016). The reasons for this variability are still open to debate, but may be associated with the methods used to record maximum and minimum temperatures, or local-scale effects of **atmospheric boundary layer** processes.

The overwhelming focus has tended to be on global mean annual near-surface air temperatures, but it is apparent that there is significant regional variability in the magnitude of temperature change across the planet (Figure 1.7). It is also evident that there is increasing inter-annual variability as mean temperatures are down-scaled to hemispheric and regional scales (Figure 1.8). It is the nature and impacts of such regional- and local-scale variability and their implications for developing adaptation strategies that is a major focus of this book.

In addition to increasing air temperatures, evidence of climate change includes shrinking ice sheets, Arctic sea ice, glaciers, and snow cover; ocean warming and acidification; and sea level rise. There is also evidence to suggest that changes are occurring in the global atmospheric circulation system, including a poleward shift of the major features since the 1970s. In contrast, trends in climate variables such as humidity, **precipitation**, and cloud cover are less clear, while changes in the occurrence of severe weather also provide a weak signal (IPCC 2021).

In summary, it is clear that global average air temperature has risen by at least 0.8 °C over the last 100 years, but this rate of change has varied regionally (larger in some areas, less in others). A further rise in global temperature by 1 °C will take us close to a 1-million-year record high, and predictions suggest that a rise of 4 °C by 2100 is possible. Responding to this warming trend requires action at a range of scales from international

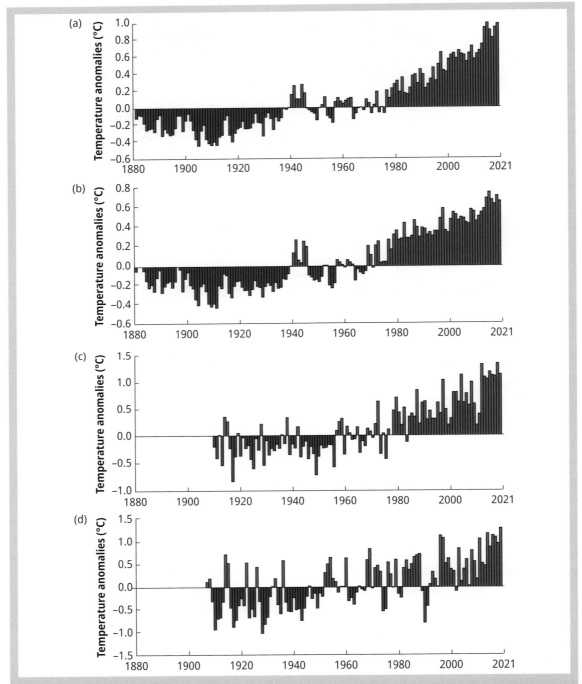

FIGURE 1.8 Mean annual temperature anomalies over (a) the whole globe, (b) the Southern Hemisphere, (c) Oceania, and (d) New Zealand, 1880 to 2021. The anomalies for the globe and the Southern Hemisphere are with reference to the 1901–2000 average, while those for Oceania and New Zealand are with reference to the 1910–2010 average

Source: based on data from the National Centers for Environmental Information and the National Institute of Water and Atmospheric Research (NIWA)

through to regional and local scales. As discussed in the following chapters, more knowledge is required of climate variability at smaller scales in a range of environments in order to allow local communities to develop appropriate adaptation strategies.

CAUSES OF CLIMATE CHANGE

The historical record indicates that there are many natural causes of climate change that have influenced temperature variations over many thousands and millions of years. For example, Figure 1.9 shows that temperature has varied by more than 10 °C over the past 400,000 years, during which time CO_2 concentrations have varied between about 180 and 280 ppm. The close relationship between CO_2 and temperature is readily apparent, and it is clear that except for the recent rapid increase in CO_2 concentrations to more than 400 ppm, human activity would have had little impact on the observed variations in both parameters.

As solar radiation is the main source of energy for processes within the Earth–atmosphere system, it is logical to consider that variation in solar radiation receipt would be a major driver of temperature change on planet Earth. **Sunspots** are dark patches that occur on the surface of the Sun that are associated with an increase in the intensity of solar radiation received on Earth. They have a cyclic variation of around 11 years and represent an obvious source of temperature variation. Variations in the orbital characteristics of the Earth around the Sun (called the **Milankovitch mechanisms**) can also explain periodic variations in solar energy receipt and their regional distribution. Meteorites are the only other important factor external to the Earth–atmosphere system that can have a significant effect on our climate, with major collisions with the Earth's surface said to have been responsible for dramatic cooling of the whole planet in the past. Such a collision about 65 million years ago is thought to have accounted for extensive extinction of plant and animal species. Factors internal to the Earth–atmosphere system that are believed to cause climate to change over the time frame of hundreds of thousands of years include volcanic activity, changes in ocean circulation, and

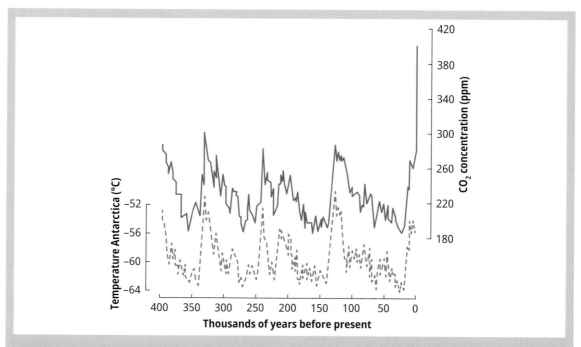

FIGURE 1.9 Temperature and CO_2 concentrations obtained from the Vostok ice core in Antarctica

Source: original data from Petit et al. (1999). Climate and atmospheric history of the past 420,000 years from the Vostok ice core, Antarctica. *Nature* 399: 429–36

internal feedback processes involving the atmosphere, ocean, and **cryosphere**.

It is now generally considered that humans are the main cause of significant recent climate change, as represented by the well-known global warming trend. The main impact of human activity appears to be through an enhancement of the naturally occurring 'greenhouse effect'. This effect is illustrated by the **atmospheric absorption spectrum** shown in Figure 1.10. The solid-coloured areas under the **spectral intensity curves** for incoming solar radiation and outgoing terrestrial radiation (the top set of graphs)

represent the amount of energy able to pass through the atmosphere in each direction. It is clear that most of the incoming solar radiation manages to pass through the Earth's atmosphere while a large part of the outgoing terrestrial radiation is absorbed by the atmosphere. The lower graphs show the contribution of trace gases in the atmosphere to absorption and **scattering** of radiation. It is evident that **water vapour** and CO_2 play a major role in absorbing particularly the outgoing radiation.

Emissions of greenhouse gases resulting from fossil fuel burning are generally considered to be responsible

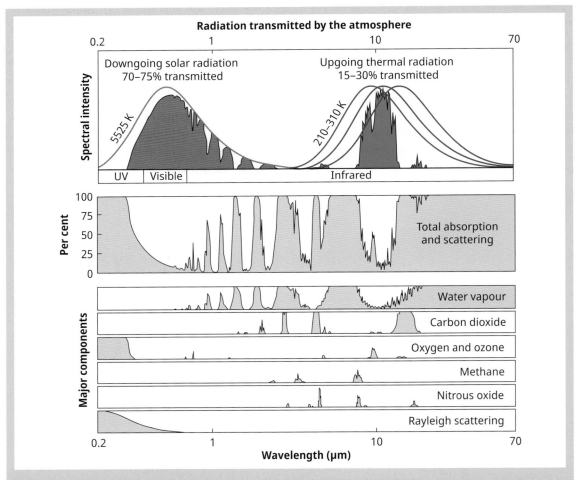

FIGURE 1.10 Atmospheric absorption spectrum, showing the effects of the Earth's atmosphere on incoming solar radiation and outgoing terrestrial radiation

Source: https://en.wikipedia.org/wiki/Absorption_band#/media/File:Atmospheric_Transmission.png

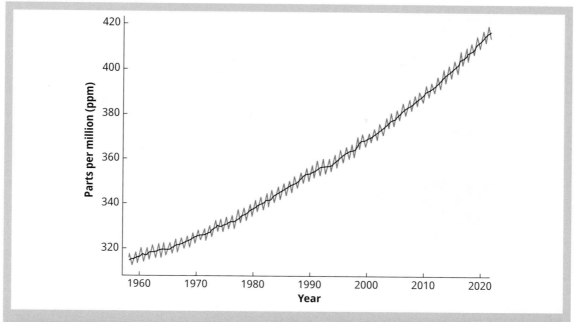

FIGURE 1.11 Recent trend in CO_2 concentration measured between 1960 and 2020 at Mauna Loa, Hawaii

Source: https://gml.noaa.gov/ccgg/trends/

for the dramatic increase in global CO_2 concentrations over the last 200 years (seen in Figure 1.11) and the related increase in global mean temperatures shown in Figure 1.3. Given the obvious relationship between CO_2 concentrations and temperatures shown in Figure 1.9, it is hardly surprising that increasing concentrations from around 270 to over 400 ppm since the start of the industrial revolution would be associated with increasing temperature. The recent data depicted in Figure 1.11 show that the trend of increasing CO_2 concentration appears to be accelerating, in spite of efforts to try to achieve international agreement over emissions reductions over several decades.

At the same time, land surface change through deforestation, plantation forestry, and agricultural and urban development can also impact on the energy budget of planet Earth. Deforestation is often associated with extensive **biomass** burning that results in CO_2 emissions, but perhaps more importantly it also results in a reduction in the capacity of the **biosphere** to take up CO_2. Typically, growing plants take up significant

quantities of CO_2 during the process of **photosynthesis**. Human activity therefore contributes to an enhancement of the greenhouse effect by increasing emissions of CO_2 into the atmosphere, while at the same time reducing the ability of the Earth–atmosphere system to extract CO_2 from the atmosphere. Figure 1.12 illustrates the variability in surface–atmosphere exchange of carbon and the effects of land-use change and emissions of fossil fuels on **carbon budget** components.

It is also evident that human activity contributes to changing atmospheric composition in other ways, typically via **air pollution** in the form of both gases and particles. Different gases have different radiative properties, while suspended particles can have a significant influence on radiation transfers as well as on the nature of cloud development, depending on their size and colour. As discussed later, some research has suggested that the emission of particles into the atmosphere may counter the warming effect of increased greenhouse gases.

Any changes in global air temperatures are ultimately determined by changes in the energy budget of the

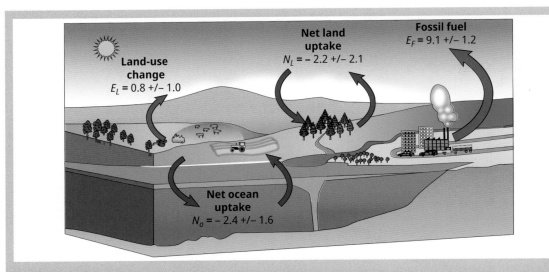

FIGURE 1.12 Estimated exchanges in the main components of the carbon budget (PgC/yr or 1 x 10^{12} g of carbon per year) in 2010. Positive values represent take-up by the atmosphere, while negative values represent loss from the atmosphere

Source: Ballantyne et al. (2015). Audit of the global carbon budget: Estimate errors and their impact on uptake uncertainty. *Biogeosciences* 12: 2565–84

Earth–atmosphere system. The energy budget is comprised of exchanges of heat energy in the form of radiation (solar and terrestrial), **sensible heat** (heat that you can feel or sense), and **latent heat** (heat typically stored in the form of water vapour). Land surface changes have an effect on these different components by changing the radiative and thermal exchange properties of the Earth's surface. For example, surface albedo (reflectivity) can be significantly modified by major landscape change (such as deforestation or urban development), resulting in an increase or decrease in the amount of solar radiation absorbed by the ground. Similarly, changes in the physical properties of the surface (e.g. increased/decreased moisture content, variations in soil compaction, and **thermal conductivity**) can result in changes in the way in which heat is transferred between the atmosphere and ground surface. A good example of this effect is the reduction of sea ice cover in polar regions, which has resulted in increased energy exchange between the atmosphere and underlying ocean.

As concluded by IPCC (2014b):

Anthropogenic greenhouse gas emissions have increased since the pre-industrial era, driven largely by economic and population growth, and are now higher than ever. This has led to atmospheric concentrations of carbon dioxide, methane and nitrous oxide that are unprecedented in at least the last 800,000 years. Their effects, together with those of other anthropogenic drivers, have been detected throughout the **climate system** and are extremely likely to have been the dominant cause of the observed warming since the mid-twentieth century.

Figure 1.13 shows simulations of the climate between 1900 and 2000 for different regions with the aim of separating the effects of natural and anthropogenic **forcing**. The agreement between observed and simulated values with anthropogenic forcing is readily apparent. Temperatures modelled with the effect of only natural forcing clearly deviate from post-1950 observations. The temperatures simulated by the models using both natural

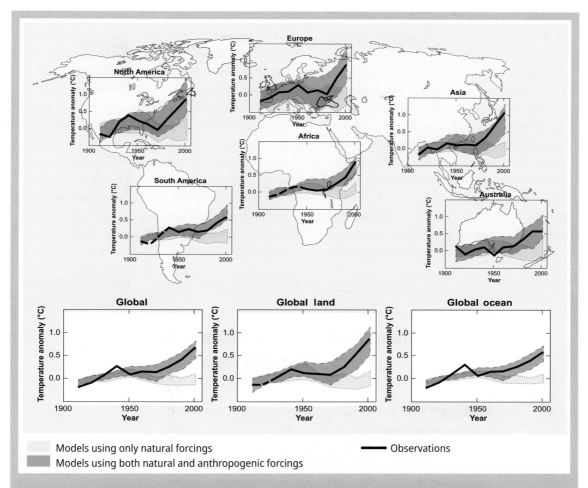

FIGURE 1.13 Comparison of observed continental- and global-scale changes in surface temperature with results simulated by climate models using natural and anthropogenic forcings

Source: IPCC (2007). *Climate Change 2007: Synthesis Report.* Contribution of Working Groups I, II and III to the Fourth Assessment Report of the Intergovernmental Panel on Climate Change (Core Writing Team, Pachauri, R. K., and Reisinger, A. (eds)). IPCC, Geneva

and anthropogenic forcing follow the post-1950 observations more closely.

TIME FRAMES OF CLIMATE CHANGE

The time frames of climate change depend on the specific characteristics of the causative factors (Figure 1.14). Clearly, periodic changes in climate are the result of processes that are dominated by a source exhibiting a cyclic variation, such as the familiar seasonal and daily cycles that are dominated by variations in solar radiation receipt. As mentioned earlier, the Milankovitch mechanisms are cyclic processes associated with changes in the orbital characteristics of the Earth around the Sun that are responsible for periodic variations of climate over a much longer time frame (tens of thousands of years). Different causes are therefore associated with differing time frames of climate response, with periodic causes associated with changes that are much more predictable than random or chaotic events (such as volcanic eruptions and meteorite strikes) that are largely unpredictable.

As mentioned earlier, it has also been established that there are cycles in sunspot activity that influence how much solar energy is received by the Earth. The dominance of the 11-year cycle of sunspot occurrence over the past 400 years is evident in Figure 1.15. The lack of sunspot activity appears to reduce solar output by approximately 2%. The '**Maunder Minimum**' of sunspot activity (shown between 1650 and 1730 in Figure 1.15) has been linked to the so-called '**Little Ice Age**', although recent evidence suggests that volcanic eruptions were the initial cause. Recent research has suggested that

sunspot activity reached a maximum towards the end of the last century and is now heading towards a minimum that may have an impact on solar radiation receipt within the next 30–40 years (Jones et al. 2012).

It should also be recognized that climate change can involve either gradual or sudden change. The current period of global warming can be considered to be a gradual response to increasing levels of greenhouse gases in the atmosphere. In contrast, sudden changes may result from unpredictable random events such as meteorite strikes or volcanic eruptions. The latter have had a measurable impact on climate within the period of recent scientific observations. For example, the eruption of Mount Pinatubo in 1991 had a significant effect on temperatures

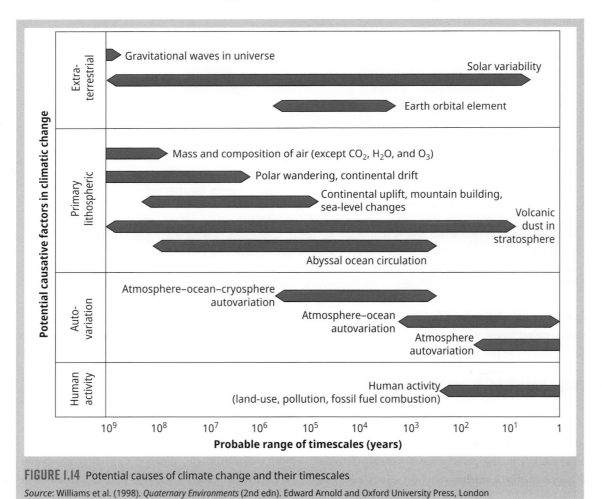

FIGURE 1.14 Potential causes of climate change and their timescales

Source: Williams et al. (1998). *Quaternary Environments* (2nd edn). Edward Arnold and Oxford University Press, London

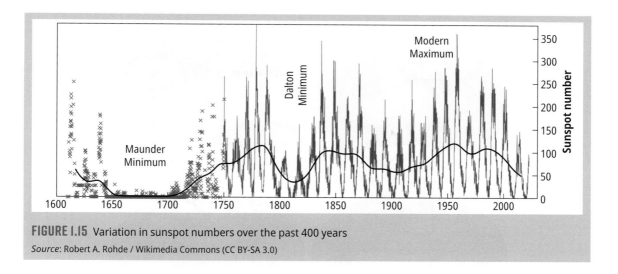

FIGURE 1.15 Variation in sunspot numbers over the past 400 years
Source: Robert A. Rohde / Wikimedia Commons (CC BY-SA 3.0)

across the globe, as shown by the **aerosol optical depth** in Figure 1.16. The **aerosol** plume initially only affected the tropical region, but within a year it had covered the entire globe. The impact of such eruptions on Earth's climate is mainly the result of the height to which the eruption reaches (the higher the aerosols reach, the further they are carried by atmospheric circulation), the latitude of the eruption (material erupted closer to the equator is more likely to reach the poles than vice versa), and the composition of the aerosols erupted into the atmosphere (dust and sulphate aerosols have different effects).

However, not all sudden changes are the result of such dramatic events, as they may also occur as a result of a previously balanced situation reaching a '**tipping point**'. This can occur when a complex system that has previously established a long-term equilibrium is forced beyond its normal operating range by a change in one or more influencing factors, so that the system suddenly shifts outside of this range. The result may be that the system effectively shifts into another state of equilibrium after a period of sudden change, or alternatively accelerates away from its original equilibrium status, causing rapid and uncontrollable change (until a new equilibrium is achieved sometime later). 'Tipping points' are effectively **non-linear** transitions, when a small change in one factor causes a major change (e.g. exponential) in another. Concern has

been expressed that the North Atlantic is one part of the globe where a tipping point could soon be reached because of the recent rapid melting of the Greenland ice cap that is changing the salinity of the water in the region. This could lead to the collapse of the Atlantic oceanic circulation, which is driven by differences in temperature and salinity of the water. Clearly, such changes tend to be rapid and irregular, making them difficult to predict.

In summary, time frames of climate change can vary significantly, depending on the causes. Natural phenomena can cause significant variations in weather and climate that can result from either external or internal factors and be short or long term in their impact (e.g. Milankovitch mechanisms, sunspot cycles, or volcanic eruptions). Single unpredictable events could clearly have more of a catastrophic effect on human society than much longer-period fluctuations or **periodicities** that are easier to predict.

TIME LAGS BETWEEN CAUSE AND EFFECT

Such changes in complex environmental systems may also be associated with time lags in system response to change. Different parts of the Earth–atmosphere system have differing sensitivity to change, so that the

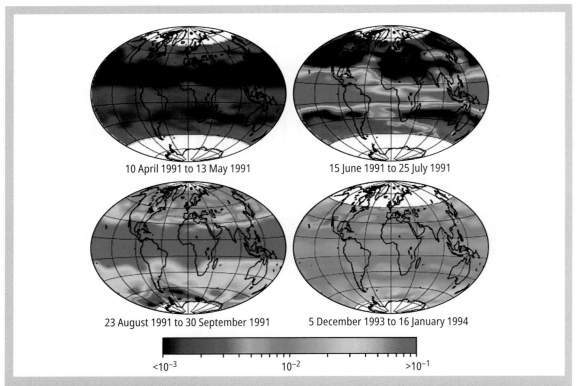

10 April 1991 to 13 May 1991

15 June 1991 to 25 July 1991

23 August 1991 to 30 September 1991

5 December 1993 to 16 January 1994

$<10^{-3}$ 10^{-2} $>10^{-1}$

FIGURE 1.16 Aerosol optical depth (a measure of aerosol load in the atmosphere) obtained by the Earth Radiation Budget Satellite showing the distribution of the aerosol plume from Mount Pinatubo between 1991 and 1994

Source: NASA Langley Research Center Aerosol Research Branch

magnitude and timing of the response to certain key factors may vary. For example, parts of the oceans respond very slowly to external **thermal forcing**, while the atmosphere responds much more quickly. The characteristic response time of the troposphere to thermal forcing is about one month, for the upper ocean it is months to years, the deeper ocean centuries, snow and ice anywhere between weeks and decades, and the biosphere seasons to hundreds of years. Table 1.1 lists the approximate residence times of key components in different environmental systems, reflecting the time it takes for each of these components to respond to change.

In terms of human impacts, it is said that the emission of ozone-destroying chemicals into the lower atmosphere can take up to 10 years to reach the lower stratosphere, in which case stopping such emissions would not have an effect until about 10 years into the future. A similar situation would occur if fossil-fuel burning were stopped tomorrow as a result of greenhouse gas reduction policies. This time lag between cause and effect is a very important factor to be taken into account in developing response strategies to climate change. It is clear, for example, that greenhouse gas reductions decided at Conferences of the Parties under the United Nations Framework Convention on Climate Change would not have an immediate effect on temperature increases.

It is therefore evident that the various parts of the Earth–atmosphere system respond to causative factors with different time lags, so that effects may not be seen until tens or hundreds of years after a particular event

TABLE 1.1 Typical response times of key components in some different environmental systems

COMPONENT	TYPICAL RESIDENCE TIME
Water vapour in the lower atmosphere	10 days
CO_2 in the lower atmosphere	5–10 days (with sea)
Aerosol particles, lower atmosphere	1 week to several weeks
Aerosol particles, upper atmosphere	Several months to several years
Water in the biosphere	2 million years
Oxygen in the biosphere	2,000 years
CO_2 in the biosphere	300 years
Groundwater	150 years (above 760 m depth)
Atlantic Ocean, surface water	10 years
Atlantic Ocean, deep water	600 years
Pacific Ocean, surface water	25 years
Pacific Ocean, deep water	1,300 years

Source: Based on data from Park, C.C. 2001: *The Environment: Principles and Applications* (2nd edition). Routledge, London and New York

or change has occurred. Over relatively long periods of time, this complex system has attempted to maintain a reasonable balance between overall gains and losses of energy in order to maintain an equilibrium. The components of the Earth–atmosphere system that respond more slowly to change tend to have a stabilizing influence that helps to minimize the rapidity of change. For example, Table 1.1 indicates that the oceans act as a moderator of climate, and this is largely because they have different thermal properties from continental areas and take longer to heat up and cool down compared with land. However, as the distribution of continents and oceans across the planet is not uniform, it could be expected that different regions will respond to global warming at different rates. The rate of warming in those regions dominated by oceanic effects, such as in the Southern Hemisphere, may well be slower than in the continental areas of the Northern Hemisphere.

FEEDBACK IN THE CLIMATE SYSTEM

Systems that readily achieve equilibrium tend to be dominated by negative feedback, in which case a factor causing a change in one direction is countered by another factor that causes a change in the opposite direction, hence creating a stable system that resists change. In contrast, positive feedback is associated with unstable systems, in which a small amount of initial forcing can lead to an accelerated response, causing rapid and major change in system status. Two common examples used to illustrate feedback in the climate system are the albedo feedback loop (Figure 1.17) and atmospheric water vapour and cloud feedback (Figure 1.18).

Figure 1.17 illustrates the situation where increasing levels of greenhouse gases result in warming of the atmosphere. Higher air temperatures result in melting of snow and ice cover, which has the effect of decreasing the albedo, or reflectivity, of land surfaces to solar radiation. More solar energy is therefore absorbed by the Earth's surface, which increases the energy gained by the atmosphere, resulting in further warming. This is therefore an example of positive feedback that, on its own, could lead to runaway warming.

Figure 1.18 provides a more complex example, in which warming generated by an enhanced greenhouse effect is predicted to lead to an increase in cloud cover because of the increased availability of water vapour in the atmosphere (due to greater evaporation of water and greater ability for the atmosphere to hold water). However, more cloud could result in either global cooling or warming depending on the nature of the cloud generated. Thin cirrus cloud located high in the troposphere (at more than 7,000 m above sea level) is highly transparent to solar radiation, but readily absorbs outgoing terrestrial radiation, leading to a net warming effect. By contrast, thick stratus and

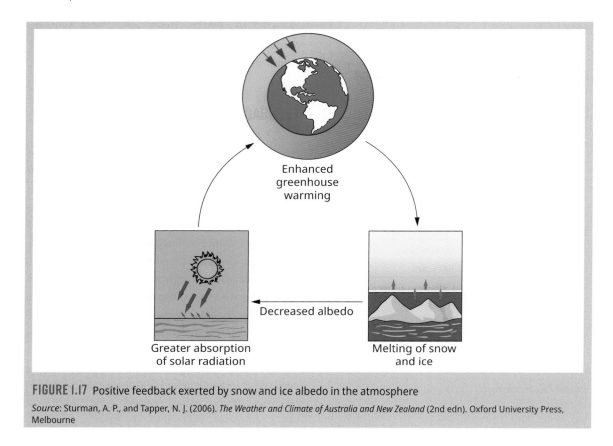

FIGURE 1.17 Positive feedback exerted by snow and ice albedo in the atmosphere

Source: Sturman, A. P., and Tapper, N. J. (2006). *The Weather and Climate of Australia and New Zealand* (2nd edn). Oxford University Press, Melbourne

stratocumulus clouds located close to the Earth's surface have a high albedo and reflect much more incoming solar radiation. They also radiate more terrestrial radiation to space than high clouds as they are much warmer, resulting in a net cooling effect on the atmosphere. It is the relative magnitude of the increased reflection of solar radiation and increased trapping of terrestrial radiation by different types of cloud that determines the final outcome of either net warming or cooling. Increased cloud cover can therefore generate either positive or negative feedback, depending on cloud characteristics.

1.3 Impacts of climate change

Impacts of climate change on both the natural environment and human activities vary over time and space. They depend on the intensity of change (e.g. the rate of temperature increase, or the increase or decrease in precipitation), but also on the **vulnerability** and adaptive capacity of different regions. The latest IPCC report showed that most of the world's natural systems have been affected by regional climate change, by increased temperature in particular (IPCC 2021).

Environmental impacts are already evident, especially on the most fragile ecosystems such as coral reefs, boreal forests, and Mediterranean ecosystems. The changing frequency of severe storms, flooding, and drought has important effects on the environment, and can be linked to such other environmental hazards as wildfires and coastal erosion. The reduction of snow and ice cover and the rise of mean sea level in the world's oceans are examples of phenomena that affect

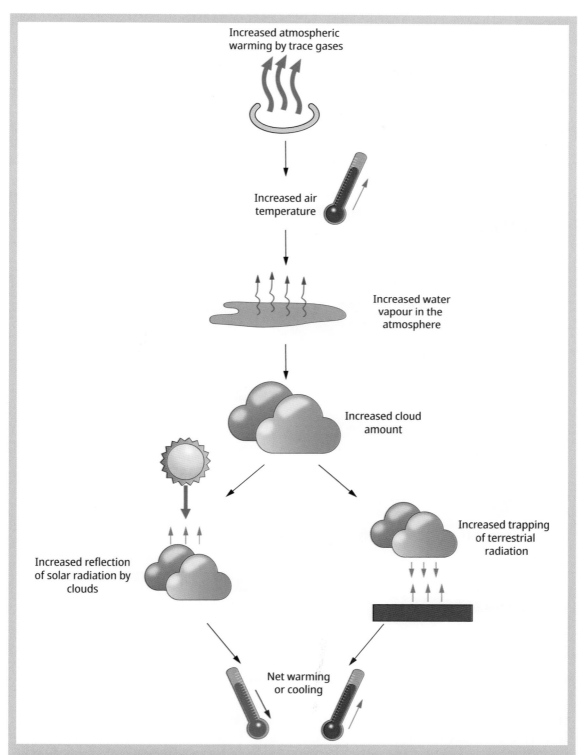

FIGURE 1.18 Role of cloud feedback processes in both warming and cooling the atmosphere, resulting in both positive and negative feedback respectively

Source: Sturman, A. P., and Tapper, N. J. (2006). *The Weather and Climate of Australia and New Zealand* (2nd edn). Oxford University Press, Melbourne

both natural and human environments to a greater or lesser degree.

Some of the areas most exposed to climate risks are coastal regions or small islands (e.g. the Maldive Islands of the Indian Ocean and the Solomon Islands of the Pacific) due to the threat of sea level rise, but also areas where populations are large and generally poor and have less capacity to adapt (e.g. sub-Saharan Africa and the Asian mega-deltas) (Parry et al. 2008). Not only are such areas subject to the direct impact of the changes in weather and climate mentioned above, they are also affected by indirect effects, including health effects associated with heat-related diseases and **vector-borne diseases** (e.g. dengue fever and malaria), and impacts on water quality, crop production, and plant pests and diseases.

A schematic summary of potential climate change impacts is provided in Figure 1.19. However, the scope of climate change impacts is more wide-ranging, and

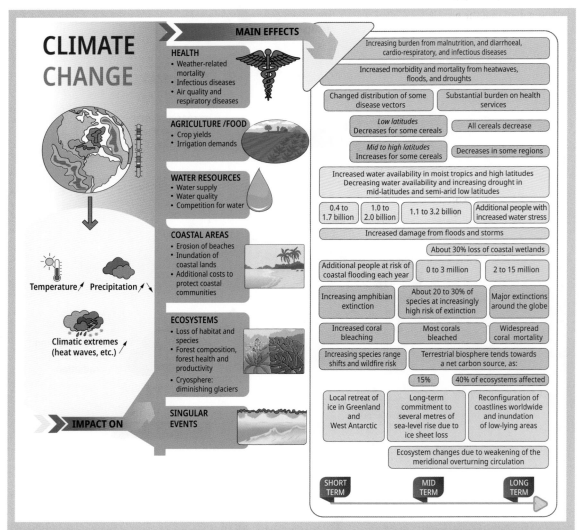

FIGURE 1.19 Schematic representation of the types of impact associated with climate change and their likely effects on people and their environment

Source: IPCC (2007). *Climate Change 2007: Synthesis Report*. Contribution of Working Groups I, II and III to the Fourth Assessment Report of the Intergovernmental Panel on Climate Change (Core Writing Team, Pachauri, R. K., and Reisinger, A. (eds)). IPCC, Geneva

includes those associated with agriculture—both live-stock and crops; energy use and generation; society—civil unrest, governance, etc.; coasts—sea level rise and coastal inundation; forests—wildfires and diseases; transportation—land, sea, and air; ecosystems—coral die-back, wildfires, flora (changing **phenology**) and fauna response; human health—heat-related diseases and vector-borne diseases; water resources—both quantity and quality; and snow and ice melt—impacts on water resources, hazards, and land surface change. It is also apparent that the nature and extent of such impacts will vary into the future, particularly if current global warming trends continue (Figure 1.19).

It should also be noted that climate change impacts on different areas such as agriculture, health, and water resources are often related in highly complex ways, thereby providing significant challenges for developing effective response or adaptation strategies. For example, the direct impacts of climate change on regional and local weather and climate interact with the indirect climate change effect on sea level rise to create particular problems for local coastal environments, as shown in Figure 1.20.

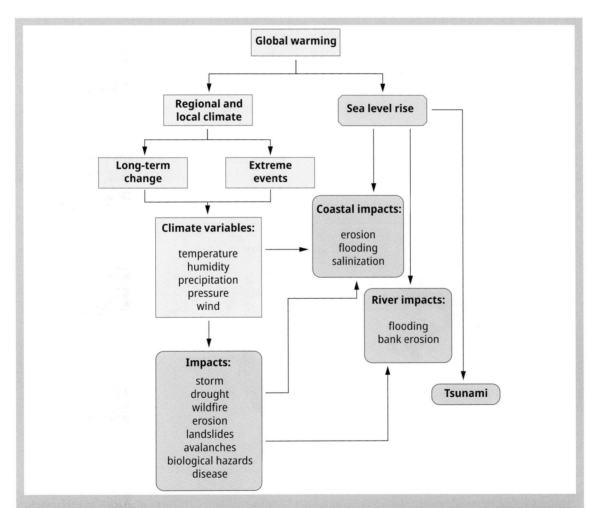

FIGURE 1.20 An illustration of regional and local impacts of global warming that are associated with direct effects on climate variables and indirect effects via sea level rise

Source: Pickering, K. T., and Owen, L. A. (1994). *An Introduction to Global Environmental Issues*. Routledge, London

1.4 Problems and uncertainty

There are various problems associated with analysing and understanding climate change that make it difficult to adequately quantify impacts and develop appropriate adaptation strategies. To begin with, the interpretation of data can sometimes be problematic, and care is required to ensure that climate station data used to investigate trends are of sufficient quality to support conclusions about climate change. For example, **urban heat island** and changing land-use effects can contaminate a climate record, providing doubt over the amount and direction of any changes in climate variables such as temperature or precipitation. Quite often these are localized effects that can be corrected for, but the standardization of processes applied to ensure scientifically supportable outcomes has required a significant amount of time and effort, and is still not perfect. Natural regional- and local-scale variability of climate can make it difficult to be absolutely confident that, first, corrections are required and, second, the magnitude of any correction is acceptable.

The distribution of climate station sites used to assess climate change may also be problematic at a much larger scale. For example, some regions are better represented in the statistics used to assess the warming trend globally, hemispherically, regionally, and locally. This is clearly evident when comparing warming trends in the Northern and Southern Hemispheres and oceanic and continental regions, as there is a distinct bias towards land-based sites in the north (Figure 1.21). Changes in the technology used to measure temperatures have helped to address this problem, as satellite remote sensing has allowed a more consistent/uniform data coverage of the Earth, although changes in measurement systems can also create problems. For example, measurement of sea surface temperature has improved in data quality and consistency over time with the use of **thermal imagery** from meteorological satellites. However, the transition from the use of buckets and glass thermometers to sensors/engine intakes on board ships, to ocean buoys, and finally to **satellite**

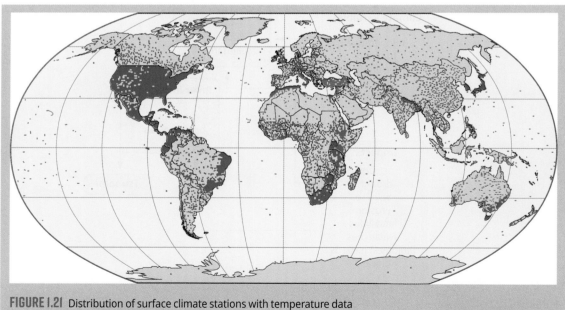

FIGURE 1.21 Distribution of surface climate stations with temperature data

Source: http://www.worldclim.org/methods1

thermography raises the issue of compatibility between the different data sets when analysing long-term trends.

Observed temperature data have identified differences in trends of daily temperature range across the globe since 1950. It was initially thought that the rising trend of mean daily temperatures was paralleled by a reduction of diurnal temperature range, with minimum temperatures rising faster than maximum temperatures. However, as mentioned earlier, recent analysis suggests that the situation is more complicated, as some regions appear to be experiencing a reduction in diurnal temperature range while others have observed an increase.

Another related issue is the possible future change in the frequency distribution of temperature. Although the focus in the literature has been very much on changing average temperatures, changes in the spread of values around the mean can cause a range of possible outcomes when it comes to impacts on the community. As shown in Figure 1.22, different shapes of the statistical distribution of temperature around the mean value can occur, accentuating or moderating the effects of the general warming trend.

Such issues create uncertainty in understanding the nature and implications of climate change for different parts of the globe. A more comprehensive understanding of the processes that influence regional- and local-scale climate variability is therefore required to comprehend spatial variability in responses to global climate change, and to develop effective response strategies at the community level.

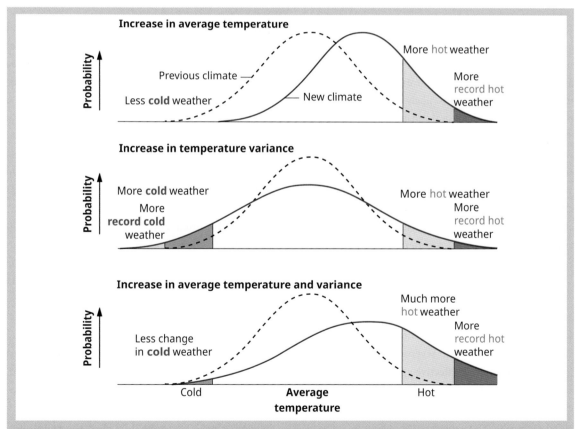

FIGURE 1.22 Schematic representation of possible changes in the statistical distribution of temperature as a result of climate change

Source: modified after https://earthobservatory.nasa.gov/features/RisingCost/rising_cost5.php

The complex interaction between natural and human factors also makes it difficult to identify causes of climate change and their significance at the regional and local scales. For example, regional causes of climate variability such as the **El Niño Southern Oscillation (ENSO)** and other **teleconnections** (hemispheric and global-scale atmosphere–ocean interactions) can have a moderating effect on the global warming signal, but only in certain regions of the world. The effect of natural processes can therefore make it difficult to clearly identify human impacts on weather and climate, although climate modellers do try to include them in future projections.

Similarly, there is the problem of evaluating magnitude versus frequency in assessing impacts of global warming on society. There has been significant discussion about more intense and more frequent tropical cyclones, droughts, heatwaves, severe storms, intense precipitation, etc. in a warmer world, but such predictions tend to be neither spatially nor temporally specific. To some extent this is due to a current limited capacity to downscale global and hemispheric effects to the regional and local scales.

1.5   How can we respond to climate change?

Responses to global climate change must be based on a thorough understanding of environmental processes in order to identify the nature of the observed change and its likely causes and downstream impacts. As mentioned in previous sections, likely causes may be complex and involve both natural and anthropogenic effects. Similarly, the impact of global-scale warming can be expected to be spatially and temporally diverse, with some parts of the globe being affected more than others and in different ways. A key challenge to development of effective regional- and local-scale responses to climate change relies on gaining as complete an understanding as possible of these complex patterns of change across a range of space and timescales.

As shown in Figure 1.23, there are only two possible types of response to climate change—mitigation and adaptation. **Mitigation** involves developing strategies to address the root causes of the observed changing climate, in order to try and reverse the change process. In contrast, adaptation effectively assumes that society needs to work out how to live with the observed climate change, and requires communities to think innovatively about how they can change their activities to minimize adverse effects or even to take advantage of new opportunities.

Mitigation has attracted significant attention from both the scientific community and popular media over the past several decades, and clearly involves responses from the major countries working internationally to address the causes of climate change, such as greenhouse gas emissions. However, although mitigation generally requires coordination at the national and international scale and the establishment of appropriate response frameworks, it also requires individuals to think more carefully about how their use of resources can be modified to reduce their cumulative impact on the environment.

In contrast, discussion of approaches to adaptation has tended to lag behind mitigation. Adaptation also involves decision-makers at the national level, but is increasingly an important problem at the community level—that is, at regional and local scales. Community-level decision-makers need to understand the processes by which larger-scale climate change is affecting their local-scale environment, and what that means for their activities (in agriculture, urban development, coastal zone management, etc.). It is therefore very important for applied climatologists to be able to work alongside stakeholders, such as local authorities and businesses, to help them understand the relationship between climate change and their activities.

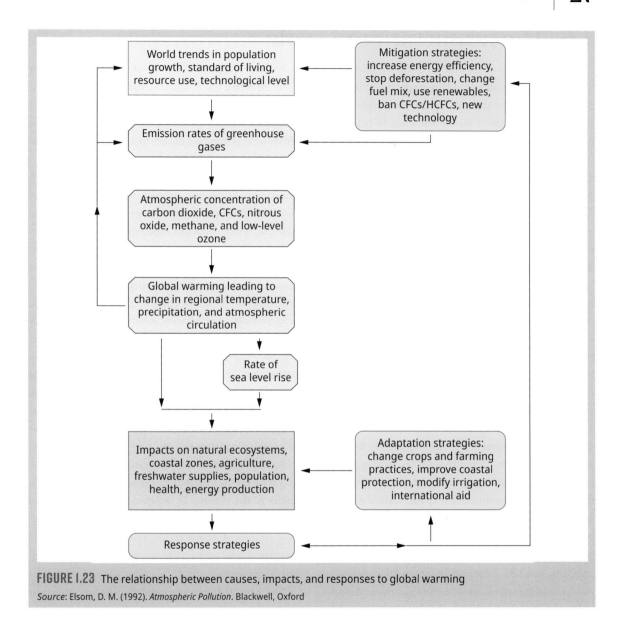

FIGURE 1.23 The relationship between causes, impacts, and responses to global warming

Source: Elsom, D. M. (1992). *Atmospheric Pollution*. Blackwell, Oxford

The following chapters therefore attempt to provide guidance for both applied climatologists and decision-makers in developing suitable adaptation strategies in response to current and future climate change. Such adaptation strategies need to be designed so that they can be applied individually or collectively in support of robust decision-making that is appropriate to the range of natural and human processes in a variety of different environments. The nature of the subject provides an opportunity for problem-based learning and community engagement to be used as practical learning tools.

1.6 The importance of scale

To understand the impact of climate change at regional and local scales, the effect of surface characteristics on the spatial variability of the climate must be taken into account. At local scales, atmospheric conditions in the lowest layer of the atmosphere (the atmospheric boundary layer) depend on surface conditions (Oke 1987). Morphology, roughness, and the nature of the surface as defined by relief, vegetation, moisture content, or human infrastructure can modify the behaviour of meteorological variables and characterize the microclimate of an area. This largely explains the strong spatial variability of the climate over small areas, especially in regions of rugged terrain. For example, in hilly terrain, the mean annual temperature difference can vary by several degrees between the top and bottom of a hill. In the climate change context, spatial variability induced by local effects such as topography and proximity to a river or lake must be integrated into adaptation strategies in response to climate change.

However, evaluating the impact of climate change at the local scale requires a multiscale approach: from the global, hemispheric, and regional to the local scale. The reasons for this approach are related to the functioning of the atmosphere. The smaller the spatial scale, the greater are the number of factors affecting the meteorological parameters such as temperature and precipitation. For that reason, the influence of factors such as topography and land use can create significant spatial variability over relatively small areas. In order to evaluate this spatial variability, the hierarchy of factors influencing the climatic variables must be identified in relation to the range of spatial and temporal scales.

Many authors have attempted to categorize these phenomena according to a spatial and temporal classification based on fixed spatial dimensions and timescales, but in reality, atmospheric phenomena are part of a continuum and fixed boundaries are very approximate. Nevertheless, the scales at which climate variables are most influenced by surface conditions are, sequentially: the *meso* or *regional* scale (from several hundred kilometres to a few kilometres, and from a few hours to a few days), the *local* scale (from tens of kilometres to a kilometre and one hour to a day), and the *micro* scale (from several hundred metres to a few centimetres, and from a few seconds to a few hours) (Figure 1.24).

The regional scale takes into account atmospheric phenomena such as regional winds influenced by mountain ranges, coastlines, large lakes, or forests. For example, a large lake can influence the climate of a region (through its temperature, humidity, wind, etc.) over several tens of square kilometres. At the local scale, these same atmospheric phenomena can be modified by other finer-scale factors. For example, inside a mountain range, a valley and adjacent mountains can cause local flows having day/night cycles (e.g. valley and mountain breezes). The microclimatic scale concerns climatic variations that are observed over shorter distances (Figure 1.24), and are often caused by differences in land use or isolated obstacles in the landscape—for example, the influence of different soil types on temperature at the scale of a single slope (Figure 1.25).

At the regional and local scales, surface roughness and type are factors that can create high spatial variability of the climate. In order to assess the impact of climate change at regional and local scales, the influence of these different factors must be prioritized and integrated into appropriate measurement and modelling frameworks.

It is important to understand the impacts of climate change at smaller scales in order to develop practical adaptation strategies that are appropriate to different aspects of human activity. Local factors (e.g. slope, exposure, soil type, distance from the sea, etc.) cause climate variations that can be greater than climate variability at a larger scale. It is this spatial–temporal variability of climate, combined with scale interaction (from macro- to microclimate), that defines living conditions for the population. An estimate of the impacts of climate change at a fine scale would allow better anticipation of possible economic and social consequences.

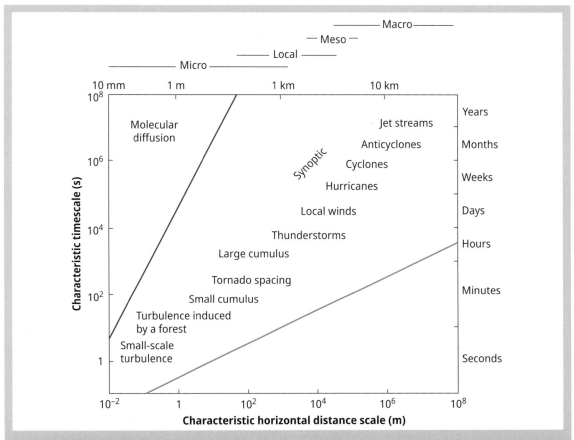

FIGURE I.24 Time and space scales of various atmospheric phenomena

Source: Hess, W. N. (1974). *Weather and Climate Modification*. Wiley, New York

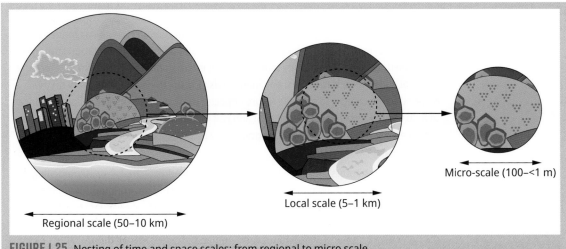

FIGURE I.25 Nesting of time and space scales: from regional to micro scale

Source: adapted from Quénol (2011). *Observation et modélisation spatiale du climat aux échelles fines dans un contexte de changement climatique*. Habilitation à Diriger des Recherches, Rennes 2 University, 91 pp

Understanding the interaction of atmospheric processes across a range of scales in different environments will provide the basis for developing comprehensive and effective adaptation strategies (Figure 1.25). This includes the problem of how to make global climate change projections relevant for local adaptation.

In the last few years, simulations of future climate have made significant progress in terms of reducing uncertainties and improving the spatial resolution of model outputs. Currently, **regional climate models** allow a spatial resolution of a few kilometres to be reached, but do not have a fine enough resolution to properly assess local-scale impacts. Improved measurement and simulation of climate change at the local scale is a key issue for developing both adaptation and mitigation methods. In this regard, it is important to know both the magnitude and location of specific local effects (e.g. changes in temperature, precipitation, cloud cover, and windiness), and how they respond to larger-scale atmospheric forcing (Le Treut 2010).

Summary

- The Earth–atmosphere system is complex (as illustrated in Figure 1.26), with many interacting human and natural factors that can cause climate to change at a range of spatial and temporal scales.

- Such change can result from the integration of many causes over differing timescales, which often makes understanding causative processes rather problematic.

- As a result of scientific research conducted over the past half-century, a lot more is now known about how the Earth–atmosphere system works. However, knowledge is still imperfect, which can make it difficult to reduce the uncertainty associated with both assessing impacts of change on a range of different regional and local environments (natural, agricultural, urban, etc.) and developing suitable adaptation strategies. For example, the influence of ENSO cycles generates complexity in specific regions of the world, making it difficult to accurately assess the regional- and local-scale impacts of the global warming signal.

- Although discussion of the causes and consequences of climate change has tended to be largely global in focus, in reality assessing impacts and developing adaptation strategies has to be done at the community scale. That is, it is a regional/local problem that requires regional authorities, businesses, and individuals to make decisions about how they will respond to observed and possible future impacts. These decision-makers need guidance to help them assess the vulnerability of and risk to their activities, as well as to identify any possible opportunities that global warming may provide, such as development of new crops.

- The following chapters therefore bring together knowledge of analysis and modelling techniques applied to regional and local climates in selected environments, with the aim of providing such guidance. This knowledge can be used to identify and quantify climate change impacts at the fine scale, as well as develop adaptation strategies based on a scientific understanding of the natural and human processes involved.

For case studies and updates, visit the online resources at:

 www.oup.com/he/sturman-quenol1e

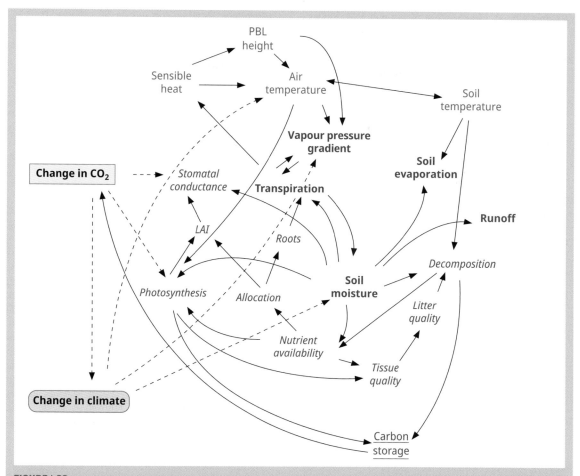

FIGURE 1.26 An illustration of the complexity of the interactions between changes in atmospheric carbon dioxide and climate and the soil, land cover, and local atmospheric systems. LAI is leaf area index, PBL is planetary (or atmospheric) boundary layer

Source: after Ehlers, E., and Krafft, T. (2001). *Understanding the Earth System: Compartments, Processes and Interactions*. Springer-Verlag, Berlin & Heidelberg

References

Ballantyne, A. P., Andres, R., Houghton, R., Stocker, B. D., Wanninkhof, R., Anderegg, W., Cooper, L. A., DeGrandpre, M., Tans, P. P., Miller, J. B., Alden, C., and White, J. W. C. (2015). Audit of the global carbon budget: Estimate errors and their impact on uptake uncertainty. *Biogeosciences* 12: 2565–84.

Ehlers, E., and Krafft, T. (2001). *Understanding the Earth System: Compartments, Processes and Interactions*. Springer-Verlag, Berlin & Heidelberg.

Elsom, D. M. (1992). *Atmospheric Pollution*. Blackwell, Oxford.

Fuhrer, J., and Gregory, P. J. (eds) (2014). *Climate Change Impact and Adaptation in Agricultural Systems*. CABI, Wallingford.

Hess, W. N. (1974). *Weather and Climate Modification*. Wiley, New York.

IPCC (2007). *Climate Change 2007: Synthesis Report*. Contribution of Working Groups I, II and III to the Fourth Assessment Report of the Intergovernmental Panel on Climate Change (Core Writing Team, Pachauri, R. K., and Reisinger, A. (eds)). IPCC, Geneva.

IPCC (2013). *Climate Change 2013: The Physical Science Basis*. Contribution of Working Group I to the Fifth Assessment Report of the Intergovernmental Panel on Climate Change [Stocker, T. F., D. Qin, G.-K. Plattner, M. Tignor, S. K. Allen,

J. Boschung, A. Nauels, Y. Xia, V. Bex and P. M. Midgley (eds)]. Cambridge University Press, Cambridge, United Kingdom and New York, NY, USA, 1535 pp.

IPCC (2014a). Summary for policymakers. In: Field, C. B., Barros, V. R., Dokken, D. J., Mach, K. J., Mastrandrea, M. D., Bilir, T. E., Chatterjee, M., Ebi, K. L., Estrada, Y. O., Genova, R. C., Girma, B., Kissel, E. S., Levy, A. N., Mac-Cracken, S., Mastrandrea, P. R., and White, L. L. (eds), *Climate Change 2014: Impacts, Adaptation, and Vulnerability. Part A: Global and Sectoral Aspects.* Contribution of Working Group II to the Fifth Assessment Report of the Intergovernmental Panel on Climate Change. Cambridge University Press, Cambridge and New York.

IPCC (2014b). *Climate Change 2014: Synthesis Report.* Contribution of Working Groups I, II and III to the Fifth Assessment Report of the Intergovernmental Panel on Climate Change (Core Writing Team, Pachauri, R. K., and Meyer, L. A. (eds)). IPCC, Geneva.

IPCC (2021). Summary for policymakers. In: Masson-Delmotte, V., Zhai, P., Pirani, A., Connors, S. L., Péan, C., Berger, S., Caud, N., Chen, Y., Goldfarb, L., Gomis, M. I., Huang, M., Leitzell, K., Lonnoy, E., Matthews, J. B. R., Maycock, T. K., Waterfield, T., Yelekçi, O., Yu, R., and Zhou, B. (eds), *Climate Change 2021: The Physical Science Basis.* Contribution of Working Group I to the Sixth Assessment Report of the Intergovernmental Panel on Climate Change. Cambridge University Press, Cambridge and New York.

Jones, G., Lockwood, M., and Stott, P. A. (2012). What influence will future solar activity changes over the 21st century have on projected global near-surface temperature changes? *Journal of Geophysical Research* 117, D05103, doi:10.1029/2011JD017013.

Jouzel, J., Masson-Delmotte, V., Cattani, O., Dreyfus, G., Falourd, S., Hoffmann, G., Minster, B., Nouet, J., Barnola, J. M., Chappellaz, J., Fischer, H., Gallet, J. C., Johnsen, S., Leuenberger, M., Loulergue, L., Luethi, D., Oerter, H., Parrenin, F., Raisbeck, G., Raynaud, D., Schilt, A., Schwander, J., Selmo, E., Souchez, R., Spahni, R., Stauffer, B., Steffensen, J. P., Stenni, B., Stocker, T. F., Tison, J. L., Werner, M. and Wolff, E. W. (2007). Orbital and Millennial Antarctic Climate Variability over the Past 800,000 Years. *Science* 317, 793–6.

Leal Filho, W. (2017). *Climate Change Adaptation in Pacific Countries. Climate Change Management.* Springer Nature, Cham, Switzerland.

Leal Filho, W., and Keenan, J. M. (2017). *Climate Change Adaptation in North America: Fostering Resilience and the Regional Capacity to Adapt.* Springer Nature, Cham, Switzerland.

Leal Filho, W., Simane, B., Kalangu, J., Wuta, M., Munishi, P., and Musiyiwa, K. (2017). *Climate Change Adaptation in Africa: Fostering Resilience and Capacity to Adapt.* Springer Nature, Cham, Switzerland.

Le Treut, H. (2010). *Modèles climatiques: certitudes, incertitudes et impacts locaux.* In: Dubreuil, V., Quénol, H., Planchon, O., and Bonnardot, V. (eds), *Risques et changement climatique.* Actes du colloque du 23e colloque de l'Association Internationale de Climatologie, Rennes, pp. 7–10.

Metz, B. (2009). *Controlling Climate Change.* Cambridge University Press, Cambridge.

Nelson, G. C., Rosegrant, M. W., Koo, J., Robertson, R., Sulser, T., Zhu, T., Ringler, C., Msangi, S., Palazzo, A., Batka, M., Magalhaes, M., Valmonte-Santos, R., Ewing, M., and Lee, D. (2009). *Climate Change: Impact on Agriculture and Costs of Adaptation*, Vol. 21. International Food Policy Research Institute, Washington, DC.

Oke, T. R. (1987). *Boundary Layer Climates.* Routledge, Abingdon, England.

Park, C. C. (2001). *The Environment: Principles and Applications* (2nd edn). Routledge, London and New York.

Parry, M., Canziani, O., and Palutikof, J. (2008). Key IPCC conclusion on climate change impacts and adaptations. *WMO Bulletin* 57(2).

Petit, J. R., Jouzel, J., Raynaud, D., Barkov, N. I., Barnola, J.-M., Basile, I., Benders, M., Chappellaz, J., Davis, M., Delayque, G., Delmotte, M., Kotlyakov, V. M., Legrand, M., Lipenkov, V. Y., Lorius, C., Pépin, L., Ritz, C., Saltzman, E., and Stievenard, M. (1999). Climate and atmospheric history of the past 420,000 years from the Vostok ice core, Antarctica. *Nature* 399: 429–36.

Pickering, K. T., and Owen, L. A. (1994). *An Introduction to Global Environmental Issues.* Routledge, London.

Quénol, H. (2011). *Observation et modélisation spatiale du climat aux échelles fines dans un contexte de changement climatique.* Habilitation à Diriger des Recherches, Rennes 2 University, 91 pp.

Simpson, M. C., Gössling, S., Scott, D., Hall, C. M., and Gladin, E. (2008). *Climate Change Adaptation and Mitigation in the Tourism Sector: Frameworks, Tools and Practices.* UNEP, University of Oxford, UNWTO, WMO, Paris.

Sturman, A., and Quénol, H. (2013). Changes in atmospheric circulation and temperature trends in major vineyard regions of New Zealand. *International Journal of Climatology* 33: 2609–21.

Sturman, A. P., and Tapper, N. J. (2006). *The Weather and Climate of Australia and New Zealand* (2nd edn). Oxford University Press, Melbourne.

Thorne, P. W., Menne, M. J., Williams, C. N., Rennie, J. J., Lawrimore, J. H., Vose, R. S., Peterson, T. C., Durre, I., Davy, R., Esau, I., Klein-Tank, A. M. G., and Merlone, A. (2016). Reassessing changes in diurnal temperature range: A new data set and characterization of data biases. *Journal of Geophysical Research: Atmospheres* 121: 5115–37.

van Noordwijk, M., Hoang, M. H., Neufeldt, H., Öborn, I., and Yatich, T. (2011). *How Trees and People Can Co-adapt to Climate Change: Reducing Vulnerability through Multifunctional Agroforestry Landscapes.* World Agroforestry Centre (ICRAF), Nairobi.

Williams, M. A. J., Dunkerley, D. L., De Deckker, P. D., Kershaw, A. P., and Stokes, T. (1998). *Quaternary Environments* (2nd edn). Edward Arnold and Oxford University Press, London.

CHAPTER **TWO**

Approaches to Regional and Local Downscaling

LEARNING OUTCOMES

Having read this chapter, you should be able to:

- understand the general concept of climate modelling and the limitations of global climate models

- comprehend the origin and application of climate change scenarios

- explain why global climate model scenarios need to be downscaled to regional and local scales

- outline the main approaches used to downscale climate change scenarios from global climate models to the regional and local scales

- describe the sources of uncertainty in climate models and ways in which it can be reduced

- explore the practicalities of predicting future climates across a range of spatial scales

- discuss the possible future development of modelling systems in order to predict climate change impacts and develop adaptation strategies

2.1 Introduction: downscaling global climate models to smaller scales

Ideally, every local community needs to be able to assess the robustness of their region to the threats posed by global climate change. In order to achieve this, decision-makers need access to reliable information based on solid scientific foundations. Although work on understanding the causes of climate change and developing mitigation policies tends to occur at the global scale (e.g. by the United Nations Framework Convention on Climate Change, and the European Union), this work has limitations that make its application less useful at the regional and local scales. In particular, complex terrain and land-use variations at fine spatial scales have traditionally been poorly captured within global models, making realistic predictions of climate change impacts at the local level unreliable, although recent improvements in computing power and complexity of global climate models have allowed finer-resolution climate predictions (IPCC 2021). In order to provide reliable information for local authorities to develop response strategies designed for the scale of their territory, simulations generated by the international community must be downscaled to regional and local levels.

Depending on the application, a number of approaches have been used to downscale the spatial and temporal resolution of global climate predictions. Table 2.1 outlines these approaches and their various applications. The users of both global climate models and these downscaling techniques are many and varied, but are frequently non-specialists (e.g. engineers and planners) who are interested in applying knowledge of climate and climate change to the development of adaptation strategies at the local and regional scales.

In this chapter we evaluate the methodological approaches to regional and local downscaling of climate predictions that provide the solid scientific foundation for developing adaptation strategies needed at local levels. We consider the limitations of global climate models and the various approaches to downscaling to smaller scales shown in Table 2.1. Users of these approaches need to be aware of the limitations of such models, and

TABLE 2.1 Spatial and temporal scales of climate models and their application

CLIMATE MODELS	SPATIAL RESOLUTION	TEMPORAL RESOLUTION	SCALE	APPLICATION
Global (GCM)	From 5° to 0.5° (500 to 50 km)	From 10 years to several hundred years	Global	Modelling of atmospheric general circulation Modelling of global warming
Global with varying resolution (VRGCM)	From 1° (lat/long) to 10–12 km	From 10 years to several hundred years	Global and regional	Weather forecasting Modelling of global warming
Regional (RCM)	From 50 km to 200 m (imbricated grids)	Hourly to several years	Regional and local	Weather forecasting Meso-scale **climate modelling**
Statistical downscaling	From several km to several metres	Hourly to several years	Regional and local	Local-scale climate modelling
Interpolation of climate data	Several metres	Hourly to several years	Local	Local-scale climate modelling

Note: GCM = global climate model, VRGCM = variable resolution global climate model, RCM = regional climate model
Source: Quénol et al. (2017). Which climatic modelling to assess climate change impacts on vineyards? *OENO One* 51: 91–7

the sources and magnitudes of the uncertainty associated with their predictions. Such issues are therefore also addressed in this chapter. Finally, we consider the next steps for regional and local downscaling, as we review the need for **complex models** that account for the myriad influencing factors behind climate change scenarios.

2.2 How can we downscale global climate models to regional and local scales?

WHAT ARE GLOBAL CLIMATE MODELS?

Global climate models (GCMs) are complex computer programs that are closely related to **weather forecasting models**. Like weather forecasting models, they attempt to represent the processes that operate in the atmosphere through application of fundamental equations of atmospheric physics. The main difference between them is that weather models simulate short-term weather and are forced (driven) by observed data, while climate models are applied over long periods of time in order to predict future climate change over periods of several decades or even hundreds of years (for which there are no data). Climate models have also been used to simulate the climate of the past as part of the model development and testing process.

Climate models include relatively simplified representations of the surface of the Earth and its atmosphere that take into account the mechanisms that govern atmospheric circulation. The planet is represented by a three-dimensional grid within which complex equations are applied to simulate the range of natural processes involved (Figure 2.1), often within sub-models representing the atmosphere, land surface interactions, ocean–atmosphere interactions, the cryosphere, and the biosphere. The atmospheric component of these models includes equations representing the mechanics of atmospheric motion, thermodynamic processes, and energy fluxes, as well as the **microphysics** associated with cloud and precipitation formation. The basic laws underlying these physical processes have been known for a long time, but the logical structure behind the current atmospheric numerical models was not developed until Lewis

Fry Richardson's work of the 1920s (Richardson 1922). Such global models are used to calculate meteorological parameters (e.g. temperature, humidity, wind, and precipitation) for each grid cell over different timescales. By integrating these equations over time, **dynamical models** attempt to predict the state of the atmosphere at some time in the future based on its current state. For example, as described in the 6th Assessment Report of the **Intergovernmental Panel on Climate Change** (IPCC 2021), climate simulations have been carried out at the global (or planetary) scale typically using a horizontal grid resolution of around 0.5° latitude and longitude (approximately 50 km resolution grid) over the period 2000–2100 (see Figure 2.1). This spatial resolution allows us to simulate the influence of different **emission scenarios** on the general circulation of the atmosphere and to estimate their impact on climate variables, such as temperature and precipitation, at a global scale. These models are the key element in any simulation of climate change and provide the starting point for assessing the impacts of climate change at finer spatial resolutions.

GREENHOUSE GAS EMISSIONS IN GLOBAL CLIMATE MODELLING

As it is not possible to represent all atmospheric processes by fundamental equations based on physical laws, some components of atmospheric models are based on statistical relationships between meteorological variables. In order to predict the effects of human activity on the current global warming trend, the main forcing used in global climate models is the estimated contribution of

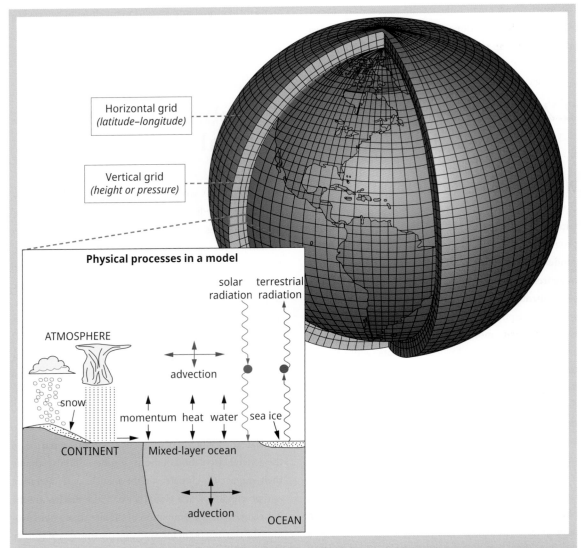

FIGURE 2.1 Schematic illustration of the three-dimensional gridded structure of a global atmospheric model

Source: http://celebrating200years.noaa.gov/breakthroughs/climate_model/modeling_schematic.html

anthropogenic emissions to modification of greenhouse gas concentrations in the atmosphere. The intensity of this greenhouse gas forcing varies in response to different future socio-economic scenarios that have been established to reflect possible evolution pathways of all human activities. The scenarios that have been used for future climate simulations, termed **Representative Concentration Pathways** (van Vuuren et al. 2011), therefore take into account several possible futures defined by a certain level of population, a certain type of industry and energy system, and growth in response to possible national and international policies (Nakićenović and Swart 2000). All of this information is used to estimate future greenhouse gas emissions. These Representative Concentration Pathways (RCPs) include both high and low greenhouse gas emission scenarios, reflecting the political will of key countries to mitigate climate change. For the Fifth IPCC Report, there were four RCPs, named after a range of possible radiation forcing values: RCP2.6, RCP4.5, RCP6, and RCP8.5. Each RCP represents a possible increase in net radiation (+2.6, +4.5, +6.0, and +8.5 W m^{-2}) expected in 2100 compared with pre-industrial values (see Table 2.2) (IPCC 2013).

It should be noted here that a scenario is not the same as a prediction, as a scenario is used to indicate in a simplified way how future conditions may change based on a set of hypothetical assumptions about the driving force of that change. For example, the scenario RCP2.6 assumed that global annual greenhouse gas emissions will peak between 2010 and 2020 and then decline substantially, while RCP4.5 assumed that emissions will peak at around 2040 before declining, RCP6 assumed that emissions will peak at around 2080 before declining, and RCP8.5 assumed that emissions will continue to rise throughout the twenty-first century. These assumptions need to be represented by varying rates of change in greenhouse gas emissions within climate models in order to provide an idea of the impact of each scenario on future climate. In comparison, short-term weather predictions or forecasts are more **deterministic estimates** of the future state of the atmosphere based on the initial conditions derived from observations and how well the model is able to represent atmospheric processes.

For the Sixth IPCC Report, a new set of scenarios termed **Shared Socioeconomic Pathways (SSP)** was created to input into the climate models used in the CMIP6 project (**CMIP** stands for Coupled Model Intercomparison Project—IPCC 2021; O'Neil et al. 2016; Riahi et al. 2017). The major contribution of this modelling project lies in the greater choice of scenarios that allow development of different socio-economic trajectories. Only RCP8.5 corresponded to the most pessimistic scenario in the earlier CMIP5 project, while additional scenarios were added in CMIP6. For example, the newer SSP3–7.0 scenario corresponds to an intermediate scenario between RCP8.5 and RCP6.0 (reflecting weak mitigation policies), while SSP1–1.9 takes into account the results of the Paris Agreement that aimed to limit global warming to 1.5 °C by 2100 compared to pre-industrial levels. The simulations carried out in CMIP6 therefore used a greater range of emission scenarios than CMIP5, as well as more powerful models. The results showed similar trends over the historical period and more intense warming for mean and extreme temperatures in the future. As shown in Figure 2.2, these different scenarios can be used to indicate the range of possible alternative outcomes based on different assumptions about changes in human behaviour and their impact.

Figure 2.3 shows the differences in global patterns of temperature and precipitation change simulated for 2081–2100 relative to 1995–2014 associated with three different SSPs reflecting maximum reduction of greenhouse gas emissions (SSP1–1.0) through to no change in human behaviour (i.e. the 'business-as-usual' scenario of SSP5–8.5). The simulations show that the greatest warming appears to be in the Arctic region and over the

TABLE 2.2 The key characteristics of the four RCPs

NAME	RADIATIVE FORCING	CONCENTRATION (PPM)	PATHWAY
RCP8.5	>8.5 W m^{-2} in 2100	>1,370 CO_2-equivalent in 2100	Rising
RCP6.0	~6 W m^{-2} at stabilization after 2100	~850 CO_2-equivalent (at stabilization after 2100)	Stabilization without overshoot
RCP4.5	~4.5 W m^{-2} at stabilization after 2100	~650 CO_2-equivalent (at stabilization after 2100)	Stabilization without overshoot
RCP2.6	Peak at ~3 W m^{-2} before 2100 and then declines	Peak at ~490 CO_2-equivalent before 2100 and then declines	Peak and decline

Source: Moss et al. (2010). The next generation of scenarios for climate change research and assessment. *Nature* 463(7282): 747–56

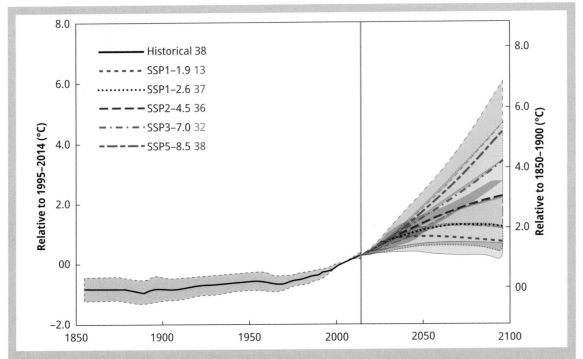

FIGURE 2.2 Evolution of global temperature change between 1850 and 2100 according to different SSP scenarios, referenced to baseline periods of 1850–1900 and 1995–2014. The black line indicates historical simulations or observations, while the coloured lines indicate modelled future temperature changes based on the different SSPs. Shading indicates the range of uncertainty

Source: Tebaldi et al. (2021). Climate model projections from the Scenario Model Intercomparison Project (ScenarioMIP) of CMIP6. *Earth System Dynamics* 12: 253–93

main continents, with lesser warming over the North Atlantic and Southern Ocean, particularly with scenario SSP5–8.5. The simulated pattern of precipitation change is more complex, with greater increases over the poles and parts of the tropical regions, and decreases over eastern parts of the oceans in the Southern Hemisphere, the central Atlantic Ocean, the Mediterranean Sea, and the Amazon regions (Tebaldi et al. 2021). Such model predictions provide a useful broad framework for the development of adaptation strategies at the regional and national scale, but more detailed information is needed to help individuals, businesses, and regional authorities respond effectively to possible future climate change.

APPROACHES TO DOWNSCALING TO SMALLER SCALES

Global climate models (GCMs) currently have a resolution of several tens to hundreds of kilometres (typically, 0.5° latitude/longitude or 55 × 55 km at the equator), so atmospheric processes and phenomena at a horizontal resolution of less than 10 km are not often well represented. In particular, they do not take into account small-scale variations in surface characteristics, such as complex terrain and land use, and the resulting spatial variability of climate. Downscaling methods are therefore used to incorporate the effects of complex surface variability and increase the spatial resolution of models

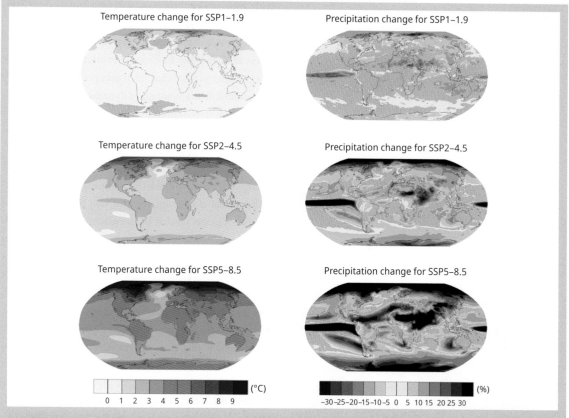

FIGURE 2.3 Differences in global temperature (left column) and precipitation change (right column) between 1995–2014 and 2081–2190 based on CMIP6 model simulations and scenarios SSP1–1.9, SSP2–4.5, and SSP5–8.5. Hatched areas are not statistically significant

Source: Tebaldi et al. (2021). Climate model projections from the Scenario Model Intercomparison Project (ScenarioMIP) of CMIP6. *Earth System Dynamics* 12: 253–93

to less than 500 metres (Figure 2.4). This provides a more accurate fine-scale prediction, allowing for improved impact assessment, and supports the development of sound adaption strategies at local levels.

Dynamical and statistical modelling systems (Figure 2.4) differ in that, while dynamical models are based on the laws of physics, **statistical models** are based on constancy of a statistical relationship between sets of measured variables derived from a specific data set. Therefore, while

dynamical models have universal application, statistical models are constrained to the data set upon which they are based. It should follow that atmospheric dynamical models perform better than statistical models for situations where the physical equations used provide a good representation of actual processes in the atmosphere. However, statistical models can be useful for situations when a specific physical relationship is poorly understood or too complex to be represented by fundamental equations in a climate model,

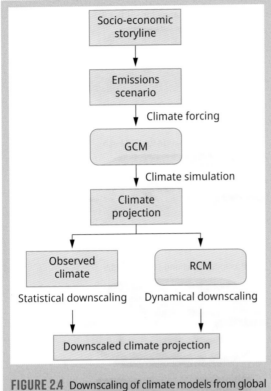

FIGURE 2.4 Downscaling of climate models from global to local scale using dynamical and statistical techniques

Source: Daniels et al. (2012). Climate projections FAQ. In: *General Technical Report*. RMRS-GTR-277WWW, Fort Collins, CO, US Department of Agriculture, Forest Service, Rocky Mountain Research Station

or when it is computationally more efficient (e.g. when conducting high-resolution simulations) (IPCC 2007). In general, the use of the dynamical approach, the statistical approach, or a dynamical/statistical combination should be based on the objectives (e.g. impact assessment at the regional or local scale), the available resources (especially computing resources), and the levels of uncertainty expected in the results (Figure 2.5).

DYNAMICAL DOWNSCALING

Dynamical downscaling allows the regionalization of GCM outputs to smaller sub-areas on the Earth's surface. It does this using the physical equations associated

with atmospheric processes and their interactions with surface characteristics, including terrain and land use. These physical equations are applied in the region of interest at a relatively fine spatial resolution (e.g. 1 km or less), so that surface characteristics are more accurately represented. The advantage of dynamical downscaling is that it attempts to represent the actual physical processes operating in the atmosphere at the finest scale possible. The disadvantage is that this approach requires significantly large computer resources.

Regional climate models (RCMs) are dynamically downscaled global climate models that aim to regionalize the outputs of global models by using nesting of model grids of increasing resolution. The first grid is thus forced at its boundaries by atmospheric fields at low resolution (often from the global climate models), while the last grid provides simulations at the finest resolution. These fine grids represent the circulation of the atmosphere at the regional scale. As the resolution of climate models increases, the effects of surface characteristics such as topography, vegetation, **hydrography**, and soil characteristics are better represented. Two types of regional atmospheric model are typically used: **variable resolution general circulation models (VRGCMs)** and regional climate models (RCMs) (see Table 2.1). VRGCMs are GCMs with improved spatial grid resolution over specific areas of interest. Variable-sized grid cells are used across the whole model domain in order to avoid the need for huge computing resources. This results in what is called a stretched grid, with variable grid spacing over different parts of the whole gridded area and higher spatial resolution for regions of interest (as shown in Figure 2.6). These models are robust because they use the same physical equations as the GCMs on which they depend. High-resolution grids cannot be applied across the whole globe because of the prohibitive demand for computational capacity, while the coarse spatial resolution of GCMs (several tens of kilometres) is not sufficiently precise for regional studies, so that the use of stretched grids provides a solution to these problems. Having said that, recent increases in computational capacity have allowed improvement in the spatial resolution of global climate models (as shown in Figure 2.7).

RCMs are also dynamical models and have a much finer spatial resolution (10–20 km) than the GCMs. This

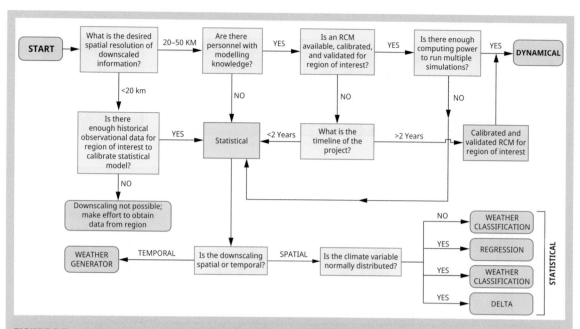

FIGURE 2.5 Logical steps in deciding between dynamical and statistical downscaling

Source: Trzaska, S., and Schnarr, E. (2014). A review of downscaling methods for climate change projections. *United States Agency for International Development by Tetra Tech ARD*, 1–42

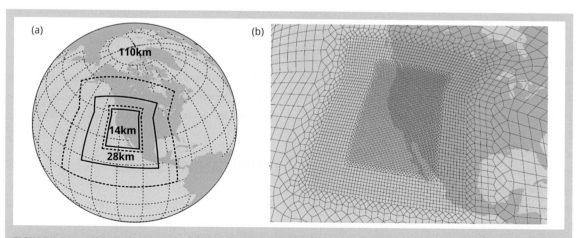

FIGURE 2.6 Variable resolution model downscaling: (a) from the global 110 km resolution mesh through two layers of refinement to 28 and 14 km, and (b) depiction of the grid structure used in the transition from the 110 km to the 14 km grid

Source: Huang et al. (2016). An evaluation of the variable-resolution-CESM for modeling California's climate. *Journal of Advanced Modeling of Earth Systems* 8: 345–69 and Wang et al. (2018). The future of wind energy in California: Future projections with the Variable-Resolution CESM. *Renewable Energy* 127, 242–57

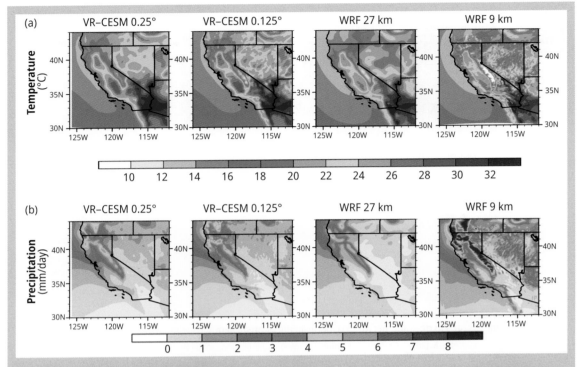

FIGURE 2.7 Evaluation of variable resolution models (VR-CESM) and a Regional Climate Model (Weather Research and Forecasting model—WRF) for modelling California's climate: (a) mean June–August temperature and (b) annual precipitation

Source: Huang et al. (2016). An evaluation of the variable-resolution-CESM for modeling California's climate. *Journal of Advanced Modeling of Earth Systems* 8: 345–69

allows a better representation of surface conditions, such as orography, land–sea contrast, vegetation, and land use. Although they simulate regional physical processes, they are much less complex than global models. RCMs can be forced at their edges by GCMs, and the results provide an important assessment of uncertainty, particularly for future climate simulations (e.g. the DRIAS platform, http://www.drias-climat.fr/). For example, regionalized multimodel simulations of the climate of France at a spatial resolution of 8 km have produced varying results. Figure 2.8 highlights different distributions of modelled temperatures depending on the model used (WRF or **Aladin-Climat**) and the period modelled (2021–2050 or 2071–2100). In this example, model bias was estimated by deriving anomalies with reference to the period 1958–2008. Bias associated with specific RCMs may be related

to their particular structure, but it can generally be identified and corrected during the downscaling process. This may be as simple as subtracting a constant value from the predicted temperatures if the relationship is **linear**.

STATISTICAL DOWNSCALING

The use of an RCM allows detailed investigation of spatial patterns obtained by global models. However, the significant computing capacity needed to run these models makes it difficult to achieve satisfactory results at a very fine scale, especially over long periods of time or for impact studies. Downscaling using statistical methods requires less computing capacity than dynamical methods, which may allow a finer spatial resolution. Such methods can also be used to

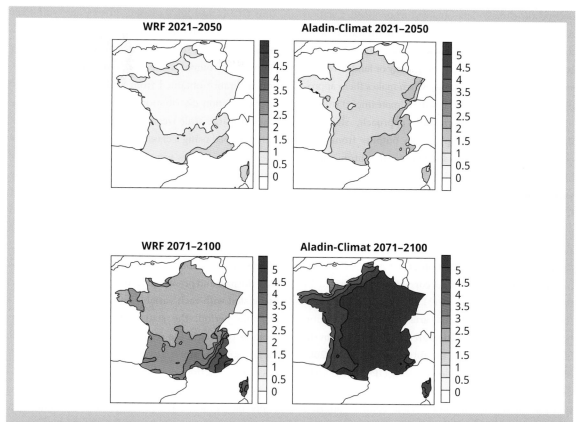

FIGURE 2.8 Evaluation of regional climate models (WRF and Aladin-Climat) at 12 km resolution for modelling summer temperature anomalies (°C) in France for 2021–2050 (top) and 2071–2100 (bottom) based on the RCP8.5 scenario, and a reference period of 1976–2005

Source: Ouzeau et al. (2014). *Le climat de la France au XXIe siècle*, Vol. 4, *Scénarios régionalisés: édition 2014 pour la métropole et les régions d'outre-mer*. Rapport, Ministere de l'Ecologie, du Developpement durable et de l'Energie

reduce biases identified in the output of dynamical models (e.g. consistently high or low temperatures, precipitation, or wind speeds), through comparison with observed data over selected model evaluation periods.

Statistical downscaling involves the application of a number of statistical techniques to identify the relationship between a selected climate variable (e.g. air temperature) and land surface characteristics (e.g. altitude, aspect, slope, or land cover). Regression or **neural network modelling** techniques have frequently been used to define the relationship between temperature and terrain, often at a spatial resolution of only tens of metres (Schoof and Pryor 2001). The advantages of statistical downscaling are that it can be used where the physical processes are not properly

understood, and it requires significantly less computer resources. However, the disadvantage is that it is only valid for the data set from which it was derived.

Approaches to statistical downscaling depend on the statistical relationship between the global-scale variables from GCMs and regional/local factors (e.g. topography, hydrography, and land use). This relationship is based on the correlation between predicted temperature over a large area and predicted temperature at the regional or local scale. Using this relationship allows the continental- and national-scale patterns to be applied to much smaller scales. Identifying this relationship can be achieved using several methods, including multiple linear regression and neural networks. These **empirical methods** typically depend on climate data obtained from weather station networks. One of the main advantages of these methods is that they incorporate the impact of the unique characteristics of specific regions (e.g. orography or land cover) on small-scale climate variations, which makes them appropriate for regional- and local-scale climate impact studies.

Using a multiple regression approach, statistical downscaling has been applied to outputs from both GCMs and RCMs in New England for the future period of 2046–2065 (Ahmed et al. 2013). In their study, the **predictands** were the expected observed climate data from weather station networks. Incorporating surface parameters at the local scale (e.g. land use and topography) was shown to improve the spatial resolution of the results, while the use of observed data in statistical downscaling also helped to correct bias generated by the RCMs (Ahmed et al. 2013). For example, Figure 2.9 shows the very high regional variability of the total number of days with precipitation greater than 10 mm in the New England region for the future period 2046–2065 obtained using statistical downscaling (IPCC 2007). The difference between the coarse-resolution GCM simulation and the statistically downscaled regional pattern is very apparent. As a result, Ahmed et al. (2013) demonstrated the usefulness of the statistical downscaling approach to create a set of climate indicators based on temperature and precipitation that can be used for regional climate change impact studies.

Other statistical downscaling methods have been based on weather regime identification using weather type classification (or **weather typing**). Weather typing generally involves classifying daily weather situations based on some sort of objective clustering of mean sea level pressure patterns. Large-scale weather patterns from GCMs and RCMs based on weather typing can be associated with specific distributions of regional climate parameters, such as temperature or precipitation. Figure 2.10 compares the coarse pattern of precipitation in France obtained from a GCM with the much finer-resolution distribution obtained using a method based on large-scale weather typing. Climate scenarios were grouped using a classification of 10 weather types. These weather types were then associated with spatial patterns of climate variables such as precipitation (liquid and solid), temperature, wind speed and direction, infrared and visible radiation, and **specific humidity** at a resolution of 8 km. The climate variables were then compared with a database of **mesoscale** meteorological observations, enabling the validation of data modelled over the past and present period, in order to assess biases associated with each variable and weather type. After a learning period, the statistical relationship between weather types and the regional distribution of climatic variables can be applied over future periods on the basis of GCM predictions.

As we have established, statistical downscaling generally allows more efficient representation of finer spatial resolutions than dynamical downscaling. However, the main weakness of the statistical approach is that it is a static model independent of atmospheric physics. Therefore, it is assumed that the statistical relationships defined from the current climate will remain unchanged in future climates. In addition to being computationally efficient, it can be used for bias correction for climate model simulations (Ahmed et al. 2013). A number of comparative studies have shown that dynamical and statistical downscaling can provide similar results (Wilby and Wigley 2000; Wood et al. 2004; Le Roux et al. 2018).

2.3 How can we deal with model uncertainty?

There are many sources of uncertainty in climate change modelling, and it should be recognized that it is impossible to know exactly what the climate will be in 2050 or 2100. This is because, first, the models that we use still do not perfectly represent all of the complex processes that operate in the atmosphere. Second, the input data that are used to initialize climate models are neither free of error nor available at sufficient spatial and temporal

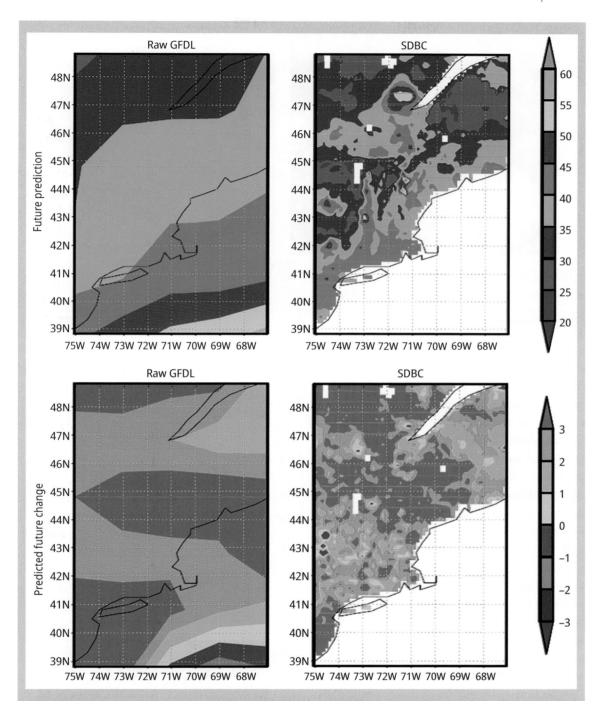

FIGURE 2.9 The mean of the total number of days in the New England region with precipitation greater than 10 mm from a GCM (left) and statistically downscaled (right) for the future (2046–2065) (top two maps), and predicted changes from present-day (1961–1999) mean values (bottom two maps)

Source: Ahmed et al. (2013). Statistical downscaling and bias correction of climate model outputs for climate change impact assessment in the U.S. Northeast. *Global and Planetary Change* 100: 320–32

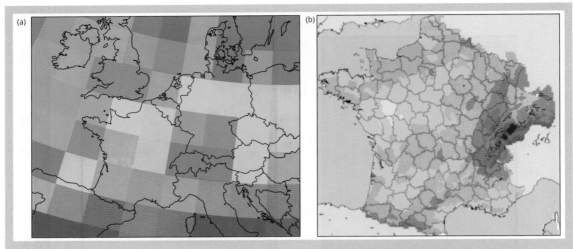

FIGURE 2.10 Example of statistical downscaling of precipitation (mm/day) in France from the spatial resolution of (a) a global climate model (with a 2.5° x 3.75° grid resolution) to (b) a spatial resolution of 8 km

Source: Page, C., and Terray, L. (2011). *Nouvelles projections climatiques à échelle fine sur la France pour le 21ème siècle: Les scénarii SCRATCH2010.* CERFACS Technical Report TR/CMGC/10/58, Toulouse, France

resolution. Third, there will always be an element of chaos in the operation of atmosphere processes which makes any predictions imperfect. Observations show us that there are regional changes in precipitation, **cloud fraction**, shifting **jet streams,** and temperature patterns that are not well represented by GCMs. It seems that the impact of different scenarios on regional-scale climate is likely to be inaccurate for precipitation intensity and frequency (e.g. floods and droughts), sea ice (especially in the Southern Hemisphere), and sea level rise (as a result of unknown ice sheet processes) (Gettelman and Rood 2016). To achieve sound adaption strategies, it is therefore important to identify the sources of uncertainty. In particular, it is important to establish the general category of the uncertainty (e.g. scientific, socio-economic, natural climate variability, or human behaviour), and its influence on the accuracy of future climate modelling.

As we have already established, downscaling methods are needed to be able to apply the predictions of global climate models to regional and local impact studies. However, the process of downscaling introduces increasing levels of uncertainty. The modelling chain illustrated in Figure 2.11 demonstrates how each new link brings increasing levels of uncertainty. This could be called a cascade of uncertainties,

in which it is clear that the increased spatial resolution of the simulations leads to greater uncertainty (Boé 2007).

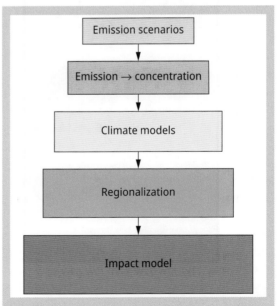

FIGURE 2.11 The concept of a cascade of uncertainties with increasing box size reflecting the increasing level of uncertainty

Source: Boe, J. (2007). *Changement global et cycle hydrologique: Une étude de régionalisation sur la France.* These de Doctorat, Universite Paul Sabatier—Toulouse III

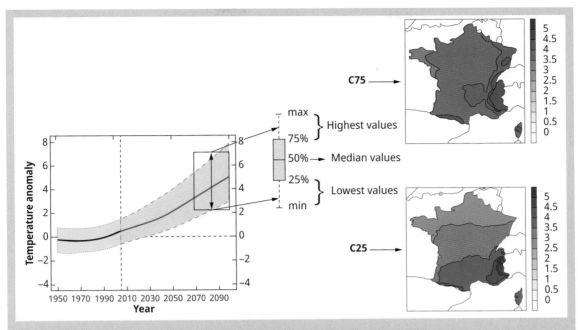

FIGURE 2.12 An illustration of the scatter associated with model predictions of temperature anomalies (from the baseline period 1976–2005) over France. C25 (first quartile) represents the value below which 25% of the distribution of temperature anomalies occurs, while C75 (third quartile) represents the value below which 75% of the distribution occurs

Source: Ouzeau et al. (2014). *Le climat de la France au XXIe siècle*, Vol. 4, *Scénarios régionalisés: édition 2014 pour la métropole et les régions d'outre-mer*. Rapport, Ministere de l'Ecologie, du Developpement durable et de l'Energie

IDENTIFYING UNCERTAINTY IN CLIMATE MODELS

The uncertainty associated with atmospheric numerical models, whether GCMs or short-term weather forecasting models, can result in significant scatter (or variation) in the predicted value of a particular climate variable (e.g. temperature or precipitation), as shown in Figure 2.12. Such uncertainty is associated with three main sources, as discussed by Hawkins and Sutton (2009) and Gettelman and Rood (2016), these being: **model uncertainty**, initial condition uncertainty, and scenario uncertainty. These are associated with model design (how well do the models represent actual environmental processes?), accuracy of our knowledge of the current state of the atmosphere (how good are the input data?), and the predictability of human behaviour into the future (how well can we predict human activity

and greenhouse gas emissions?). Attempts can be made to quantify these uncertainties, but we first need to identify where they come from before we can take steps to reduce them.

MODEL UNCERTAINTY

Uncertainty can be both implicit in the model itself, as well as in how the model is applied. These uncertainties are defined as model uncertainty, as they are associated with the workings of the model itself. This includes incorrect or inaccurate formulation of important processes (e.g. via **parameterization** of less well-understood processes). Scale is an important factor in this regard, as there is typically uncertainty associated with the representation of **sub-grid-scale processes** (processes that operate at a finer spatial and temporal resolution than the model grid), such as the role of cloud. This is because the practicality associated with

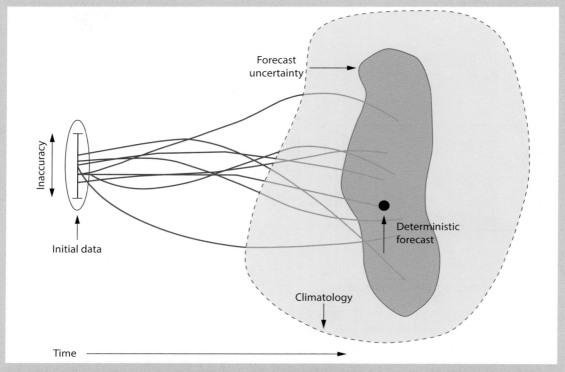

FIGURE 2.13 Schematic illustration of initial condition uncertainty

Source: modified after Slingo, J., and Palmer, T. (2011). Uncertainty in weather and climate prediction. *Philosophical Transactions of the Royal Society A* 369(1956): 4751–67

running atmospheric models on often limited computer facilities makes it unfeasible to directly represent all atmospheric processes, so that parametrization becomes necessary to deal with finer spatial and temporal resolutions.

INITIAL CONDITION UNCERTAINTY

This is associated with inaccuracy of the input data used to initialize the model, including representation of the **boundary conditions** (Figure 2.13). Initial condition uncertainty is considered less of a problem with regard to GCMs, as climate predictions typically cover several decades. However, it does have an impact on the reliability of short-term weather forecasts in data-scarce parts of the world, for example. Any small errors in representing the initial state of the atmosphere can propagate to become major errors over time.

SCENARIO UNCERTAINTY

There is also uncertainty associated with the assumptions that are used to generate the scenarios that provide what may be plausible future outcomes of climate change (shown earlier in Figure 2.2). The basis for the four main scenarios, expressed as Representative Concentration Pathways (RCPs), is discussed earlier in Table 2.2 and the associated text. These RCPs, and the more recent SSPs, are based on socio-economic models that reflect such things as changes in population, economic growth, adoption of clean technologies, public perception and attitudes, and changing energy-use patterns. These scenarios therefore largely depend on the degree to which humans as policy-makers or individuals respond to the need to reduce greenhouse gas emissions by cutting back on the use of fossil fuels. The responses can vary between the most extreme scenario reflected in RCP8.5 (representing

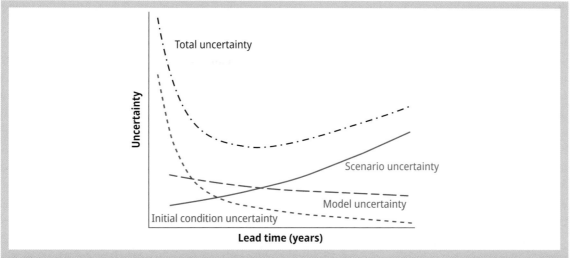

FIGURE 2.14 Different contributions to climate model uncertainty

Source: Hawkins, E., and Sutton, R. (2009). The potential to narrow uncertainty in regional climate prediction. *Bulletin of the American Meteorological Society* 90: 1095–107

'business as usual'—little is done by individuals or the community to mitigate the problem) and RCP2.6 (which represents a situation in which significant public concern results in drastic cuts in fossil-fuel emissions).

As illustrated in Figure 2.14, the total uncertainty associated with a climate model is at first dominated by initial condition uncertainty and later scenario uncertainty (Gettelman and Rood 2016). Model uncertainty stays relatively constant and is largely dependent on how well the model represents the physical processes operating in the Earth–atmosphere system.

REDUCING UNCERTAINTY IN CLIMATE MODELS

GCMs have improved significantly over the past several decades, through both better representation of key atmospheric processes in model design, and a rapid increase in high-performance computing capability. However, there is still uncertainty associated with model representation of a number of atmospheric processes. These include those involving water vapour and cloud feedback, the cryosphere (snow and ice cover), and radiation exchanges. The relationship between some of these processes can be quite

complex, making it difficult to incorporate them into a GCM. For example, there is a complex relationship between water vapour, cloud, and radiation, which also involves atmospheric aerosol content. There is therefore much effort to try and identify the main sources of uncertainty in GCM predictions and to determine their relative magnitude (e.g. Gordon et al. 2000; Crook and Forster 2014; Fasullo and Trenberth 2012; Qu et al. 2014; Sherwood et al. 2014; Tian et al. 2015; Huber and Zanna 2017). This work suggests that although GCMs appear to be getting the large-scale climate roughly right, much more work is needed before smaller-scale climate is reliability predicted.

A number of modelling experiments have been conducted to try to address the issue of model uncertainty, particularly in relation to providing realistic scenarios at a range of scales. For example, data assimilation can be used to reduce uncertainty in weather forecasting models. This involves using available observations to constrain models when forecasts start to go astray. However, when looking at climate, GCMs aim to predict so far into the future that it is not possible to use real measurements to help the model stay on track.

Bias correction has also been considered as a way of reducing uncertainty. There may be a consistent bias evident between model predictions and observations, as has been recognized with a negative bias in temperatures predicted by the WRF model by Steele et al. (2014) and Hu et al. (2010). If this is the case then it is possible to make a simple correction for this bias—for example, by adding or subtracting the average difference between observation and prediction. However, this is not often a reliable fix as the bias may vary with season or under different weather conditions. There is also significant uncertainty with the prediction of extremes, such as the impact of tropical cyclones, floods, and droughts. This makes the process of bias correction to reduce uncertainties difficult.

The most common approach to reducing uncertainty in climate models is to use groups of different models. These ensembles (groups) are created by conducting multiple model runs using a range of different settings (Figure 2.15) (Lutz et al. 2016; McSweeney and Jones 2016). This approach can be used to investigate uncertainty associated with different scenarios, model types/designs, and initial conditions. For example, several different GCMs designed by different research laboratories can be run using the same input data and basic set-up configurations. Alternatively, the same model can be run using a range of different settings or input data sets (Figure 2.16), while a range of different models could be run using a set of different scenarios (e.g. of future greenhouse gas emissions) as initial assumptions. Analysis of the resulting ensembles of model runs can provide a good insight into the uncertainty associated with the various different sources (model design, initial conditions, scenarios of future impacts of humans on climate). For example, by using several different models it is possible to assess which models are more consistent in their representation of both past and future temperatures, as shown in Figure 2.15. Similarly, different data sets can be used to initialize the same model in order to assess how different sources of

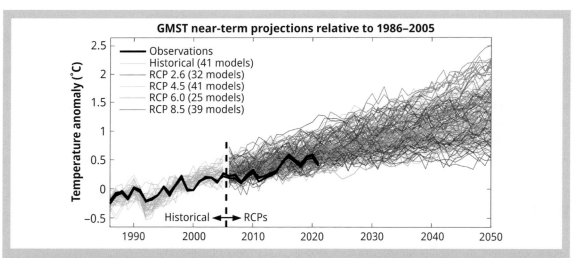

FIGURE 2.15 An example of the application of ensembles based on up to 42 different models and four different scenarios illustrating differences in uncertainty associated with predicted temperature anomalies. GMST is global mean surface temperature; updated using recent observations from https://www.climate-lab-book.ac.uk/comparing-cmip5-observations/

Source: IPCC (2013). *Climate Change 2013: The Physical Science Basis*. Contribution of Working Group I to the Fifth Assessment Report of the Intergovernmental Panel on Climate Change (Stocker, T. F., Qin, D., Plattner, G.-K., Tignor, M., Allen, S. K., Boschung, J., Nauels, A., Xia, Y., Bex, V., and Midgley, P. M. (eds)). Cambridge University Press, Cambridge and New York; updated using recent observations from https://www.climate-lab-book.ac.uk/comparing-cmip5-observations/

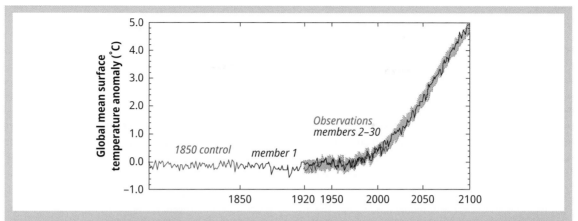

FIGURE 2.16 An example of a single **model ensemble** generated by small differences in initial conditions that resulted in 30 simulations starting in 1920 using the same model

Source: Kay et al. (2015). The Community Earth System Model (CESM) large ensemble project: A community resource for studying climate change in the presence of internal climate variability. *Bulletin of the American Meteorological Society* 96: 1333–49

data can impact on future predictions of climate. Such work helps to assess the causes of divergence or spread between model predictions, so that the best performing models and the most appropriate data sets can be selected to try and reduce the uncertainty. This might also include making improvements to model design, or enhancing understanding of likely human responses to changing climate.

REDUCING OTHER FORMS OF UNCERTAINTY

Initial condition and scenario uncertainty are two main sources of uncertainty for which models need to allow. Uncertainty associated with initial conditions needs to be addressed by improving the accuracy of input data provided to the model at the start of a model run. The more accurate the initial information provided to the climate model, the better the prediction of the future state of the climate. The accuracy of the initial data on the current state of the atmosphere is limited by the data available from global measurement networks. There are

much more data available for some parts of the world (e.g. continental North America and western Europe) than others (the Southern Hemisphere oceans and the polar regions), and these data gaps will generate uncertainty that is not limited to those regions. This situation is not likely to improve significantly in the near future because of the large areas of ocean in the Southern Hemisphere and the logistical difficulties involved in deploying equipment in such areas.

Scenario uncertainty depends on how well we can predict the changes in society that affect our future consumption of fossil fuels and emission of greenhouse gases into the atmosphere. It is therefore dependent on a range of socio-economic factors, as well as changes in technology and human behaviour. The huge number of unknowns makes it very difficult to accurately predict how changes in human activity may influence the future state of the climate. Human behaviour is one of the most difficult things to predict. This is why different SSPs have been used in recent assessments of future climate trends (as shown in Figure 2.2). How models could incorporate human-influenced scenarios

CASE STUDY 2.1
Southern Hemisphere sea ice

Figure 2.17 shows the disparity that is evident between observed and model-predicted sea ice extent around the Antarctic continent. Although various models and different scenarios suggest that sea ice should be decreasing, actual measured trends are much more erratic and lack a clear downward trend. This situation is markedly different from that of the Arctic region, where extensive sea ice melting is consistent with model predictions. The inability of the current GCMs to predict observed changes in Antarctic sea ice extent demonstrates that they are still unable to accurately represent the processes most significant for sea ice development and decay in Antarctica. The scarcity of climate data available in the Antarctic and Southern Ocean region makes it difficult to both accurately initialize the models and validate model predictions, although satellite remote-sensing techniques are increasingly used to obtain both climate and sea ice data. Whatever the cause of the lack of fit to model predictions, there is something different about the southern polar region that makes it difficult for larger-scale climate models to accurately represent observed trends in sea ice area. As argued previously, there is therefore a need to improve downscaling from the global to the regional scale in order to understand the cause of the difference between the two polar regions and before being able to develop an appropriate response strategy.

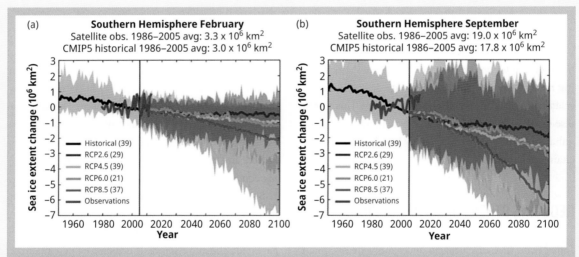

FIGURE 2.17 Model predictions of past and future sea ice distribution in (a) February and (b) September, showing the predicted impact of different scenarios compared with actual observations

Source: IPCC (2013). *Climate Change 2013: The Physical Science Basis*. Contribution of Working Group I to the Fifth Assessment Report of the Intergovernmental Panel on Climate Change (Stocker, T. F., Qin, D., Plattner, G.-K., Tignor, M., Allen, S. K., Boschung, J., Nauels, A., Xia, Y., Bex, V., and Midgley, P. M. (eds)). Cambridge University Press, Cambridge and New York

moving forward will be discussed later in the chapter. For now, it is clear that although we can try to reduce uncertainty by improving the design of climate models and the quality of the data that we use to initialize them, we will always have to live with a significant amount of uncertainty.

WHAT ABOUT UNCERTAINTY IN MEASUREMENTS?

Measurements of climate variables are frequently used to assess model performance, but only when models are applied to past situations. It is generally assumed that if a model is able to accurately represent past climate conditions, then it should be able to provide a useful idea of future climates as well. However, there are many problems associated with past climate data, including the effects of the use of new technology for making the measurements (e.g. the transition from glass thermometers to electronic sensors for measuring temperature), and changing land use around long-term measurement sites (e.g. large-scale urban development and deforestation). A lot of work has been done to address such problems, through comparison and standardization of data-collection methods, and selecting sites that have experienced minimal long-term change in their surroundings. Evaluation of uncertainty associated with different GCMs is therefore a tricky business, which is a key reason for using ensembles to provide a range of possible outcomes.

2.4 Why is it important to investigate climate variability across different spatial scales?

The significant spatial variability of climate in very small areas (such as in rugged terrain) can be similar to, if not greater than, future temperature increases simulated by GCMs and estimated by IPCC scenarios. For example, the mean temperature difference between a city and its periphery (resulting from the urban heat island effect)[1] can be several degrees. Knowledge of such spatial variability of climate at fine scales provides a major advantage when developing ways of adapting to climate change. The higher the resolution at which we are able to map such climate variables as temperature and precipitation, the more refined we can make any adaptation strategy. For example, specific sub-areas within a region can be targeted rather than wasting resources applying adaptation tools across the whole region.

To account for this, spatial variability of climate must be integrated into climate change models. This reduces model uncertainties (when comparing predicted and actual climate data) and improves the spatial resolution of model outputs. The study of spatial variability of climate at local scales requires the application of a measurement and modelling methodology that takes into account the influence of local factors (e.g. topography and land use) on climate and may incorporate the nesting of scales (from regional to local scale; see Chapter 1).

WHY IS THE LOCATION OF MEASUREMENT POINTS IMPORTANT FOR SPATIAL VARIABILITY?

Understanding climate variability at local scales requires a network of measurements to study the effect of surface characteristics on the spatial variability of the climate. However, weather stations in national networks are installed according to standards (defined by the World Meteorological Organization) that are established to reduce the influence of local factors. For example, weather stations must be in open areas far from any obstructions, such as large vegetation

---

[1] 'An urban heat island (UHI) is a metropolitan area which is significantly warmer than its surroundings. This temperature difference is usually larger at night than during the day and larger in winter than in summer, and is most apparent when winds are weak. The main causes are changes in the land surface by urban development along with waste heat generated by energy use' (https://scied.ucar.edu/longcontent/urban-heat-islands).

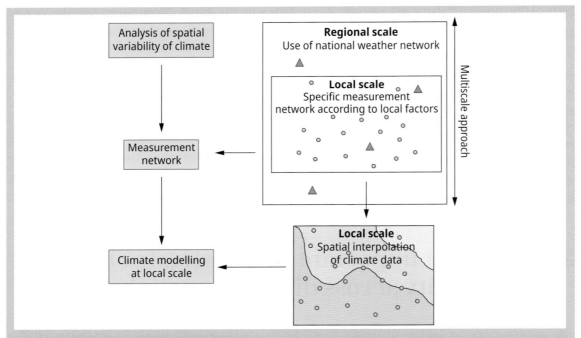

FIGURE 2.18 Analysis of climate variability at the local scale, based on measurements from the national weather station network (shown as green triangles) and a local network established to reflect local factors (shown as mauve dots)

and buildings, with measurements made over short grass. Where the objective is to determine the influence of local factors on weather variables, the location of measuring stations should not be defined by these standards. The observation of climate variability at local scales therefore often requires the installation of a specific measurement network. Measurement points should be well distributed across the study area (in order to provide uniform cover to allow spatial modelling), as well as in relation to small-scale landscape features affecting the local climate, such as topography (e.g. representing a range of aspects, altitudes, and slopes) (see Figure 2.18).

USING STATISTICAL METHODS FOR MODELLING SPATIAL CLIMATE VARIABILITY

Statistical methods are particularly appropriate for modelling spatial variability of climate at the local scale. They can be used to perform spatial interpolation (filling in gaps in the coverage) of climate data obtained at such fine scales. As discussed earlier, these methods are based on establishing the relationship between surface characteristics (e.g. landscape morphology and land use) and weather variables. In this type of study, the existence of a link between climate elements and surface characteristics is then evaluated spatially across a study site using a **geographic information system (GIS)**. For example, Figure 2.20 provides an illustration of urban heat island modelling in the Rennes metropolitan area (France). The temperatures recorded by 22 weather stations were modelled using a multivariate regression method. The first step was to statistically analyse the land-use variables and select the most relevant variables to create the regression model. Then the second step involved application of the regression model to the study site. The results of the measurements and spatial modelling identified high spatial variability

CASE STUDY 2.2
The Loire Valley, France

Figure 2.19 illustrates a multiscale approach to the installation of a network of meteorological stations in the wine-growing region of the Loire Valley (France). This climate network was established at regional and local scales in order to study the spatial variability of climate at vineyard scale in the context of climate change. The national network of meteorological stations (operated by Météo France) allows study of the spatial variability of climate at the regional scale, including the influence of oceanic and continental effects on the Loire river valley (Figure 2.19(a)). At the scale of local wine-growing areas (in this case, Quart de Chaumes), the meteorological sensors were installed according to the topography (slope, altitude, and exposure), soil type, and distance to the river (Figure 2.19(b) and (c)).

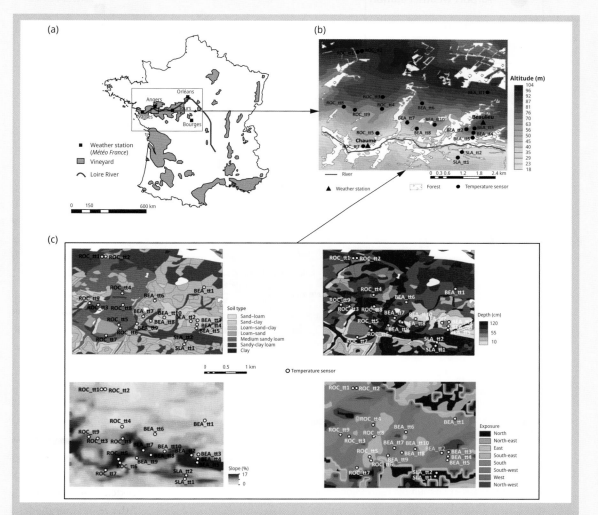

FIGURE 2.19 Measurement networks at (a) regional and (b) local scales in the Loire Valley (France), and (c) the local factors (soil type, soil depth, slope, and exposure) used to determine the location of measurement points

Source: Quénol et al. (2014). Modelisation spatiale des temperatures dans le vignoble des coteaux du Layon. *Revue Internationale de Géomatique*, 377, 400 and Bonnefoy et al. (2014). Modelisation spatiale des temperatures dans le vignoble des coteaux du Layon. *Revue Internationale de Géomatique*, 377, 400

that developed between the city and the countryside and also within the city itself as a result of the urban heat island effect (Foissard et al. 2019). Figure 2.20(a) shows the measurement network, while Figure 2.20(b) presents a map of the temperature anomaly field created by the urban area.

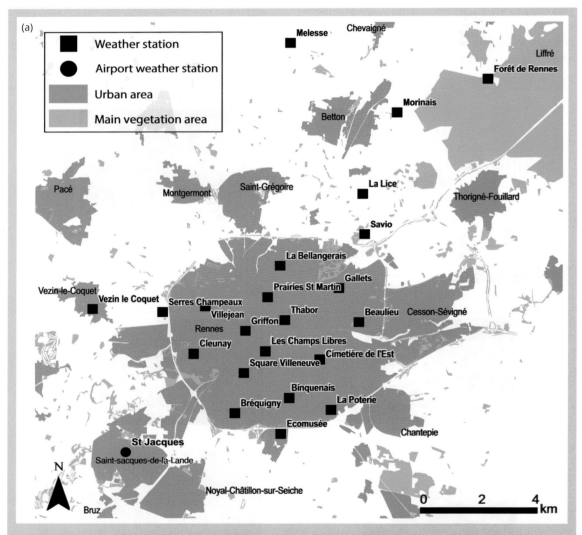

FIGURE 2.20 (a) Weather measurement network in Rennes metropolitan area, and (b) spatial interpolation of the mean UHI in 2011, based on multiple regression between the temperatures recorded by weather stations and land-use factors (land use and low vegetation)

Source: Foissard et al. (2019). Defining scales of the land use effect to map the urban heat island in a mid-size European city: Rennes (France). *Urban Climate*, 29, 100490

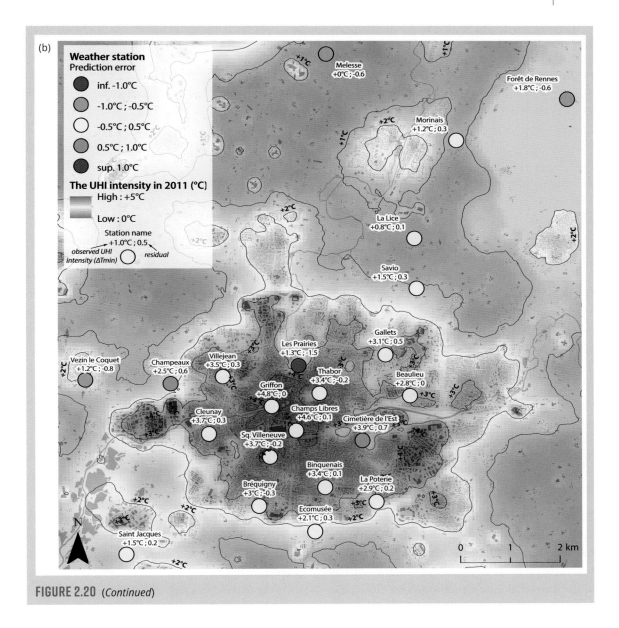

FIGURE 2.20 (*Continued*)

INTEGRATING LOCAL CLIMATE SPATIAL VARIABILITY INTO CLIMATE CHANGE MODELS

Fine-scale climate analysis based on measurement and spatial modelling cannot estimate the future climate. However, integrating local climate variability (validated by measuring actual data) into regional and local climate change models reduces uncertainties for climate change impact studies. Figure 2.21 provides a schematic representation of the scientific approach used to integrate local-scale spatial climate variability into regional climate models. Le Roux (2017) applied this modelling approach to the vineyard areas of Saint-Émilion (France) and Marlborough (New Zealand) in order to take into account effects of local climatic variability on the characteristics of the wines.

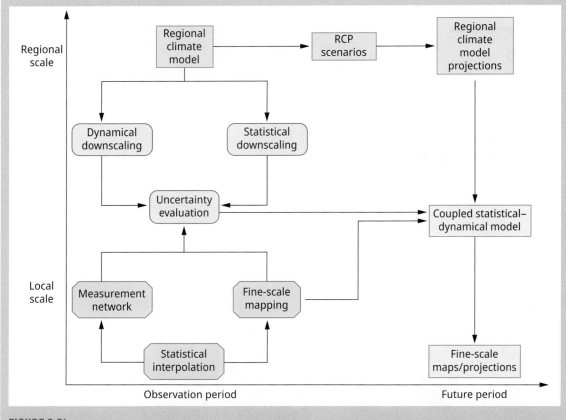

FIGURE 2.21 Schematic representation of fine-scale climate modelling in the context of climate change

Source: modified after Le Roux, R. (2017). *Modélisation climatique à l'échelle des terroirs viticoles dans un contexte de changement climatique.* These de Doctorat, Universite Rennes 2, Rennes, France

Figure 2.22 illustrates how such fine-scale modelling can be used to provide much more detail of the spatial variability of a **bioclimatic index** (the Winkler index) that is frequently used to assess the suitability of the thermal climate for growing specific grape varieties. From such examples, it is clear that the spatial variability of climate at fine scale must be considered in developing adaptation strategies for a range of human activities. This approach involves merging climate change modelling and analysis of climate at fine scales in order to develop adaptation strategies and support rational decision-making.

2.5 What are the next steps in regional and local downscaling?

GCMs are based on certain assumptions about future concentrations of greenhouse gases that rely on further assumptions about socio-economic activity and human behaviour. As mentioned earlier, as a result of the uncertainty associated with these assumptions, a series of scenarios are typically modelled to provide a range of

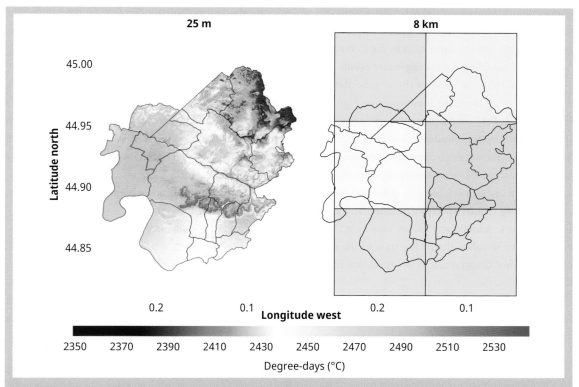

FIGURE 2.22 Modelling of the Winkler index in the Saint-Émilion wine region at a resolution of 8 km according to the RCP8.5 scenario for the period 2081–2100 (on the right) and at 25 m resolution using statistical downscaling from the large-scale model output (on the left)

Source: modified after Le Roux, R. (2017). *Modélisation climatique à l'échelle des terroirs viticoles dans un contexte de changement climatique.* These de Doctorat, Universite Rennes 2, Rennes, France

possible outcomes for some period in the future. GCMs themselves are purely physically based models, and there is no allowance for changing attitudes, technology, and economic activity (except through the different RCPs). To allow for this, the most recent IPCC reports use SSPs (Figure 2.2), representing a range of possible increases in net radiation resulting from various human attempts to reduce greenhouse gas emissions. However, it is highly likely that the assumptions behind these SSPs will become increasingly invalid as time passes, which makes development of long-term adaptation strategies for specific industries or sectors of the community fraught with difficulty. This has been recognized by increasing amounts of research into linking models of human behaviour with climate models (e.g. Beckage et al. 2018).

INCORPORATING NATURAL AND HUMAN COMPONENTS INTO COMPLEX MODELS

Monier et al. (2017) identified the need to combine human dimensions with environmental dynamics in order to develop integrated assessment models that provide a sound basis for adaptation to future climate change. Figure 2.23 schematically summarizes the relationship between possible different model types that incorporate human and natural components. The vertical axis represents the continuum between empirical (observation-based) and theoretical (process-based) models. Empirical models are frequently based on statistical techniques that quantify the relationship between a range of measured climate variables, while global climate change models are typical process-based models, as discussed earlier. Empirical models are dependent on the observations used in their creation, so have limitations when simulating future events as they lie outside of the time frame of the original data. This is the 'out-of-sample' issue mentioned in Figure 2.23 (Monier et al. 2017). Complex process-based models such as **Earth-system models** are dependent on how well the fundamental environmental (physical, chemical, biological) processes are represented in the model design. They can be very complex pieces of computer code and may require careful validation and calibration in order to address any biases. However, they are better able to simulate the future state of the climate as they are not constrained by observations made in the past.

The horizontal axis represents models that range from those attempting to simulate the roles of individuals or organizations (agents) within a system to the integration of multiple models (e.g. climate, hydrological, economic, and social) into large and complex systems models (such as integrated Earth-system models). So the left-hand end of the axis in Figure 2.23 represents the more simplistic models that focus on the role of single individuals in environmental change, such as a person's attitude to recycling and energy use. Much more complex models are situated at the other end, integrating the effects of many individuals and major stakeholder organizations, via their socio-economic activities, with the complex biophysical processes that impact on climate and society.

A specific model may lie anywhere in this diagram (Figure 2.23). For example, simplistic models with a small number of observed input variables and dealing with the effects of single agents only would lie in the bottom left of the diagram, while the most complicated modelling systems that integrate processed-based climate models with socio-economic

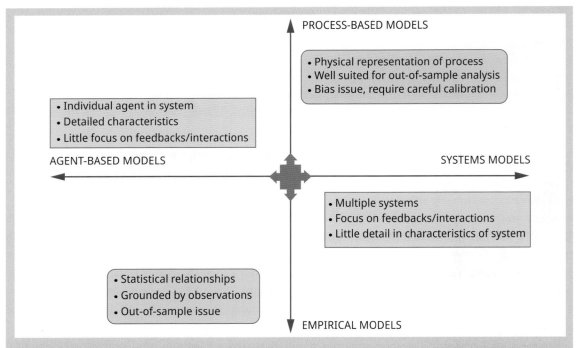

FIGURE 2.23 Illustration of the relationship between different model types used to assess climate change impacts on people and the environment

Source: Monier et al. (2017). A review of and perspectives on global change modelling for northern Eurasia. *Environmental Research Letters* 12: 083001

and human response models would lie in the top right. A visual perspective of the key components involved in such a fully integrated human–Earth-system model, often called an integrated assessment model, is provided in Figure 2.24. Few attempts have been made to fully integrate a physics-based GCM with a model based on human behaviour and economic activity (which are largely responsible for the increased levels of emission of greenhouse gases). Typically, integrated assessment models have been based on simplistic coupling (linking or connecting) of climate and economic development models. However, increases in computing power should allow development of more complex integrated models that can provide a more comprehensive representation of both natural and anthropogenic processes.

Yet, even if the GCMs were able to accurately predict future climates using physical equations, it is much more difficult to predict changes in economic activity, energy use, demand for food and materials, or human attitudes to their environment (all factors that influence greenhouse gas emissions). Although there are scientific laws governing many of the natural processes occurring in the environment, no such laws exist to explain human behaviour or economic activity. It should also be remembered that these human-based processes will vary significantly between different parts of the world, so there are no universal rules that can be applied.

In response to this problem, Monier et al. (2017) provided an example of an integrated assessment model that involved the coupling of a human activity model with an Earth-system model in order to investigate three key relationships: human health, land-use change, and water use (Figure 2.25). The incorporation of a human-system and an Earth-system model into such an integrated framework increases the uncertainty associated with predicted future climate change outcomes, creating a challenge for development of sound adaptation strategies.

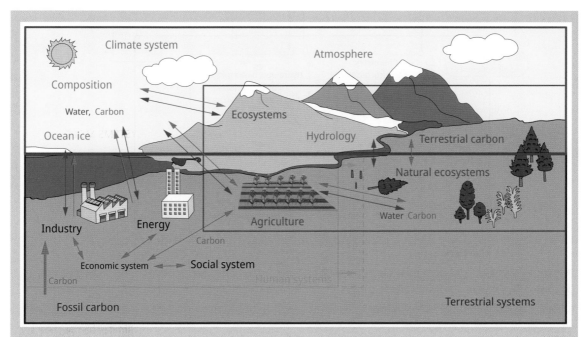

FIGURE 2.24 Schematic illustration of the interaction between key components of the human and environmental systems

Source: Gettelman, A., and Rood, R. B. (2016). *Demystifying Climate Models: A User's Guide to Earth System Models*. Earth Systems Data and Models, Vol. 2. Springer-Verlag GmbH, Berlin and Heidelberg

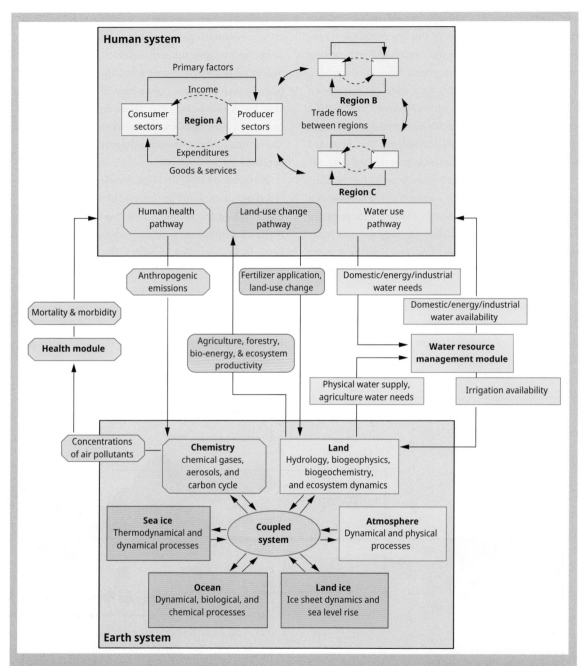

FIGURE 2.25 An example of an integrated assessment model, incorporating human and Earth systems, with a focus on human health, land-use change, and water use

Source: Monier et al. (2017). A review of and perspectives on global change modelling for northern Eurasia. *Environmental Research Letters* 12: 083001

2.6 What knowledge do we need to develop sound adaptation strategies?

In order to develop sound adaptation strategies, it is clear that we really need models that integrate both physical and human components. Changes in human attitudes to the environment are difficult to predict, as are changes in socio-economic and commercial activity. As such, the subject of climate change adaptation, or the capacity to manage the consequences of climate change for a specific area or region, requires a multiscale approach.

Ultimately, sound adaptation strategies require both top-down and bottom-up processes that incorporate an understanding of both human and physical processes (see Figure 2.26). The 'top-down' approach involves downscaling large-scale climate models in order to estimate climate impacts at the scale of the studied region. Although downscaling accentuates the uncertainties associated with the various stages of climate modelling (as described in previous sections), it provides the essential

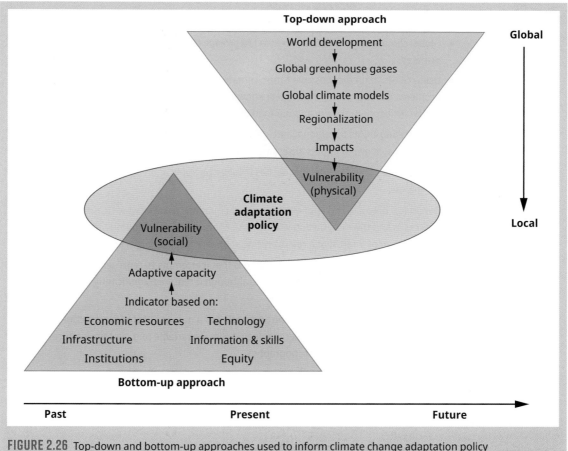

FIGURE 2.26 Top-down and bottom-up approaches used to inform climate change adaptation policy

Source: Dessai, S., and Hulme, M. (2004). Does climate adaptation policy need probabilities? *Climate Policy* 4: 107–28

regionalized climate data for use in **impact models** used to simulate regional changes.

In an ideal multiscale approach these data are then combined with the 'bottom-up' approach to assess the exposure and vulnerability of a region based on an analysis of the current and past state of local socio-ecosystems (Pacteau and Joussaume 2013). This integrated approach would provide the reliable data local authorities need to create action plans adapted to the scale of their region.

In the context of climate change adaptation policies, many countries, along with the European Union and the United Nations, have created 'climate services'. In 2011, the Global Framework for Climate Services (GFCS) was established by the World Meteorological Organization (WMO) in order to provide access to climate services to assist decision-making in different sectors, such as agriculture and food security, disaster risk reduction, energy, cities, and health, and water.[2] Climate organizations in several countries (e.g. NOAA,[3] DRIAS,[4] UKCIP,[5] and GERICS[6]) have started to provide decision-making tools for adaptation and access to regionalized climate change scenarios through climate services websites.

Summary

- Global climate models (GCMs) are used to provide a large-scale view of possible future climates.

- Using GCMs to predict possible future climate at regional and local scales is fraught with problems because of our incomplete knowledge of the complex processes operating in the Earth–atmosphere system and our inability to represent these processes at fine scales.

- Downscaling GCMs to regional and local scales provides more accurate fine-scale predictions, allowing impact assessment and supporting sound adaptation strategies.

- The two main downscaling approaches involve the application of dynamical or statistical techniques.

- Dynamical downscaling applies the physical equations associated with atmospheric processes and their interaction with surface characteristics (including terrain and land use) in the region of interest at a relatively fine spatial resolution (e.g. 1 km or less).

- The advantage of dynamical downscaling is that it attempts to represent the actual physical processes operating in the atmosphere, although it requires significantly more computer resources.

- Statistical downscaling involves the application of a number of statistical techniques to identify the relationship between a selected climate variable (e.g. air temperature) and land surface characteristics (e.g. topography).

---

[2] https://gfcs.wmo.int/.
[3] https://www.climate.gov/#climateWatch.
[4] www.drias-climat.fr/.
[5] http://www.ukcip.org.uk/.
[6] http://www.climate-service-center.de/.

- The advantages of statistical downscaling are that it can be used where the physical processes are not properly understood, and it requires significantly less computer resources. However, it is only valid for the data set from which it was derived.

- There is significant uncertainty associated with GCMs that can be categorized as model uncertainty, initial condition uncertainty, and scenario uncertainty.

- Model uncertainty is being addressed by using model ensembles to try and constrain the range of possible outcomes.

- Advances in technology allow the collection of climate observations at much higher spatial resolution, which can then be used to test model performance at regional and local scales. Such observations can also be integrated with model predictions to provide a more accurate high-resolution assessment of the possible impacts of climate change.

- In order to develop sound adaptation strategies, we need models that integrate both physical and human components.

- Recent research has investigated integrated assessment models, which incorporate human and Earth systems with a focus on such areas as human health, land-use change, and water use.

- Sound adaptation strategies require both top-down and bottom-up processes that incorporate an understanding of both human and physical processes.

- Regional and local community organizations do not have access to perfect knowledge of their environments, and a lot of work is needed to provide improved insights into how climate change is likely to affect them.

- Ideally, the local community needs to be able to assess the robustness or sustainability of their regions in response to climate change, and to define the range of possible outcomes at the regional and local scales.

For case studies and updates, visit the online resources at:

 www.oup.com/he/sturman-quenol1e

References

Ahmed, K. F., Wang, G., Slinader, J., Wilson, A. M., Allen, J. M., Horton, R., and Anyah, R. (2013). Statistical downscaling and bias correction of climate model outputs for climate change impact assessment in the U.S. Northeast. *Global and Planetary Change* 100: 320–32.

Beckage, B., Gross, L. J., Lacasse, K., Carr, E., Metcalf, S. S., Winter, J. M., Howe, P. D., Fefferman, N., Franck, T., Zia, A., Kinzig, A., and Hoffman, F. M. (2018). Linking models of human behaviour and climate alters projected climate change. *Nature Climate Change* 8: 79–84.

Boé, J. (2007). *Changement global et cycle hydrologique: Une étude de régionalisation sur la France*. Thèse de Doctorat, Université Paul Sabatier—Toulouse III.

Bonnefoy, C., Madelin, M., and Quénol, H. (2014). Modélisation spatiale des températures dans le vignoble des coteaux du Layon. *Revue Internationale de Géomatique*, 377, 400.

Crook, J. A., and Forster, P. M. (2014). Comparison of surface albedo feedback in climate models and observations. *Geophysical Research Letters* 41: 1717–23.

Daniels, A. E., Morrison, J. F., Joyce, L. A., Crookston, N. L., Chen, S. C., and McNully, S. G. (2012). Climate projections FAQ. In: *General Technical Report*. RMRS-GTR-277WWW, Fort Collins, CO, US Department of Agriculture, Forest Service, Rocky Mountain Research Station.

Dessai, S., and Hulme, M. (2004). Does climate adaptation policy need probabilities? *Climate Policy* 4: 107–28.

Fasullo, J. T., and Trenberth, K. E. (2012). A less cloudy future: The role of subtropical subsidence in climate sensitivity. *Science* 338(6108): 792–4.

Foissard, X., Dubreuil, V., and Quénol, H. (2019). Defining scales of the land use effect to map the urban heat island in a mid-size European city: Rennes (France). *Urban Climate*, 29, 100490.

Gettelman, A., and Rood, R. B. (2016). *Demystifying Climate Models: A User's Guide to Earth System Models*. Earth Systems Data and Models, Vol. 2. Springer-Verlag GmbH, Berlin and Heidelberg.

Gordon, C., Cooper, C., Senior, C. A., Banks, H., Gregorz, J. M., Johns, T. C., Mitchell, J. F. B., and Wood, R. A. (2000). The simulation of SST, sea ice extents and ocean heat transports in a version of the Hadley Centre coupled model without flux adjustments. *Climate Dynamics* 16: 147–68.

Hawkins, E., and Sutton, R. (2009). The potential to narrow uncertainty in regional climate prediction. *Bulletin of the American Meteorological Society* 90: 1095–107.

Hu, X. M., Nielsen-Gammon, J. W. and Zhang, F. (2010). Evaluation of three planetary boundary layer schemes in the WRF model. *Journal of Applied Meteorology and Climatology* 49: 1831–44.

Huang, X., Rhoades, A. M., Ullrich, P. A. and Zarzycki, C. M. (2016). An evaluation of the variable-resolution-CESM for modeling California's climate. *Journal of Advanced Modeling of Earth Systems* 8: 345–69.

Huber, M. B., and Zanna, L. (2017). Drivers of uncertainty in simulated ocean circulation and heat uptake. *Geophysical Research Letters* 44: 1402–13.

IPCC (2007). *Climate Change 2007: The Physical Science Basis*. Contribution of Working Group I to the Fourth Assessment Report of the Intergovernmental Panel on Climate Change (Solomon, S., Qin, D., Manning, M., Chen, Z., Marquis, M., Averyt, K. B., Tignor, M., and Miller, H. L. (eds)). Cambridge University Press, Cambridge and New York.

IPCC (2013). *Climate Change 2013: The Physical Science Basis*. Contribution of Working Group I to the Fifth Assessment Report of the Intergovernmental Panel on Climate Change (Stocker, T. F., Qin, D., Plattner, G.-K., Tignor, M., Allen, S. K., Boschung, J., Nauels, A., Xia, Y., Bex, V., and Midgley, P. M. (eds)). Cambridge University Press, Cambridge and New York.

IPCC (2021). Summary for policymakers. In: Masson-Delmotte, V., Zhai, P., Pirani, A., Connors, S. L., Péan, C., Berger, S., Caud, N., Chen, Y., Goldfarb, L., Gomis, M. I., Huang, M., Leitzell, K., Lonnoy, E., Matthews, J. B. R., Maycock, T. K., Waterfield, T., Yelekçi, O., Yu, R., and Zhou, B. (eds), *Climate Change 2021: The Physical Science Basis*. Contribution of Working Group I to the Sixth Assessment Report of the Intergovernmental Panel on Climate Change. Cambridge University Press, Cambridge and New York.

Kay, J. E., Deser, C., Phillips, A. S., Mai, A., Hannay, C., Strand, G., Arblaster, J. M., Bates, S. C., Danabasoglu, G., Edwards, J., Holland, M., Kushner, P., Lamarque, J.-F., Lawrence, D., Lindsay, K., Middleton, A., Munoz, E., Neale, R., Oleson, K., Polvani, L., and Vertenstein, M. (2015). The Community Earth System Model (CESM) large ensemble project: A community resource for studying climate change in the presence of internal climate variability. *Bulletin of the American Meteorological Society* 96: 1333–49.

Le Roux, R. (2017). *Modélisation climatique à l'échelle des terroirs viticoles dans un contexte de changement climatique*. Thèse de Doctorat, Université Rennes 2, Rennes, France.

Le Roux, R., Katurji, M., Zawar-Reza, P., Quénol, H., and Sturman, A. (2018). Comparison of statistical and dynamical downscaling results from the WRF model. *Environmental Modelling and Software* 100: 67–73.

Lutz, A. F., ter Maat, H. W., Biemans, H., Shrestha, A. B., Wester, P., and Immerzeel, W. W. (2016). Selecting representative climate models for climate change impact studies: An advanced envelope-based selection approach. *International Journal of Climatology* 36: 3988–4005.

McSweeney, C. F., and Jones, R. G. (2016). How representative is the spread of climate projections from the 5 CMIP5 GCMs used in ISI-MIP? *Climate Services* 1: 24–9.

Monier, E., Kicklighter, D. W., Sokolov, A. P., Zhuang, Q., Sokolik, I. N., Lawford, R., Kappas, M., Paltsev, S. V., and Groisman, P. Y. (2017). A review of and perspectives on global change modelling for northern Eurasia. *Environmental Research Letters* 12: 083001.

Moss, R. H., Edmonds, J. A., Hibbard, K. A., Manning, M. R., Rose, S. K., Van Vuuren, D. P., Carter, T. R., Emori, S., Kainuma, M., Kram, T., Meehl, G. A., Mitchell, J. F. B., Nakicenovic, N., Riahi, K., Smith, S. J., Stouffer, R. J., Thomson, A. M., Weyant, J. P., and Wilbanks, T. J. (2010). The next generation of scenarios for climate change research and assessment. *Nature* 463(7282): 747–56.

Nakićenović, N., and Swart, R. (2000). *Special Report on Emissions Scenarios*. A Special Report of Working Group III of the Intergovernmental Panel on Climate Change. Cambridge University Press, Cambridge.

O'Neill, B. C., Tebaldi, C., Vuuren, D. P. V., Eyring, V., Friedlingstein, P., Hurtt, G., Knutti, R., Kriegler, E., Lamarque, J.-F., Lowe, J., Meehl, G. A., Moss, R., Riahi, K., and Sanderson, B. M. (2016). The scenario model intercomparison project (ScenarioMIP) for CMIP6. *Geoscientific Model Development* 9: 3461–82.

Ouzeau, G., Déqué, M., Jouini, M., Planton, S., and Vautard, R. (2014). *Le climat de la France au XXIe siècle*, Vol. 4, *Scénarios régionalisés: édition 2014 pour la métropole et les régions d'outre-mer*. Rapport, Ministère de l'Écologie, du Développement durable et de l'Énergie.

Pacteau, C., and Joussaume, S. (2013). Adaptation au changement climatique. In: *Le développement durable à découvert*. CNRS Éditions, Paris, pp. 268–9.

Pagé, C., and Terray, L. (2011). *Nouvelles projections climatiques à échelle fine sur la France pour le 21ème siècle: Les scénarii SCRATCH2010*. CERFACS Technical Report TR/CMGC/10/58, Toulouse, France.

Qu, X., Hall, A., Klein, S. A., and Caldwell, P. (2014). On the spread of changes in marine low cloud cover in climate model simulations of the 21st century. *Climate Dynamics* 42: 2603–26.

Quénol, H. (2014). *Changement climatique et terroirs viticoles*. Lavoisier, Tec & Doc, Paris, 444 pp.

Quénol, H., de Cortazar Atauri, I. G., Bois, B., Sturman, A., Bonnardot, V., and Le Roux, R. (2017). Which climatic modelling to assess climate change impacts on vineyards? *OENO One* 51: 91–7.

Riahi, K., van Vuuren, D. P., Kriegler, E., Edmonds, J., O'Neill, B. C., Fujimori, S., Bauer, N., Calvin, K., Dellink, R., Fricko, O., Lutz, W., Popp, A., Crespo Cuaresma, J., Samir, K. C., Leimbach, M., Jiang, L., Kram, T., Rao, S., Emmerling, J., Ebi, K., Hasegawa, T., Havlik, P., Humpenöder, F., Da Silva, L. A., Smith, S., Stehfest, E., Bosetti, V., Eom, J., Gernaat, D., Masui, T., Rogelj, J., Strefler, J., Drouet, L., Krey, V., Luderer, G., Harmsen, M., Takahashi, K., Baumstark, L., Doelman, J., Kainuma, M., Klimont, Z., Marangoni, G., Lotze-Campen. H, Obersteiner, M., Tabeau, A., and Tavoni, M. (2017). The shared socioeconomic pathways and their energy, land use, and greenhouse gas emissions implications: An overview. *Global Environmental Change* 42: 153–68.

Richardson, L. F. (1922). *Weather Prediction by Numerical Process*. Cambridge University Press, Cambridge.

Schoof, J. T., and Pryor, S. C. (2001). Downscaling temperature and precipitation: A comparison of regression-based methods and artificial neural networks. *International Journal of Climatology* 21: 773–90.

Sherwood, S. C., Bony, S., and Dufresne, J. L. (2014). Spread in model climate sensitivity traced to atmospheric convective mixing. *Nature* 505(7481): 37–42.

Slingo, J., and Palmer, T. (2011). Uncertainty in weather and climate prediction. *Philosophical Transactions of the Royal Society A* 369(1956): 4751–67.

Steele, C. J., Dorling, S., von-Glasow, R., and Bacon, J. (2014). Modelling sea-breeze climatologies and interactions on coasts in the southern North Sea: Implications for offshore wind energy. *Quarterly Journal of the Royal Meteorological Society* 141: 1821–35.

Tebaldi, C., Debeire, K., Eyring, V., Fischer, E., Fyfe, J., Friedlingstein, P., Knutti, R., Lowe, J., O'Neill, B., Sanderson, B., van Vuuren, D., Riahi, K., Meinshausen, M., Nicholls, Z., Tokarska, K. B., Hurtt, G., Kriegler, E., Lamarque, J.-F., Meehl, G., Moss, R., Bauer, S. E., Boucher, O., Brovkin, V., Byun, Y.-H., Dix, M., Gualdi, S., Guo, H., John, J. G., Kharin, S., Kim, Y., Koshiro, T., Ma, L., Olivié, D., Panickal, S., Qiao, F., Rong, X., Rosenbloom, N., Schupfner, M., Séférian, R., Sellar, A., Semmler, T., Shi, X., Song, Z., Steger, C., Stouffer, R., Swart, N., Tachiiri, K., Tang, Q., Tatebe, H., Voldoire, A., Volodin, E., Wyser, K., Xin, X., Yang, S., Yu, Y., and Ziehn, T. (2021). Climate model projections from the Scenario Model Intercomparison Project (ScenarioMIP) of CMIP6. *Earth System Dynamics* 12: 253–93.

Tian, D., Guo, Y., and Dong, W. (2015). Future changes and uncertainties in temperature and precipitation over China based on CMIP5 models. *Advances in Atmospheric Sciences* 32: 487–96.

Trzaska, S., and Schnarr, E. (2014). A review of downscaling methods for climate change projections. *United States Agency for International Development by Tetra Tech ARD*, 1–42.

van Vuuren, D. P., Edmonds, J., Kainuma, M. L. T., Riahi, K., Thomson, A., Matsui, T., Hurtt, G., Lamarque, J.-F., Meinshausen, M., Smith, S., Grainer, C., Rose, S., Hibbard, K. A., Nakicenovic, N., Krey, V., and Kram, T. (2011). Representative concentration pathways: An overview. *Climatic Change* 109: 5–31.

Wang, M., Ullrich, P. and Millstein, D. (2018). The future of wind energy in California: Future projections with the Variable-Resolution CESM. *Renewable Energy* 127, 242–257.

Wilby, R. L., and Wigley, T. M. L. (2000). Precipitation predictors for downscaling: Observed and general circulation model relationships. *International Journal of Climatology* 20: 641–61.

Wood, A. W., Leung, L. R., Sridhar, V., and Lettenmaier, D. P. (2004). Hydrologic implications of dynamical and statistical approaches to downscaling climate model outputs. *Climatic Change* 62: 189–216.

CHAPTER **THREE**

Urban Environments, Air Pollution, and Human Health

LEARNING OUTCOMES

Having read this chapter, you should be able to:

- explain what is unique about the urban climatic environment

- describe possible effects of climate change on urban heat islands

- identify direct and indirect climate change impacts on urban air pollution

- discuss other likely effects of climate change on the urban environment

- critically evaluate possible climate change adaptation strategies specifically for urban areas

3.1 Introduction: the urban environment in the context of climate change

More than 50% of the Earth's human population live and work in an urban environment. This chapter therefore examines the factors operating at the urban scale that create the unique climatic environment of these regions.

A growing global population and the migration of people from rural regions into large urban areas has resulted in a well-recognized modification of the local climate known as the *urban heat island*. Intensive urbanization and related commercial and industrial activity have also caused significant reductions in air quality. The causes of these effects on local climate are examined here, along with their significance for human health and well-being, and the likely impact of climate change on the urban environment. For example, urban environments can have significant impacts on human health via temperature and humidity effects on human comfort, especially through the development of extreme conditions (such as heatwaves), as well as impacts on general well-being. The interaction between climate change impacts such as heatwaves, flooding, and drought, as well as effects on changes in air pollution (e.g. airborne particulates and ozone) and human health are discussed. Climate change-induced sea level rise also represents a significant threat to major cities of the world because so many of them are located on vulnerable coastlines.

The urban environment is inherently extreme when considering such factors as heat, moisture, and windiness. Heatwaves can have a significant impact on the population of metropolitan areas because of the effects of the urban fabric on heat transfer. Similarly, impermeable urban surfaces are designed to shed water rapidly, leaving a more arid environment than the surrounding rural land, while the complexity of the urban landscape can create areas of both strong and weak winds due to the interaction between the overlying airflow and buildings of varying shapes and sizes.

The results of recent research are therefore used here to illustrate the nature of the processes operating within urban areas, the likely impacts of climate change on these processes, and development of suitable adaptation strategies for this unique environment. In order to develop appropriate responses to climate change in urban areas for the future well-being of the urban population, it is obvious that an integrated analysis is required that encompasses urban climate, air pollution, and public health (Salmond et al. 2018).

3.2 How does urban development affect local climate?

THE URBAN HEAT ISLAND—ITS ORIGINS AND CHARACTERISTICS

The spatio-temporal variability of urban climate is the result of very strong heterogeneity of urbanized space, which contains horizontal and vertical surfaces that modify the physical characteristics of the atmospheric boundary layer (the near-surface layer). The considerable expansion of urbanized areas during the twentieth century has had significant effects on local climate, with impacts over larger regions where more extensive metropolitan areas have developed. These climatic effects are largely thermal, although climate elements such as wind, precipitation, and atmospheric humidity are also affected. The most concrete expression of the change in the surface energy exchanges is through creation of the urban heat island.

The urban heat island is characterized by higher temperatures in the city compared to the surrounding rural area, and is often distinguished by an urban air dome or plume which represents the impact of the city on the overlying layer of the atmosphere (Figure 3.1). More than a simple 'centre/periphery' distinction, the urban heat island is created in response to the different types of urban surface and land use. The centre is generally characterized by dense, tall buildings dominated by dry vertical surfaces of concrete and glass, while the periphery comprises horizontal surfaces that are often partly vegetated and moister. In between, the urban surface can be quite complex with the juxtaposition of sealed housing areas and vegetated parks and open areas that create their own microclimatic effects.

Cities are therefore often several degrees warmer than their surrounding rural areas. The impact of urbanization on the formation of the urban heat island has led to numerous studies in major metropolitan areas such as Athens (Kastoulis and Theoharatos 1985), Delhi (Mohan et al. 2009), Melbourne (Morris and Simmonds 2000), New York (Gaffin et al. 2008), and Tokyo (Hung et al. 2006). In the largest cities, the urban heat island can extend beyond the periphery by up to several tens of kilometres.

The creation of urban heat islands is the result of the specific effects of urban surfaces, including buildings and ground cover, on radiative and sensible heat transfer. It depends on the absorption of solar radiation by surface materials during the day and its slow release in the form of sensible heat during the night, with **evapotranspiration** being reduced in the city compared to the surrounding countryside because of the lack of available surface moisture. The urban heat island is therefore the result of an **energy balance** modified by artificial urban surfaces, as well

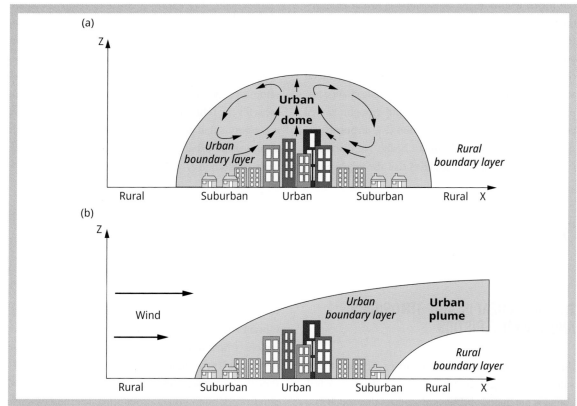

FIGURE 3.1 Modification of the overlying atmosphere by an urban area, showing the development of an urban (a) dome or (b) plume carried downwind by the prevailing airflow
Source: adapted from Oke 1987

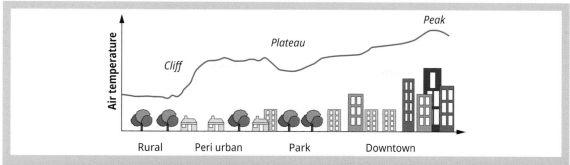

FIGURE 3.2 Typical air temperature characteristics in rural and dense urban areas. The spatial variation of temperature is often composed of the "cliff" at the rural–urban transition, the "plateau" in the suburban area, and the "peak" over the city centre, with cool islands forming over vegetated parks and lakes
Source: adapted from Oke 1987

as the emission of gases from fuel combustion which can also affect energy exchanges, both resulting in the observed urban–rural temperature differences. More generally, the urban heat island is characterized not only by a temperature gradient between the city centre and the periphery (Oke 1987) but also by often quite complex variations in climate within urban areas created by differences in land use (e.g. buildings, roads, green spaces, lakes, etc.) (Figure 3.2). In addition to these spatial variations across the city, there can often be distinct temporal variations in the nature and strength of the urban–rural temperature contrast, as shown schematically in Figure 3.3.

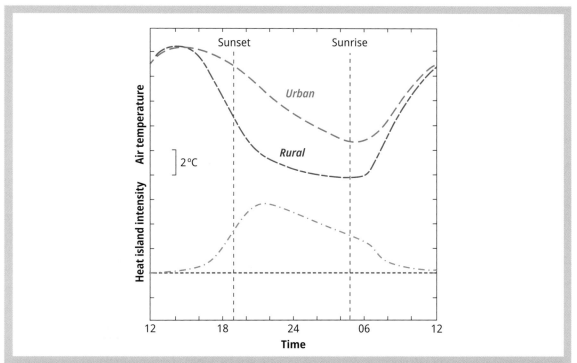

FIGURE 3.3 Schematic representation of diurnal variations in urban and rural temperatures (top) and their difference (bottom) for an idealised city under clear, calm weather conditions
Source: adapted from Oke, T. R. (1987). *Boundary Layer Climates*. Second edition, Routledge, London and New York; and Runnalls and Oke 2000

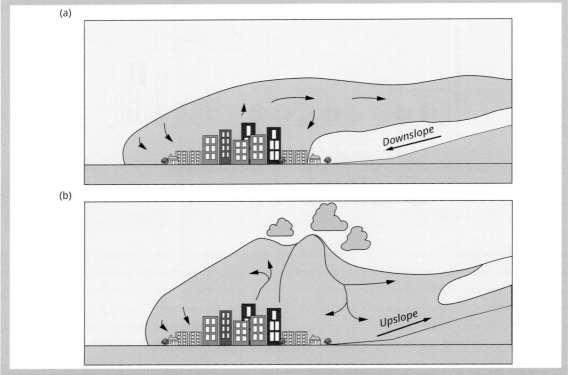

FIGURE 3.4 The potential influence of local airflow generated by nearby mountain slopes on urban heat island development during (a) night time, and (b) daytime

Source: adapted from Wanner, H., and Filliger, P. (1989). Orographic influence on urban climate. *Weather and Climate* 9: 22–8

The intensity and spatial variability of the urban heat island depends on several factors:

- *geographic location* (e.g. topography and proximity to sea or lake surfaces);

- *surface characteristics* such as urban morphology (e.g. the density and shape of buildings, the unique properties of urban materials, and urban geometry);

- *human activities* (e.g. industrial activities, road traffic, winter heating and summer air conditioning);

- *weather/climatic conditions*, particularly the typical succession of atmospheric circulation systems experienced in a region (Oke 1987).

GEOGRAPHIC LOCATION

Geographic location strongly influences urban heat island formation, particularly the regional topography or the proximity of large bodies of water or forests in the vicinity of the urban area. These larger-scale factors determine the city's climate and thus influence the characteristics of the urban heat island. For example, cities located in mountain regions are often influenced by local winds that can be strong enough to mix the air and limit the intensity of the urban heat island (Wanner and Filliger 1989) (Figure 3.4). This phenomenon is similar for coastal cities where the proximity of the sea and its associated land/sea breeze circulation limits development of the rural–urban temperature difference.

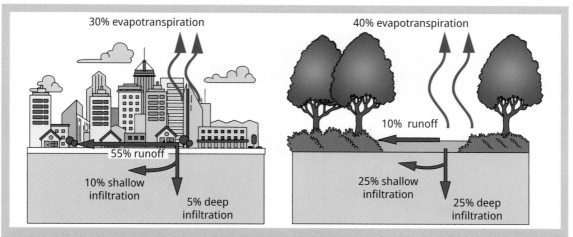

FIGURE 3.5 The effects of impervious urban surfaces on water availability for evaporative cooling (left) compared with a rural area (right)

Source: adapted from Federal Interagency Stream Restoration Working Group 1998, courtesy of the Environmental Protection Agency

SURFACE CHARACTERISTICS

The unique surface characteristics associated with the nature and morphology of urban areas are the main factors generating the urban heat island. Reduced vegetation cover in urban areas and extensive impervious artificial surfaces reduce evapotranspiration, contributing to the urban heat island through the consequent reduced evaporative heat loss (Figure 3.5). This effect is increased by the low albedo (reflectivity) of urban surfaces as a result of the very different radiative properties of urban materials. A greater proportion of incoming solar energy is therefore absorbed by the urban fabric.

Urban geometry also contributes to the urban heat island effect, as cities are typically designed to be dense and compact, which prevents adequate release of heat by either radiative heat loss or the effects of airflow. The height of the buildings and the spacing of the streets between the buildings modify the energy absorption and emission (Figure 3.6). The 'urban canyon' phenomenon illustrates the complexity of the influence of urban geometry on solar and terrestrial radiation. During daytime, the tall buildings that frequently occur in city centres can cause shading on surrounding buildings and in the street canyons between them, resulting in a negative effect on surface

temperatures. At the same time, sunlight can be reflected off the vertical sidewalls of the modern buildings, which are often highly reflective. Multiple reflection can occur with solar radiation being bounced off many different surfaces until it is eventually absorbed within the urban canopy layer, ultimately lowering the overall urban albedo and increasing temperatures. At night time, the urban environment is dominated by radiative cooling of the different surfaces. The urban canyons can reduce the effective heat loss from the urban canopy layer as the complex structure of the urban landscape is able to obstruct the transfer of radiative heat from the different urban surfaces to the overlying atmosphere (Sailor and Fan 2002).

HUMAN ACTIVITY

Heat produced by human activities also contributes to development of urban heat islands. Anthropogenic heat is released from a range of sources, such as transportation, industrial activities, or space heating in winter. The effects of waste heat are accentuated by the urban structure, with high building density and small spaces. Studies have shown that heat produced by human activities can increase the urban heat island by up to 1 °C (Zhang et al. 2013). The emission of air pollutants can also impact on radiative energy exchanges in the urban

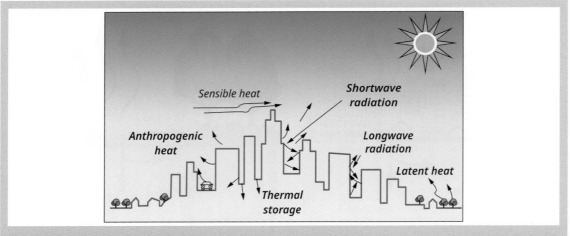

FIGURE 3.6 The effect of urban geometry on energy exchanges within cities

Source: USEPA 2008, adapted from Sailor, D. J., and Fan, H. (2002). Modeling the diurnal variability of effective albedo for cities. *Atmospheric Environment* 36: 713–25

atmosphere, resulting in more energy being retained close to the ground.

WEATHER/CLIMATE CONDITIONS

The development and intensity of the urban heat island are affected by atmospheric conditions at different temporal and spatial scales. Urban heat islands are more intense under clear skies and light winds, when the magnitude of the urban–rural temperature difference of large cities, with populations greater than about 1 million (e.g. New York, Delhi, Sydney, and Moscow), can be more than 6 °C (Oke 1997). Cloud cover blocks incoming solar radiation and reduces daytime warming in cities. Strong winds may also moderate temperature differences between urban and rural areas by mixing the air. The temporal variability of the urban heat island is mainly caused by the alternation between day and night (over a 24-hour time frame), the succession of weather types (over a few days), and seasonal variability (over a few months). For most of the year, the urban heat island is a mainly nocturnal phenomenon due to greater daytime mixing of the atmosphere, which tends to reduce the temperature contrast. Although daytime temperatures can be higher in the city, the temperature differences between the city and surrounding countryside are

generally greater at night, when warmer urban surfaces retain their heat because of their geometry and thermal properties (Figure 3.6). However, as shown in Figure 3.7, there is significant variability in the nature of urban heat islands in different climatic regions of the world, depending on seasonal changes in weather patterns and their effect on cloud cover and airflow over urban areas, as well as on the dominant land surface characteristics in the surrounding regions (Chakraborty and Lee 2019).

The characteristics of the urban heat island over any given city are therefore the result of a combination of the above factors (geographic location, surface characteristics, human activity, and weather/climate conditions) operating at different spatial and temporal scales (Figure 3.8).

THE URBAN HEAT ISLAND AND CLIMATE CHANGE

One important impact of climate change in cities is the accentuation of the urban heat island by absorbing the increased radiation trapped in the atmosphere by the enhanced greenhouse effect. This is likely to result in higher temperatures in the urban core of major cities.

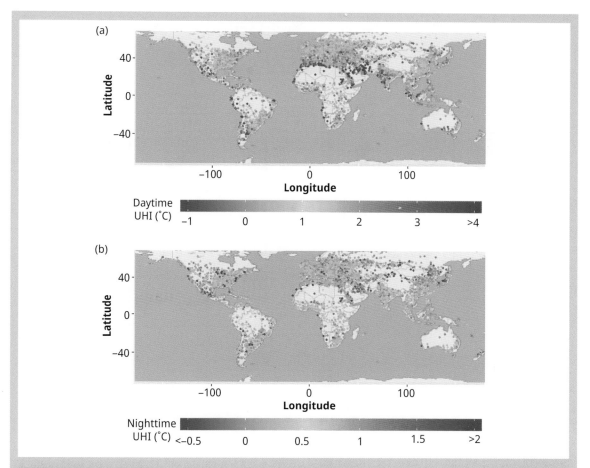

FIGURE 3.7 Map of variations in urban heat island intensity during (a) daytime, and (b) nighttime across the globe based on satellite measurements of more than 7,000 urban clusters

Source: Chakraborty, T., and Lee, X. (2019). A simplified urbanextent algorithm to characterize surface urban heat islands on a global scale and examine vegetation control on their spatiotemporal variability. *International Journal of Applied Earth Observation and Geoinformation* 74: 269–80

Mean annual temperatures in 39 cities increased between 0.12 and 0.45 °C per decade over the 1961–2010 period, and annual temperatures in major cities worldwide were expected to increase by 0.7 °C (RCP4.5) to 1.5 °C (RCP8.5) by 2020, 1.3 to 3.0 °C by 2050, and 1.7 to 4.9 °C by 2080 (Rosenzweig et al. 2015). The high temperatures caused by the combined influence of global warming and the localized urban heat island effect have negative impacts on the health and comfort of city residents, energy demand (resulting from increased energy demand for cooling in summer), and urban ecosystems (causing disappearance of urban species). For example, the urban heat island effect increases the intensity and duration of heatwaves in urban areas and, consequently, increases heat stress mortality rates (Tan et al. 2010; Li and Bou-Zeid 2013). 'The 2003 European heat wave is estimated to have resulted in 22,000–35,000 premature deaths that were concentrated among already socially vulnerable populations, such as the poor and elderly' (Schar and Jendritzky 2004).

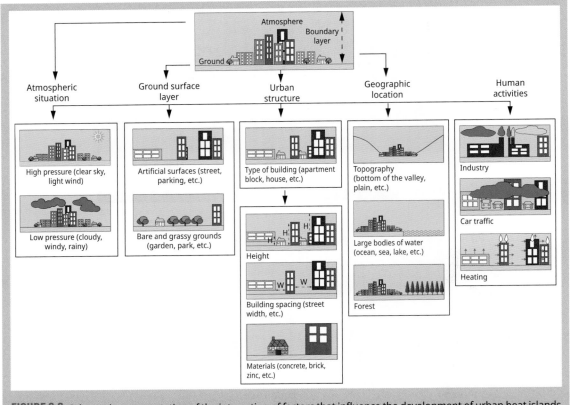

FIGURE 3.8 Schematic representation of the interaction of factors that influence the development of urban heat islands

USING MULTISCALE MODELS TO ANALYSE THE EFFECTS OF CLIMATE CHANGE ON URBAN HEAT ISLANDS

Climate projections predict a temperature increase and more frequent **extreme events** such as heatwaves. Urban populations will therefore be increasingly exposed to thermal risks. Recent research has attempted to estimate the evolution of the urban heat island according to different climate change scenarios in order to implement adaptation policies. Multiscale nested approaches have been used to take into account the interaction of global climate change and urban heat islands (see Chapter 2). However, spatial differences of temperature inside a city can be as large as the projected global changes. The urban heat island intensities in Tokyo, Shanghai, and Delhi (ranging from 3 to 12 °C) already exceed the mean temperature increases projected for these cities by the 2080s

(1.5–2.5 °C) (Blake et al. 2011). Such multiscale approaches allow downscaling between regional and local climate variability (due to the urban heat island) to be taken into account in relation to global climate change scenarios. Dynamical downscaling models regionalize the outputs of global climate models by nesting model grids of increasing resolution (see Figure 2.6 in Chapter 2). At the finest scale, the outputs of a regional model can be coupled with an urban microclimate model, which is used to simulate the surface–plant–air interactions over the urban landscape. In this way, modelling of the environment within city blocks can be achieved with a resolution of just a few metres. These urban microclimate models consider the relationship between the factors that determine the urban microclimate, such as urban morphological characteristics, and the distribution of vegetation

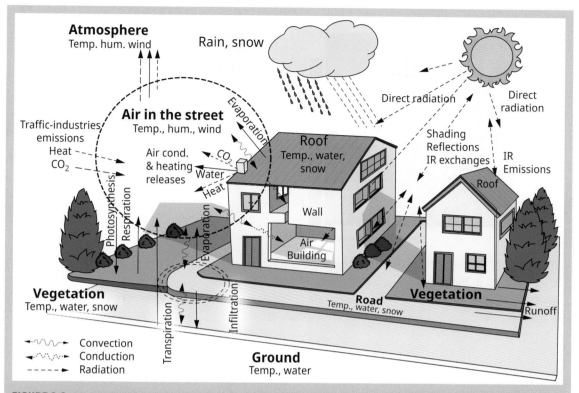

FIGURE 3.9 Energy exchanges between the atmosphere and urban environment represented by the "Town Energy Balance" (TEB) model. 'Temp.' and 'hum.' represent temperature and humidity, respectively, while IR stands for infrared
Source: https://www.umr-cnrm.fr/spip.php?article199&lang=en

and water in the landscape. They can be used to simulate the energy and water exchanges between the city and the overlying atmosphere (Figure 3.9). Several cities (e.g. Helsinki, Tokyo, and Berlin) have established specific climate-monitoring networks in order to observe and forecast urban climate variability, but also to build and validate climate models (see Figure 2.20 in Chapter 2).

Conry et al. (2015) used this **multiscale model approach** to study the impact of climate change on the urban heat island in Chicago. Downscaling was achieved by combining a dynamical global (200 km resolution) and a regional model (from 900 to 300 m resolution) with a microscale model (2 m resolution), taking into account the components of the urban microclimate.

The application of this approach to the specific case of Chicago has highlighted the effect of the lake breeze on the urban heat island in present and future climates (e.g. the RCP8.5 scenario over the years 2076–2081) and its impact on temperature regulation at the city and urban block scale (Figures 3.10 and 3.11). Analysis of the difference between the present and future temperatures at block scale show that sheltered regions of the domain with low wind speeds experience the most heating at 1200 LST in the future August, while at night time (0000 LST) more significant temperature increases occur than during daytime, resulting in an enhanced UHI intensity (Figure 3.11).

Climate modelling that couples regional models with urban climate models makes it possible

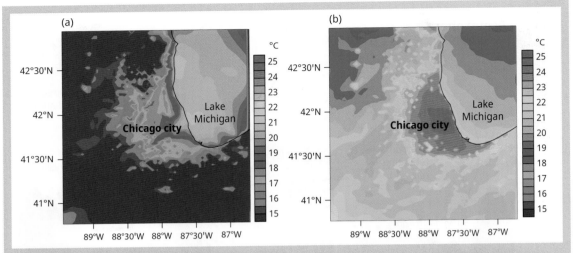

FIGURE 3.10 Modelling of the mean temperature during night time (0200–0500 LST) in the Chicago area for (a) present August, and (b) future August

Source: Conry et al. (2015). Chicago's heat island and climate change: Bridging the scales via dynamical downscaling. *Journal of Applied Meteorology and Climatology* 54: 1430–48

to estimate the impacts of climate change on the urban heat island in relation to different scenarios. Such model downscaling approaches are also used for prospective purposes in order to test different urban development scenarios, in order to limit the effect of the urban heat island in the climate change context. The application of this systemic modelling methodology requires an interdisciplinary approach involving climatologists, architects, economists, social scientists, and others to investigate the interactions between climate change, urban structures, and urban economies (Masson et al. 2014). In this way, modelling can be used to assess several long-term adaptation strategies for different socio-economic scenarios and urban development patterns (Figure 3.12).

For example, in Paris, different urban planning scenarios were studied in the context of adaptation to heatwaves by using an interdisciplinary modelling chain, including a socio-economic model of land use and transport interaction, and a physically based model of urban climate (Lemonsu et al. 2015). The results from these different scenarios showed that logically the urban heat island is always higher at night and most commonly affects the city centre. However, the distribution and intensity of the urban heat island may vary according to the selected urban planning scenarios, and this may be of significance when evaluating heatwave risk. In particular, compact cities tend to concentrate inhabitants into the areas most affected by the urban heat island, making them more vulnerable to the impacts of high temperatures. Such interdisciplinary modelling studies provide important tools to help urban areas to mitigate or adapt to the effects of future climate change, in particular the current global warming trend.

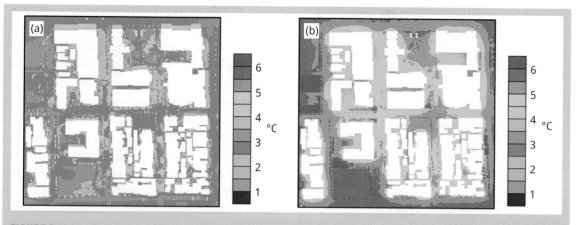

FIGURE 3.11 The temperature increase between present and future August at block scale in Chicago at (a) 1200 LST, and (b) 0000 LST

Source: Conry et al. (2015). Chicago's heat island and climate change: Bridging the scales via dynamical downscaling. *Journal of Applied Meteorology and Climatology* 54: 1430–48

3.3 What is the impact of climate on urban air quality?

AIR POLLUTION—ITS SOURCES AND EFFECTS

Urban air pollution can be defined as any situation in which atmospheric constituents in urban areas are modified, causing detrimental impacts on human health and the environment. It is normally the result of human activities, such as vehicle use, domestic heating and air conditioning, and a range of industrial processes. These activities can result in the emission of a number of different air pollutants, including the greenhouse gases that contribute to global warming. Consequently, the accumulated effect of many cities across the globe contributes massively to the enhanced greenhouse effect (about 75% of global emissions—Stern 2007) and the observed warming trend (discussed in Chapter 1). It is also evident that there are feedback processes by which urban areas are increasingly thought to be adversely affected by global warming. These effects include extremely high temperatures and enhancement of air pollution levels, with their consequent impacts on health, including respiratory problems such as asthma, heatstroke, and premature deaths. **Urban air quality** and climate change are therefore closely related.

There are many different types of air pollutant that can affect human health and the urban environment, including fine particles (airborne particulates) such as smoke and dust, nitrogen oxides, carbon monoxide, carbon dioxide, ozone, and a range of other gases and compounds (the most important of which are listed in Table 3.1). Atmospheric processes can affect the emission, transport, dispersion, chemical transformation, and deposition of pollutants through the action of several key meteorological variables (Figure 3.13), the most important being temperature, humidity, precipitation, wind, turbulence,

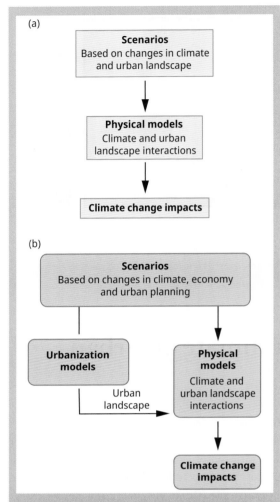

FIGURE 3.12 Schematic representation of (a) a simple impact model based solely on scenarios of future climate and physical models, and (b) a systemic model incorporating an interdisciplinary approach to investigating interactions between climate change and urban development

Source: modified after Masson et al. (2014). Adapting cities to climate change: A systemic modelling approach. *Urban Climate* 10: 407–29

and vertical mixing. The amount of air pollution concentrations in an urban environment is effectively the result of the balance between pollutant emission rates and the ability of the atmosphere to disperse or remove atmospheric contaminants. Local air pollution problems are therefore created when the natural cleaning mechanisms of the atmosphere become overloaded.

IMPACTS OF CLIMATE CHANGE

It is obvious, then, that air pollution affects, but is also strongly affected by, climate. The burning of fossil fuels and emission of both atmospheric particulates and greenhouse gases can cause climate change through their effects on the planet's energy budget (discussed in Chapter 1). For example, increased concentrations of black carbon in the atmosphere can reduce the amount of solar radiation reaching the ground surface, at the same time increasing the amount of energy absorbed in the atmosphere above. Consequent changes in the vertical temperature structure of the atmosphere can lead to changes in atmospheric processes with downstream effects on storm intensity and precipitation patterns.

Both primary and secondary air pollutants occur in the urban environment, with the most abundant being airborne particulates, nitrogen dioxide, and ozone from a range of sources (see Table 3.1). **Primary pollutants** are those that are emitted and occur in the atmosphere in their original form, while **secondary pollutants** are those that result from reactions that take place between primary pollutants (e.g. particulates, nitrogen oxides, volatile organic compounds, and carbon monoxide) and naturally occurring gases and aerosols, producing **photochemical smog** (e.g. ozone) and secondary particulates (e.g. sulphate aerosols). Increased global temperatures can alter the concentration and distribution of these anthropogenic air pollutants. However, efforts to reduce air pollution in major urban areas of the world have meant that pollutant concentrations are generally declining due to better controls on emissions, although there are significant differences between developed and less-developed countries (as shown in Figure 3.14). Research conducted in some areas has therefore tended to focus on the possible effects of climate change in reducing the observed declining urban pollution trend (Pénard-Morand and Annesi-Maesano 2004; Orru et al. 2017). Nevertheless, it is clear that the impact of climate change on air quality will vary globally, so that it is important that regional- and local-scale assessments are undertaken based on downscaling future climate scenarios obtained from global climate models. This is particularly important for less developed areas of the globe where air quality is consistently poor and there

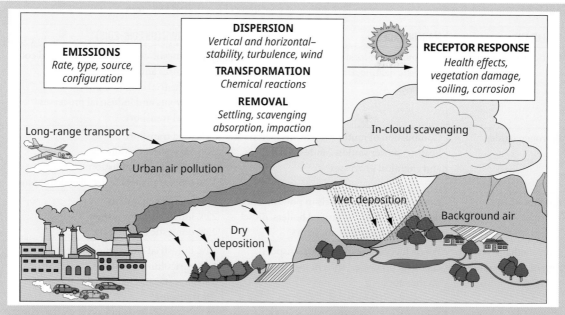

FIGURE 3.13 The most important components of an air pollution problem

Source: adapted from Oke, T. R. (1987). *Boundary Layer Climates*. Second edition, Routledge, London and New York; and Penard-Morand, C., and Annesi-Maesano, I. (2004). Air pollution: From sources of emissions to health effects. *Breathe* 1: 108–19

is little funding and infrastructure to address the problem. Such regional- and local-scale investigations should involve the application of consistent methodologies to allow valid comparisons of differing regional responses of air quality to climate change.

DIRECT EFFECTS

Direct effects of climate change on air pollution in urban areas are the result of changes in the key meteorological variables described earlier. They include factors immediately affecting the sources of pollutants, including emission types and rates, as well as the characteristics of the atmosphere that determine air pollution transport and dispersion, and its chemical transformation and subsequent removal (shown in Figure 3.13). The increase or decrease in the ability of the atmosphere to disperse or remove atmospheric pollutants is largely a function of changes in atmospheric temperature, vertical temperature structure, wind, and precipitation regimes. For example, situations where climate change results in stronger winds and increased precipitation should result in an improvement in air quality due to greater dispersion and removal of pollution. In areas

likely to experience increased occurrence of drought, air pollution may worsen due to reduced removal of pollutants by rainfall, as well as through the impacts of dust storms and wildfires. The possible impacts of climate change on the key meteorological factors affecting air pollution concentrations at the regional and local scales are described systematically in the following paragraphs (and represented schematically in Figure 3.15).

Temperature and vertical temperature structure

The ambient temperature within urban areas has an impact on both the amount and type of air pollution emission. In cooler climates, higher temperatures could result in decreased burning of fuels for domestic heating and therefore decreased emission of associated pollutants (e.g. airborne particulates and carbon monoxide), so that global warming would be expected to reduce air pollution levels. However, in warmer climates, higher temperatures associated with global warming are likely to cause greater use of air conditioners, which may result in higher pollutant emissions and therefore ambient concentrations.

Temperature also plays a significant role in the atmospheric chemistry processes that result in the creation of

TABLE 3.1 The main types and sources of air pollution in urban areas of the United Kingdom

POLLUTANT	MAIN SOURCES	BREAKDOWN (UK 2016–2018)*
Particulate material	Combustion of fossil fuels in power stations, domestic heating, transport, and industrial processes	38% domestic combustion (wood and coal) in open fires and solid fuel stoves 16% industrial combustion 13% solvents and industrial processes 12% road transport
Nitrogen oxides	Combustion of motor vehicle fuels, domestic heating, power stations, industrial boilers, and chemical processes	35% road transport 22% energy generation 19% industrial combustion 17% other transport (e.g. rail and shipping)
Sulphur dioxide	Combustion of fossil fuels in power stations, domestic heating, industrial boilers, diesel vehicles, and waste incinerators	37% energy generation 22% industrial combustion 22% domestic burning
Non-methane volatile organic compounds (VOCs)	Fossil-fuel combustion (e.g. transport), chemical processes, solvent use, waste incinerators	54% industrial emissions 14% agriculture 8% domestic and industrial combustion 5% transport
Carbon monoxide	Incomplete combustion, especially transport and industry	27.6% stationary combustion 27.4% domestic combustion 18.0% road transport 11.0% other transport 7.9% production processes 6.8% iron and steel production 1.4% agriculture/waste
Ozone	Produced as a secondary pollutant through photochemical reactions involving nitrogen oxides and VOCs	See nitrogen oxides and volatile organic compounds

*DEFRA (2018) https://www.gov.uk/government/publications/air-quality-explaining-air-pollution/air-quality-explaining-air-pollution-at-a-glance#what-air-quality-means; NAEI (2016) http://naei.beis.gov.uk/overview/pollutants?pollutant_id=4

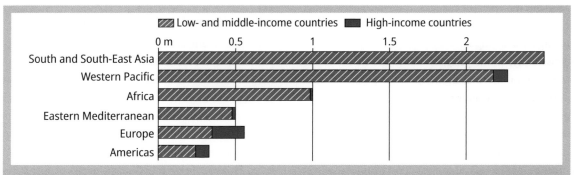

FIGURE 3.14 Estimated number of deaths caused by indoor and outdoor air pollution (in millions) in different parts of the world, and for richer and poorer countries

Source: Data courtesy of World Health Organization

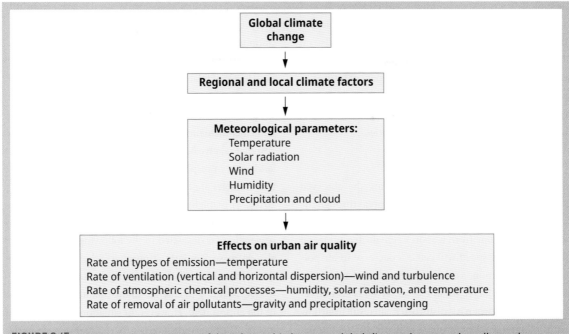

FIGURE 3.15 Schematic representation of the relationship between global climate change and smaller-scale meteorological effects on air pollution

secondary pollutants such as ozone and sulphate aerosols, with higher temperatures resulting in more rapid chemical reactions, so that the production of photochemical smog is expected to increase with global warming. Concentrations of ozone and fine particulates should therefore increase in the vicinity of urban areas. However, it should be noted that there is a time delay between the emission of the primary pollutants in urban areas (e.g. nitrogen oxides) and the formation of secondary pollutants (e.g. ozone), so that the highest concentrations of photochemical smog tend to be located on the periphery or downstream of major urban areas, rather than in city centres.

The temperature near the Earth's surface is also important because of its effect on the generation of turbulence and vertical mixing. However, it is the vertical profile of temperature above the surface that controls the extent to which air pollutants can be mixed upwards through the lower atmosphere, thereby reducing near-surface concentrations. The possible effects of climate change on the near-surface vertical temperature profile are difficult to predict, being made more complicated by the two-way relationship between air pollution and local climate. For example, a warming trend is likely to occur throughout the lower layers of the atmosphere, but it may also be associated with a reduction in the emission of pollution within urban areas, which could modify the energy exchanges in the atmosphere over the city. For instance, higher near-surface temperatures and lower pollution concentrations in the air above the urban area are likely to result in a destabilizing of the lowest layers, resulting in greater vertical mixing of pollutants (reducing pollution levels close to the ground).

Sunshine and solar radiation

Solar radiation is a contributor to atmospheric chemistry processes, with those involving sunlight called photochemical processes. Secondary pollutants such as ozone are often created through the combined effect of solar radiation and temperature increasing the efficacy of reactions involving primary pollutants. However, the formation of photochemical smog is dependent on sufficient amounts of sunlight and may take several hours to develop. The intensity and duration of solar radiation is dependent on geographic location, but also on cloud cover, which is generally less under anticyclonic weather patterns. Consequently, the impact of future climate change on the occurrence and trajectories followed by the main weather systems could determine future air pollution trends in the world's major cities.

Wind

Wind plays a major role in determining the observed concentration of air pollutants in urban areas through the processes of dilution, turbulence, and vertical mixing. If pollution emissions from a source remain the same, an increase in wind speed will cause a decrease in air pollution concentration, as the same number of molecules are mixed into a larger volume of air. Wind is also three-dimensional and when it is disturbed it can result in airflow that is highly turbulent, moving in many different directions. The greater the turbulence, the greater the mixing of air, which helps to dilute pollutant concentrations. However, vertical motion is affected by **atmospheric stability**, with a stable atmosphere restricting vertical motion (either upwards or downwards). Atmospheric stability varies as a result of changing weather systems and the daily cycle of surface heating and cooling, and is determined by the vertical temperature profile. Even under a very stable atmosphere, air pollution can still be transported horizontally by the low-level wind. However, air pollution dispersion is much greater in unstable situations when both horizontal motion and vertical mixing can occur in association with increased turbulence. The strength of the wind and atmospheric stability are the result of the major weather systems dominant over a given area, and the occurrence and tracking of these weather systems are likely to change under future climatic scenarios. So, as mentioned above, it is important to understand the relationship between predicted changes in global circulation and their downscaled impact at the regional and local scales in order to develop effective adaptation strategies.

Humidity/atmospheric moisture

Atmospheric moisture content is strongly related to prevailing weather conditions over a given area, so that there is a generally strong relationship between **relative humidity** and precipitation, and therefore low air pollution concentrations. This is because rainfall is a major factor in removing pollutants from the atmosphere and is associated with high levels of relative humidity. However, relative humidity may also have an impact on atmospheric chemistry and the production of secondary pollutants (Jia and Xu 2014). Global climate model predictions of future climates suggest that relative humidity will decrease substantially over land areas in response to rising air temperature, as these two variables are inversely related (Byrne and O'Gorman 2016). This might suggest that precipitation will be reduced over these areas and therefore pollution removal by scavenging (as discussed in the following section) would also decrease. Similarly, atmospheric chemistry processes that rely on high relative humidity would also be less effective, resulting in changes to the pollutant composition in the atmosphere. However, in situations where there is plenty of surface moisture (e.g. over oceans), evaporative uptake of water by the warmer air may mean little change or even an increase in relative humidity. So again, regional variation in climate change impacts on atmospheric moisture content should be expected and incorporated into appropriate response strategies.

Precipitation and cloud

The microphysical processes that result in cloud and precipitation formation (e.g. rain, snow, or hail) require the occurrence of **condensation nuclei**, onto which water vapour can condense when the air temperature drops below the dew-point temperature. These nuclei are typically naturally occurring aerosols suspended in the atmosphere, such as fine dust, pollen, and sea salt. However, the nuclei over urban areas are frequently made up of anthropogenic particles that have been emitted by motor vehicles, domestic heating, or industrial processes, or those that have resulted as secondary particulates through chemical reactions in the atmosphere. Condensation of water that occurs onto these pollution aerosols frequently results in removal of pollutants from the atmosphere through a process called scavenging, as rainout or washout. Rainout is an in-cloud process whereby the pollutant aerosols act as condensation nuclei which grow to become water droplets and then fall from the clouds to the ground, while washout occurs when water droplets falling from clouds intercept pollutant aerosols below, which are then carried to the ground (see Figure 3.13). The combination of these two processes is termed 'wet deposition', as opposed to dry deposition, which occurs solely due to the effects of gravity. Wet deposition is the most important mechanism for the removal of air pollutants from the atmosphere.

Given the complex relationship between possible future climates as predicted by global climate models, consequent changes in the tracks of different weather systems, and their effects on cloud type and height, it is extremely difficult to predict the likely regional and local effects of changing precipitation processes on air pollution concentrations in urban areas. Given that precipitation is the most important process for the removal of air pollutants, any increases or decreases in precipitation can result in more or less pollutants being removed from the air. As mentioned earlier, global climate model predictions suggest a future decline in relative humidity over land areas, from which it could be inferred that cloud and precipitation will also decline over these areas. If this were the case, then the scavenging of pollution would be reduced, resulting in higher concentrations remaining in the atmosphere. However, it would be unwise to apply such a wide-ranging prediction to all parts of the globe, as there would be substantial regional and local variability (e.g. between continental and oceanic areas), and until the problem of accurately downscaling the relevant processes is solved considerable uncertainty will remain (as discussed in Chapter 2).

There are clearly a number of ways in which large-scale climate change can affect pollution concentrations between their initial source and their ultimate sink, which may be located either within or outside urban areas (see Figure 3.13). Investigating such effects at the regional and local scales requires careful downscaling of predictions based on large-scale global climate models to specific regions to ensure that the future state of the key meteorological variables is realistically represented. For example, it is thought that climate change is responsible for a decreasing frequency of cyclonic systems in mid-latitudes (Jacob and Winner 2009) and more frequent occurrence of anticyclones, resulting in weaker winds. Downscaled impacts of global-scale climate change on wind, temperature, precipitation, and solar radiation at the regional and local scales could therefore vary significantly, so it is important to investigate possible effects on smaller-scale climate in order to develop appropriate response strategies. As discussed in Chapter 2, there is therefore significant uncertainty associated with predicting the future impacts of climate change on air quality at regional and local scales.

INDIRECT EFFECTS

There are many possible indirect effects of climate change on air pollution concentrations, some being more obvious than others. For example, in some parts of the world, fossil-fuel combustion may decline as a result of rising temperatures due to a reduction in the need for space heating, although this effect may be countered by an increased need for air conditioning. There is also evidence that in some regions (e.g. in Europe and North America) climate change could improve air quality as a result of changes in long-range and regional transport of air pollution. Similarly, higher temperatures combined with more frequent droughts in some parts of the world could result in increased natural emissions from wildfires and wind-blown dust that may significantly reduce air quality in nearby urban areas. Global climate change may also interfere with the seasonal occurrence of natural allergenic pollens in the atmosphere by prolonging the warmer seasons, although such effects are likely to vary from one region to another (D'Amato et al. 2016). Other biological effects include changes in the emission of naturally occurring **biogenic volatile organic compounds** due to higher temperatures, which can then impact on the production of secondary pollutants within urban areas. Increases in such secondary pollutants as ozone due to global warming can also have a significant impact on crop yields in areas surrounding major cities, with subsequent effects on food security and public health through malnutrition in poorer regions (Orru et al. 2017).

Another indirect effect of climate change on air pollution involves the impact of humans responding to the issue of climate change by reducing their greenhouse gas emissions (Stowell et al. 2017). Clearly, greater awareness of and sensitivity to possible future impacts of climate change have resulted in people reducing their reliance on fossil-fuel consumption and consequently reducing the emission of pollutants into the atmosphere. This positive environmental action has the dual effect of both reducing the rate of the current global warming trend, but also improving air quality.

The effect of weather changes on air pollution in the United States suggests that increased temperature and decreased wind speeds between 1994 and 2012 have resulted in higher levels of ozone and particulate material in the atmosphere than would otherwise have been the case, with consequent effects on human health (Jhun et al. 2015). However, it is evident that the air pollution problem in urban areas involves many complex interactions between human activity and environmental factors, often involving synergistic effects that are not completely understood, which makes predicting the impacts of climate change very difficult.

3.4 Other climate change impacts on the urban environment

SEA LEVEL RISE

A large number of the world's cities are located at or near sea level, with an increasing proportion of the global population living within 100 km of the coast. Sea level rise is an indirect effect of global warming, resulting from the melting of large volumes of land-based ice as global temperatures have increased, as well as thermal expansion of the warming oceans. Figure 3.16 shows the change in global mean sea level from a baseline in

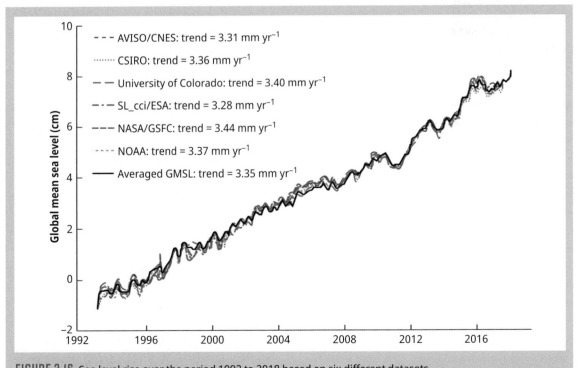

FIGURE 3.16 Sea level rise over the period 1993 to 2018 based on six different datasets

Source: WCRP Global Sea Level Budget Group (2018). Global sea-level budget 1993–present. *Earth System Science Data* 10: 1551–90

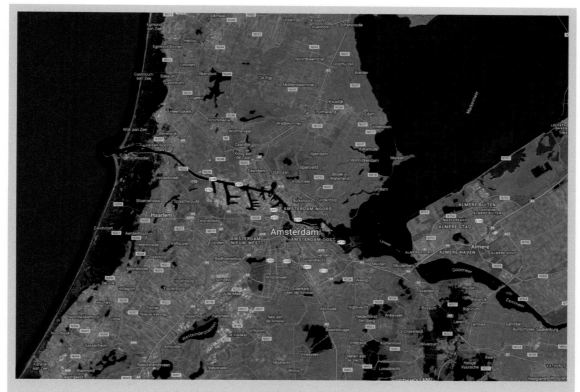

FIGURE 3.17 Projections of sea level rise for the city of Amsterdam by 2100. The blue colour represents areas expected to be below annual flood level based on a scenario of moderate cuts to greenhouse gas emissions
Source: https://coastal.climatecentral.org/

1993 to 2018 derived from six different data sets that are based on a combination of satellite remote sensing, *in situ* observations, and model estimates (WCRP Global Sea Level Budget Group 2018). There is a consistent upward trend of around 8 cm over this relatively short period, with an average sea level rise of more than 3 mm per year. Although these figures sound small, the impact on low-lying areas can be significant, and future climate change scenarios suggest that sea level rise could accelerate over coming decades, threatening large metropolitan areas and their growing populations. Examples of cities where there is significant concern over current or future problems associated with rising sea level are the cities of Amsterdam (Figure 3.17) and Bangkok (Figure 3.18), but there is also significant concern about the future of some Pacific Island states, which could disappear under water if the current trend of rising sea level continues.

3.5 Impacts of the urban environment on public health

It is evident from previous sections that the creation of extensive city landscapes has caused significant anthropogenic effects on the local environment, which undoubtedly impact on the welfare of the people who live within them. Maintaining human health and well-being in urban conurbations is therefore a serious challenge

FIGURE 3.18 Projections of sea level rise for the city of Bangkok by 2100. The blue colour represents areas expected to be below annual flood level based on a scenario of moderate cuts to greenhouse gas emissions

Source: https://coastal.climatecentral.org/

that is compounded by the global warming trend, which has the capacity to make the urban environment more extreme. As previously mentioned, human activities within cities create air pollution emissions that have both health impacts on local inhabitants, as well as contributing to the enhanced greenhouse effect that is the main cause of global warming. Poor air quality is thought to be the cause of more than 4 million premature deaths per annum worldwide, as well as having a significant range of other health effects on the urban population (Salmond et al. 2018). This represents a significant cost to the community that is exacerbated by the growing thermal effects of urban heat islands. The combination of poor air quality with high temperatures within cities has health consequences that can contribute to socio-economic effects that impact on the well-being of predominantly the poorer and more disadvantaged members of the urban community. The urban population is particularly exposed to respiratory illnesses related to inhalation of suspended particles (smoke and dust), emitted gases such as nitrogen oxides and sulphur dioxide, and products of atmospheric chemical reactions such as ozone. The increasing frequency of heatwaves not only increases stress on the human cardiovascular system but also can contribute to increased emissions of biogenic volatile organic compounds, as well as the rate of atmospheric chemical reactions. Heatwaves can therefore have wide-ranging negative impacts on human health, as demonstrated by the 2003 heatwave in Europe that was estimated to have caused 70,000 excess deaths (Tong et al. 2021). There are effects not only on respiratory illness, but also on kidney disease and mental health, with older, poorer, and more disadvantaged sections of the community being worse affected.

3.6 How can we develop effective adaptation strategies for major cities?

The complex interactions between urban climate, air pollution, and public health and well-being in the context of climate change remain poorly understood and difficult to predict. However, in order for cities to adapt to climate change, adaptation policies must be quickly defined and implemented. Although urban climatologists have been studying this theme for decades, community interest in and concerns about possible impacts are more recent. This increased attention to environmental and health issues related to rising temperatures has helped to advance the development of heat island reduction strategies, mainly through urban planning initiatives. Local-scale climate and pollution measurement networks, the development of urban climate models, and a series of pilot projects involving scientists, engineers, and practitioners are helping to define strategies for adapting cities to climate change. The amount of research in this area has increased rapidly since 2015, with a particular emphasis on addressing problems associated with thermal comfort and urban heat island mitigation (Graça et al. 2022). Current policy efforts are therefore focused on encouraging strategies to change urban geometry and materials, as well as anthropogenic heat generation in communities to reduce urban heat islands. Figure 3.19

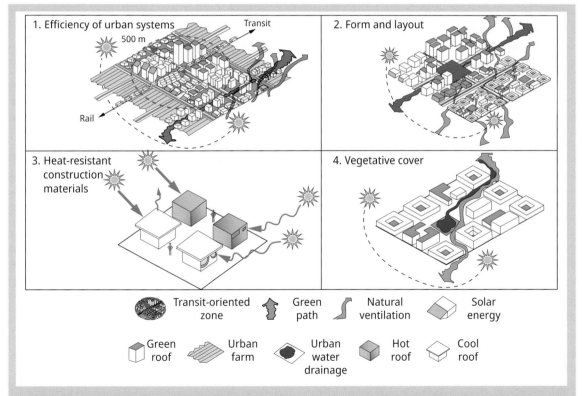

FIGURE 3.19 Main strategies used by urban planners and designers to facilitate integrated climate change mitigation and adaptation in cities

Source: Rosenzweig et al. (2015). *ARC3.2 Summary for City Leaders*. Urban Climate Change Research Network, Columbia University, New York

shows that the main strategies integrated into urban planning projects concern improvements in the efficiency of urban infrastructure, the modification of the form and layout of buildings, the increase in vegetation cover and water in the urban landscape, and the use of heat-resistant building materials and reflective surface coatings. A key general aim of such strategies would be to modify the layout of urban areas in order to provide cooling and better ventilation.

The integration of climate change scenarios into urban planning projects makes it possible to test and propose different climate change adaptation strategies to local authorities in line with urban policies. Many studies are being carried out, particularly on the use of green spaces to reduce the effects of climate change on human health (de Munck et al. 2018; Salmond et al. 2018). Xu et al. (2017) have shown that in a sub-tropical city like Hong Kong, the effect of green space on the air reduces the intensity of the urban heat island, as well as reducing mortality by improving quality of life. Many cities have focused on green infrastructure within built-up areas in their urban planning in order to address climate change adaptation. For example, in London:

> The Green Grid for East London seeks to create a network of interlinked, multi-purpose open spaces to support the wider regeneration of the sub-region, enhancing the potential of existing and new green spaces to connect people and places, absorb and store water, cool the vicinity, and provide a mosaic of habitats for wildlife. (GLA 2008, p. 80)

The use of water spaces also reduces the intensity of the urban heat island. The form and location of water bodies affect their evaporative cooling efficiency and their ability to improve thermal comfort. A 'water-sensitive urban design' approach to spatial planning makes it possible to improve management of urban water (stormwater, groundwater, and wastewater management, as well as water supply), in addition to thermal comfort. Figure 3.20 indicates the temperature differences in relation to urban structure, land cover characteristics, and proximity to water bodies in a residential suburb of Adelaide (Australia). The results showed that water-affected sites were cooler than dryer urban sites.

One of the important factors increasing the urban heat island is the low albedo of the urban fabric. A method of adaptation is therefore to increase the albedo (reflectivity) of urban surfaces. Jandaghian and Akbari (2018) showed that by increasing the surface albedo of roofs, walls, and pavements in a climate model, simulated air temperatures decreased by more than 2 °C in urban areas and by 1 °C in suburban areas. With the same objective of reducing the temperature increase using reflective materials, the City of Los Angeles painted some of its streets with a white coating that absorbs less heat. Other large cities have promoted the development of 'cool roofs' (covered with reflective paint) or green roofs (covered in vegetation).

In responding to the impacts of climate change, the choice of specific adaptation and mitigation measures must be made by recognizing the complex interaction between the many processes that operate within the city. Urban planning in response to climate change requires a clear understanding of the interactions between the social, economic, cultural, and physical processes that take place in cities and how they affect urban land use in space and time. Adaptation strategies based on reducing the urban heat island often also improve air quality and therefore public health, and are likely to contribute to reducing greenhouse gas emissions while improving the **resilience** of cities. It is difficult to reduce human susceptibility to air pollutants in urban areas, so that protecting community health under predicted warmer climatic conditions will require the application of stricter air quality controls, such as establishment of clean air zones. These, in turn, will help to reduce greenhouse gas emissions. In many cities of the world, such actions have already been shown to reduce the levels of pollutants in urban

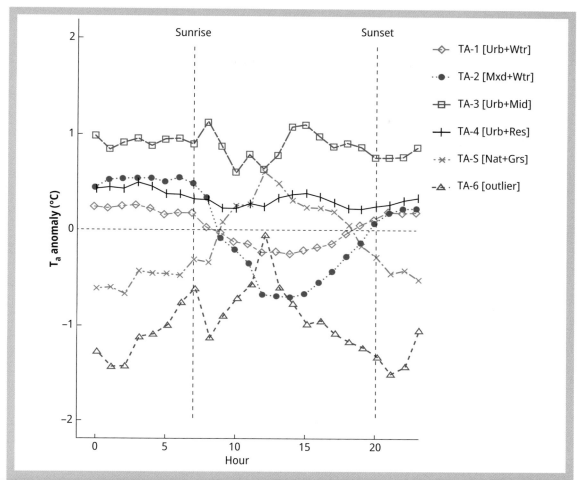

FIGURE 3.20 Hourly differences from the mean air temperature (T$_a$) for different urban sites associated with different land cover characteristics in Mawson Lakes (Australia). TA-1 represents urban sites with nearby water, TA-2 mixed-land-use sites with nearby water, TA-3 mid-rise urban sites, TA-4 urban residential sites, TA-5 natural grass-dominated sites, and TA-6 a single outlier site

Source: Broadbent et al. (2018). The microscale cooling effects of water sensitive urban design and irrigation in a suburban environment. *Theoretical and Applied Climatology* 134: 1–23

areas over recent decades (as shown for London and Birmingham in Figure 3.21), and it is expected that regulation, along with technological changes, such as the increased use of electric vehicles, will ensure that environmental impacts of air pollution continue to reduce. The COVID-19 pandemic of 2020–2022 will complicate the problem of identifying effects of emissions-reduction strategies and climate change on ambient air pollution concentrations because of its significant impact on human behaviour, including in changing people's work habits (such as increased working at home).

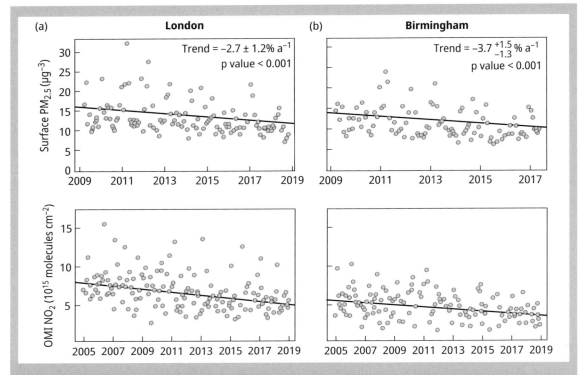

FIGURE 3.21 Recent trends in ambient $PM_{2.5}$ and NO_2 concentrations in (a) London and (b) Birmingham in response to the application of emissions controls. PM is particulate material

Source: adapted from Vohra et al. (2021). Long-term trends in air quality in major cities in the UK and India: A view from space. *Atmospheric Chemistry and Physics* 21: 6275–96

CASE STUDY 3.1
Climate change adaptation and urban planning

Climate change adaptation strategies in cities are the most complex to implement as they have to take into account the impacts of the climate on different sectors that are concentrated in limited spaces (Knieling and Klindworth 2016). Adaptation policies must ensure the safety and security of the inhabitants, but also their well-being, while maintaining appropriate economic and environmental conditions. Due to their characteristics (e.g. size, population, economic activity, and concentration), cities are very vulnerable to climate impacts. Many climate impacts are accentuated in built-up areas, in relation to various infrastructure sectors, including transport and communications (e.g. roads, railways,

bridges, subways, phone and fibre networks), energy and water supply (e.g. drinking water and electricity), and waste and sewage disposal (e.g. stormwater and wastewater). Cities must integrate these various sectors into their current and future development and management plans in order to reduce climate risks. With the growth of urban population, many cities have had to adopt an integrative approach to incorporating climate change considerations into current management and future construction of infrastructure (see also Chapter 4). For new infrastructure, building norms or planning laws typically already incorporate consideration of possible climate change effects. For example, in response to rising temperatures and more frequent heatwaves, building design standards recommend the use of materials that limit the impact of heat on the population and incorporate the growth of urban green spaces. Drainage and sewerage systems are designed to handle potential flood risks while transportation and energy supply infrastructure can be protected by storm protection structures. Such urban planning approaches to reducing impacts on infrastructure are mainly implemented in cities in developed countries, while the situation is much more complicated in developing countries, often because of lack of finance, uncontrolled urban sprawl, and poor governance of urban planning processes and implementation. Breitmeier et al. (2009) conducted a comparative study of urban infrastructure management plans for current and future climate risks for the coastal cities of Lagos (Nigeria), Dhaka (Bangladesh), and Hamburg (Germany). The infrastructure of these cities is regularly threatened by major floods and these risks will be greatly exacerbated by the predicted rise in sea level due to climate change.

Hamburg has developed a sophisticated comprehensive strategy for adapting to climate change by implementing a policy of flood protection, water management, and port planning over the short, medium, and long term. HafenCity's project planning for Hamburg city centre is a result of this approach, with the buildings located on 'artificial dwelling mounds' well above the highest expected flood level. The different types of infrastructure are defined according to specific standards that take into account the highest flood risk (according to climate change scenarios) with optimal access for emergency assistance in the event of extreme events (Monbaliu et al. 2014; Huang-Lachmann and Lovette 2016). This strategy is being developed jointly with the municipality and the population to raise awareness of the need to adapt urban infrastructure to current and future climate risks. The involvement of the population makes it possible to raise awareness of the need for resilience to the impacts of climate change. Figure 3.22 presents the urban development plan for the HafenCity

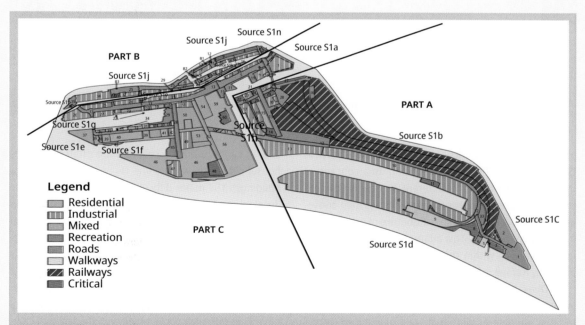

FIGURE 3.22 Land-use map of the HafenCity area in Hamburg, Germany based on source–pathway–receptor modelling, derived from the development scheme and land-use plan for the year 2010

Source: Monbaliu et al. (2014). Risk assessment of estuaries under climate change: Lessons from western Europe. *Coastal Engineering* 87: 32–49

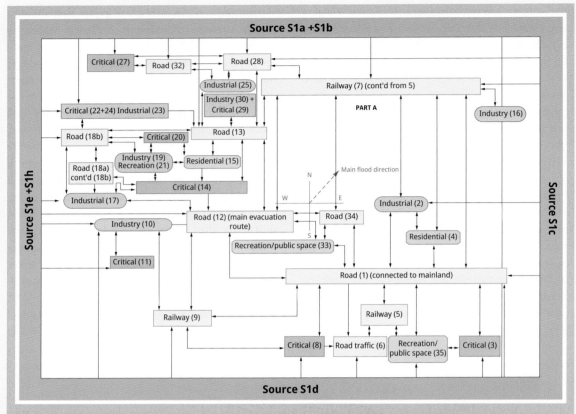

FIGURE 3.23 Source–pathway–receptor model applied to Part A of the HafenCity area in Hamburg, Germany (shown in Figure 3.22)

Source: Monbaliu et al. (2014). Risk assessment of estuaries under climate change: Lessons from western Europe. *Coastal Engineering* 87: 32–49

area based on the results of source–pathway–receptor (SPR) modelling. This involves setting up a conceptual model that identifies the different sources of climate risk (in this case, floods) and then evaluates their consequences according to the specific nature of urban development (Figure 3.23). This adaptation strategy was set up in Hamburg within the climate change adaptation planning framework adopted by Europe and Germany.

In Dhaka and Lagos, strategies for adapting urban infrastructure to climate impacts are much more complicated to define, with high and unplanned urban growth complicating the implementation of climate risk management plans. Poor segments of the population tend to settle in flood-prone areas and the urban infrastructure is not even adapted to current climate risks

(e.g. in Lagos, drainage channels are often blocked by household waste, while some channels are blocked by buildings). The major difficulties faced by megacities in developing countries in managing current climate risks make it difficult to implement adaptation strategies for addressing problems created by future climate change. A study by Breitmeier et al. (2009) highlighted the virtual lack of awareness of and preparedness for the impacts of climate change in cities in developing countries. This is particularly related to poor governance of urban planning. These problems, combined with the fact that cities in developing countries are often in regions with high climate risks, make strategies to reduce climate impacts on urban infrastructure much more difficult to establish than in developed countries.

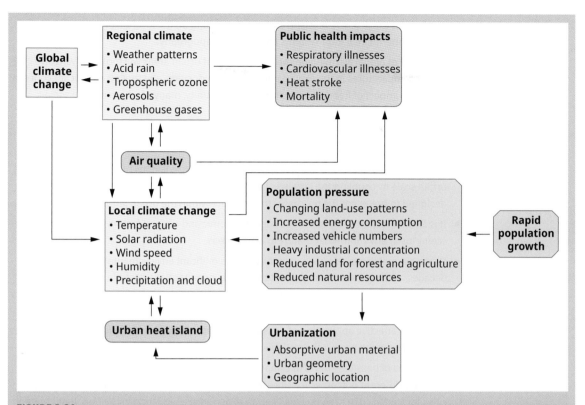

FIGURE 3.24 Complex interactions between global climate change and urban air quality and urban heat island effects

Source: adapted from Hassan et al. (2016). Impact of climate change on air quality and public health in urban areas. *Asia-Pacific Journal of Public Health* 28: 38–48

Summary

- The adaptation of cities to climate change should be undertaken at the local level within the context of regional, national, and international policies and initiatives.

- In order to develop effective adaptation strategies, it is first important to evaluate the degree of vulnerability and the nature of climate risks (e.g. sea level rise, heatwaves, and air pollution) to which each city is exposed.

- It is therefore important to gain a good understanding of the relevant processes operating in urban areas and their significance for the specific city under consideration. Figure 3.24 illustrates the complex interaction of processes within the urban environment that needs to be understood.

- Any changes in global climate will feed through to the regional and local scales, and along with other physical and human processes will impact on both the urban heat island and urban air quality.

- The urban heat island is itself a localized change of climate created by anthropogenic modification of land surface characteristics, resulting in modification of the energy exchanges over the city. It tends to create a warmer and more arid climate within urban areas, with rural–urban temperature differences often exceeding 6 °C.

- The form of the urban heat island can vary depending on the location of the city in relation to atmospheric circulation systems and regional topography.

- The effect of global warming on the local climate of urban areas will most likely involve higher temperatures in the central parts of the major cities, and there is significant concern about the impact of heatwaves on the local community, many of whom may be socio-economically disadvantaged.

- However, cities currently located in cooler parts of the globe may benefit from warmer temperatures, resulting in better health outcomes for the community and its environment.

- Attempts have been made to downscale global model predictions of future climate to the urban scale by coupling the larger-scale climate models with fine-scale models specifically designed to represent the processes that operate within the urban landscape.

- It is also important to try to include socio-economic and cultural factors in developing future scenarios of environmental change in urban areas.

- Urban air quality has also been recognized as a significant environmental problem for many decades, and it is therefore important to try and understand the possible impacts of global warming on air pollution levels in urban areas, as climate is a major factor affecting air quality.

- In more developed economies there has generally been a decline in air pollution levels as a result of effective application of emission controls in urban areas, so for some cities it is a matter of trying to predict the possible impacts of global warming on this declining trend.

- Predictions of possible effects of climate change on air pollution also need to recognize the likely different outcomes for cities located in different parts of the world. For example, cities located in colder regions are likely to experience a reduction in the pollutant emissions associated with space heating, while those located in hotter regions may produce more emissions due to the greater need for air conditioning.

- There may also be changes in the nature of the pollutants in the atmosphere associated with changes in the rates and types of emission, as well as changes in the atmospheric processes (e.g. increases in secondary pollutants such as ozone due to higher temperatures and increased solar radiation).

- Because of the difficulties in downscaling from global models to the regional level, it is not easy to predict what changes in atmospheric circulation may occur in different parts of the world. Some areas may experience windier conditions, while others may have more precipitation, resulting in a cleaner atmosphere and better air quality. Recent research suggests that land (continental) areas of the globe are likely to be dryer and presumably less cloudy, resulting in a reduction in the atmosphere's ability to remove pollutants. There may also be increased frequency of dust storms and wildfires, resulting in higher concentrations of aerosols over such areas.

- Sea level rise is another indirect effect of global climate change that is likely to impact on coastal cities. Clearly, adaptation options in response to this issue are both difficult and very expensive, involving either large-scale construction of coastal barriers or the relocation of those areas most susceptible to the impact of encroachment of the sea.

- The development of climate change adaptation strategies for urban areas needs to consider the interaction of a range of factors, both environmental and socio-economic. It also requires the development of urban climate models that accurately represent the processes that operate within the city, but also that can be coupled to larger-scale models that are able to represent changes in atmospheric circulation affecting the surrounding region. The application of such models should involve scientists, engineers, planners, and other practitioners.

- The main components of an urban adaptation strategy should include: improvements in the efficiency of urban infrastructure; the modification of the form and layout of buildings; the increase of vegetation cover and surface water in the urban landscape; and the use of heat-resistant building materials and reflective surface coatings.

For case studies and updates, visit the online resources at:

 www.oup.com/he/sturman-quenol1e

References

Blake, R., Grimm, A., Ichinose, T., Horton, R., Gaffin, S., Jiong, S., Bader, D. A., and Cecil, L. D. (2011). Urban climate: Processes, trends, and projections. In: Rosenzweig, C., Solecki, W. D., Hammer, S. A., and Mehrotra, S. (eds), *Climate Change and Cities: First Assessment Report of the Urban Climate Change Research Network*. Cambridge University Press, Cambridge, pp. 43–81.

Breitmeier, H., Kuhn, J., and Schwindenhammer, S. (2009). Analyzing urban adaptation strategies to climate change: A comparison of the coastal cities of Dhaka, Lagos and Hamburg. In: *Contribution to the Panel, Regieren im Klimawandel Section, Regierungssystem und Regieren in der Bundesrepublik Deutschland* (Vol. 21, p. 25). DVPW-Kongress, Berlin.

Broadbent, A. M., Coutts, A. M., Tapper, N. J., Demuzere, M., and Beringer, J. (2018). The microscale cooling effects of water sensitive urban design and irrigation in a suburban environment. *Theoretical and Applied Climatology* 134: 1–23.

Byrne, M. P., and O'Gorman, P. A. (2016). Understanding decreases in land relative humidity with global warming: Conceptual model and GCM simulations. *Journal of Climate* 29: 9045–61.

Chakraborty, T., and Lee, X. (2019). A simplified urban-extent algorithm to characterize surface urban heat islands on a global scale and examine vegetation control on their spatiotemporal variability. *International Journal of Applied Earth Observation and Geoinformation* 74: 269–80.

Conry, P., Sharma, A., Potosnak, M. J., Leo, L. S., Bensman, E., Hellmann, J. J., and Fernando, H. J. (2015). Chicago's heat island and climate change: Bridging the scales via dynamical downscaling. *Journal of Applied Meteorology and Climatology* 54: 1430–48.

D'Amato, G., Vitale, C., Lanza, M., Molino, A., and D'Amato, M. (2016). Climate change, air pollution, and allergic respiratory diseases: An update. *Current Opinion in Allergy and Clinical Immunology* 16: 434–40.

de Munck, C., Lemonsu, A., Masson, V., Le Bras, J., and Bonhomme, M. (2018). Evaluating the impacts of greening scenarios on thermal comfort and energy and water consumptions for adapting Paris city to climate change. *Urban Climate* 23: 260–86.

FISRWG (1998). *Stream Corridor Restoration: Principles, Processes, and Practices*. Federal Interagency Stream Restoration Working Group (FISRWG) (15 Federal agencies of the US government). GPO Item No. 0120-A; SuDocs No. A 57.6/2:EN 3/PT.653.

Gaffin, S. R., Rosenzweig, C., Khanbilvardi, R., Parshall, L., Mahani, S., Glickman, H., Goldberg, R., Blake, R., Slosberg, R. B., and Hillel, D. (2008). Variations in New York City's urban heat island strength over time and space. *Theoretical and Applied Climatology* 94: 1–11.

GLA (2008). *The London Climate Change Adaptation Strategy: Draft Report*. Greater London Authority (GLA), London.

Graça, M., Cruz, S., Monteiro, A., and Neset, T-S. (2022). Designing urban green spaces for climate adaptation: A critical review of research outputs. *Urban Climate* 42: 101126.

Hassan, N. A., Hashim, Z., and Hashim, J. H. (2016). Impact of climate change on air quality and public health in urban areas. *Asia-Pacific Journal of Public Health* 28: 38–48.

Huang-Lachmann, J. T., and Lovett, J. C. (2016). How cities prepare for climate change: Comparing Hamburg and Rotterdam. *Cities* 54: 36–44.

Hung, T., Uchihama, D., Ochi, S., and Yasuoka, Y. (2006). Assessment with satellite data of the urban heat island effects in Asian mega cities. *International Journal of Applied Earth Observation and Geoinformation* 8: 34–48.

Jacob, D. J., and Winner, D. A. (2009). Effect of climate change on air quality. *Atmospheric Environment* 43: 51–63.

Jandaghian, Z., and Akbari, H. (2018). The effect of increasing surface albedo on urban climate and air quality: A detailed study for Sacramento, Houston, and Chicago. *Climate* 6: 19.

Jhun, I., Coull, B. A., Zanobetti, A., and Koutrakis, P. (2015). The impact of nitrogen oxides concentration decreases on ozone trends in the USA. *Air Quality, Atmosphere and Health* 8: 283–92.

Jia, L., and Xu, Y. (2014). Effects of relative humidity on ozone and secondary organic aerosol formation from the photo-oxidation of benzene and ethylbenzene. *Aerosol Science and Technology* 48(1): 1–12.

Katsoulis, B. D., and Theoharatos, G. A. (1985). Indications of the urban heat island in Athens, Greece. *Journal of Climate and Applied Meteorology* 24: 1296–302.

Knieling, J., and Klindworth, K. (2016). Climate adaptation governance in cities and regions: Framework conditions, theoretical concepts and research questions. In: Knieling, J. (ed.), *Climate Adaptation Governance in Cities and Regions: Theoretical Fundamentals and Practical Evidence.* John Wiley, Hoboken, NJ, pp. 1–20.

Lemonsu, A., Viguie, V., Daniel, M., and Masson, V. (2015). Vulnerability to heat waves: Impact of urban expansion scenarios on urban heat island and heat stress in Paris (France). *Urban Climate* 14: 586–605.

Li, D., and Bou-Zeid, E. (2013). Synergistic interactions between urban heat islands and heat waves: The impact in cities is larger than the sum of its parts. *Journal of Applied Meteorology and Climatology* 52: 2051–64.

Masson, V., Marchadier, C., Adolphe, L., Aguejdad, R., Avner, P., Bonhomme, M., Bretagne, G., Briottet, X., Bueno, B., de Munck, C., Doukari, O., Hallegatte, S., Hidalgo, J., Houet, T., Le Bras, J., Lemonsu, A. Long, N., Moine, M.-P., Morel, T., Nolorgues, L., Pigeon, G., Salagnac, J-L., Viguié, V., and Zibouche , K. (2014). Adapting cities to climate change: A systemic modelling approach. *Urban Climate* 10: 407–29.

Mohan, M., Kikegawa, Y., Gurjar, B. R., Bhati, S., Kandya, A., and Ogawa, K. (2009). Assessment of urban heat island intensities over Delhi. The 7th International Conference on Urban Climate, Japan, Yokohama, 2 June–3 July 2009. http://www.5dstudios.com/clients/gcca/wp-content/uploads/2012/05/Delhi-UHI.pdf.

Monbaliu, J., Chen, Z., Felts, D., Ge, J., Hissel, F., Kappenberg, J., Narayan, S., Nicholls, J, Ohle, N., Schuster, S., Sothmann, J., and Willems, P. (2014). Risk assessment of estuaries under climate change: Lessons from western Europe. *Coastal Engineering* 87: 32–49.

Morris, C. J. G., and Simmonds, I. (2000). Associations between varying magnitudes of the urban heat island and the synoptic climatology in Melbourne, Australia. *International Journal of Climatology* 20: 1931–54.

New York City Panel on Climate Change (NPCC) (2015). *Building the Knowledge Base for Climate Resiliency.* New York City Panel on Climate Change 2015 Report, Annals of the New York Academy of Sciences.

Oke, T. R. (1987). *Boundary Layer Climates.* Second edition, Routledge, London and New York.

Oke, T. R. (1997). Urban climates and global environmental change. In: Thompson, R. D. and A. Perry (eds), *Applied Climatology: Principles and Practices.* Routledge, New York, pp. 273–87.

Orru, H., Ebi, K. L., and Forsberg, B. (2017). The interplay of climate change and air pollution on health. *Current Environmental Health Reports* 4: 504–13.

Penard-Morand, C., and Annesi-Maesano, I. (2004). Air pollution: From sources of emissions to health effects. *Breathe* 1: 108–19.

Rosenzweig, C., Solecki, W., Romero-Lankao, P., Mehrotra, S., Dhakal, S., Bowman, T., and Ali Ibrahim, S. (2015). *ARC3.2 Summary for City Leaders.* Urban Climate Change Research Network, Columbia University, New York.

Sailor, D. J., and Fan, H. (2002). Modeling the diurnal variability of effective albedo for cities. *Atmospheric Environment* 36: 713–25.

Salmond, J., Sabel, C. E., and Vardoulakis, S. (2018). Towards the integrated study of urban climate, air pollution, and public health. *Climate* 6(1): 14.

Schär, C., and Jendritzky, G. (2004). Climate change: Hot news from summer 2003. *Nature* 432(7017): 559.

Stern, N. (2007). *The Economics of Climate Change: The Stern Review.* Cambridge University Press, Cambridge.

Stowell, J. D., Kim, Y. M., Gao, Y., Fu, J. S., Chang, H. H., and Liu, Y. (2017). The impact of climate change and emissions control on future ozone levels: Implications for human health. *Environment International* 108: 41–50.

Tan, J., Zheng, Y., Tang, X., Guo, C., Li, L., Song, G., Zhen, X., Yuan, D., Kalkstein, A. J., Li, F., and Chen, H. (2010). The urban heat island and its impact on heat waves and human health in Shanghai. *International Journal of Biometeorology* 54: 75–84.

Tong, S., Prior, J., McGregor, G., Shi, X., and Kinney, P. (2021). Urban heat: An increasing threat to global health. *British Medical Journal* 375:n2467.

United States Environmental Protection Agency (USEPA) (2008). *Reducing Urban Heat Islands: Compendium of Strategies* (draft). https://www.epa.gov/sites/production/files/2017-05/documents/reducing_urban_heat_islands_ch_1.pdf.

Vohra, K., Marais, E. A., Suckra, S., Kramer, L., Bloss, W. J., Sahu, R., Gaur, A., Tripathi, S. N., Van Damme, M., Clarisse, L., and Coheur, P.-F. (2021). Long-term trends in air quality in major cities in the UK and India: A view from space. *Atmospheric Chemistry and Physics* 21: 6275–96.

Wanner, H., and Filliger, P. (1989). Orographic influence on urban climate. *Weather and Climate* 9: 22–8.

WCRP Global Sea Level Budget Group (2018). Global sea-level budget 1993–present. *Earth System Science Data* 10: 1551–90.

Xu, L., Ren, C., Yuan, C., Nichol, J. E., and Goggins, W. B. (2017). An ecological study of the association between area-level green space and adult mortality in Hong Kong. *Climate* 5: 55.

Zhang, H., Qi, Z.-F., Ye, X.-Y., Cai, Y.-B., Ma, W.-C., and Chen, M.-N. (2013). Analysis of land use/land cover change, population shift, and their effects on spatiotemporal patterns of urban heat islands in metropolitan Shanghai, China. *Applied Geography* 44: 121–33.

CHAPTER **FOUR**

Energy and Infrastructure

LEARNING OUTCOMES

Having read this chapter, you should be able to:

- describe trends in global and national energy use and its relationship to climate

- critically assess the options available for future energy generation with the aim of reducing fossil-fuel emissions

- identify climate impacts on infrastructure and approaches to reducing vulnerability

- explore possible approaches to adapting energy and infrastructure systems for future climate change

4.1 Introduction: energy and infrastructure in the context of climate change

The relationship between energy use and climate variability is well known, and provides the rationale for investigating ways in which humans can develop **renewable energy sources** and move away from unsustainable use of fossil fuels for energy generation. The practical application of alternative energy sources such as wind, solar radiation, and hydropower relies on investigations undertaken at the local and regional scale, and knowledge of atmospheric processes at this scale is very important for making efficient use of available energy resources. The use of renewable energy as part of mitigation and adaptation strategies will be discussed in this chapter. The problems created by the increased development of renewable resources for energy distribution infrastructure will be examined, as the availability of such energy sources as wind and solar can vary erratically. The possible impact of future climate change on the viability of renewable energy systems will also be explored.

Electricity is a major source of energy used across the planet, but there is a fundamental problem in getting energy from generators to consumers. This is because the electricity-using population tends to be concentrated in a few areas of the world, often along coastlines, while the capacity to generate energy is more widely distributed. In the past, the strategy has been to locate power plants close to areas of high population and import the energy in the form of fossil fuels (especially coal, oil, and natural gas) to the generators for consumption. This is not practicable for renewable energy sources such as hydro, wind, and solar, so that electricity needs to be generated close to the energy source and then transferred to the consumers via the power distribution network. This adds significant cost and complexity.

The infrastructure that we all rely on in our everyday lives (e.g. energy, food, and water distribution; road, rail, and air transportation; waste disposal; and communication networks) is closely related to energy generation and its use, and is therefore an obvious topic for discussion in this chapter. Its sensitivity to variations in weather and climate at the regional and local scales creates unique problems that can only be solved through understanding atmospheric processes that operate at this relatively small scale. Possible changes in climatic conditions could impact on this infrastructure, creating costly problems for the day-to-day operations of society.

The increasing sophistication of human society over the past 100 years has resulted in the development of an infrastructure that is increasingly complex and reliant on the generation and delivery of energy, alongside the transport of other materials, such as food and waste, often over long distances. The need to reduce our consumption of fossil fuels and turn to renewable energy sources has resulted in some changes in the configuration and management of energy distribution networks, due to an increase in local energy production and usage. This is especially so with regard to solar and sometimes wind generation, so that electricity generation and distribution networks have become less centralized to some extent as a result.

This chapter therefore investigates the relationship between climate, energy, and infrastructure with the aim of developing adaptation strategies in response to current and future climate change at the regional and local scales.

4.2 Energy use and climate

The relationship between climate and energy consumption is complex because energy is consumed in several different sectors of society (the main ones being residential, commercial, industrial, and transport) which have differing sensitivity to the main climate factors, such as temperature, humidity, wind, and rainfall. In addition, in developed economies, regions experiencing higher temperatures tend to consume electricity for air conditioning to cool residential and commercial buildings, while those experiencing lower temperatures tend to consume fuels such as gas, oil, and wood for space heating. The use of energy in developing economies, however, is less clearly differentiated on the basis of regional differences in the thermal climate. So, energy consumption in different climatic zones tends to reflect both the general climate characteristics of the region (especially temperature) and the socio-economic attributes of the community (e.g. the relative dominance of residential, commercial, and industrial activities, and general financial well-being).

The relationship between industrial and transport activities and energy consumption tends to differ significantly from that between residential and commercial activities and energy use. This is mainly because of the often-important role of energy as an input to industrial processes, as well as in the operation of transport networks (road, rail, sea, and air). Many industries require significant amounts of energy as part of the production processes—for example, industries involved in metal smelting. In such situations, energy usage tends to be independent of such climate factors as air temperature, and more related to economic activity. However, climate variability may become important where changing precipitation regimes result in a reduction in the availability of water for hydropower, for example.

Because of the complex relationship between human activity and energy use, the impact of the global warming trend experienced over the past few decades on energy use is difficult to identify clearly. Although there is increasing use of renewable energy sources internationally, about 80% of global energy consumption is currently generated from fossil fuels, primarily natural gas, oil, and coal (Figure 4.1). The burning of fossil fuels is therefore a major component of the energy generation

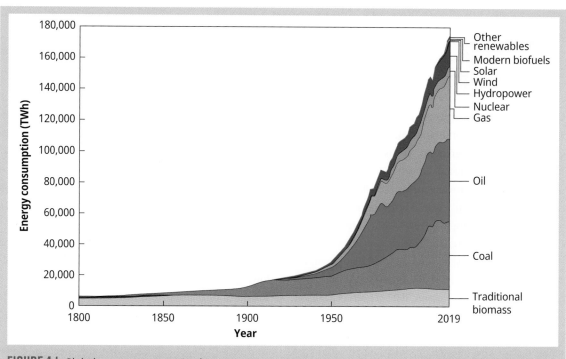

FIGURE 4.1 Global energy consumption by source

Source: https://ourworldindata.org/global-energy-200-years

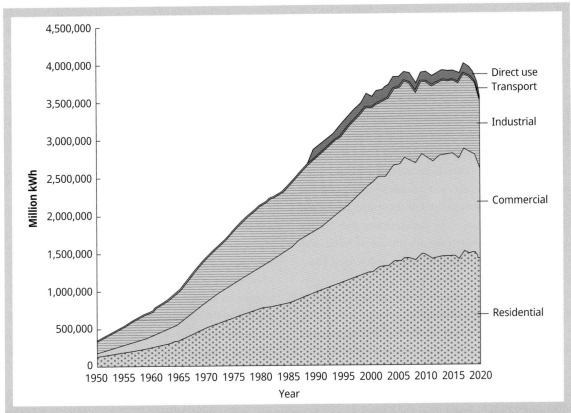

FIGURE 4.2 Electricity retail sales (million kWh) in the United States by major sector and by all direct users (entities that use the energy they generate themselves) over the period 1950–2021

Source: US Energy Information Center, Monthly Energy Review, February 2022, https://www.eia.gov/totalenergy/data/monthly/

infrastructure, and energy use contributes about 35% of all carbon emissions (https://www.epa.gov/ghgemissions/global-greenhouse-gas-emissions-data). It is therefore an important contributor to global warming, so that any improvements in the efficiency of energy production and use would be of significant benefit to international attempts to reverse the impacts of the enhanced greenhouse effect.

Recent data suggest that, in spite of rising temperatures, electricity use in the United States has stayed relatively constant since about 2007 (Figure 4.2). Over recent decades, the need for air conditioning has tended to increase, while the requirement for space heating has reduced, which has affected the energy-use profile of the whole country. The current approximate breakdown of

electricity usage in the United States is residential 37%, commercial 34%, industrial 25%, and other 4%, with overall usage staying roughly constant between 2007 and 2020 (US Energy Information Administration 2022). A noticeable drop in consumption associated with the COVID-19 pandemic has occurred since then (Figure 4.2).

The overall per capita energy consumption in the United States appears to be on a downward trend following several decades of mostly stable values (US Energy Information Administration 2022), so there is little evidence to suggest that the current warming trend is associated with an increased use of energy resources. In contrast, it is highly likely that any effects of global warming are being countered by improved efficiency in the production and use of energy, and the changing energy-type breakdown. In the latter case, a general shift has occurred in the need for energy use from heating to cooling, while technology changes have resulted in switches from fossil-fuel use to electricity.

The efficiency of energy production depends on climate because of its influence on the provision of hydro, solar, and wind power through the availability of precipitation, solar radiation, and wind. It also has an indirect effect on fossil-fuel and nuclear power generation because of the need for cooling during the generation process. Rising air temperatures will clearly reduce the effectiveness of the cooling systems operating in such power plants.

As mentioned earlier, in most inhabited climate regions outside of the tropics the need for space heating and cooling tends to be seasonal. Consequently, the effect of a general warming trend would be to create a shift in the balance between the heating and cooling needs of specific regions. For example, in parts of North America and Europe there should be a greater need for air conditioning during the summer, with a compensating decrease in demand for winter heating. This is likely to have implications for meeting peak demand for electricity during hot periods during summer time, when demand for electricity has traditionally been low. In contrast to the dominant role of electricity in air conditioning, space heating in winter can be supplied using various fuels, such as coal, oil, wood, or electricity. A reduction in the demand for fossil fuels for space heating during winter would obviously be beneficial in addressing the underlying causes of the current global warming trend. It is therefore highly likely that different climate regions will experience a changing mix of fuels used to meet their energy needs (e.g. shifting from heating oils to cooling electricity), with a general move away from dirty fuels to cleaner energy. Some climate regions will be affected more than others, with those experiencing continental climates likely to be more affected than maritime locations.

However, greater demand for electricity generation associated with higher temperatures could cause problems for current modes of production that often require the use of cooling towers, which would be less effective and less able to meet increased demand. In addition, the need to reduce the use of fossil fuels at the same time as increasing electricity production will require a major shift towards cleaner renewable energy, such as solar, wind, and hydropower.

4.3 Is renewable energy a viable solution?

The atmosphere is at the centre of the most important environmental crisis the world has seen—global warming. However, it can also provide some solutions to this problem as it is a significant source of renewable energy, and most of the forms of energy available in the atmosphere can be harnessed with negligible contributions to global warming. By transferring from the use of fossil fuels to renewable forms of energy, we can contribute to the mitigation of the enhanced greenhouse effect by reducing carbon dioxide emissions. The investment in alternative energy sources has increased over the past two decades in parallel with increasing concerns about possible impacts of global warming (Figure 4.3), although the trend over the past decade has tended to level off. Not all alternative forms of energy are clean and renewable, with those involving the burning of **biofuels** being a prime example. The cleanest and most environmentally friendly renewable energy sources are those associated with hydro, wind, and solar power, while the use of energy obtained from geothermal resources and biofuels often results in the emission of atmospheric pollutants, as well as having other environmental impacts.

Figure 4.3 shows a change in the renewable energy mix over recent decades, with differing rates of uptake of the main source types. The proportion of new investment in wind and solar energy generation increased

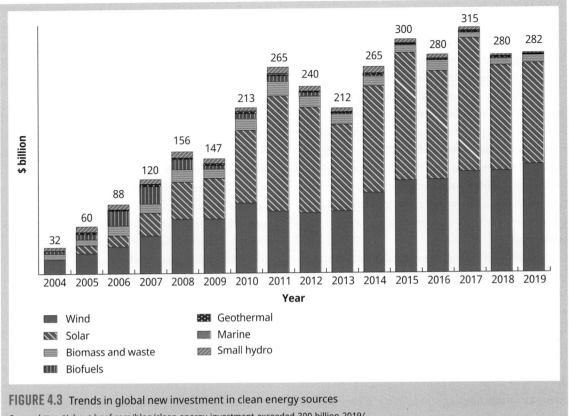

FIGURE 4.3 Trends in global new investment in clean energy sources

Source: https://about.bnef.com/blog/clean-energy-investment-exceeded-300-billion-2019/

from a combined total of about 50% of total investment in 2004 to more than 75% in 2018, with, for example, investment in biofuel production increasing until 2007 and then declining significantly afterwards.

RENEWABLE ENERGY SOURCES

HYDROPOWER

Hydropower is one of the earliest sources of electricity generation and currently a major contributor to global power needs, contributing about 16% of global production (Berga 2016). It is sensitive to dry spells or drought, but has an advantage over some other forms of renewable energy (e.g. wind and solar) as it has the inherent ability to store energy in the form of water behind a dam, which can then be turned into electricity when it

is required. The downside is that large areas of land have often been flooded in order to set up a hydropower system at the outset, and the downstream natural stream-flow regime can be severely disrupted (e.g. the Three Gorges Dam project in China, and the Bakun Dam in Sarawak, Malaysia). There are therefore often significant effects on local ecosystems and human communities. In addition, hydro lakes tend to fill up with sediment over time, reducing the amount of water (and therefore energy) able to be stored behind the dam. It is also of concern that the environmental impacts of hydro dam development may constrain the ability of local communities to adapt to climate change.

Hydropower is obviously only a feasible option in regions where there is sufficient precipitation (rain or snow) to keep hydro lakes recharged. Therefore, once hydropower generation schemes are established, the main

CASE STUDY 4.1

US federal hydro schemes: climate change impacts and adaptation

Aim: To identify potential climate change effects on power generation within the main federal hydropower generation regions and suggest response strategies.

Methodology: Available data included power generation, streamflow, meteorology, and global climate model output. Global climate model output available at

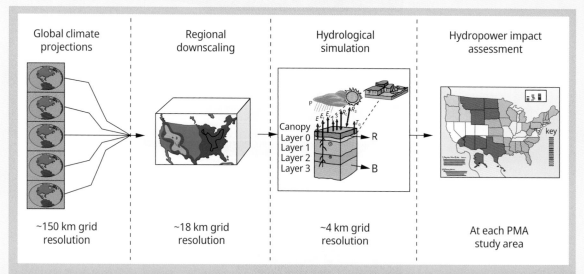

FIGURE 4.4 Modelling methodology used to predict changes in hydropower generation caused by future climate change. PMA = Power Marketing Administration

Source: US Department of Energy (2017). *Effects of Climate Change on Federal Hydropower: The Second Report to Congress, January 2017*. Washington, DC

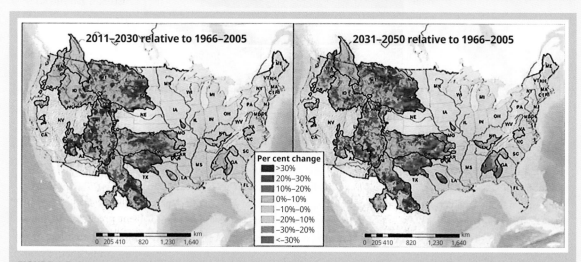

FIGURE 4.5 Maps of the projected future changes in runoff in US federal catchments over the United States for the periods 2011–2030 and 2031–2050

Source: US Department of Energy (2017). *Effects of Climate Change on Federal Hydropower: The Second Report to Congress, January 2017*. Washington, DC

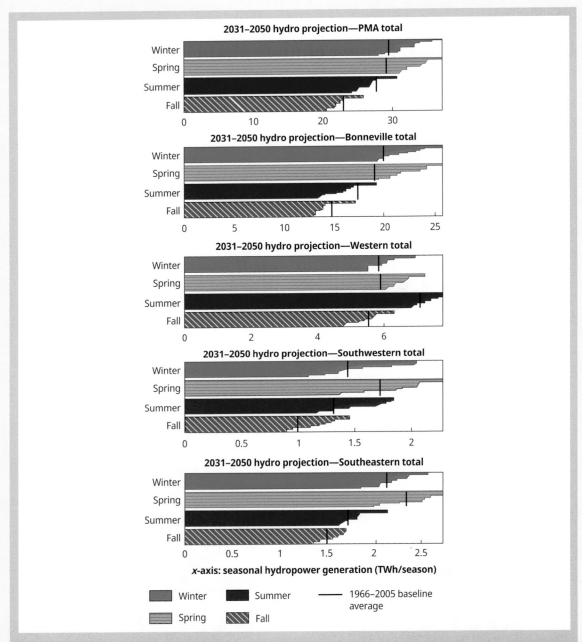

FIGURE 4.6 Projected changes in seasonal power generation in US federal hydro regions for the period 2031–2050 (compared with a 1966–2005 baseline) based on the RCP8.5 emissions scenario and a 10-member GCM ensemble. The horizontal bar for each season is made up of the projection from each of the ten ensembles organized from highest to lowest. The vertical black line is the multi-model average for the period 1966–2005. GCM = global climate model, RCP = Representative Concentration Pathway (see Chapter 1), PMA = Power Marketing Administration, TWh = terawatt hour

Source: US Department of Energy (2017). *Effects of Climate Change on Federal Hydropower: The Second Report to Congress, January 2017*. Washington, DC

over 150 km resolution was dynamically downscaled to the regional level (18 km resolution) using a regional climate model (RegCM version 4) and then bias-corrected and coupled with a hydrological model that incorporated water and energy budgets, as well as **runoff** at catchment scale (at 4 km grid resolution) (Figure 4.4). A 10-member ensemble of IPCC AR5 GCMs was selected using the business-as-usual emissions scenario RCP8.5 (US Department of Energy 2017).

Results: The main factors affecting future power generation are changes in precipitation, runoff, and air temperature. The effect of predicted temperature changes is mostly on the proportion of precipitation stored as snow and the timing of snowmelt, which is expected to be much earlier.

The model predictions indicated significant spatial variability of precipitation, and therefore runoff, across the US federal catchments (as shown in Figure 4.5). There is also expected to be significant seasonal variability across all regions, with downstream effects on power generation (Figure 4.6). Much of the inter-regional variability can be accounted for by differences in the contribution of snow-melt and rainfall, resulting in shifts in the timing of water availability. Over time, as rising temperatures cause a year-on-year reduction in the amount of snow cover, inflows into the hydro lakes will be more directly related to the occurrence of precipitation-producing weather systems. Climate change is likely to impact on the characteristics and movement of such systems across hydro catchments, with effects that may be difficult to predict. Although there appeared to be a slight shorter-term decline in water available for hydro generation, this study showed an overall trend towards wetter conditions by 2031–2050 (US Department of Energy 2017) (Figure 4.7).

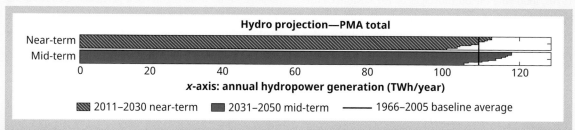

FIGURE 4.7 Summary of total predicted hydropower generation for US federal areas. The horizontal bar for each season is made up of the projection from each of the ten ensembles organized from highest to lowest. The vertical black line is the multi-model average for the period 1966–2005. Abbreviations as for Figure 4.6

Source: US Department of Energy (2017). *Effects of Climate Change on Federal Hydropower: The Second Report to Congress, January 2017*. Washington, DC

negative impact of climate change would be a change in the precipitation regime, resulting in a significant decrease of rain or snow in a given hydro catchment. In some particularly dry countries, such as Australia, research has been conducted into the effect of high temperatures on evaporative water loss from reservoirs, but the negative effect of rising temperatures on water loss in hydro systems would be small in comparison with the effect of increased drought conditions.

In cold regions where snow and ice melt provide a significant input to hydro schemes, a warming trend will initially lead to higher stream flows and therefore more water available for power production. However, it is also likely to cause changes in the annual hydrological regime of the catchments fed by snow and ice melt, which could have implications for the ongoing management of the electric power resource. For example, instead of water intake being mostly due to summertime snow/ice melt, it will tend to be more evenly spread throughout the year. Increasing glacier melt may also result in higher fine-sediment loads in the water that can cause more rapid abrasion of turbines, as well as sedimentation of the hydro lakes.

Overall, it is felt that hydropower systems may benefit from the anticipated climate change, mostly through increased inflows, although the impact is expected to vary regionally (Berga 2016). There is also plenty of potential for mitigating fossil-fuel emissions through the establishment of new hydro schemes.

WIND POWER

The human exploitation of wind power has been around for a long time, starting with the use of sailing ships to navigate the oceans and other water bodies, and windmills to grind flour and pump water in the Middle East, Central Asia, and China more than 1,000 years ago. Windmills have evolved from purely mechanical operation to electricity generation since the early 1900s, although the most rapid rate of installation of wind turbines for electricity generation has occurred since the 1970s, following the oil shortages of 1973. Modern turbines evolved from those used in rural applications in Denmark, and there has been a growing global market since the 1970s due to climate change fears associated with excessive fossil-fuel combustion and greenhouse gas emissions. Germany, Spain, the United States, India, and China are big players in developing new generation capacity, with global installed capacity reaching almost 750 GW by 2020 (https://wwindea.org/information-2/information/).

The maximum amount of power that can theoretically be harvested from the wind is proportional to the cube of the wind velocity, as illustrated by the following simple equation and Figure 4.8:

$$P_w = \frac{1}{2}\rho A v^3 \qquad [4.1]$$

where P_w is wind power (W), ρ is air density (kg m^{-3}), A is the area swept by the turbine blade (m^2), and v is the wind velocity (m s^{-1}). However, the actual amount of electricity generated by a specific turbine is also a function of its efficiency. Equation 4.1 demonstrates that even a small change in the wind regime of a particular area resulting from climate change that causes an increase or decrease in the mean wind velocity could have a significant impact on the viability of wind energy generation.

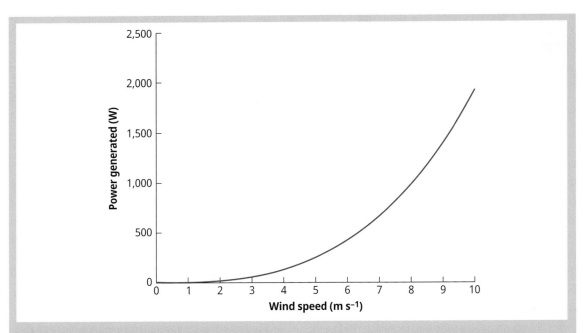

FIGURE 4.8 Theoretical maximum amount of power that can be generated by a range of wind velocities, as calculated from Equation 4.1 using an air density of 1.225 kg m^{-3} and turbine rotor diameter of 2 m

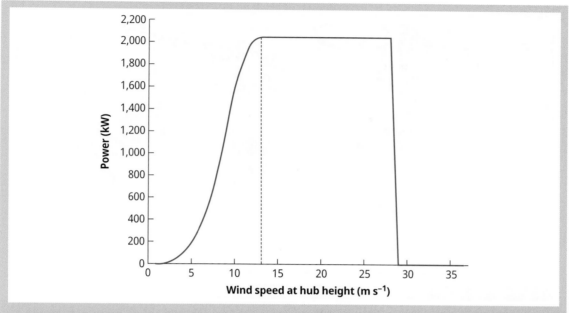

FIGURE 4.9 A typical wind turbine power curve (in kW) across a range of wind speeds from 0 to above the turbine cut-out velocity (28 m s⁻¹). Note that the turbine has a rated (maximum) power of 2050 kW at a wind speed of 13 m s⁻¹ (indicated by the vertical dashed line), and that the turbine rotor diameter is 82 m and the cut-in velocity is 3 m s⁻¹
Source: Santos et al. (2015). Projected changes in wind energy potentials over Iberia. *Renewable Energy* 75: 68–80

It should also be noted that each wind turbine has specific design characteristics that affect its ability to generate power across a range of wind speeds. This is evident from Figure 4.9, which shows that a turbine only generates power across a limited range of wind speeds. That is, the turbine blades only start moving once wind speed exceeds the cut-in velocity and they stop once wind speed reaches the cut-out speed, when the blades are 'feathered' (twisted) to make them stop rotating in order to avoid damage.

The annual average wind speed for a particular area or site is often used to assess the viability of wind generation projects. This can be used as a starting point for evaluating climatic change adaptation options for different parts of the world (Figures 4.10 and 4.11), although regional and local variability of the wind resource can be significant and needs to be assessed using high-resolution atmospheric models, validated by wind observations from individual sites.

Figure 4.10 shows that the global wind resource is much greater over the oceans and particularly over the mid to high latitudes in the Southern Hemisphere, while it is much less over continental and tropical regions. When examining smaller regions, the wind resource is very variable at much higher spatial resolutions over land areas, where the effects of terrain can be significant. It is evident that the annual average wind speed over the United States is much higher over the central regions east of the Rocky Mountains, with average annual speeds of more than 8 m s⁻¹, but even there it can show significant variability (Figure 4.11).

It is at the regional and local scales that climate change could have an impact on the wind resource in different areas. This is because the warming world appears to be associated with a poleward shift in the larger-scale atmospheric circulation which affects the tracking of day-to-day weather systems and the way in which they interact with the underlying terrain. Changes in the magnitude of the wind resource are therefore likely, with some regions being subject to increased mean winds while others experience a reduction.

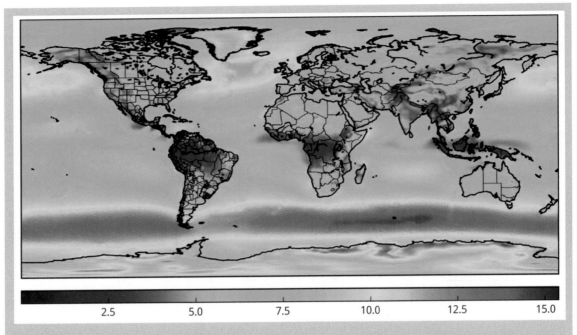

FIGURE 4.10 Global distribution of average wind speed (m s⁻¹) at 100 m above the surface for the period 2007–2016
Source: Dupont et al. (2018). Global available wind energy with physical and energy return on investment constraints. *Applied Energy* 209, 322–38

Wind energy generation as a climate change mitigation and adaptation tool

There are two key issues facing the development of wind farms—first, finding sites where electricity generation will be most efficient; and second, the integration of wind power with other sources of energy generation. The variation of wind speed over time and space can create problems for the development and use of wind energy potential. The most efficient sites occur where average wind speeds are consistently high, with little variation over time, but they also need to be close enough to the electricity network to minimize costs of getting the power to the users. For many highly populated countries, extensive use of wind power is not possible without saturating the environment with wind turbines, resulting in conflicts with other land uses. As a result, many recent European wind farms have been located offshore, over adjacent seas, although this typically doubles the cost of installation.

In spite of these limitations, wind power has become a popular alternative to other sources of energy generation in Europe, to the extent that some countries like Denmark have generated more electricity than they actually need, and so end up exporting power to nearby countries. This is not possible for all countries, particularly those lacking land borders with other countries (e.g. New Zealand), so that the development of wind power as a renewable energy resource needs to be carefully integrated with other forms of energy generation to maximize its efficient use. For example, wind and hydropower work well together, as there is the potential to use wind energy when it is available and use hydropower when wind speeds fall. It is therefore important to be able to predict short-term variations in wind speed accurately across a region.

The use of wind to generate electricity has grown rapidly since 2000, as demonstrated by the trend in global installed capacity shown in Figure 4.12. In 2020, China set a new world record for the addition of wind generation capacity with a total of 52 GW, as seen in Table 4.1. Other major players are the United States and Germany, although the growth of wind energy capacity has been

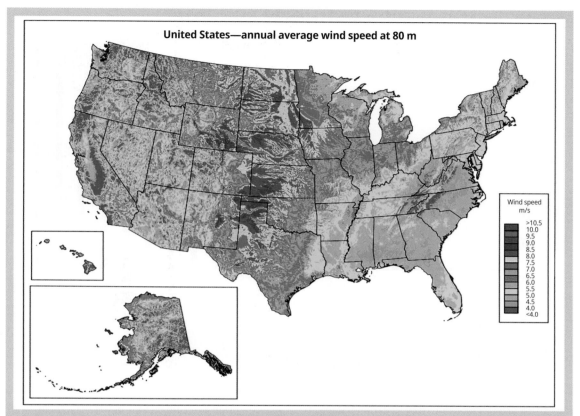

FIGURE 4.11 Annual average wind speed at 80 m above ground level at 2.5 km resolution over the United States based on model estimates provided by AWS Truepower

Source: Department of Energy, data courtesy of AWS Truepower and National Renewable Energy Laboratory

TABLE 4.1 List of the main countries involved in developing wind energy capacity in 2020

COUNTRY/REGION	INSTALLED CAPACITY (GW)	NEW ANNUAL CAPACITY (GW)
China	290.0	52.0
United States	122.3	16.9
Germany	62.8	1.4
India	38.6	1.1
Spain	27.4	1.6
United Kingdom	24.2	0.65
Brazil	18.0	2.6
France	17.9	1.3
Canada	13.6	0.175
Italy	10.9	0.28
Turkey	9.3	1.2
Rest of the world	110.0	14.0

Source: https://wwindea.org/information-2/statistics-news/

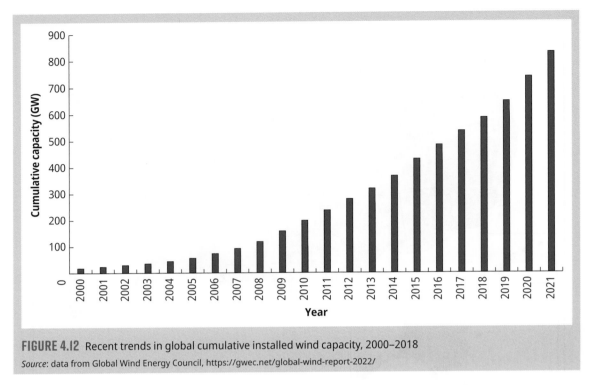

FIGURE 4.12 Recent trends in global cumulative installed wind capacity, 2000–2018

Source: data from Global Wind Energy Council, https://gwec.net/global-wind-report-2022/

lacklustre in Germany since 2000. In fact, Figure 4.13 shows that development of wind generation capacity stalled after 2017 and that significant new development is required for Germany to reach its goal of 80% electricity from renewable sources by 2030. In 2021, a new coalition government took power in Germany, with significant support for actions to reduce emissions of greenhouse gases. This change in government policy,

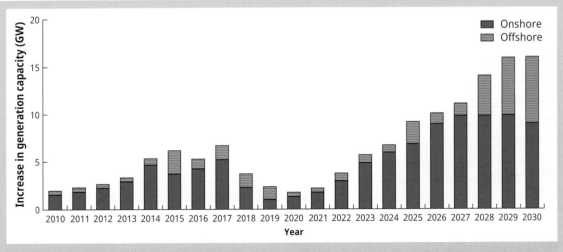

FIGURE 4.13 Trend in new wind energy generation capacity in Germany since 2010 and the annual development of new capacity required to achieve the goal of 80% renewable electricity by 2030

Source: https://gwec.net/global-wind-report-2022/

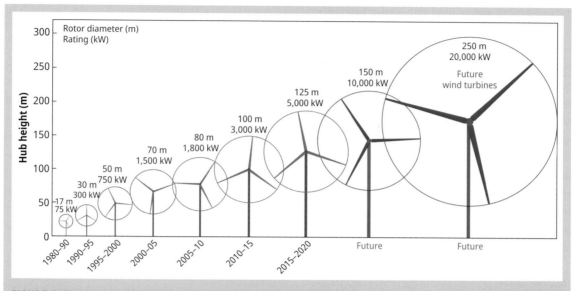

FIGURE 4.14 Trends in typical turbine size and capacity since the 1980s

Source: Padmanathan et al. (2019). Conceptual framework of antecedents to trends on permanent magnet synchronous generators for wind energy conversion systems. *Energies* 12: 2616

combined with the recent conflict in Ukraine, may well accelerate progress in developing wind energy capacity, as the use of fossil fuels from Russia declines.

A noticeable aspect of the global growth of wind energy has been the increase in size and capacity of individual turbines installed at wind farm sites (Figure 4.14). This growth in size reflects the efficiency gains achieved by a large turbine over several small ones. By 2020, wind turbines with blade diameters greater than 150 m were being produced by several manufacturers, representing a swept area (*A* in Equation 4.1) of greater than 17,000 m^2, and even bigger turbines are planned.

The feasibility of exploiting the wind resource as a replacement for fossil-fuel burning depends on a range of factors that need to be considered for each region. The average wind speed varies globally because of the large-scale circulation systems that make up the global atmospheric circulation, including the tropical circulation, sub-tropical anticyclones, the westerly wind belt and the mid-latitude cyclonic weather systems (Figure 4.10). The geographic location of regions relative to these systems therefore largely establishes their background level

of wind resource. However, the effects of local terrain on airflow patterns and altitude on average wind speed need to be considered when developing individual wind farms. It is well known that wind speed normally increases with altitude, as the effect of friction with the surface is reduced. It is also evident that the nature of the terrain can cause the wind to speed up or slow down. There can therefore be significant variability in the wind resource across relatively small areas, and it is important that this is considered when developing wind farms. It is also important that predictions of the future wind resource are obtained at a high-enough resolution over given regions to be able to accurately assess the future impacts of climate change on the viability of wind energy generation.

The temporal variability of the wind resource also needs to be considered when exploiting wind energy. Ideally, the average wind speed should remain consistently high, with little variation over time. However, except for some remote areas of the world, the wind typically varies significantly because of both the influence of changing day-to-day weather patterns and the daily cycle of heating and cooling. Other effects can include seasonal variability associated with the annual north–south movement of the main atmospheric circulation systems, as well as longer-term inter-annual and inter-decadal effects associated with such phenomena as the El Niño Southern Oscillation (ENSO). The best areas are those experiencing few extreme peaks or periods of calm. As mentioned earlier, wind turbines have a cut-in wind speed below which they will not turn, as well as a maximum wind speed above which the blades are 'feathered' (turned so as to reduce the area facing the wind) and locked. Changes in weather pattern that result in greater extremes in wind speed are therefore problematic for wind energy generation.

Although the most efficient locations of wind farms are close to the users of electricity, land-based locations in highly populated areas are often impracticable. Consequently, offshore wind farms have been developed in many parts of the world, but particularly in Europe, in spite of the cost of development being double that of land-based wind farms. These sites experience less variability in wind speeds than onshore locations as a result of the smoother ocean surface and its thermal properties, so are generally a more reliable source of electricity. For example, offshore wind farms are less affected by hurricane damage.

How sensitive is wind power generation to climate change?

In regard to climate change, the focus internationally has been on the impacts of rising temperatures. However, it is increasingly evident that human communities will have to adapt to changes in other climate parameters, such as wind. As mentioned earlier, and as is evident from Equation 4.1, a small change in the average wind speed can cause a significant change in the available wind energy resource. There is clear evidence that as the world heats up there will be changes in the large-scale atmospheric circulation that will have an impact on the wind regime at the regional and local scales (Karnauskas et al. 2018). The effect of regional changes in available wind power predicted by an ensemble of GCMs for the twenty-first century can be seen in Figure 4.15. It is evident from the projections that some regions may

benefit from increased wind speeds while others will be negatively impacted by a reduction in the available wind resource. Consequently, when planning to include wind energy in climate change adaptation strategies, it is important to downscale the large-scale predictions of future wind climates obtained from GCMs to the regional and local scales to provide an idea of the sustainability of existing or planned wind energy generation systems into the future (e.g. Alonso Díaz et al. 2019). It is also important not to restrict the focus solely to average wind speed, as changes in the statistical distribution of wind speeds can have a significant impact on the wind energy produced, while increases in the frequency of extreme storms associated with more intense weather systems could also threaten the viability of wind farms through damage to turbines.

SOLAR POWER

Solar power can be generated and used at a range of scales, from extensive solar farms, providing large amounts of energy using concentrated solar power to the national electricity grid, to small clusters of solar **photovoltaic** panels installed on residential or commercial buildings. Figure 4.16 shows a solar farm located in a desert environment, where there are typically many days of sunshine. This solar farm uses photovoltaic panels that convert solar energy directly to electricity using semiconductor technology, similar to smaller photovoltaic panels typically installed on urban buildings. Other large solar farms use mirrors to focus the Sun's energy onto tubes containing liquid (creating concentrated solar power) which drives turbine-powered generators.

Considering their environmental impact, it should be noted that solar farms take up a lot of land which cannot be used for other purposes, unlike wind farms, while the manufacture of photovoltaic solar panels does result in the emission of a small amount of greenhouse gases. In spite of these effects, solar energy generation and use provides a net positive benefit for the environment and society in general through reducing energy costs and carbon emissions.

The timing of solar energy generation is obviously daytime only, with a maximum occurring around solar

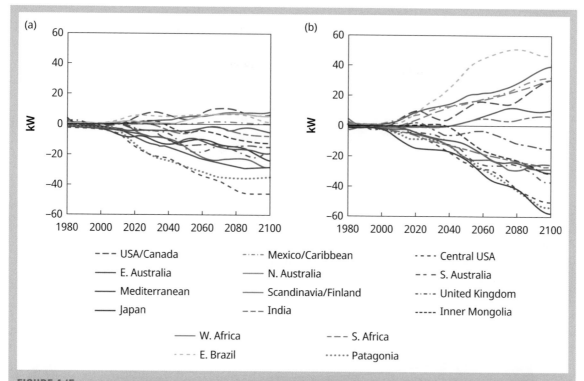

FIGURE 4.15 Predicted evolution of available wind power for different regions during the twenty-first century based on ten CMIP5 coupled GCMs under the (a) RCP4.5 and (b) RCP8.5 scenarios. CMIP = Coupled Model Intercomparison Project, GCM = global climate model, and RCP = Representative Concentration Pathway

Source: modified from Karnauskas et al. (2018). Southward shift of the global wind energy resource under high carbon dioxide emissions. *Nature Geoscience* 11: 38–43

noon, and seasonal variation depending on the latitudinal location of the generating plant. There can also be significant regional differences in solar energy potential due to cloud-cover effects that are largely a function of the prevailing weather patterns experienced over a given region. The global pattern of available solar energy is shown in Figure 4.17, while a regional map of the United States is provided in Figure 4.18.

Solar and hydro electricity generation require different weather conditions to be effective, with the latter providing power when there is adequate precipitation to fill the reservoirs, while solar energy generation needs sunshine and therefore a lack of precipitation. However, some hydro dams are located in catchments downstream of regions where precipitation typically occurs (e.g. on the leeside of major mountain systems), so the two

renewable generation systems are not necessarily mutually exclusive. A key difference between the two forms of renewable energy is that solar power must be used immediately or stored for later use (e.g. using batteries, fuel

FIGURE 4.16 A large solar farm generating photovoltaic solar power

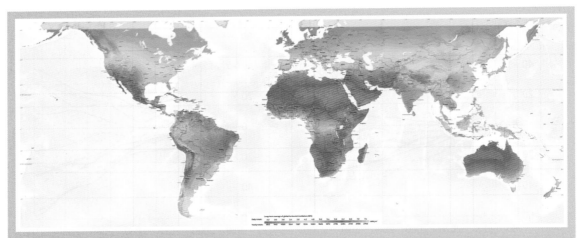

FIGURE 4.17 Global distribution of available solar energy as represented by incoming solar radiation on a horizontal surface, based on available data for the period 1994–2018

Source: Global Solar Atlas (CC BY 4.0)

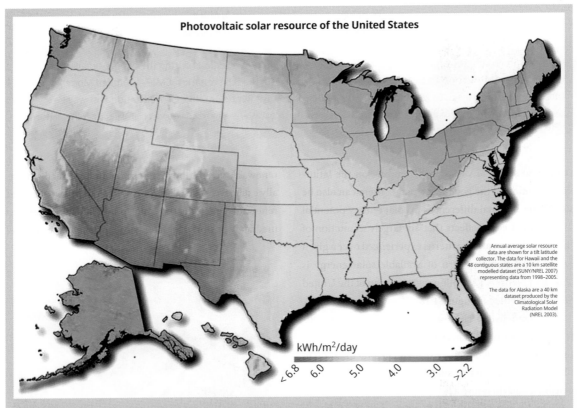

FIGURE 4.18 Regional map of the solar energy resource over the United States, based on data for 1996–2005

Source: National Renewable Energy Laboratory for the US Department of Energy

cells, or through conversion to hydrogen), which can be practicable for both small-scale solar systems such as on residential dwellings and large-scale energy storage.

Using solar energy to replace fossil-fuel combustion requires careful regional resource assessment and site evaluation (Choi et al. 2019). Atmospheric models can be used to map incident solar radiation expected over an area, while Geographic Information System software can be used to provide a more detailed evaluation of individual sites, taking into consideration local terrain effects, the existing power distribution network, and connectivity to potential sites.

Like wind power, using solar power as a climate change adaptation tool relies on the availability of solar energy being maintained or increased into the future. Higher air temperatures would be beneficial to concentrated solar power systems as their operation depends on the application of heat. However, photovoltaic systems are less efficient at higher ambient temperatures, so investigations have been undertaken to assess the likely effect of climate change on solar energy production. These predictions are generally based on climate model output, including changes in temperature and cloud cover. Global assessments suggest that in parts of Europe, China and East Asia, and North America the amount of photovoltaic power generation could potentially increase under a warmer regime (e.g. Jerez et al. 2015; Müller et al. 2018), while the Arctic and the sub-Antarctic regions would experience the greatest reduction (Figure 4.19), although the percentage changes are very small. Investigation of differences between the

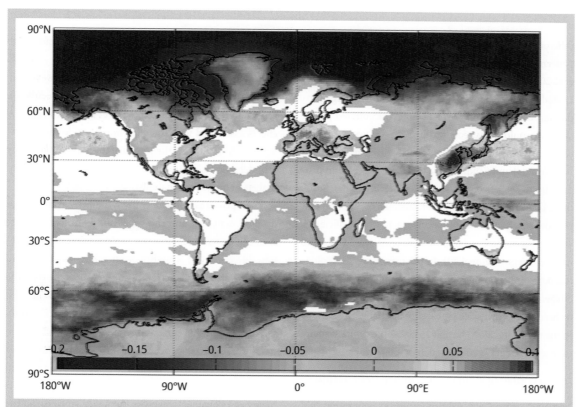

FIGURE 4.19 Global map of median predicted percentage change per annum of photovoltaic power output over the period 2006–2049 (white areas indicate no significant trend)

Source: Wild et al. (2015). Projections of long-term changes in solar radiation based on CMIP5 climate models and their influence on energy yields of photovoltaic systems. *Solar Energy* 116: 12–24

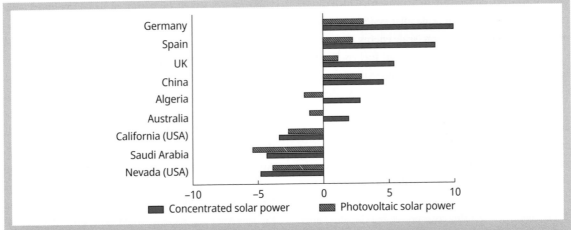

FIGURE 4.20 Predicted percentage change in solar energy output using different technologies (photovoltaic and concentrated power systems) and in different countries by 2080

Source: adapted from Crook et al. (2011). Climate change impacts on future photovoltaic and concentrated solar power energy output. *Energy and Environmental Science* 4: 3101–9

different solar technologies and regions reveals a complex pattern of possible changes, as shown in Figure 4.20 (Crook et al. 2011). In many European countries (e.g. Germany, the United Kingdom, and Spain) and China solar energy production using both photovoltaic and concentrated power systems would be expected to increase by up to 10%. In contrast, parts of the western United States (e.g. California and Nevada) and Saudi Arabia would be expected to produce up to 5% less energy using both technologies. Some other countries (e.g. Algeria and Australia) could find that photovoltaic panels would decrease in their efficiency, while concentrated solar power systems would become more efficient (Figure 4.20). In the meantime, technological developments continue to improve photovoltaic panel efficiency. There is therefore an obvious need to develop techniques to downscale global climate change predictions to the regional scale to be able to assess the future viability of renewable energy sources such as solar power.

OTHER FORMS OF RENEWABLE POWER GENERATION

There are several other forms of power generation that can be used as part of a combined mitigation and adaptation strategy in response to greenhouse gas-induced climate change. These include geothermal power, tidal and wave power, and biofuels. Geothermal power potential is limited to those areas where volcanic activity occurs, such as in the United States, Iceland, Indonesia, New Zealand, Kenya, and parts of Central America. It is, however, associated with the release of small amounts of greenhouse gases and there is some concern over the environmental effects associated with the depletion of underground reserves of hot water. As the source of this renewable energy is underground, future changes in climate will have minimal effect on its sustainability.

Tidal power is not widely used, mainly due to its high development cost and the small number of sites where it would be feasible. However, unlike other forms of renewable energy, it is highly predictable, resulting from the gravitational attraction of the moon as it orbits the Earth. Ideal sites experience a large variation in tidal height and strong tidal currents, often due to characteristics of the shoreline and seabed, particularly where narrow constrictions occur. The first major tidal power station was constructed on the La Rance estuary in northern France in 1966, although many larger plants have been constructed across the world since then. The main environmental concern with tidal power plants is the effect of the turbine blades on marine life. As with geothermal power generation, the effect of climate change on tidal power is likely to be minimal.

Although wave energy is potentially a considerable source of electricity, it is less predictable than other sources as it is generated by the effect of the wind on the surface of the ocean. Although a number of assessments of the wave energy resource have been conducted, such as along the east coast of the United States (Allahdadi et al. 2019; see Figure 4.21) and around Australia (Hughes and Heap 2010; see Figure 4.22), the technology is expensive and not well developed, so that a number of large projects have failed (including the Aguçadoura Wave Farm off the coast of Portugal and Scotland—https://www.bbc.com/news/uk-scotland-scotland-business-30560980). If wave energy generation were to develop as a sustainable source of renewable energy, it would be sensitive to changes in wind speed, so that any changes in atmospheric circulation could potentially increase or decrease the amount of energy available.

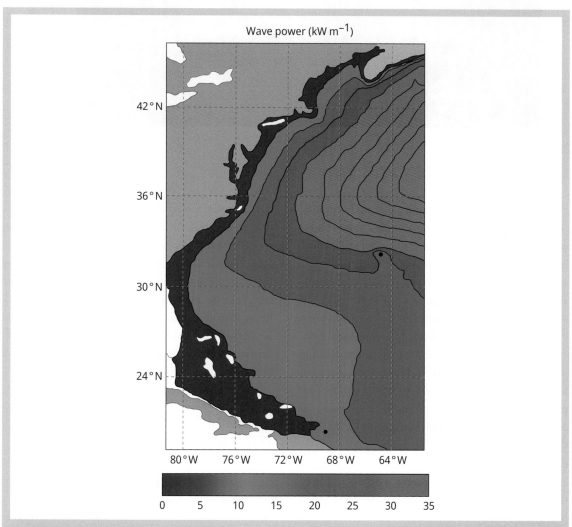

FIGURE 4.21 Mean monthly wave power (kW m⁻¹) off the eastern coast of the United States for January 2009 based on simulation of significant wave height and energy period

Source: Allahdadi et al. (2019). Development and validation of a regional-scale high-resolution unstructured model for wave energy resource characterization along the US East Coast. *Renewable Energy* 136: 500–11

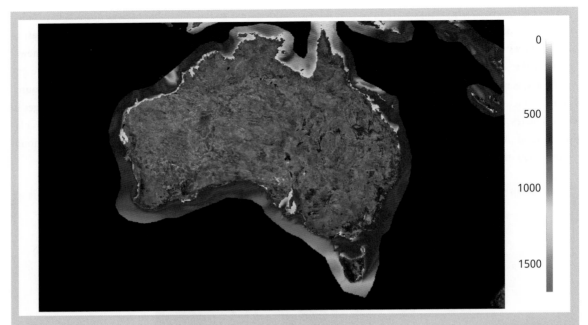

FIGURE 4.22 Maximum wave energy flux (kW m^{-1}) around the coat of Australia based on data for 1980 to 2010
Source: https://nationalmap.gov.au/renewables#share=s-gGd5ztFcxe2ysy9f

In the first decade of this century, biofuels were touted as a sustainable and clean alternative and renewable energy source, particularly as a replacement for fossil fuels in internal combustion engines. Crops such as maize, sugar cane, and vegetable oils can be used to make ethanol, and initially some countries provided subsidies to encourage biofuel production as it was seen as a viable option for reducing greenhouse gas emissions. However, it was soon realized that there were significant issues with this energy source, including the competition between the growing of crops for fuel and that for food production; the destruction of forests, ecosystems, and conservation areas through land conversion; the emission of greenhouse gases during the production and use of biofuels; impacts on soil, air, and water quality; impacts on human rights and poverty in developing countries; and the economics of production during falling oil prices. The production and use of biofuels has therefore tended to be a diversion on the road to developing environmentally and socially acceptable alternatives to fossil fuel. Figure 4.3 indicates that biofuels had a significant share of the renewable energy market in the mid-2000s,

but since then have declined, with development and use of biofuels largely limited to a relatively small group of countries (e.g. the United States, Brazil, and in South-East Asia). Their major role was to introduce an alternative transport fuel at a time of high oil prices, thereby moderating price fluctuations. In regard to potential impacts of future climate change, the production of biofuel would be affected like any other cropping system, with significant events such as drought and floods having negative impacts on its future sustainability.

INTEGRATING RENEWABLE ENERGY WITH TRADITIONAL SOURCES

As is evident from the previous sections, there are various forms of renewable energy that can play differing roles in developing adaptation strategies in response to climate change, although they each have varying sensitivity to predicted future climates. While most of these energy sources are associated with minimal greenhouse gas emissions, they still need to be integrated into

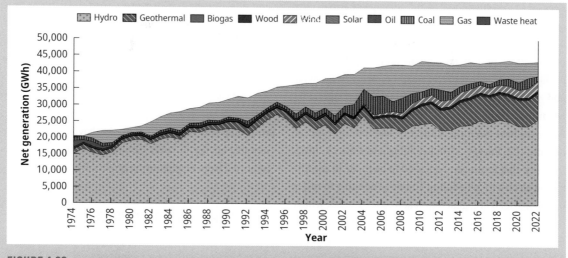

FIGURE 4.23 Electricity generation in New Zealand from all sources between 1974 and 2022

Source: original graph created from data obtained from the NZ Ministry for Business, Immigration and Employment, https://www.mbie.govt.nz/building-and-energy/energy-and-natural-resources/energy-statistics-and-modelling/energy-statistics/electricity-statistics/

an energy distribution and usage system that currently involves some sources that rely on the burning of fossil fuels of one form or another (coal, oil, or natural gas), as well as nuclear power. As a result of the unique characteristics of the different types of renewable energy (hydro, wind, solar, etc.), their integration into the electricity network by the power system operator can often provide significant challenges. As previously mentioned, there can be significant synergies between energy sources such as wind, solar, and hydropower. In some countries, such as New Zealand, the majority of electricity is generated by renewable sources (84% of total electricity generation in 2018), in this case dominated by hydropower supported by wind, geothermal, and a small but increasing amount of solar energy (Figure 4.23). The burning of fossil fuels is used to top up the network when there is insufficient renewable energy available. An interesting feature of the trend shown in Figure 4.23 is the levelling off of electricity generation since about 2005 as improvements have been made in energy conservation. This is consistent with international experience in other developed countries.

A trend associated with increasing use of renewable energy is that there has been a movement away from centralized energy generation, using large power stations with extensive distribution networks, towards more localized generation based on smaller, local renewable energy resources, such as wind farms, solar farms, and numerous photovoltaic panels on domestic houses. Although this creates more complexity in matching supply and demand, it does make the network less susceptible to major power outages when a single power plant fails.

Although it is easier for the system operator to control, an electricity network tends to be less robust in response to major events when it involves a single large source of power that may be some distance from power users when compared with a network of multiple smaller, dispersed power generators. In the former case, if the generation plant fails all users are affected, and if a major supply line is damaged a large number of users may be without power. In the latter case, power users are closer to generation sites and therefore less likely to be affected when extreme weather, such as strong winds, lightning, or snow loading, brings down power lines some distance away on the network.

However, operating an electricity distribution network that consists of many different generators of varying sizes and types (fossil fuel, wind, solar, geothermal, etc.) and widely dispersed users creates significant challenges. The demand from users needs to be met from a range of generators, and their ability to supply electricity may change rapidly as a result of weather changes (e.g. solar and wind). As a result, the issues facing system operators when integrating renewable energy into existing power networks have been the subject of research over recent decades (GE Energy 2010; Reichling and Kulacki 2008). It is clear that improvements need to be made in coordinating electricity scheduling among generators in order to balance load and generation across wide areas, which would require increased flexibility among generators in the supply of electricity. A key issue is the ability of the system operator to be able to use reserve generation to account for variability in wind and solar. In this regard, not only does short-term forecasting of wind and solar radiation need to be improved, but so do predictions of network load resulting from user demand for electricity.

In a network supplied by both fossil-fuel-based and renewable electricity generation systems, the fossil-fuel-based power stations can be used to cover the base load, with renewable energy generation covering the rest. In a totally renewable energy network, the base load can be covered by those forms of generation that show the least short-term fluctuation, such as hydropower and geothermal. Other forms of renewable energy, such as tidal current generation, can then be added, while those that experience the greatest intermittency (wind, solar, and wave power) can be added on top.

A number of studies have evaluated the use of a combination of different renewable energy forms to meet the electricity needs of particular regions at a range of scales. Gormally et al. (2012) completed a geospatial investigation of the potential for community-based renewable energy generation in the Cumbria region of the United Kingdom, examining a range of different sources including hydropower, wind, solar, and bioenergy in relation to the pattern of demand. At a much larger scale, Barrington-Leigh and Ouliaris (2017) produced a provincial-level analysis of the potential for renewable energy in Canada. This too took a geospatial approach, applied to onshore and offshore wind, hydropower, solar, tidal, ocean wave power, geothermal, and bioenergy, and included an analysis of generation in relation to the pattern of demand for power. Several provinces (British Columbia, Saskatchewan, Manitoba, New Brunswick, Nova Scotia, and Prince Edward Island) were estimated to have significantly more renewable energy capacity than their demand for power, with only Alberta and Ontario not having sufficient renewable energy to cover demand (although it could be imported from neighbouring provinces).

RENEWABLE ENERGY STORAGE

As recognized with solar energy generation, a key issue with the different forms of renewable energy is how to store it during periods of surplus generation for later use when demand increases. Electricity generation from solar and wind power is normally very variable, as it depends on day-to-day weather changes, so how can we make the most of it to reduce energy generation using fossil fuels? There are several options being developed to address this problem of renewable energy storage, from very short-term storage using capacitors and flywheels to longer-term storage using compressed gases, pumped storage hydro systems, thermal energy storage in liquids or solids, conversion of electrical energy to hydrogen, and the use of batteries.

Pumped storage hydro systems represent the largest method of storing renewable energy. In this case, two reservoirs are used to store surplus energy, with water being pumped from a lower to an upper reservoir during periods of surplus electricity generation on the network, especially using solar and wind energy that would otherwise go to waste. The additional water in the upper reservoir is then available to be used when demand for electricity generation increases (e.g. under cold conditions at night and when the wind drops and there is no solar power) (Figure 4.24).

There is significant disagreement regarding the effectiveness of the use of hydrogen as a form of energy storage. The first thing to note is that more than 90% of

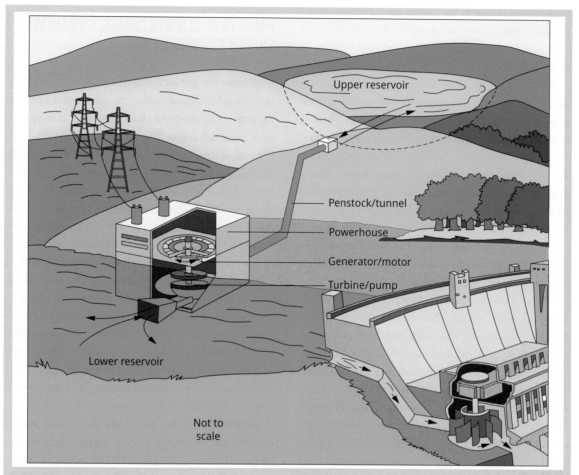

FIGURE 4.24 Schematic diagram of a pumped storage hydropower system

Source: adapted from https://www.energy.gov/eere/water/pumped-storage-hydropower

hydrogen production is currently from fossil fuels, especially natural gas (producing 'grey hydrogen'). However, it can be produced from solar and wind power via electrolysis, splitting the water molecule into hydrogen ('green hydrogen') and oxygen, but this is more than twice as expensive to produce. Although it can be stored as a gas and used later as a fuel to generate electricity, or for use in fuel cell vehicles and aircraft for transport, it is generally considered more effective to use electricity directly than convert it to hydrogen. Hydrogen can also be converted into ammonia and methane, allowing a range of other applications in energy generation and industry, and can be stored for relatively long periods (days to months) and transported some distance from the source of generation. However, handling hydrogen is not without significant infrastructure costs, as storage and transport is not easy, with long-distance transport via pipeline unviable. In addition, it uses a large amount of water to create hydrogen via electrolysis, making it impracticable in desert regions where water is scarce. Currently, generating hydrogen from renewable sources is still significantly more expensive than from fossil fuels, but the cost may reduce significantly over the next decade. The debate for and against its use and storage is likely to continue in the meantime. It may eventually become a viable source of power for some applications, such as in aviation, heavy transport, and a range of industries.

Batteries are also being increasingly used as energy storage, from small-scale installations as part of domestic solar generation systems to much larger-scale battery facilities capable of storing energy from a range of different forms of generation (wind, hydro, and solar, in addition to fossil-fuel burning). The largest battery system in the world was established in January 2021 at the Moss Landing Energy Storage Facility in California. It is made up of numerous lithium-ion batteries that together can generate 300 megawatts of power (https://www.weforum.org/agenda/2021/04/renewable-energy-storage-pumped-batteries-thermal-mechanical/).

Electric cars are effectively small batteries on wheels that derive their energy from a range of different generation sources, both renewable and fossil-fuel generated. In an ideal world, they should use only renewable energy in order to reduce greenhouse gas emissions, otherwise the current transition to electric vehicles would have little effect on global warming. However, from a comparison of the efficiency of electric cars powered by renewable energy with that of cars powered by hydrogen fuel cells, it is clear that electric cars are significantly more efficient. In countries dominated by renewable generation of electricity (such as Albania, Iceland, Namibia, Paraguay, Norway, and New Zealand), it would therefore be more sensible to use that energy to charge the batteries of electric vehicles directly than to convert it to hydrogen to be used in fuel cell vehicles (unless that energy would otherwise go to waste).

Clearly, there are many issues with the storage of surplus energy, whether generated renewably or through the burning of fossil fuels. In order to reduce impacts on climate, the ideal situation is one in which renewable generation is the main source of energy and the storage of energy generated is adapted to regional or local circumstances.

IMPACTS OF CLIMATE CHANGE ON RENEWABLE ENERGY RESOURCES

It is evident that global climate change will result in changing atmospheric circulation patterns and therefore changing patterns of wind and cloud cover (and consequently solar radiation) across different parts of the world. There is therefore significant interest in trying to understand the likely future impacts of climate change on energy production and supply at the regional and local scales, and downstream effects on adaptation strategies (Cronin et al. 2018). As mentioned above, not only will climate change affect the pattern of demand for power, it will also affect the ability of renewable energy generation to supply it. Shifting weather patterns are likely to cause changes in the average amount and variability of wind power, as well as in solar radiation and the supply of water into hydropower catchments. It may also impact on bioenergy crop sustainability, as well as the cooling and transmission requirements of power plants and electricity networks. This is in addition to the effects of more extreme weather conditions on power production and distribution.

However, there are some key issues that involve considerable uncertainty. These include the effects of climate change on the quantity and timing of energy from renewable sources, as well as on the efficiency of production and delivery of power from both traditional and renewable sources. Also, the relationship between changing climate and renewable energy generation is complex. For example, hydropower is vulnerable to the amount, timing, and spatial pattern of precipitation, as well as the effect of temperature on evaporation and snowmelt across hydro catchments. Similarly, although Figure 4.8 illustrates the theoretical contribution of increasing wind speed to increased power production, in reality increased wind speeds result in greater energy only up to a certain limit when the turbines are feathered to stop damaging effects of high winds (Figure 4.9). So, above a certain threshold, power production would drop to zero. As suggested in Chapter 2, there is much uncertainty, not only with the output of global climate models but also with attempting to simulate the effect of predicted future climates on renewable energy production from a range of sources at the regional and local scales.

A number of studies have been conducted at a range of scales to investigate this problem. These include assessment of the vulnerability of renewable energy (hydro, wind, and solar) to climate change over different regions in China (Wang et al. 2014), as well as several investigations of the future viability of wind power over different regions (e.g. California—Rasmussen et al. 2011; Spain—Santos et al. 2015; Oklahoma—Stadler et al. 2015; Europe—Tobin et al. 2016). In the Chinese study, exposure was defined as the extent to which renewable energy generation is subject to climate change effects; sensitivity was defined as the extent to which a region is dependent on renewable energy; while adaptive capacity is a region's potential to respond to impacts of climate change on renewable energy through mitigation or adaptation techniques (Wang et al. 2014). Figure 4.25 illustrates

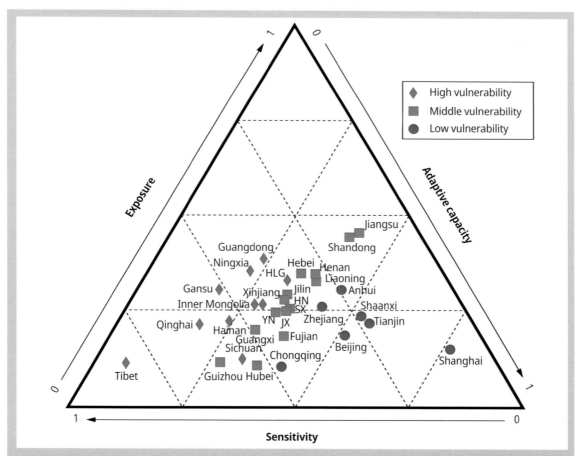

FIGURE 4.25 An assessment of vulnerability to the potential effects of climate change on renewable energy generation in different regions of China. HLG, HN, SX, JX and YN represent Heilongjiang, Hunan, Shanxi, Jiangxi and Yunnan

Source: Wang et al. (2014). China's regional assessment of renewable energy vulnerability to climate change. *Renewable and Sustainable Energy Reviews* 40: 185–95

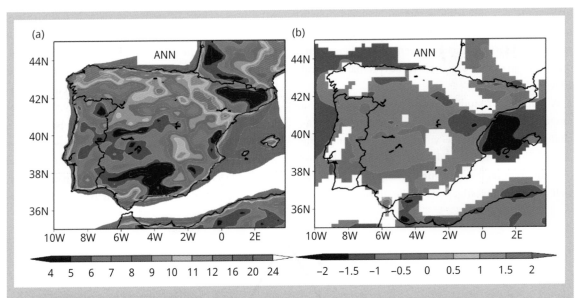

FIGURE 4.26 (a) Average annual wind energy potential (MWh day^{-1}) over the Iberian Peninsula for the period 2041–2070 (emissions scenario A1B—representing a balance between fossil-fuel and non-fossil fuel development of energy technologies), and (b) the statistically significant (95% confidence level) differences between the future and 1961–2000 values

Source: Santos et al. (2015). Projected changes in wind energy potentials over Iberia. *Renewable Energy* 75: 68–80

the significant differences in the potential impact of climate change on renewable energy across different regions in China based on this analysis.

Two studies of the likely impact of climate change on wind energy generation demonstrated the complex pattern of changing wind resource that could occur over parts of Europe (Santos et al. 2015; Tobin et al. 2016). Figure 4.26 provides an assessment for the Iberian Peninsula showing a slight decrease in wind energy potential by the middle of the present century over most of the area, except for the Straits of Gibraltar. Figure 4.27 predicts a more complex pattern of change over the wider European area by the end of the century, with eastern Europe and parts of the eastern Mediterranean experiencing increased wind energy potential while the western and south-western areas show a decline.

4.4 Climate impacts on infrastructure

Infrastructure is closely linked to energy production and use through, for example, the use of road, rail, and air transport networks for the distribution of energy, food, and people. The vulnerability of different types of infrastructure to weather and climate variations is associated with both their structure (highways, port wharves, railway lines, etc.) and the transported product (energy, food, waste, and people). Assessment of climate change impacts on such facilities can only be achieved by understanding atmospheric processes at regional and local scales in the context of larger-scale global warming. The previous sections have highlighted the strong link between climate

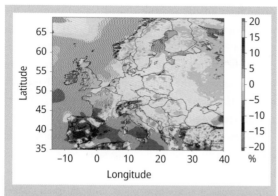

FIGURE 4.27 Percentage changes in wind energy potential over the European region for 2071–2100 relative to the 1971–2000 period under the 'business-as-usual' scenario RCP 8.5. RCP = Representative Concentration Pathway

Source: Tobin et al. (2016). Climate change impacts on the power generation potential of a European mid-century wind farms scenario. *Environmental Research Letters* 11: 034013

and energy. Here, we illustrate that the infrastructure used to transport energy is also strongly affected by the spatial and temporal variability of climatic factors.

The level of climate risk for infrastructure varies depending on the type of infrastructure and the climatic factors involved (e.g. mean values or extreme events), but also according to the location (e.g. urban, rural, coastal, or mountain), the level of economic development of the region, and the capacity for resilience to climate risk. Consequently, the adaptation of infrastructure to climate risk requires a comprehensive climate impact analysis that includes all of these parameters.

The location of a piece of infrastructure strongly determines its sensitivity to climate risk and its adaptation capacity. Urban areas are more sensitive than rural areas in that they concentrate many different types of infrastructure (e.g. transport, energy, water supplies, communications, and buildings) in small areas. Urban infrastructure is sensitive to many impacts, particularly extreme weather events, some of which are accentuated by the characteristics of the city. Climate impacts on infrastructure are also expected to be most significant in coastal and mountainous areas due to rising sea levels, increased extreme weather events, and melting glaciers, which make cities

located in coastal and some mountain regions more exposed to the impacts of climate change. The locational characteristics are therefore very important in assessing the climate vulnerability of infrastructure.

CLIMATE VULNERABILITY OF INFRASTRUCTURE

Vulnerability and sensitivity to climate risk depend on the type of infrastructure. In the transport sector, climate change affects road, rail, air, and maritime networks. Rising temperatures and sea levels, as well as the increasing frequency and intensity of extreme weather events (e.g. storms, heatwaves, and floods) have a significant impact on the functioning of all types of transport infrastructure (European Commission 2013). Periods of heavy rainfall produce floods and landslides that can directly affect all transport systems. Soil erosion directly impacts structures such as roads, bridges, and railway embankments, while high temperatures can also have an influence on the materials used in transport networks, such as railway lines and tarmac on roads. During the heatwaves of August 2003 and June 2019, rail traffic in France was severely disrupted, as temperatures above 40 °C caused expansion and deformation of the rails and wires. Climate change can also have an impact on port infrastructure and marine navigation, as they are sensitive to storms and wind and wave conditions as well as sea level in ports and waterways (Policy Research Corporation 2009). Inland waterway transport can also be affected due to low water levels in areas severely affected by drought.

In some regions, the potential impacts of climate change on infrastructure can be positive. In mountains or in regions with cold climates, the decrease in snowfall or the decrease in freezing episodes provides more favourable conditions for transport, but these positive effects can also have negative repercussions. In Canada, warmer winters and increased freeze–thaw cycles are accelerating the deterioration of transportation infrastructure (IMG-Golder Corporation Environmental Consulting 2012). The increased frequency of hot days in summer and the decrease in **permafrost** thickness limit the reliability and stability of transportation routes (Lemmen and Warren 2004). These findings of the climate vulnerability of transport infrastructure also apply to buildings and structures. The resistance of buildings to the future impacts of climate change is essential. Extreme weather events affect the durability of materials and buildings, and this has an impact on people's safety and quality of life.

We can therefore identify various potential positive and negative climate impacts (Haurie et al. 2009; Hulme et al. 2009; Cochran 2009). The development of catalogues of climate vulnerability according to climatic factors and types of infrastructure makes it possible to assess the potential risks associated with the monitoring and maintenance of transport infrastructure (Table 4.2). Managing these climate risks for infrastructure involves a very significant cost. In Europe, road transport infrastructure and climate constraints account for 30–50% of current road maintenance costs (€8–13 billion per year). About 10% of these costs are related to extreme weather events alone, with extreme rains and floods making the primary contribution (European Commission 2013).

For effective infrastructure vulnerability management and adaptation planning, a good understanding of current and projected climate risks is required.

APPROACHES TO REDUCING IMPACTS ON INFRASTRUCTURE

Climate has an impact on the stability and performance of infrastructure, and must therefore be taken into account when making investment decisions so that new infrastructure and upgrades to existing infrastructure are resilient to climate change. A good understanding of current and projected climate risks is required to ensure effective infrastructure vulnerability management and adaptation planning. The vulnerability of infrastructure networks (e.g. transport, energy, communication, and drinking water) to climate change has been assessed in some countries (notably the Scandinavian countries, the Netherlands, the United Kingdom,

Australia, Canada, and the United States) through the use of science-based studies (Boyle et al. 2013; Lindgren et al. 2009; van Ierland et al. 2007). These national reports enable the climate vulnerability of infrastructure to be assessed at the national or regional level and operating strategies to be established in the context of current and future climate change.

The assessment of climate risk and possible impacts on infrastructure should be undertaken at regional and local scales, and the results used to establish infrastructure network management plans. Bubeck et al. (2019) evaluated the current and future railway flooding risks at the European level for different regionalized climate change scenarios using a specific damage model for railway infrastructure. The analysis was carried out over a historical period (1976–2005), making it possible to estimate the risks in terms of annual damage to the rail network for each European country (Figure 4.28(a)), and as a function of the size of the rail network (Figure 4.28(b)). Future modelling, based on several climate projections (+1.5 °C, +2 °C, and +3 °C) according to the RCP8.5 scenario, has shown that the direct risks of flooding on rail networks are expected to increase significantly due to climate change. The expected annual damage to European railways is projected to increase by 255% under a temperature increase of +1.5 °C (between 2025 and 2031), by 281% with +2 °C (between 2037 and 2046), and 310% with +3 °C (between 2055 and 2069) (Figures 4.28 and 4.29). The researchers' final conclusions were:

> To cover the risk increase due to climate change, European member states would need to increase expenditure in transport by €1.22 billion annually under a 3 °C warming scenario without further adaptation. Limiting global warming to the 1.5 °C goal of the Paris Agreement would result in avoided losses of €317 million annually. (Bubeck et al. 2019, p. 1)

In countries with cold climates, rising temperatures are a major concern because of their effect on permafrost melting and consequent impacts on road infrastructure. Higher air temperatures reduce the extent and thickness of permafrost, which can compromise

TABLE 4.2 Climate risk and the main impacts on transport infrastructure in Europe

TYPE	CLIMATIC HAZARD	RISK
General	Various	• Reduced security • Increased repair and maintenance costs • Disruption in the delivery of goods and passengers
Rail infrastructure	Extreme heat/cold	• Rail buckling • Instability of embankments • Increased wildfires can damage infrastructure • Ice on rails and wires *Positive*: Rail would freeze more rarely in regions with cold climates.
	Extreme precipitation	• Damage to infrastructure due to flooding and/or landslides
	Extreme storms	• Damage to infrastructure such as signals, power cables, etc. (e.g. due to falling trees and power lines)
Road infrastructure	Extreme heat	• Pavement deterioration • Increased wildfires can damage infrastructure
	Extreme storms	• Damage to infrastructure • Roadside trees/vegetation can block roads
	Coastal roads: Sea level rise/ extreme storms/extreme precipitation	• Damage to infrastructure due to flooding • Coastal erosion • Road closure
	Mountain roads: Permafrost degradation	• Decrease of stability, rock falls, landslides • Road closure
	Sewerage systems: Extreme precipitation	• Overloaded sewerage systems can cause road flooding and water pollution
Aviation infrastructure	Extreme heat	• Degradation of runways and runway foundations • Decreased lift for aircraft and increased runway lengths
	Extreme precipitation	• Flood damage to runways and other infrastructure
	Extreme storms	• Wind damage to terminals, navigation equipment, and signage
	Coastal airports: Sea level rise	• Flooding of runways, outbuildings, and access roads
Shipping infrastructure	High river flow (due to extreme precipitation and/or snowmelt)	*Inland shipping* • Problems for passage under bridges • Speed limitations because of dyke instability • Some restrictions on the height of vessels
	Low river flow (e.g. drought)	• Severe restrictions on loading capacity • Navigation problems and speed reduction
	Change in ice cover	• Damage to navigation signs and infrastructure (e.g. locks) *Positive*: Shorter periods of ice cover can be expected
	Reduced sea ice	*Maritime shipping* • Improved access • Longer shipping season • New shipping routes
	Sea level rise and extreme storms	*Maritime shipping* • Navigability could be affected by changes in sedimentation rates and location of shoals • More severe storms and extreme waves might affect ships *Ports* • Destruction of infrastructure • Interruptions and bottlenecks in the flow of products through ports

(continued)

TABLE 4.2 (*Continued*)

TYPE	CLIMATIC HAZARD	RISK
Urban infrastructure	Extreme heat	• Increase of the urban heat island effect (causing melting and deterioration of asphalt, thermal expansion on bridge expansion joints and paved surfaces, and damage to bridge structure material)
	Extreme precipitation	• Damage to infrastructure due to flooding, property at risk due to location, heavy water runoff
	Extreme storms	• Damage and increased maintenance costs
	Coastal cities: Sea level rise and storm surge flooding	• Risk of inundation of road infrastructure and flooding of underground tunnels • Degradation of the road surface and base layers from salt penetration
Energy transmission and distribution infrastructure	Extreme heat	• Decreased network capacity (electrical transmission) • Reduced throughput capacity in gas pipelines (oil and gas transmission)
	Snow and storms	• Increased likelihood of damage to energy networks and blackouts
	Extreme precipitation	• Mass movement (landslides, mud and debris flows) causing damage
	Sea level rise and storms	• Damage to coastal infrastructure (e.g. refineries and coastal pipelines)

Source: Data from the European Commission report on 'Adapting infrastructure to climate change' (European Commission, (2013). *Adapting Infrastructure to Climate Change*. Commission Staff working document 137, European Union, Brussels. https://eur-lex.europa.eu/legal-content/EN/TXT/PDF/?uri=CELEX:52013SC0137), annex 1

the stability of transportation routes and structures. Hjort et al. (2018) modelled the possible effect of global warming on permafrost in the Arctic and predicted future hazard potential for infrastructure, such as transport networks, oil pipelines and settlements (Figure 4.30).

4.5 How can we design adaptable energy and infrastructure systems for future climates?

Climate change is expected to affect infrastructure and therefore the way society interacts with it. The infrastructure on which we all depend in our daily lives is closely linked to the production and use of energy. Adaptation planning is therefore essential to anticipate the impacts of climate change and to know how to adapt infrastructure to ensure access to energy and transport for the population (Chappin and van der Lei 2014).

Climate change is altering both supply capacity and energy demand and infrastructure use. Designing energy and infrastructure systems that can be adapted to future climates is complex. This requires a comprehensive approach that in many cases must take into account the interdependence between different types of infrastructure (e.g. transport, energy, communication networks, and waste-disposal networks), given that they are generally concentrated in small areas with a large population (i.e. urban areas). Figure 4.31 highlights a socio-technical approach to planning infrastructure adaptation measures to climate change. This approach consists of developing economic, social, and technical strategies that are consistent with each other. By following this socio-technical approach, designing energy and infrastructure systems that can be adapted to future climates adopts a logical step-by-step process (Figure 4.32).

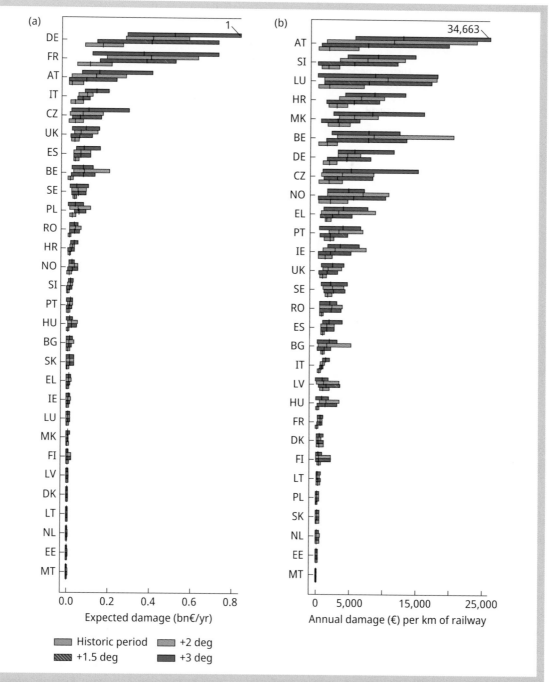

FIGURE 4.28 Country aggregated (a) expected annual damage (billion euros per year) and (b) annual relative damage (based on the length of the railway network in each European country) for the historic period and three warming scenarios (mean value and ensemble spread) using the RCP8.5 scenario. RCP = Representative Concentration Pathway, countries: Austria (AT), Belgium (BE); Bulgaria (BG), Croatia (HR), Czechia (CZ), Denmark (DK), Estonia (EE), Finland (FI), France (FR), Germany (DE), Greece (EL), Hungary (HU), Ireland (IE), Italy (IT), Latvia (LV), Lithuania (LT), Luxembourg (LU), Malta (MT), Netherlands (NL), North Macedonia (MK), Norway (NO), Poland (PL), Portugal (PT), Romania (RO), Slovakia (SK), Slovenia (SI), Spain (ES), Sweden (SE), United Kingdom (UK)

Source: Bubeck et al. (2019). Global warming to increase flood risk on European railways. *Climatic Change* 155: 19–36

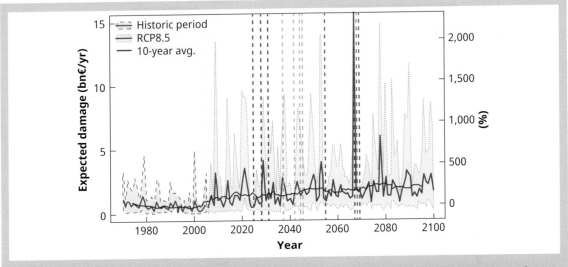

FIGURE 4.29 Simulated monetary cost of damage to European railway infrastructure per year, relative change from the historic period, and 10-year moving average. Purple and blue shades show the ensemble spread provided by seven climate model simulations. The vertical green (+1.5 °C), orange (+2 °C), and red (+3 °C) lines indicate when the specific warming levels are reached according to several regional climate models. RCP = Representative Concentration Pathway

Source: after Bubeck et al. 2019

ASSESSING RISKS AND VULNERABILITY IN RELATION TO CLIMATE IMPACT PROJECTIONS

Identifying and quantifying climate risks according to their magnitude and probability of occurrence is the first step in planning adaptation options. What are the climate-related risks in the region associated with infrastructure and energy generation and access? To be able to assess the robustness of infrastructure at a territorial scale, climate risk must be assessed at regional and local scales using the climate measurement and modelling approaches described in Chapter 2. A fine-scale climate analysis makes it possible to identify accurately the locations of the most vulnerable sectors. Then, downscaled simulations of the future climate according to the IPCC's various socio-economic scenarios make it possible to estimate the evolution of these risks by taking into account the uncertainties associated with the models. This phase should make it possible to assess the vulnerability of all the infrastructure within a territory (Table 4.2). This must be done in relation to the analysis of all climate impacts that may

affect the functioning of the area studied and the well-being of the population. This systemic analysis provides the basis for planning climate change adaptation processes.

IDENTIFYING AND IMPLEMENTING ADAPTATION OPTIONS

Identifying energy and infrastructure systems that can be adapted to future climates requires defining priority areas and sectors, and then designing a range of options that address the uncertainty inherent in the magnitude of climate change impacts, as well as the uncertainty of future socio-economic scenarios. Rational adaptation planning provides the possibility to apply several options depending on the intensity of the climate impact. The Thames 2100 project aimed to define a long-term adaptation plan (with the time horizon of 2100) for floods in the Thames Estuary, taking into account the uncertainty of climate projections (Ranger et al. 2013). Managing the uncertainty associated with climate projections presents

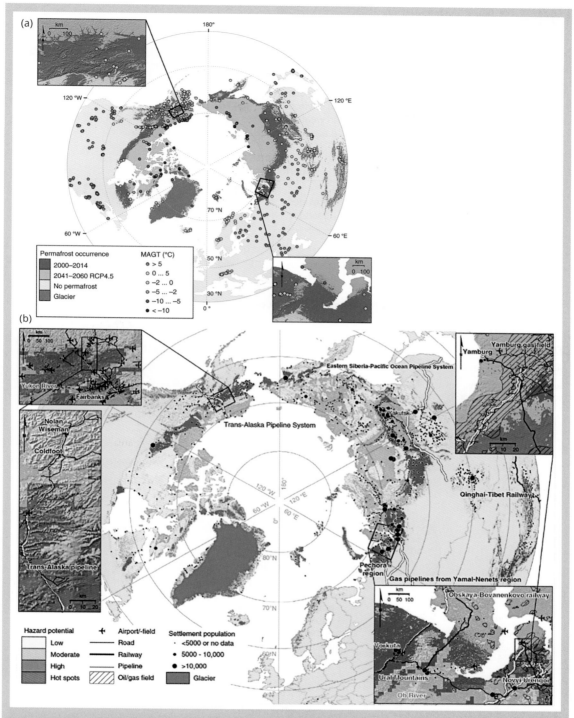

FIGURE 4.30 (a) Distribution of permafrost under contemporary (2000–2014) and predicted future (2041–2060) climate under the RCP4.5 scenario. The contemporary extent of permafrost includes both blue and green areas. Data points (boreholes) of observed mean annual ground temperature (MAGT) are indicated by coloured circles. (b) Predicted hazard potential for infrastructure (2041–2060) resulting from climate change

Source: Hjort et al. (2018). Degrading permafrost puts Arctic infrastructure at risk by mid-century. *Nature Communication* 9: 5147

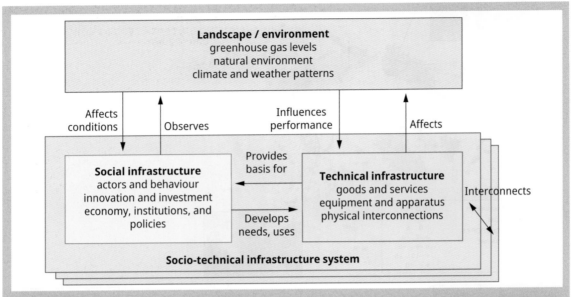

FIGURE 4.31 Schematic illustration of the socio-technical system associated with infrastructure affected by climate. Adaptation involves a change in the components of the socio-technical infrastructure system

Source: Chappin, E. J., and van der Lei, T. (2014). Adaptation of interconnected infrastructures to climate change: A socio-technical systems perspective. *Utilities Policy* 31: 10–17

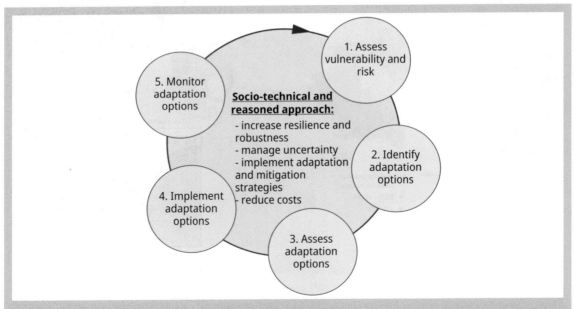

FIGURE 4.32 Different stages of adaptation planning to address the impacts of climate change on energy and infrastructure systems

Source: adapted from EEA and EC, 2012 - https://climate-adapt.eea.europa.eu/

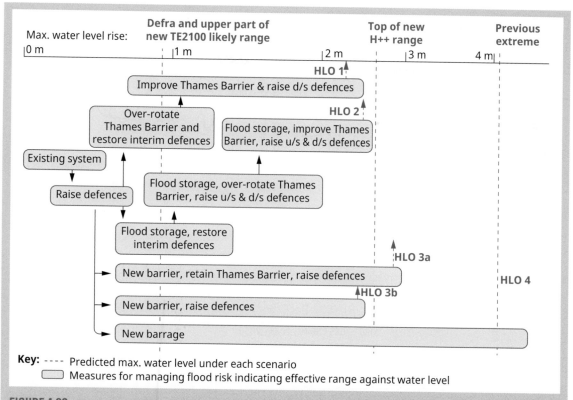

FIGURE 4.33 Long-term planning scheme for adaptation to flooding of the Thames River resulting from sea level rise. d/s represents downstream while u/s represents upstream. HLO1 to HLO4 represent High Level Options reflecting low to high impact

Source: Ranger et al. (2013). Addressing 'deep' uncertainty over long-term climate in major infrastructure projects: Four innovations of the Thames Estuary 2100 Project. *EURO Journal on Decision Processes* 1(3–4): 233–62

significant challenges for major infrastructure projects where decisions made today can have long-term impacts (e.g. when designing infrastructure replacement or upgrades). In the Thames project, each option in the adaptation plan was defined according to different sea level rise thresholds. This approach aimed to develop flexible strategies that can be modified over time as knowledge is improved and conditions change (Figure 4.33).

In general, increasing the resilience and robustness of regions is an important objective in the implementation of options for adapting infrastructure and energy systems to climate change. This allows decision-makers or project managers to anticipate risks and choose the technical solutions that will reduce the effects of climate change in order to restore a balanced situation. This requires regulations and standards that evolve as knowledge improves. Taking this approach, increasing and reinforcing resilience through the implementation of adaptation strategies requires the establishment of specific infrastructure construction standards and long-term planning of developments that consider all the socio-economic parameters of the region.

This approach has been applied in projects on climate resilience of transport, energy, and water infrastructure in Africa. While several African countries were preparing to invest massively in infrastructure development and renovation, the World Bank implemented the 'Enhancing the Climate Resilience of Africa's Infrastructure' programme in order to anticipate the consequences of climate change by renovating existing and adapting new infrastructure. To support planners in determining the most cost-effective and appropriate adaptation strategy for each situation,

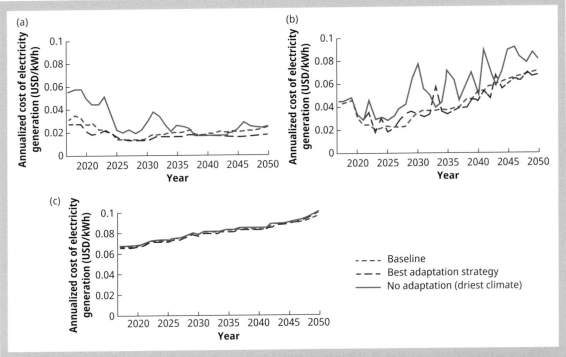

FIGURE 4.34 Impact of climate on the cost of electricity generation in Africa, illustrating the annualized cost of electricity generation (USD/kWh) for three scenarios: the baseline, a no-adaptation strategy for the driest climate, and the most resilient adaptation strategy for three countries: (a) Uganda, (b) Tanzania, and (c) Egypt

Source: Sridharan et al. (2019). Resilience of the Eastern African electricity sector to climate driven changes in hydropower generation. *Nature Communications* 10: 302

this study developed a method to compare the cost of inaction with the cost of a preventive adaptation approach (Cervigni et al. 2015, 2016). The results showed that by planning climate change adaptation strategies now, the cost would be much lower than the cost of inaction. However, the relevance of specific adaptation strategies will depend heavily on the financial, technical, and institutional capacities of individual countries. This adaptation planning has been applied to the road transport network and the development of renewable energies (including hydroelectricity) in order to reduce Africa's current high dependence on fossil fuels. Several hydropower adaptation strategies based on different climate change scenarios (e.g. dry or wet climatic conditions affecting water availability) and the geographical position of the territories have made it possible to assess the vulnerability of potential hydropower infrastructure expansion plans to climate change. Despite the high uncertainty associated with future climate conditions, this approach reduces climate risks through appropriate adjustments in the planning and design process. Compared to a non-resilient approach, such as planning based on past climate, the study showed that taking a resilient approach would reduce costs by at least half. This study also highlighted the contribution of renewable energies to climate change mitigation and adaptation strategies. Figure 4.34 compares the cost of electricity production in Uganda, Tanzania, and Egypt using resilient and no-adaptation strategies in response to climate change. The results show significant fluctuations in electricity costs in the scenarios without adaptation. The cost differences between the different strategies differ from country to country (e.g. little cost difference in Egypt because the share of hydroelectric-power electricity is very low). In general, it should also be noted that the most resilient strategy includes adaptation in all of the energy, water, and agriculture sectors (Sridharan et al. 2019).

MONITORING AND EVALUATING ADAPTATION MEASURES

The previous steps (shown in Figure 4.32) make it possible to develop long-term climate risk adaptation strategies for infrastructure and energy accessibility. The effectiveness of adaptation solutions requires flexible planning that allows for adjustments or modifications to be made in response to the intensity of climate change impacts, but also for the integration of new knowledge resulting from technological developments and innovation. The implementation of this system therefore requires regular monitoring and long-term evaluation of adaptation measures. The process of reviewing the different actions can improve the effectiveness of adaptation measures. It also provides knowledge that can be conceptualized and applied to other regions. For example, the CLIMATE-ADAPT platform (https://climate-adapt.eea.europa.eu/) provides detailed information on each of the steps (as well as data, tools, and guidance documents) in planning adaptation measures for European countries.

Summary

- Infrastructure is closely associated with energy production and use, such as in the role of road, rail, and air transport infrastructure and the distribution of energy, food, and people.

- There is a need to change energy sources as part of a climate change adaptation and mitigation strategy. The increasing substitution of fossil fuels (which are unsustainable and contribute significantly to climate change) by renewable energies is changing the systems for acquiring and transporting energy.

- Renewable energies (e.g. hydroelectricity, wind power, and solar energy) are dependent on weather and climate variations at regional and local scales. Climate measurements and modelling studies at regional and local scales allow the potential for each type of energy to be assessed and mapped according to each meteorological parameter (i.e. wind, temperature, solar radiation, and precipitation).

- Infrastructure and energy production are strongly impacted by climate change. There is a need to simulate the impacts of climate change on energy efficiency capacities and infrastructure vulnerability in different parts of the world. It is important to understand regional- and local-scale variations in climate in order to develop appropriate adaptation strategies.

- Both benefits and costs will come with climate change. For example, increased temperatures and solar radiation will increase the potential of solar energy while increased droughts will have a negative impact on the development of hydropower. It is therefore necessary to evaluate very precisely the advantages and disadvantages associated with the different types of energy production and the geographical areas within which they are used.

- Energy and infrastructure need to be both resilient to today's needs as well as responsive to the needs of the future.

- Climate change will affect the structure of electricity demand and also the ability to produce renewable energy to supply it. Adaptation requires integration of a range of options designed to ensure that each component operates as sustainably as possible in response to a changing climate. For example, renewable energy networks can be integrated with fossil fuels when available renewable energy production is insufficient.

- Climate change adaptation plans should be defined to limit infrastructure vulnerability and ensure access to energy for the population.

- Economic, social, and technical strategies that are consistent with each other should be developed. This requires a logical and flexible process to provide alternative options depending on the level of climate risk, thereby taking into account the uncertainties associated with the different climate scenarios.

- Increased resilience and robustness should be a major goal of the implementation of adaptation strategies.

For case studies and updates, visit the online resources

 www.oup.com/he/sturman-quenol1e

References

Allahdadi, M. N., Gunawan, B., Lai, J., He, R., and Neary, V. S. (2019). Development and validation of a regional-scale high-resolution unstructured model for wave energy resource characterization along the US East Coast. *Renewable Energy* 136: 500–11.

Alonso Díaz, Y., Bezanilla, A., Roque, A., Centella, A., Borrajero, I., and Martinez, Y. (2019). Wind resource assessment of Cuba in future climate scenarios. *Wind Engineering* 43: 311–26.

Barrington-Leigh, C., and Ouliaris, M. (2017). The renewable energy landscape in Canada: A spatial analysis. *Renewable and Sustainable Energy Reviews* 75: 809–19.

Berga, L. (2016). The role of hydropower in climate change mitigation and adaptation: A review. *Engineering* 2: 313–18.

Boyle, J., Cunningham, M., and Dekens, J. (2013). *Climate Change Adaptation and Canadian Infrastructure: A Review of the Literature*. International Institute for Sustainable Development, Winnipeg, Manitoba.

Bubeck, P., Dillenardt, L., Alfieri, L., Feyen, L., Thieken, A. H., and Kellermann, P. (2019). Global warming to increase flood risk on European railways. *Climatic Change* 155: 19–36.

Cervigni, R., Liden, R., Neumann, J. E., and Strzepek, K. M. (2015). *Enhancing the Climate Resilience of Africa's Infrastructure: The Power and Water Sectors*. World Bank, Washington, DC.

Cervigni, R., Losos, A. M., Neumann, J. L., and Chinowsky, P. (2016). *Enhancing the Climate Resilience of Africa's Infrastructure: The Roads and Bridges Sector*. World Bank, Washington, DC.

Chappin, E. J., and van der Lei, T. (2014). Adaptation of interconnected infrastructures to climate change: A socio-technical systems perspective. *Utilities Policy* 31: 10–17.

Choi, Y., Suh, J., and Kim, S.-M. (2019). GIS-based solar radiation mapping, site evaluation, and potential assessment: A review. *Applied Science* 9: 1960.

Cochran, I. (2009). *Climate Change Vulnerabilities and Adaptation Possibilities for Transport Infrastructures in France*. Climate Report 18. http://www.caissedesdepots.fr/fileadmin/PDF/finance_carbone/etudes_climat/UK/09-09_climate_report_n18_-_transport_infrastructures_in_france.pdf.

Cronin, J., Anandarajah, G., and Dessens, O. (2018). Climate change impacts on the energy system: A review of trends and gaps. *Climate Change* 151: 79–93.

Crook, J. A., Jones, L. A., Forstera, P. M., and Crook, R. (2011). Climate change impacts on future photovoltaic and concentrated solar power energy output. *Energy and Environmental Science* 4: 3101–9.

Dupont, E., Koppelaar, R., and Jeanmart, H., (2018). Global available wind energy with physical and energy return on investment constraints. *Applied Energy* 209, 322–38.

European Commission (2013). *Adapting Infrastructure to Climate Change*. Commission Staff working document 137, European Union, Brussels. https://eur-lex.europa.eu/legal-content/EN/TXT/PDF/?uri=CELEX:52013SC0137.

GE Energy (2010). *Western Wind and Solar Integration Study*. Prepared for the National Renewable Energy Laboratory, Golden, Colorado (Report no. NREL/SR-550-47434, 981991). https://doi.org/10.2172/981991.

Gormally, A. M., Whyatt, J. D., Timmis, R. J., and Pooley, C. G. (2012). A regional-scale assessment of local renewable energy resources in Cumbria, UK. *Energy Policy* 50: 283–93.

Haurie, L., Sceia, A., and Thénié, J. (2009). *Inland Transport and Climate Change: A Literature Review*. Informal document no. WP29-149–23, United Nations Economic Commission for Europe.

Hjort, J., Karjalainen, O., Aalto, J., Westermann, S., Romanovsky, V. E., Nelson, F. E., Etzelmüller, B. and Luoto, M. (2018). Degrading permafrost puts Arctic infrastructure at risk by mid-century. *Nature Communication* 9: 5147.

Hughes, M. G., and Heap, A. D. (2010). National-scale wave energy resource assessment for Australia. *Renewable Energy* 35: 1783–91.

Hulme, M., Neufeldt, H., and Colyer, H. (eds) (2009). *Adaptation and Mitigation Strategies: Supporting European Climate Policy—The Final Report from the ADAM Project*. Tyndall Centre for Climate Change Research, University of East Anglia, Norwich.

IMG-Golder Corporation Environmental Consulting (2012). *Nunavut Regional Adaptation Collaborative: Vulnerability Assessment of the Mining Sector to Climate Change*. Task 1 Report No. 11-1334-0020. https://www.climatechangenunavut.ca/sites/default/files/task1_final.pdf.

Jerez, S. R., Tobin, I., Vautard, R., Montavez, J. P., Lopez-Romero, J. M., Thais, F., Bartok, B., Christensen, O. B., Collette, A., Deque, M., Nikulin, G., Kotlarski, S., van Meijgaard, E., Teichmann, C., and Wild, M. (2015). The impact of climate change on photovoltaic power generation in Europe. *Nature Communication* 6: 10014.

Karnauskas, B., Lundquist, J. K., and Zhang, L. (2018). Southward shift of the global wind energy resource under high carbon dioxide emissions. *Nature Geoscience* 11: 38–43.

Lemmen, D., and Warren, F. (eds) 2004 *Climate Change Impacts and Adaptation: A Canadian Perspective*. Natural Resources Canada, Ottawa.

Lindgren, J., Jonson, D. K., and Carlsson-Kanyama, A. (2009). Climate adaptation of railways: Lessons from Sweden. *European Journal of Transport and Infrastructure Research* 9: 164–81.

Müller, J., Folini, D., Wild, M., and Pfenninger, S. (2018). CMIP-5 models project photovoltaics are a no-regrets investment in Europe irrespective of climate change. *Energy* 171: 135–48.

Padmanathan, K., Kamalakannan, N., Sanjeevikumar, P., Blaabjerg, F., Holm-Nielsen, J. B., Uma, G., Arul, R., Rajesh, R., Srinivasan, A., and Baskaran, J. (2019). Conceptual framework of antecedents to trends on permanent magnet synchronous generators for wind energy conversion systems. *Energies* 12: 2616.

Policy Research Corporation (2009). *The Economics of Climate Change Adaptation in EU Coastal Areas: Summary Report*. Director-General for Maritime Affairs and Fisheries, European Commission, Luxembourg.

Ranger, N., Reeder, T., and Lowe, J. (2013). Addressing 'deep' uncertainty over long-term climate in major infrastructure projects: Four innovations of the Thames Estuary 2100 Project. *EURO Journal on Decision Processes* 1(3–4): 233–62.

Rasmussen, D. J., Holloway, T., and Nemet, G. F. (2011). Opportunities and challenges in assessing climate change impacts on wind energy: A critical comparison of wind speed projections in California. *Environmental Research Letters* 6: 024008.

Reichling, J. P., and Kulacki, F. A. (2008) Utility scale hybrid wind–solar thermal electrical generation: A case study for Minnesota. *Energy* 33: 626–38.

Santos, J. A., Rochinha, C., Liberato, M. L. R., Reyers, M., and Pinto, J. G. (2015). Projected changes in wind energy potentials over Iberia. *Renewable Energy* 75: 68–80.

Sridharan, V., Broad, O., Shivakumar, A., Howells, M., Boehlert, B., Groves, D. G., Rogner, H-H., Taliotis, C., Neumann, J. E., Strzepek, K. M., Lempert, R., Joyce, B., Huber-Lee, A., and Cervigni, R. (2019). Resilience of the Eastern African electricity sector to climate driven changes in hydropower generation. *Nature Communications* 10: 302.

Stadler, S., Dryden, J. M., and Greene, J. S. (2015). Climate change impacts on Oklahoma wind resources: Potential energy output changes. *Resources* 4: 203–26.

Tobin, I., Jerez, S., Vautard, R., Thais, F., van Meijgaard, E., Prein, A., Déqué, M., Kotlarski, S., Maule, C. F., Nikulin, G., Noël, T., and Teichmann, C. (2016). Climate change impacts on the power generation potential of a European mid-century wind farms scenario. *Environmental Research Letters* 11: 034013.

US Department of Energy (2017). *Effects of Climate Change on Federal Hydropower: The Second Report to Congress, January 2017*. Washington, DC.

US Energy Information Administration (2022). *February 2022 Monthly Energy Review*. DOE/EIA-0035 (the latest and previous monthly reviews can be found at https://www.eia.gov/totalenergy/data/monthly/).

van Ierland, E. C., De Bruin, K., Dellink, R. B., and Ruijs, A. (2007). *A Qualitative Assessment of Climate Adaptation Options and Some Estimates of Adaptation Costs*. Report on the Routeplanner projects 3, 4, and 5. Netherlands Policy Programme ARK, Wageningen.

Wang, B., Ke, R.-Y., Yuan, X.-C., and Wei, Y.-M. (2014). China's regional assessment of renewable energy vulnerability to climate change. *Renewable and Sustainable Energy Reviews* 40: 185–95.

Wild, M., Folini, D., Henschel, F., Fischer, N., and Mueller, B. (2015). Projections of long-term changes in solar radiation based on CMIP5 climate models and their influence on energy yields of photovoltaic systems. *Solar Energy* 116: 12–24.

Wright, J. F., Duchesne, C., Nixon, M., and Côté, M. (2002). *Ground Thermal Modeling in Support of Terrain Evaluation and Route Selection in the Mackenzie River Valley*. Report prepared for the Climate Change Action Fund, Natural Resources Canada, Ottawa.

CHAPTER **FIVE**

Climate Change and Agriculture

LEARNING OUTCOMES

Having read this chapter, you should be able to:

- describe the complex relationship between climate and agriculture

- critically assess ways of defining optimal climate conditions for crops and livestock

- explain the relative impact of extreme weather events versus average climate conditions on crop and livestock production

- evaluate possible climate change impacts on agricultural systems

- discuss possible climate change adaptation strategies for agricultural activities

5.1 Introduction: climate change and agriculture

The sensitivity of **primary biological industries** to variations in climate is covered in this chapter, using appropriate examples from agriculture because of its major role in providing food for a growing global population. The latest IPCC report suggests that up to 10% of agricultural land will be unsuitable for agriculture in the near future (IPCC 2022). The link between changing environmental conditions and viability of arable crops is obvious, although the sensitivity of different crops to climate change can vary considerably. For example, evaluation of impacts and development of adaptation strategies can be expected to differ between annual and perennial crops. Viticulture and orcharding are good examples of agricultural industries that are highly sensitive to variations in climate, as the quantity and quality of the harvest are dependent on both average climate conditions and the occurrence of much

shorter-term weather events throughout the **growing season** (e.g. late/early frosts and weather during flowering and harvest). Similarly, the expansion of the dairy industry into marginal climatic environments and the grazing of livestock in regions that are becoming increasingly hot can create significant environmental stress for cattle. The impact of climate on other land uses (e.g. forestry) is also important, and it is expected that land-use change will be needed under future climates to ensure the right combination of resources to support population needs. Examples of contemporary research will provide the basis for understanding the relationships between climate change and agriculture, including an assessment of impacts and development of adaptation strategies in response to climate change.

At the outset, it should be noted that there is a two-way relationship between climate and agriculture (Figure 5.1),

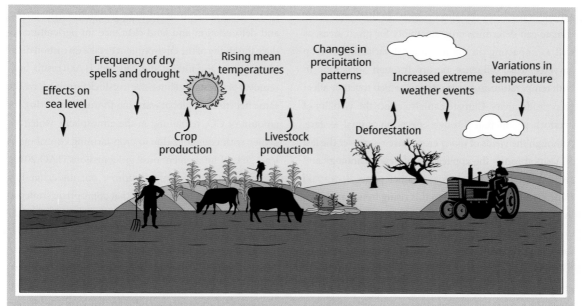

FIGURE 5.1 The two-way relationship between climate variability and agriculture. The effect of climate change on agriculture is indicated by the downward-pointing arrows, while the upward-pointing arrows represent the impact of agriculture on climate change

Source: adapted from FAO 2017

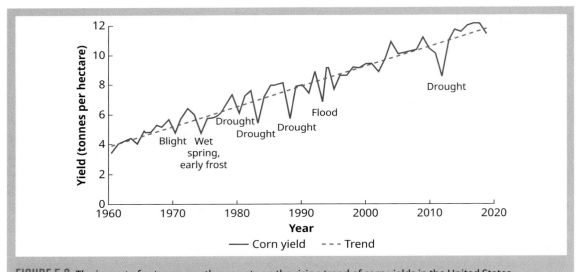

FIGURE 5.2 The impact of extreme weather events on the rising trend of corn yields in the United States

Source: adapted from https://www.iowafarmbureau.com/Article/Corn-Yields-in-the-Midwest-in-2019-A-Tale-of-Uncertainty-and-Differences; & USGCRP (2009). *Global Climate Change Impacts in the United States: 2009 Report*. US Global Change Research Program, Washington, DC. https://nca2009.globalchange.gov/agriculture/index.html

as it is evident both that climate affects agriculture and that agricultural activity can affect climate. In the former case, climate can determine crop suitability for given areas, as well as impacting on the interannual variability of crop harvests. This influence occurs through variations in both temperature and precipitation, which together affect crop productivity. Climate can also affect the viability of livestock production through effects on animal welfare. Although the yields of many crops have risen over the last 50 years through the application of new technology and farming methods, short-term weather patterns can still cause significant disruption to this rising trend (as shown in Figure 5.2). Extreme events, such as storms, floods, and droughts, can severely impact on our ability to provide food and raw materials for a growing global population. It is also clear that agriculture can be a major emitter of greenhouse gases, especially methane, which is emitted mostly by farmed livestock, carbon emissions from the use of fossil fuels in crop production, and through land clearance (Figure 5.1). This contributes to the enhancement of the greenhouse effect, which is the main cause of the

observed rising trend in global air temperatures. In addition, forests are considered to be the lungs of the planet, and deforestation and land clearance for agriculture reduce the ability of the environment to take up carbon dioxide (CO_2), as also indicated in Figure 5.1. As a result, both removal of forests and intensive livestock farming have the same net effect on global warming through increasing the amount of CO_2 remaining in the atmosphere, which together with emissions due to crop farming contribute at least 20% of total greenhouse gas emissions (FAO 2016). It is therefore important to improve our understanding of this two-way relationship so that appropriate strategies can be put in place to ensure the future sustainability of the farming industry.

The following sections will start by examining the climate variables that influence productivity in agriculture, and then discuss ways in which climate change could affect future sustainability in this area. The chapter will conclude by using examples to show how adaptation strategies can be developed in response to future climate change.

5.2 Defining optimal climatic conditions for crops and livestock

Climate has an impact on agriculture through the effects of such variables as solar radiation, temperature, and rainfall. Future climate change is likely to impact particularly on the temperature requirements of different varieties of crop. However, the relationship between crop development and temperature can be quite complex. There are several temperature-related factors that influence the growth and yield of a specific crop. These include what are called the **cardinal temperatures**: the base temperature (Table 5.1), optimal temperature (Table 5.2), and maximum temperature (Cho et al. 2008). The base temperature is the temperature above which plant development can occur, while the optimum temperature is the temperature at which the rate of crop development is the greatest. The maximum temperature represents the upper limit to plant development. Conversely, the minimum temperature represents the lower limit to plant development. All of these temperatures vary between different crops and their varieties (e.g. different varieties of carrot, wheat, or rice). The relationship between temperature and crop growth is made complex by there being more than one response curve, depending on the phase of development of the

TABLE 5.1 Some example base temperatures obtained for various vegetable crops

SPECIES	BASE TEMPERATURE (°C)
Cabbage	0–6.5
Carrot	1–2.15
Chinese cabbage	0
Onion	1.4–5.9
Radish	1.2
Red beet	5.6

Source: Goodger, R. A. (2013). *Cardinal Temperatures and Vernalisation Requirements for a Selection of Vegetables for Seed Production.* Bachelor of Agricultural Science dissertation, Lincoln University

TABLE 5.2 Optimal temperature requirements of different crops

MEAN MONTHLY TEMPERATURES (°C)			VEGETABLES
OPTIMUM	MINIMUM	MAXIMUM	
COOL-SEASON CROPS			
12–24	7	29	Chive, garlic, leek, onion, shallot
15–18	5	24	Beetroot, broad bean, broccoli, Brussels sprout, cabbage, horseradish, kohlrabi, parsnip, radish, spinach, Swiss chard, turnip
15–18	7	24	Artichoke, carrot, cauliflower, celeriac, celery, Chinese cabbage, lettuce, mustard, parsley, pea, potato
WARM-SEASON CROPS			
15–21	10	27	Lima bean, green bean
15–24	10	35	Sweetcorn, New Zealand spinach
18–24	10	32	Pumpkin, squash, vegetable marrow
18–24	15	32	Cucumber, muskmelon, sweet melon
21–24	18	27	Sweet pepper, tomato
21–29	18	35	Chili, eggplant, okra, sweet potato, watermelon

Source: https://www.kzndard.gov.za/images/Documents/Horticulture/Veg_prod/climatic_requirements.pdf

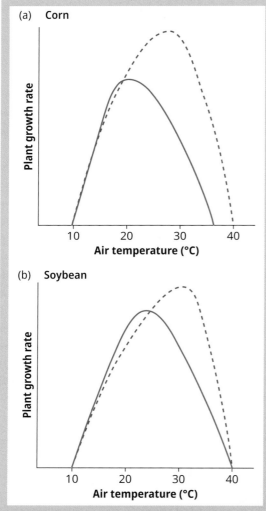

FIGURE 5.3 Temperature response curves for (a) corn and (b) soybean showing the temperature ranges for the reproduction phase (solid red line) and the vegetative growth phase (dashed blue line)

However, the temperature during the growing season of an annual or perennial crop is not the only influence. **Vernalization** (winter chilling) and changing day length during the growing season (**photoperiodic** variations) are also important. Vernalization is the cooling of plant seed during a period of low temperatures, which for some crops is required to initiate plant development through to flowering. A photoperiodic signal can also help to stimulate flowering of the plant. A lack of winter chilling can delay or inhibit flowering in some crops. Grapevines, for example, require a period of temperatures between about 0 and 7 °C during winter, and inadequate winter chilling can result in delayed budburst and poor flowering (Dokoozlian 1999).

The optimal thermal regime often varies between different varieties of a specific crop, such as the grapevine (e.g. Pinot noir, Sauvignon blanc, Merlot, Syrah, etc.). Figure 5.4 provides an illustration of the different mean growing season temperatures associated with the main wine grape varieties, as defined by Jones (2006), based on climate data obtained from areas where these varieties are currently grown. It should be noted that the current distribution of grapevines is not necessarily climatically optimal, as there are many reasons why specific grape varieties are grown where they are, including historical, cultural, and regulatory (e.g. as a result of the *appellation d'origine contrôlée* system in France). Notwithstanding this limitation, the general principle illustrated in Figure 5.4 can still provide a useful guide to the influence of growing season temperatures on the cultivation of different grape varieties. It is clear that those varieties associated with a narrow temperature range such as Pinot noir will be less able to adapt to global warming than varieties with a greater range, such as Riesling. In the case of wine production, there are likely to be two main effects of a warming trend. The first would be a change in the style of wine produced in a given region, as higher temperatures would have an impact on the aromatic qualities of the grape juice. The second is the need to change grape varieties when the temperature becomes too hot to support optimal grapevine growth. Similar

plant. Figure 5.3 provides response curves for both corn and soybean, showing that the optimal temperatures (indicated by the peak in each curve) tend to be lower for the reproduction phase compared to the vegetative growth stage. The base temperature in both crops (corn and soybean) is considered to be around 10 °C.

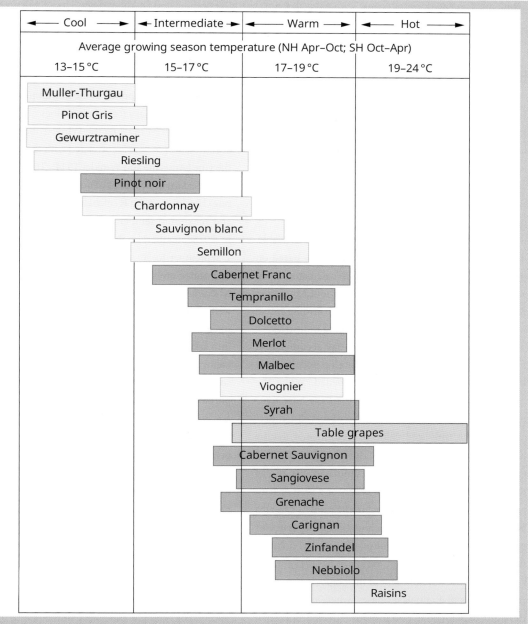

FIGURE 5.4 Mean growing season temperature ranges for different varieties of wine grape. The horizontal bars indicate the range of mean growing season temperatures required to produce a viable harvest based on data obtained from major vineyard regions of the world. White grape varieties are indicated in yellow, red grape varieties in red, table grapes in purple, and grapes for raisins in blue. NH is Northern Hemisphere and SH is Southern Hemisphere

Source: Jones, G. V. (2006). *Climate and terroir: Impacts of climate variability and change on wine*. In: Macqueen, R. W., and Meinert, L. D. (eds), *Fine Wine and Terroir: The Geoscience Perspective*. Geoscience Canada Reprint Series Number 9. Geological Association of Canada, St. John's, Newfoundland, pp. 203–16

problems occur with other crops, such as apples, apricots, peaches, and kiwifruit.

BIOCLIMATIC INDICES

In addition to identifying constraints on crop growth and development based on raw temperatures, a number of bioclimatic indices have been developed to evaluate the suitability of climatic conditions for particular crops. These indices are often based on heat accumulation during the growing season, but may also include other factors such as precipitation, although sensitivity to precipitation is reduced where irrigation is available. The most frequently used indices tend to be based on **growing degree-day** accumulation, calculated from daily temperature data. Such indices should therefore respond directly to the observed global warming trend, with obvious implications for all cropping industries.

Indices based on growing degree-day accumulation assume, first, that a plant will only develop once its base/threshold temperature has been exceeded. When the mean daily temperature is higher than the base temperature, the difference between the observed temperature and the threshold value is accumulated day by day through the growing season. It is also assumed that each plant requires a specific accumulated degree-day total for it to reach maturity, in order for a seed or fruit crop to be harvested. Such bioclimatic models can also be used to relate daily heat accumulation with particular growth phases, such as the time taken to reach budburst, flowering, or fruit ripening (Parker et al. 2013). These key stages in the development of the grapevine are often referred to as phenological phases, where phenology is the study of plant or animal responses to environmental changes throughout the growing season.

The record of bioclimatic indices over many growing seasons can provide an indication of the impact of a changing climate. Table 5.3 provides a list of some of the commonly used bioclimatic indices in relation to crop productivity, in this case of grapevines. For example, the main indices based on sums of degree-days are the Winkler and Huglin indices. The Winkler index (also called 'growing degree-days') is the sum of the mean daily temperatures above 10 °C during the period from 1 April to 31 October in the Northern Hemisphere (1 October to 30 April in the Southern Hemisphere). The base temperature of 10 °C corresponds to the minimum temperature considered necessary for the physiological activity of the vine. The interest in using the Winkler index is that the accumulation of heat is correlated with the phenology of the vine (Amerine and Winkler 1944). The Huglin index, still based on the concept of degree-days, is more elaborate (Huglin 1978). It is calculated from the sum of mean and maximum temperatures above 10 °C from 1 April to 30 September in the Northern Hemisphere (from 1 September to 30 April in the Southern Hemisphere). This index gives more weight to daytime temperatures, when most vine development takes place, and correlates well with the sugar content of the grapes at harvest. By integrating a latitude coefficient, the Huglin index takes into account the duration of sunshine, a very important factor in vine growth. The length of the frost-free season (including the dates of first and last frost) is also important in temperate regions where frost-sensitive crops are grown, while the cool night index is an indicator of conditions just before grape harvest, when cool temperatures have an effect on the aromatic qualities of the wine (Table 5.3). Such bioclimatic indices can be applied to a range of different crops, while similar indices have been developed in relation to livestock welfare and productivity (Sejian et al. 2012). These are typically based on various temperature–humidity relationships that reflect the thermal comfort of domestic animals (examples are provided in Table 5.4). Different livestock species have different sensitivities to ambient temperature and humidity. For example, the ability to tolerate heat stress is much higher in native breeds, particularly under higher temperatures and lower humidity, than in crossbred animals. These indices are therefore used to define animal management strategies in relation to current climatic conditions, and can also provide an indication of how livestock may be impacted under predicted future climate change.

TABLE 5.3 Bioclimatic indices frequently used to assess crop suitability for viticulture and the relationship between climate and crop development, with T representing air temperature (°C)

INDEX	FORMULA	PERIOD	RANGE OF VALUES	
Average growing season temperature (Jones 2006)	$GST = \sum_{d=1}^{n} \dfrac{[T_{max} + T_{min}]/2}{n}$	April–October (NH) October–April (SH)	Too cool	<13°C
			Cool	13–15°C
			Intermediate	15–17°C
			Warm	17–19°C
			Hot	19–21°C
			Very hot	21–24°C
			Too hot	>24°C
Growing degree-days (Winkler index) (Winkler et al. 1974)	$GDD = \sum_{d=1}^{n} max\left[\dfrac{T_{max} + T_{min}}{2} - 10,0\right]$	April–October (NH) October–April (SH)	Too cool	<850
			(Region I)	850–1389
			(Region II)	1389–1667
			(Region III)	1667–1944
			(Region IV)	1944–2222
			(Region V)	2222–2700
			Too hot	>2700
Huglin index (Huglin 1978)	$HI = \sum_{d=1}^{n} max\left[\dfrac{T_{mean} + T_{max}}{2} - 10,0\right]K$	April–September (NH) October–March (SH)	Too cool	<1200
			Very cool	1200–1500
			Cool	1500–1800
			Temperate	1800–2100
			Warm temperate	2100–2400
			Warm	2400–2700
			Very warm	2700–3000
			Too hot	>3000
Cool night index (Tonietto 1999)	$CI = \sum_{d=1}^{n} \dfrac{[T_{min}]}{n}$	September (NH) March (SH)	Very cool nights	≤12°C
			Cool nights	12–14°C
			Temperate nights	14–18°C
			Warm nights	>18°C

Note: NH and SH refer to the Northern Hemisphere and Southern Hemisphere, respectively

Clearly, climate has a major impact on agricultural production through its effect on the thermal and moisture conditions within which the plants and animals are produced. However, the increased use of irrigation in agriculture has somewhat reduced the sensitivity to changes in rainfall, although severe droughts can affect the supply of water to such schemes. Agricultural crops that are not routinely irrigated are obviously more sensitive to rainfall variability. In contrast to moisture requirements, it is more difficult to modify the thermal environment of a crop in response to the current global warming trend, although manipulation of both the soil and plant canopy can be used to lessen impacts of moderate temperature increases.

Defining the optimal climatic conditions for maximum crop or livestock productivity has been the subject of numerous biometeorological investigations. The various indices described above provide valuable tools that

TABLE 5.4 Selected heat stress indices used to assess climate impacts on livestock

INDEX	FORMULA
Temperature–humidity index (THI; Amundson et al. 2006)	$THI = T - \left(0.55 - \left(0.55 \times \left(\dfrac{RH}{100}\right)\right) \times (T - 58)\right)$
Black globe humidity index (BGHI; Buffington et al. 1981)	$BGHI = T_{BG} + 0.36 \times T_{DP} + 41.5$
Temperature, humidity, and velocity index (THVI; Tao and Xin 2003)	$THVI = (0.85 \times T + 0.15 \times T_{WB}) \times V^{-0.058}$
Wind black globe temperature index (WBGTI; Al-Tamimi 2005)	$WBGTI = (0.7 \times T_{WB}) + (0.2 \times T_{BG}) + (0.1 \times T)$
Heat load index (HLI; Gaughan et al. 2008)	If $T_{BG} > 25$: $HLI = 8.62 + (0.38 \times RH) \times (1.55 \times T_{BG}) - (0.5 \times V) + (e^{2.4-V})$ If $T_{BG} < 25$: $HLI = 10.66 + (0.28 \times RH) + (1.3 \times T_{BG}) - V$

Note: T is air temperature, RH is relative humidity, T_{BG} is the temperature of a black globe, T_{DP} is dew-point temperature, T_{WB} is wet-bulb temperature, and V is wind velocity

Source: Adapted from Sejian et al. (2012). Ameliorative measures to counteract environmental stresses. In: Sejian, V., Naqvi, S. M. K., Ezeji, T., Lakrtitz, J., and Lal, R. (eds), *Environmental Stress and Amelioration in Livestock Production.* Springer, Dordrecht, pp. 153–80

can be used to assess crop or livestock suitability to different climatic environments. However, the use of mean values or totals over a growing season does not provide a complete picture of the effect of climate variability on crop or livestock productivity, as the impact of single weather events causing heavy rainfall or extreme temperatures during specific phases of the growing season (e.g. during crop flowering or cattle pregnancy) can often have a greater impact than the longer-term averages and totals calculated over the whole growing season. The following section examines the potential effects of extreme events on agriculture because these are potentially devastating.

5.3 The impact of extreme events

Extreme events such as heatwaves, frosts, wind storms, floods, and droughts can have catastrophic effects on agriculture, to the extent that the US Department of Agriculture estimates that 90% of crop losses are related to extreme weather (https://www.forbes.com/sites/jimfoerster/2019/02/15/todays-extreme-winter-weather-can-impact-tomorrows-crop-farming/#1daf484efbce). Increases in the frequency of extreme events can also have a significant effect on the viability of a crop. For example, Table 5.5 indicates the sensitivity of different crops to frost. It is clear that the impact of such extreme events will vary depending on the phase of development of the crop. When frosts occur in late spring, they tend to be much more damaging than in late winter or early spring, while heavy rainfall events during the harvest period can cause a significant reduction in yield. Although most future climate scenarios suggest that frosts will decline in frequency in most areas, changes in atmospheric circulation and their effect on daily temperature range have already been associated with an increase in frost frequency in some regions. For example, the southward shift of the sub-tropical high-pressure belt in the vicinity of Australia over recent decades is thought to have contributed to an increasing frequency

TABLE 5.5 Sensitivity of different crops to frost

A. COOL-SEASON CROPS

1. Hardy (can withstand moderate frosts)

Asparagus	Garlic	Radish
Broad bean	Horseradish	Rhubarb
Broccoli	Kohlrabi	Spinach
Brussels sprout	Mustard	Turnip
Cabbage	Parsley	
Chive	Pea (flowers and pods are more sensitive to frost	

2. Half-hardy (can withstand light frosts)

Beetroot	Chinese cabbage	Potato
Carrot	Globe artichoke	Swiss chard
Cauliflower	Lettuce	
Celery	Parsnip	

B. WARM-SEASON CROPS

1. Tender (sensitive to frosts and low temperatures)

New Zealand spinach	Sweetcorn	Tomato
Green bean		

2. Very tender (very sensitive to low temperatures)

Chili	Okra	Sweet pepper
Cucumber	Pumpkin	Sweet potato
Eggplant	Squash	Vegetable marrow
Lima bean	Sweet melon	Watermelon

Source: https://www.kzndard.gov.za/images/Documents/Horticulture/Veg_prod/climatic_requirements.pdf

of frosts in the wheat belt of Australia and some vineyard regions of New Zealand because of less cloud and increased nocturnal cooling (Crimp et al. 2016; Sturman and Quénol 2013). It should also be remembered that earlier development of crops due to warmer average temperatures can put them at much higher risk of significant damage when late frosts do occur. It is therefore important not to focus entirely on future changes in average climate conditions, as any changes in the frequency of extreme events are likely to have a much greater impact.

It is thought that greater variability in crop yields over recent decades is directly related to increases in extreme weather conditions, particularly when these weather events occur during key phases of crop development (Motha 2011). Weather events, such as droughts, floods, hurricanes, severe storms, heatwaves, freezes and wildfires, have caused many billions of dollars of damage to the US agricultural economy over the past few decades, in addition to death and destruction within the wider community. It is therefore important that the agricultural industry carefully assesses the potential impacts of possible future climate change on crop and livestock production, and develops appropriate strategies to increase its resilience in the face of such serious threats.

5.4 Climate change effects on agricultural systems

There is plenty of evidence of the impacts of climate change on agricultural systems in the historical record, including food shortages and famines in many parts of the world (Slavin 2016). Some crops may benefit from warmer conditions caused by climate change (e.g. melon, sweet potato), while others may suffer (e.g. potato, lettuce, brassicas), and the impact is likely to vary regionally. Figure 5.5 illustrates the variation in response of different agricultural crops in California. Some crops are predicted to show a largely positive response to warming over the next few decades (e.g. alfalfa and maize), while others show an immediate negative response (e.g. cotton and sunflower), or very little response at all (e.g. rice and tomato). Moreover, adaptation capacity differs between different countries, and some countries are more dependent on agriculture than others, so economic impacts will vary internationally. It appears that the situation will be more difficult for low-income, less developed countries, especially in the tropics and sub-tropics, while higher-latitude countries may actually be better off. The main impacts of climate change on agriculture are summarized in the following sections.

CHANGES IN MEAN CLIMATE

These include changes in temperature, rainfall, humidity, cloud, and solar radiation. Optimal temperature ranges for crops differ depending on whether they are grown for seed production or vegetative growth. The daily temperature range may be an important factor for some crops. For example, high night-time temperatures can increase **respiration** rates and loss of carbon for plant development, and if they occur during pollination and grain-filling they can cause a reduction in grain or fruit production (Hatfield et al. 2014). Rising temperatures also lead to increased water use by plants and therefore affect the water budget of a crop. Global warming can also lead to a lack of winter chilling for some crops, as well as earlier crop development, leading to greater susceptibility to frost damage. The winter chilling requirements vary between crops, with grapes needing about 90 hours, peaches 225 hours, apples 400 hours, and cherries over 1,000 hours (with temperatures between about 0 and 10 °C). Maps of the predicted reduction in winter chilling hours for Central Valley, California, due to global warming are shown in Figure 5.6.

Increased storms at harvest time can create practical problems associated with equipment use in difficult conditions and the spoiling of the crop being harvested. Livestock productivity can be adversely affected by higher temperatures because of heat stress, which can be made worse if humidity also increases. As mentioned previously, it is likely that there would also be changes in the amount of solar radiation, although this would vary regionally. Solar radiation is the driver of photosynthesis in plants, so such changes could have a significant effect. More than 80% of global agriculture is rain-fed and future projections suggest high latitudes will have greater precipitation and lower latitudes will have less, but regional uncertainty is high because of the difficulty in predicting changes in atmospheric circulation (Gornall et al. 2010). Changes in the seasonality of precipitation may actually be more important than total annual amounts.

CHANGES IN EXTREME CLIMATE

Increased frequency of weather extremes such as floods, drought, frosts, and heatwaves, as well as greater interannual variability, can be more important than changes in the average climate conditions.

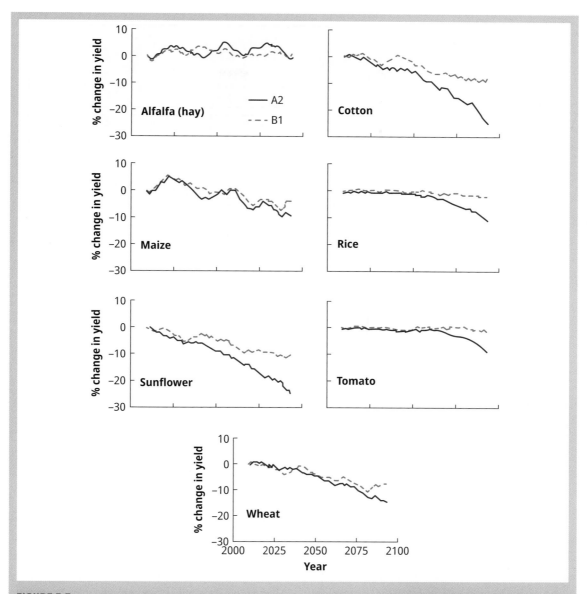

FIGURE 5.5 Percentage change in yield for various crops in Central Valley, California predicted by medium-high (A2) and low greenhouse gas emissions (B1) scenarios. A2 scenarios reflect rapid future economic growth, while B1 scenarios reflect levelling off of growth

Source: Lee et al. (2011). Effect of climate change on field crop production in California's Central Valley. *Climatic Change* 109 (Suppl. 1), S335–53

As mentioned earlier, the timing of extreme events can be crucial (e.g. heavy rainfall during flowering), so that a shift in the climate regime causing a change in the timing or intensity of such events could be devastating for some producers. Obviously, the impact of severe drought and flood events may be disastrous. Floods can completely destroy crops, or cause waterlogging and the spread of fungal diseases. Similarly, high winds associated, for example, with tropical cyclones can also be destructive.

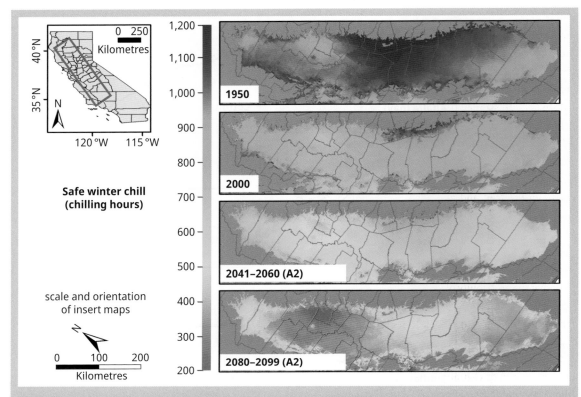

FIGURE 5.6 Predicted changes in the number of hours of winter chilling in Central Valley, California for the past (1950), recent (2000), and future time periods (2040–2060 and 2080–2099) under a medium-high greenhouse gas emissions scenario (A2)

Source: Luedeling et al. (2009). Climatic changes lead to declining winter chill for fruit and nut trees in California during 1950–2099. *PLoS ONE* 4: e6166

Livestock can suffer under high temperatures, so a warmer world can be detrimental to farm animals such as cattle and sheep. Heat stress can have a significant impact on livestock production, while drought has a direct impact on the quantity and quality of the pastures available for grazing. A warming world can also result in the spread of parasites and diseases of livestock.

CHANGES IN GROWING SEASON

Observed higher temperatures have been seen to change the length of the growing season, with earlier germination, flowering, and harvesting of many crops. These changes in the length of the growing season can have negative consequences. With the growing of most fruit, the warming trend is associated with a shortening of the growing season and earlier budburst, crop ripening, and harvesting. This impact on crop phenology could impose new agronomic choices in order to avoid harvesting too early during the hot season. Such consequences for the growing cycle may also adversely affect other crops such as vegetables, causing major shortages in the future (Scheelbeek et al. 2018). The earlier vegetative cycle can also cause an increase in risks related to extreme weather conditions. Spring frosts that occur after the budburst of grapevines or fruit trees constitute a significant risk for these crops. As the budburst is tending to occur earlier, the probability of having negative temperatures during budburst is much higher (as, in spite of rising average temperatures, the length of time during which nocturnal cooling can occur does not change) and this can cause significant damage to the harvest in a given year. In spring 2017, most European vineyards suffered very severe frost damage, contributing to a 17% reduction in production (45% in the Bordeaux region). Frost damage also affected all crops in Europe during spring 2021, especially in France with the destruction of 80% of the fruit and grape wine crops in some regions. Future simulations of spring frost in relation to grapevine budburst dates show an increased risk of frost damage to northern French vineyards (e.g. Alsace, Burgundy, and Champagne) (Sgubin et al. 2018). They also show that the probability of exceptional frost events during the growing season would increase considerably in a climate characterized by global warming of 2 °C relative to pre-industrial levels (Vautard et al. 2023).

It should not be forgotten that a changing temperature regime may also allow the introduction of new crops. However, although such new crops may benefit from higher temperatures, future climates may also bring more extreme weather (more heatwaves, storms, floods, and droughts), so that any advantages in crop production provided by the warming trend may be countered by weather-related losses.

CHANGES IN PESTS AND DISEASES

Insects, parasites, fungi, and bacteria can significantly affect crops and livestock. As a result of the projected climate change in temperate regions, crop pests and diseases are expected to be more frequent and potentially spread to areas that were not previously affected. Changes in mean climate conditions can cause a geographical expansion of diseases and pests for both animals (livestock) and plants (forests and plant crops). The areas of disease and pathogen occurrence are strongly related to the climatic conditions favourable for their adaptation. The changing climate also facilitates the emergence of

totally new diseases in regions where current climatic conditions do not allow their establishment. The incursion of these new diseases or pests in a given area is often facilitated by other vectors of spread such as transport of people and goods from one geographical area to another. Bluetongue, an insect-borne viral disease affecting livestock, appeared dramatically in southern Europe after 1998 and in northern Europe from 2006 onwards. Even if climate change is not the only factor behind its appearance, it seems that a rise in temperature also increases the transmission of bluetongue (Baylis et al. 2017). Figure 5.7 shows the evolution of the risk of bluetongue transmission between 1961 and 2008 based on changing climatic conditions, with the infection rate (R_0) being the number of cases of bluetongue resulting from the introduction of one infected host. In this case, global warming appears to have caused an increase in the number of insects that carry the viral disease. Regional climate simulations have highlighted the emergence and spread of the disease in north-western Europe since the early 1990s, with future projections from a set of 11 regional climate models predicting an increased risk of bluetongue emergence in most of western Europe by 2050 (Guis et al. 2011). Increased temperatures are also likely to have accelerated the life cycle of insects such as the codling moth (the main pest threat for apples). Regional modelling of the impact of climate change has highlighted changes in the occurrence and duration of life phases of this pest. In southern Switzerland, the phenomenon of three generations of the moth per season is only very rarely observed under current climatic conditions, but it is expected to become normal between 2045 and 2074 (Hirschi et al. 2012). A higher frequency of extreme climatic events (e.g. drought, heatwaves, and heavy rainfall) increases the vulnerability of plants to diseases and pests. In 2016, wheat yields in France reached their lowest level since 1950, although yield forecasting systems were unable to anticipate this event. Ben-Ari et al. (2018) highlighted that it was the combination of abnormally warm temperatures in late autumn and abnormally wet conditions in the following spring that increased the spread of pests and diseases. Based on climate projections, it is thought

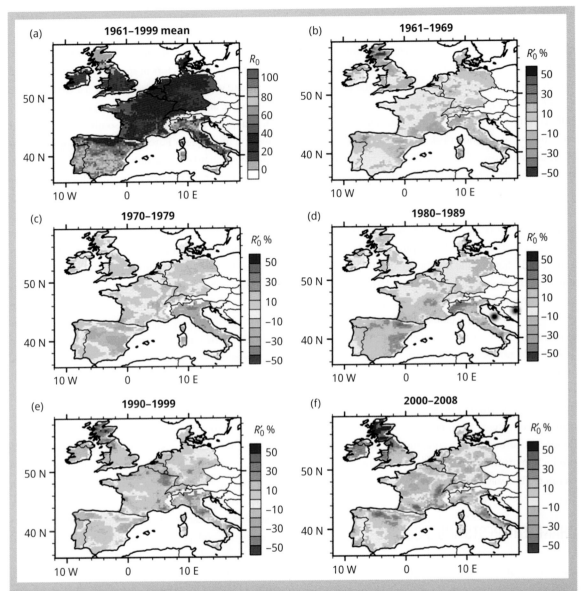

FIGURE 5.7 Long-term mean and modelled decadal changes in the infection reproduction rate (R'_0) for bluetongue disease. (a) Long-term mean R_0 for the August to October season. (b) to (f) R_0 percentage anomalies with respect to the 1961–1999 mean for different decades. R_0 is estimated from an observed climate dataset

Source: Guis et al. (2011). Modelling the effects of past and future climate on the risk of bluetongue emergence in Europe. *Journal of the Royal Society Interface* 9: 339–50

that the combination of such extreme events is expected to become more frequent in the future.

Recent research has shown that there is significant spatial variability in the impact of climate change on agriculture, with some regions gaining significant benefits while others may be adversely affected. Figure 5.8 maps the predicted impacts of climate change by the 2080s for different parts of the world based on an

FIGURE 5.8 A global assessment of the climate-induced percentage change in agricultural productivity between 2003 and the 2080s

Source: Cline, W. (2008). Global warming and agriculture. *Finance and Development*, March, 23–7

analysis by Cline (2008) that included effects of CO_2 enrichment. Higher CO_2 concentrations associated with the global warming trend may be beneficial to crop growth through their impacts on photosynthesis and transpiration, but this effect may be countered by other associated factors (e.g. higher temperatures, and water or nutrient constraints).

It is evident that, at the global scale, it is the regions closest to the equator that are likely to suffer most as a result of climate change (Figure 5.8). In contrast, some regions at higher latitudes may benefit substantially from a continued warming trend. Typically, the populations of the lower-latitude, less developed economies are more reliant on agricultural production than those in the wealthier countries at higher latitudes, so are likely to be more adversely impacted by climate change. On the basis of the 2015 Paris Agreement to 'holding the increase in the global average temperature

to well below 2 °C above pre-industrial levels and pursuing efforts to limit the temperature increase to 1.5 °C', Schleussner et al. (2016) produced projections of agricultural yields for the main crops required to maintain sufficient nutrition for the global population. The results showed that tropical regions would face significant reductions in local yields, particularly for wheat and maize (Figure 5.9).

As a result of the complex relationship between climate and agriculture, the implementation of policies to assess and limit the impacts of climate change is challenging. It is evident that the significant regional variability in impacts (e.g. lower yields in the most populated and poorest areas) must be taken into account at the global scale so that food security can be ensured for all. However, recognizing that agriculture, deforestation, and other land-use changes are responsible for more than 20% of greenhouse gas emissions, adaptation policies should also be

		1.5 °C	2 °C
		Changes in local crop yields over global and tropical present-day agricultural areas including the effects of CO_2-fertilization [%]	
Wheat	Global	2 [–6; 17]	0 [–8; 21]
	Tropics	–9 [–25; 12]	–16 [–42; 14]
Maize	Global	–1 [–26; 8]	–6 [–38; 2]
	Tropics	–3 [–16; 2]	–6 [–19; 2]
Soy	Global	7 [–3; 28]	1 [–12; 34]
	Tropics	6 [–3; 23]	7 [–5; 27]
Rice	Global	7 [–17; 24]	7 [–14; 27]
	Tropics	6 [0; 20]	6 [0; 24]

Projected yield reductions are largest for tropical regions, while high-latitude regions may see an increase. Projections not including highly uncertain positive effects of CO_2-fertilization project reductions for all crop types of about 10% globally already at 1.5 °C and further reductions at 2 °C.

FIGURE 5.9 Summary of expected differences in climate impacts on selected agricultural crops for the whole globe and just the tropics resulting from a warming of 1.5 °C and 2 °C above pre-industrial levels, based on stylized scenarios over the twenty-first century. Square brackets give the likely (66%) range of possibilities

Source: Schleussner et al. (2016). Differential climate impacts for policy-relevant limits to global warming: The case of 1.5 °C and 2 °C. *Earth System Dynamics* 7: 327–51

integrated with mitigation activities, taking into account the differences in vulnerability between diverse regions of the world. To meet these challenges, innovative solutions must be developed that will require political and financial support. Any solutions must consider the whole food system, in order to improve agricultural production at the same time as limiting negative impacts on the climate (Torquebiau et al. 2016).

5.5 How can we identify climate change impacts and develop adaptation strategies?

Decision-makers need reliable information based on solid scientific foundations in order to identify the impacts of current and future climate change on agriculture and thus implement adaptation strategies. These adaptation strategies should be based on a sound understanding of the relationship between different agricultural systems and climate, and must be specific to particular locations. Various indicators (e.g. bioclimatic indices) that are currently used to link climate and arable crop viability and productivity can be integrated into modelling of future climate change. Simulations can then be used to assess potential trends for the future and to develop appropriate adaptation strategies. As mentioned in Chapter 2, it is extremely important to accurately downscale climate projections provided by global climate models to the regional and local scales so that appropriate responses can be formulated. Farmers need high-resolution spatial simulations of future climate in order to be able to implement short-term to long-term adaptation strategies for their region.

RESPONDING TO CLIMATE CHANGE: SMART AGRICULTURE/AGROFORESTRY

There is a general need to make agricultural systems more resilient in order to reduce risk associated with a changing climate. However, it is clear that adaptation capacity varies depending on both socio-economic and environmental conditions in different parts of the world. For example, some regions experience a range of different climates as a result of the complexity of the terrain, and therefore have greater capacity to adapt than those in which climate conditions are more uniform across large areas. Similarly, there is great diversity in the efficiency of production in different parts of the world, which makes the impact of climate change more variable and the development of adaptation strategies more complex.

General approaches to adaptation involve both changing the types or varieties of crop and changing farming operations. In the former case, good knowledge is needed of future climates so that rational decisions can be made about the selection of new crops, including the development of new heat- and drought-adapted hybrid varieties. Changing farming operations includes varying fertilizer application and the timing of cropping activities, crop canopy management, soil management, and irrigation and water management. Later planting dates can help reduce negative effects of faster growth, but there may still be marketing issues because of the change in timing of harvest (Yohannes 2016).

However, there are constraints that may limit the ability of an agricultural production system to adapt to new climatic conditions, so that in some cases there may be total collapse of the food production system. Historically, this could be reflected in the occurrence of famines and droughts that caused significant loss of life. The capacity to adapt therefore depends on the rate and nature of the changing climate and the timescale over which adaptation is possible. Typically, there are several short-term or long-term actions that can be taken to help a given production system to respond effectively. However, perennial crops with a long life cycle (e.g. olives) may be very slow to adapt and therefore more affected by rapid change, and there is little that can be done over the short term. Key constraints include the time that it takes to make changes, the costs of making changes, cultural resistance to change, and various practical problems of implementing change (e.g. the lack of infrastructure, labour, water, and information).

A logical response to the threat of climate change has resulted in the concept of **smart agriculture**. Climate-smart agriculture is defined by FAO (2010, page iii) as 'agriculture that sustainably increases productivity, enhances resilience (adaptation), reduces/removes GHGs (mitigation) where possible, and enhances achievement of national food security and development goals'. Figure 5.10 illustrates this concept in relation to the main objective of achieving food security and development goals by developing strategies to both mitigate the effects of climate change and adapt to future changing climates (Lipper et al. 2014).

Agroforestry is also a rational method of adaptation to climate change, referring to farming practices that combine trees, crops, and livestock on agricultural plots. By conserving trees on these plots, farmers promote climate change mitigation because of the forestry component accumulating CO_2, at the same time as contributing to climate change adaptation. Several studies conducted by agricultural research organizations have highlighted agroforestry systems as economically and ecologically sustainable practices, particularly in terms of improving overall productivity (of biomass), fertility, and soil conservation, but also in terms of the effect of the modified microclimate on crop production (Fanish and Priya 2013; Toppo and Raj 2018).

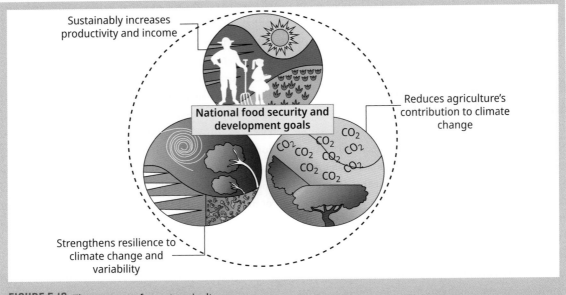

Sustainably increases productivity and income

National food security and development goals

Reduces agriculture's contribution to climate change

Strengthens resilience to climate change and variability

FIGURE 5.10 The concept of smart agriculture

Source: after Papusoi, I., and Faraby, J. A. (2013). Climate smart agriculture. Seminar on Climate Change and Risk Management, 6 May. https://www.slideshare.net/jimalfaraby/climatesmart-agriculture-20675751, image courtesy of Jimly Al-Faraby

CASE STUDY 5.1
Climate change and viticulture

A multiscale approach to the development of climate change adaptation strategies is currently being applied in the wine sector. Viticulture is a very reliable indicator of the impact of climate change for several main reasons:

- The climate affects both grapevine growth and the characteristics of the wines—that is, both the size of the harvest and the sugar and alcohol content and acidity of the resulting grape juice.

- The vine is a perennial crop that is generally planted for several decades. Harvest records over this time frame allow long-term monitoring of the consequences of the changing climate on both the plant and the characteristics of the wines produced.

- The phenology of the grapevine has been the focus of scientific study since the 1940s with various bioclimatic indices used to investigate the correlation between vine growth stages and climatic factors (particularly temperature—see Table 5.3). Analysis of the relationship

between bioclimatic indices and phenological stages enables the climatic conditions associated with each vintage to be established.

Monitoring of phenological stages and grapevine physiology alongside climate observations and predictions provided by global climate models allows assessment of the adaptability of viticulture in response to scenarios of future climate change for wine-growing regions. Many wine-producing areas are located in regions of complex terrain, which means that any adaptation strategy needs scenarios of future climate to be downscaled to the vineyard scale, as described in this case study.

RECENT CLIMATE TRENDS IN WORLD WINE-GROWING REGIONS

Although the vine is a resistant plant, its ability to grow and produce a viable crop is defined by specific climatic conditions, particularly in relation to water availability and heat. The high latitude limit for viticulture is defined by conditions where the average annual temperature is not high enough to enable the grapes to ripen properly, while at low latitudes temperatures are too high and often marked by periods of severe drought. The current limit of vine cultivation is therefore located in a latitudinal band between about 30 °N and 50 °N for the Northern Hemisphere and 20 °S and 50 °S for the Southern Hemisphere. This zonation corresponds to the 13–24 °C isotherms of the average growing season temperature, as shown in Table 5.3 (Jones 2006).

Climate change has caused a shift in this latitudinal band of possible vine cultivation towards the north in the Northern Hemisphere, and towards the south in the Southern Hemisphere. For example, in Europe, vineyards are now being developed in England, Sweden, and Denmark, while in South America, the southern lands of Patagonia are experiencing strong growth in vineyard planting. Although the quality of the wines from these new regions needs improvement, future temperature conditions will certainly be favourable for the production of good wine. This latitudinal shift is not the only geographical transformation, as extension to higher altitudes is also happening (Delay et al. 2015). Indeed, the current climatic conditions of high-altitude vineyards (>2,000 m) are much more favourable than they were twenty years ago. An increase in the average growing season temperature by 1 to 2 °C particularly favours the ripening of the grapes.

More generally, an increase in the global average temperature of 1 °C is considered to be equivalent to a potential displacement of viticulture by about 200 km towards higher latitudes or 150 m in altitude.

The changing dates of vine growth phases in relation to climate data from meteorological station networks have been studied using both raw data and bioclimatic indices in wine-growing regions around the world, which has enabled the characterization of vineyard climate types (Tonietto and Carbonneau 2004). The observed increase in temperature is reflected by an increase in bioclimatic indices that can lead to a change in the classification of regions in relation to the types of wine-growing climate shown in Table 5.3.

CLIMATE MODELLING OF FUTURE WINE-GROWING REGIONS

The observed warming climate with earlier phenological stages, the shortening of the vine growth cycle, and changes in the characteristics of the wines (e.g. increased alcohol content, changing aromatic qualities) have raised a number of questions about the impact of climate change on viticulture, which is why simulations of future climate and its impact on wine production need to be carried out. The calculation of bioclimatic indices based on data from global climate models has predicted significant changes in the distribution of vineyards by 2070–2100, with the disappearance of some viticulture areas such as in southern Australia and some Mediterranean countries, as well as the advent of new wine-growing areas such as in northern Europe and southern South America. The use of global climate models and the 'Mean growing season temperature' bioclimatic index has indicated a decrease of 25–73% (according to RCP4.5 and RCP8.5) in the area suitable for viticulture in the main wine-growing regions of the world by 2050 (Hannah et al. 2013). The significant decrease in wine-growing suitability would affect many traditional wine-producing regions (e.g. Bordeaux and the Rhône Valley regions in France, and Tuscany in Italy). However, it is important to be careful when using bioclimatic indices. These indices only provide indications of the theoretical limits for the cultivation of vines and the production of quality wines, but these indications do not take into account some important factors, such as the vine's physiological capacity to adapt to future climate. For example, van Leeuwen et al. (2013) calculated the average temperature during the growing season during 1971–1999 and 2000–2012 for three major wine regions: Rheingau (Germany), Burgundy (France), and the Rhône Valley (France). Burgundy has been producing great Pinot noir wines since 2000, although the average growing season temperature is already above the upper temperature limit cited by Hannah et al. (2013). The results are similar for the Rheingau with Pinot gris and the Rhône Valley with Syrah.

Recent work has focused on integrating crop models with climate models. Fraga et al. (2016) analysed the suitability of viticulture in Europe for recent (1980–2005) and future (2041–2070) climates using the STICS crop model (Simulateur mulTIdisciplinaire pour les Cultures Standard or 'multidisciplinary simulator for standard crops') in relation to RCP scenarios 4.5 and 8.5 (as described in Chapter 2). The crop model was used to simulate parameters related to vine physiology such as phenology, leaf area index, yield indices, and water and nitrogen stress indices. The researchers concluded that future climate change should result in climate suitability for grapevines being extended to 55°N, allowing development of new wine-producing areas (Fraga et al. 2016).

Although there was much regional variability, future projections suggest that the timing of phenological events such as budburst, flowering, véraison, and harvest will be advanced significantly, in some cases by more than a month (Fraga et al. 2016) (Figure 5.11).

These studies, based specifically on climate simulations, suggest that fairly 'brutal' methods are needed for viticulture to adapt to climate change, including moving wine-growing regions or changing grape varieties. However, most previous studies of the impact of climate change have addressed the problem only from a global perspective, without taking into account the spatial variability of climate that occurs at much finer scales within vineyard regions. At the scale of a vineyard region, variations in atmospheric parameters can be very significant over relatively small areas

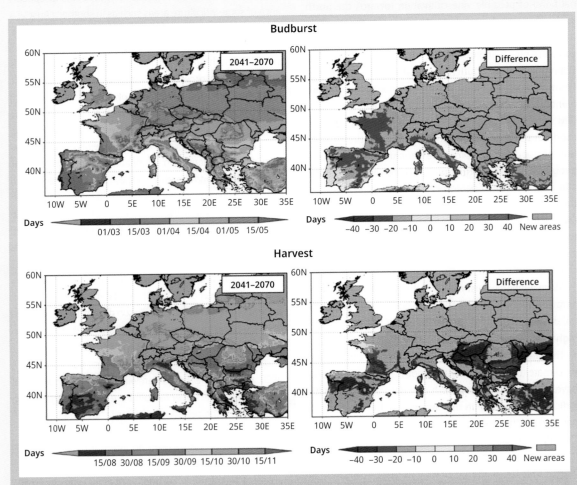

FIGURE 5.11 STICS crop model simulations for the timings of grapevine budburst and harvest over Europe (2041–2070), along with the respective differences from the recent past (1980–2005)

Source: Fraga et al. (2016). Modelling climate change impacts on viticultural yield, phenology and stress conditions in Europe. *Global Change Biology* 22: 3774–88

(from a few kilometres to a few metres) and the quality of the grapes or wine is often related to local characteristics (e.g. altitude, slope angle and aspect, or soil).

CLIMATE VARIABILITY AT VINEYARD SCALE

Local factors (e.g. slope, exposure, altitude, type of soil, distance from the sea, etc.) cause climate variations that can be greater than climate variability predicted at a larger scale (as discussed in Chapter 2). This spatio-temporal variability of climate, combined with the inter-linking of scales (from macro- to microclimate), often provides the optimal conditions required for the cultivation of different grape varieties and characterizes the unique-ness of a wine-growing terroir. The consequences of cli-mate change therefore need to be investigated at a fine scale, taking into account the characteristics of the land and the skills of the viticulturists and winemakers. This would allow a better anticipation of possible economic and social consequences than relying on more general-ized scenarios based solely on global-scale predictions.

To address this aim, regional climate models (RCMs) with a spatial resolution of 1 km to a few hundred metres have been used to investigate the climate in wine-growing regions in Burgundy (Xu et al. 2012), South Africa (Soltan-zadeh et al. 2017), and New Zealand (Sturman et al. 2017). However, the use of RCMs requires powerful computing resources to enable the development of future climate change scenarios at very fine scales.

The application of geostatistical methods to investigate climate variability at very fine spatial scales using the out-puts of RCMs enables the influence of local factors to be taken into account without the need for high-performance computers. In Chapter 2, Figure 2.22 illustrates how climate change modelling and climate analysis can be merged at fine scales to develop adaptation strategies and support decision-making. This approach to integrating local-scale spatial climate variability into regional climate models has been applied to several European vineyards. The spatial resolution of a few tens of metres allows the winegrow-ers to be provided with information adapted to the scale of their vineyards. The very high spatial variability of the climate due to local effects would more clearly identify the sections of the landscape that are more or less favour-able for quality viticulture. For example, regional-scale modelling of bioclimatic indices according to the RCP8.5

scenario ('business-as-usual' leading to highest green-house gas emissions) in 2100 has shown unfavourable changes for the Saint-Émilion wine region, corresponding to over-ripe conditions that are unfavourable for the pro-duction of quality wines from the current grape varieties. However, when examined at a much finer scale, the high spatial variability of the Saint-Émilion area would still pro-vide favourable conditions in the coolest parts of the re-gion, such as the northern section, but also provide them on the lower slopes of the vineyards (Figure 2.22).

ADAPTATION FOR VINE AND WINE

The ability of vineyards to adapt to climate change is crit-ical as the grapevine, unlike annual crops, is planted for several decades and the choice of variety must be adapted as soon as possible to both current and expected future climate conditions. Available adaptation methods used in viticulture vary depending on the intensity of climate change, but can loosely be divided into short-term and long-term responses (Figure 5.12). Climate simulations undertaken at a regional scale, combined with knowledge of local climates, make it possible to define various sce-narios of grapevine adaptability to climate change at dif-ferent spatial and temporal scales. For example, climate projections at a regional level predict significant changes in the location of vineyard areas over the long term (2070–2100), and the adaptation strategies recommended are fairly 'brutal', as indicated under long-term responses in Figure 5.12. They mark a break with existing wine-growing systems, and include changes in the vine population, tech-nological developments (e.g. irrigation), and, ultimately, modification of the world atlas of wine as we know it.

Given the many uncertainties about future climate change (described in Chapter 2), a good knowledge of the local environment can help in defining appropriate adaptation methods. The significant spatial variability of climate over very small areas is similar to, if not higher than, the rise in temperature simulated in IPCC scenar-ios. Winemakers know how to adapt to spatial climate variability, notably through their growing practices, such as those indicated under short-term responses in Figure 5.12. However, prior knowledge of climate varia-bility at fine spatial scales in vineyard regions is a major advantage when developing ways of adapting to climate change over the medium to long term.

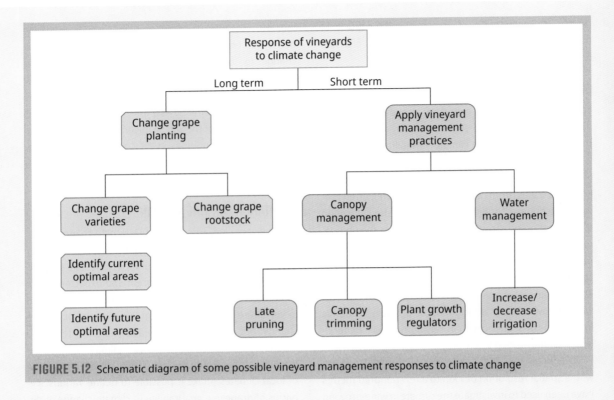

FIGURE 5.12 Schematic diagram of some possible vineyard management responses to climate change

In the short and medium term, detailed knowledge of the climate and of the consequences of climate change for viticulture help development of climate change adaptation methods based on changes in viticultural techniques (e.g. soil and plant management) and oenological practices (e.g. winemaking and the management of the wine's alcohol content). Regular review of agricultural practices allows a more measured response to the impact of climate change over the short and medium term, so as to prepare for bigger changes in the longer term should warming become too intense. 'These adaptations in practices aim to preserve existing production areas and the varietals that are grown there without changing the respective proportions or the quality and character of the wines produced' (Barbeau et al. 2015, p. 72). As a result, improving knowledge of climate–viticulture relationships at such a fine scale allows the development of a range of vineyard management responses to be applied more gradually as the extent of climate change intensifies (Neethling et al. 2017).

This approach based on the derivation of agroclimatic indicators or the application of crop models using regional or local projections of future climate can be applied to a range of crops. A general framework can therefore be developed for predicting future crop production, as shown in Figure 5.13 (Roudier et al. 2011). Many studies are being carried out using such techniques in vulnerable regions where there is an urgent need to better understand the impact of climate change on crop yields. In West Africa, for example, regional simulations based on different scenarios have predicted yield losses for the main crops such as sorghum and millet. Simulations from crop models have allowed the identification of potential adaptation strategies involving adjustment of cropping systems such as changing varieties, modifying sowing dates and densities, using irrigation, or through fertilizer management (Sultan and Gaetani 2016).

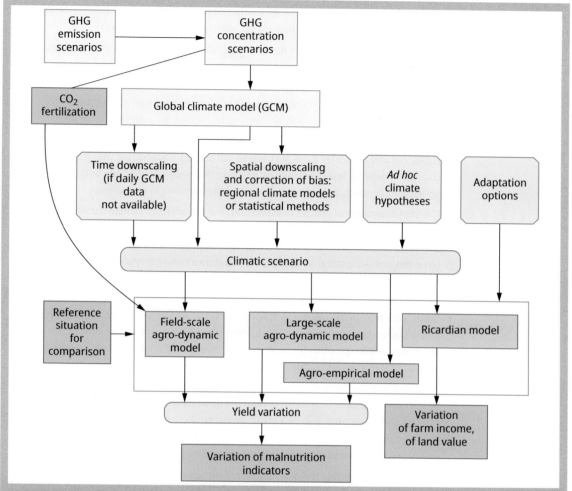

FIGURE 5.13 Outline of a working approach for investigating the impacts of climate change on crop yields. GHG—greenhouse gas

Source: Roudier et al. (2011). The impact of future climate change on West African crop yields: What does the recent literature say? *Global Environmental Change* 21: 1073–83

Summary

- The relationship between climate and agricultural systems is complex. Climate changes can have an impact on agriculture, but changing farming practices and the crops grown in response to climate change, and other factors (e.g. commercial/economic factors), can also impact on climate feedback processes.

- The sensitivity of the primary biological industries differs according to crop types (perennial or annual), species and varieties, and climate variables. There is a need to establish optimal climatic conditions for agricultural production more clearly by calculating indicators (e.g. bioclimatic indices) to estimate the current and future impacts of climate change.

- The impacts of climate change on agriculture can be both direct (e.g. through climate risks such as droughts) and indirect (e.g. via the emergence of new diseases).

- It is evident that climate change has both positive and negative impacts on agriculture depending on such things as crop type, latitudinal location, and the socio-economic situation in different parts of the world.

- As a result of the previous point, the impact of climate change on agriculture is very different from one region to another, with some regions deriving significant benefits and others potentially suffering negative effects.

- Equatorial and tropical regions are likely to suffer most from current trends in climate change. In general, less developed countries in these regions are more dependent on agricultural production, and could face significant declines in crop yields.

- The implementation of policies to assess and limit the effects of climate change is a complex task. Food security for all people must be ensured as a priority. However, agriculture, deforestation, and other land-use changes are responsible for more than 20% of greenhouse gas emissions. Adaptation policies should therefore also be integrated with mitigation activities, taking into account differences in vulnerability between different parts of the world. Finding innovative solutions (e.g. smart agriculture) will require political and financial support.

- Social, economic, and environmental policy reforms are needed to strengthen farmers' incentives to achieve sustainable productivity growth while achieving climate change mitigation and adaptation objectives. Further investment in research and development is needed to stimulate innovation in climate-friendly sustainable agriculture.

- Any change in the global climate will have regional and local repercussions and will have an impact on agriculture in terms of both the quantity and quality of products produced. Attempts have been made to downscale model predictions of future global climate to a local spatial scale by coupling larger-scale climate models with regional- and local-scale models specifically designed to simulate finer-scale climate variability.

- A multiscale approach to the development of climate change adaptation strategies is being applied in agriculture, especially in the wine sector. This approach enables the development of rational adaptation strategies based on global climate change scenarios downscaled to the regional and local scales, and incorporating traditional farming practices. Such adaptation strategies are more or less constrained depending on the rate of climate change and the timescale (short, medium, and long term) of the required response.

For case studies and updates, visit the online resources
www.oup.com/he/sturman-quenol1e

References

Al-Tamimi, H. J. (2005). Effect of solar radiation on thermo-physiological and growth parameters of indigenous black bedwin goat kids in Southern Jordan. *Journal of Biological Science* 5: 724–8.

Amerine, M. A., and Winkler, A. J. (1944). Composition and quality of musts and wines of California grapes. *Hilgardia* 15: 493–675.

Amundson, J., Mader, T. L., Rasby, R. J., and Hu, Q. S. (2006). Environmental effects on pregnancy rate in beef cattle. *Journal of Animal Science* 84: 3415–20.

Barbeau, G., Neethling, E., Ollat, N., Quénol, H., and Touzard, J. M. (2015). Adapting to climate change in grapevine agronomy. *Agronomie, Environnement et Sociétés* 5: 67–75.

Baylis, M., Caminade, C., Turner, J., and Jones, A. E. (2017). The role of climate change in a developing threat: The case of bluetongue in Europe. *Revue Scientifique et Technique (Office Internationale des Epizooties)* 36: 467–78.

Ben-Ari, T., Boé, J., Ciais, P., Lecerf, R., Van der Velde, M., and Makowski, D. (2018). Causes and implications of the unforeseen 2016 extreme yield loss in the breadbasket of France. *Nature Communications* 9: 1627.

Buffington, D. E., Collazo-Arocho, A., Canton, G. H., Pitt, D., Thatcher, W. W., and Collier, R. J. (1981). Black Globe-Humidity Index (BGHI) as comfort equation for dairy cows. *Transactions of the ASAE* 24: 711–14.

Cho, Y. Y., Bae, J. H., and Son, J. E. (2008). Use of parabolic function to calculate cardinal temperatures in pak-choi (*Brassica campestris* ssp. *chinensis*). *Horticulture, Environment and Biotechnology* 49: 145–148.

Cline, W. (2008). Global warming and agriculture. *Finance and Development*, March, 23–7.

Crimp, S. J., Zheng, B., Khimashia, N., Gobbett, D. L., Chapman, S., Howden, M., and Nicholls, N. (2016). Recent changes in southern Australian frost occurrence: Implications for wheat production risk. *Crop and Pasture Science* 67: 801–11.

Delay, E., Piou, C., and Quénol, H. (2015). The mountain environment, a driver for adaptation to climate change. *Land Use Policy* 48: 51–2.

Dokoozlian, N. K. (1999). Chilling temperature and duration interact on the budbreak of 'Perlette' grapevine cuttings. *Hortscience* 34: 1054–6.

Fanish, S. A., and Priya, R. S. (2013). Review on benefits of agro forestry system. *International Journal of Education and Research* 1: 1–12.

Fraga, H., García de Cortázar Atauri, I., Malheiro, A. C., and Santos, J. A. (2016). Modelling climate change impacts on viticultural yield, phenology and stress conditions in Europe. *Global Change Biology* 22: 3774–88.

FAO (2010). *'Climate-Smart' Agriculture: Policies, Practices and Financing for Food Security, Adaptation and Mitigation*. Food and Agriculture Organization, Rome.

FAO (2016). *The State of Food and Agriculture 2016 (SOFA): Climate Change, Agriculture and Food Security*. Food and Agriculture Organization, Rome.

Gaughan, J. B., Holt, S. M., Mader, T. L., and Lisle, A. (2008). A new heat load index for feedlot cattle. *Journal of Animal Science* 86: 226–34.

Goodger, R. A. (2013). *Cardinal Temperatures and Vernalisation Requirements for a Selection of Vegetables for Seed Production*. Bachelor of Agricultural Science dissertation, Lincoln University.

Gornall, J., Betts, R., Burke, E., Clark, R., Camp, J., Willett, K., and Wiltshire, A. (2010). Implications of climate change for agricultural productivity in the early twenty-first century. *Philosophical Transactions of the Royal Society B: Biological Sciences* 365: 2973–89.

Guis, H., Caminade, C., Calvete, C., Morse, A. P., Tran, A., and Baylis, M. (2011). Modelling the effects of past and future climate on the risk of bluetongue emergence in Europe. *Journal of the Royal Society Interface* 9: 339–50.

Hannah, L., Roehrdanz, P. R., Ikegami, M., Shepard, A. V., Shaw, M. R., Tabor, G., Zhi, L., Marquet, P. A. and Hijmans, R. J. (2013). Climate change, wine, and conservation. *Proceedings of the National Academy of Sciences* 110: 6907–12.

Hatfield, J., Takle, G., Grotjahn, R., Holden, P., Izaurralde, R. C., Mader, T., Marshall, E., and Liverman, D. (2014). *Agriculture*. In: Melillo, J. M., Richmond, T. C., and Yohe, G. W. (eds), *Climate Change Impacts in the United States: The Third National Climate Assessment*. US Global Change Research Program, Washington, DC, pp. 150–74.

Hirschi, M., Stoeckli, S., Dubrovsky, M., Spirig, C., Calanca, P., Rotach, M. W., Fischer, A. M., Duffy, B., and Samietz, J. (2012). Downscaling climate change scenarios for apple pest and disease modeling in Switzerland. *Earth System Dynamics* 3: 33–47.

Huglin, P. (1978). Nouveau mode d'évaluation des possibilités héliothermiques d'un milieu viticole. *Comptes-rendus de l'Académie d'Agriculture de France* 64: 1117–26.

IPCC (2022). *Climate Change 2022: Impacts, Adaptation, and Vulnerability.* Contribution of Working Group II to the Sixth Assessment Report of the Intergovernmental Panel on Climate Change (H.-O. Pörtner, D. C. Roberts, M. Tignor, E. S. Poloczanska, K. Mintenbeck, A. Alegría, M. Craig, S. Langsdorf, S. Löschke, V. Möller, A. Okem, B. Rama (eds)). Cambridge University Press, Cambridge.

Jones, G. V. (2006). *Climate and terroir: Impacts of climate variability and change on wine.* In: Macqueen, R. W., and Meinert, L. D. (eds), *Fine Wine and Terroir: The Geoscience Perspective*. Geoscience Canada Reprint Series Number 9. Geological Association of Canada, St. John's, Newfoundland, pp. 203–16.

Lee, J., De Gryze, S., and Six, J. (2011). Effect of climate change on field crop production in California's Central Valley. *Climatic Change* 109 (Suppl. 1), S335–53.

Lipper, L., Thornton, P., Campbell, B. M., Baedeker, T., Braimoh, A., Bwalya, M., Caron, P., Cattaneo, A., Garrity, D., Henry, K., Hottle, R., Jackson, L., Jarvis, A., Kossam, F., Mann, W., McCarthy, N., Meybeck, A., Neufeldt, H., Remington, T., Sen, P. T., Sessa, R., Shula, R., Tibu, A., and Torquebiau, E. F. (2014). Climate-smart agriculture for food security. *Nature Climate Change* 4: 1068–72.

Luedeling, E., Zhang, M., and Girvetz, E. H. (2009). Climatic changes lead to declining winter chill for fruit and nut trees in California during 1950–2099. *PLoS ONE* 4: e6166.

Motha, R. P. (2011). The impact of extreme weather events on agriculture in the United States. USDA-ARS/UNL Faculty, no. 1311. http://digitalcommons.unl.edu/usdaarsfacpub/1311.

Neethling, E., Petitjean, T., Quénol, H., and Barbeau, G. (2017). Assessing local climate vulnerability and winegrowers' adaptive processes in the context of climate change. *Mitigation and Adaptation Strategies for Global Change* 22: 777–803.

Papusoi, I., and Faraby, J. A. (2013). Climate smart agriculture. Seminar on Climate Change and Risk Management, 6 May. https://www.slideshare.net/jimalfaraby/climate-smart-agriculture-20675751.

Parker, A. K., García de Cortázar-Atauri, I., Chuine, I., Barbeau, G., Bois, B., Boursiquot, J.-M., Cahurel, J.-Y., Claverie, M., Dufourcq, T., Gény, L., Guimberteau, G., Hofmann, R. W., Jacquet, O., Lacombe, T., Monamy, C., Ojeda, H., Panigai, L., Payan, J.-C., Rodriquez Lovelle, B., Rouchaud, E., Schneider, C., Spring, J.-L., Storchi, P., Tomasi, D., Trambouze, W., Trought, M., and van Leeuwen, C. (2013). Classification of varieties for their timing of flowering and veraison using a modelling approach: A case study for the grapevine species *Vitis vinifera* L. *Agricultural and Forest Meteorology* 180: 249–64.

Roudier, P., Sultan, B., Quirion, P., and Berg, A. (2011). The impact of future climate change on West African crop yields: What does the recent literature say? *Global Environmental Change* 21: 1073–83.

Scheelbeek, P. F., Bird, F. A., Tuomisto, H. L., Green, R., Harris, F. B., Joy, E. J., Chalabi, Z., Allen, E., Haines, A., and Dangour, A. D. (2018). Effect of environmental changes on vegetable and legume yields and nutritional quality. *Proceedings of the National Academy of Sciences* 115: 6804–9.

Schleussner, C.-F., Lissner, T. K., Fischer, E. M., Wohland, J., Perrette, M., Golly, A., Rogelj, J., Childers, K., Schewe, J., Frieler, K., Mengel, M., Hare, W., and Schaeffer, M. (2016). Differential climate impacts for policy-relevant limits to global warming: The case of 1.5 °C and 2 °C. *Earth System Dynamics* 7: 327–51.

Sejian, V., Valtorta, S., Gallardo, M., and Singh, A. K. (2012). Ameliorative measures to counteract environmental stresses. In: Sejian, V., Naqvi, S. M. K., Ezeji, T., Lakrtitz, J., and Lal, R. (eds), *Environmental Stress and Amelioration in Livestock Production*. Springer, Dordrecht, pp. 153–80.

Sgubin, G., Swingedouw, D., Dayon, G., de Cortázar-Atauri, I. G., Ollat, N., Pagé, C., and van Leeuwen, C. (2018). The risk of tardive frost damage in French vineyards in a changing climate. *Agricultural and Forest Meteorology* 250: 226–42.

Slavin, P. (2016). Climate and famines: A historical reassessment. *Wiley Interdisciplinary Reviews: Climate Change* 7: 433–47.

Soltanzadeh, I., Bonnardot, V., Sturman, A., Quénol, H., and Zawar-Reza, P. (2017). Assessment of the ARW-WRF model over complex terrain: The case of the Stellenbosch Wine of Origin district of South Africa. *Theoretical and Applied Climatology* 129: 1407–27.

Sturman, A., and Quénol, H. (2013) Changes in atmospheric circulation and temperature trends in major vineyard regions of New Zealand. *International Journal of Climatology* 33: 2609–21.

Sturman, A., Zawar-Reza, P., Soltanzadeh, I., Katurji, M., Bonnardot V., Parker, A., Trought, M., Quénol, H., Le Roux, R., Gendig, E., and Schulmann, T. (2017). The application of high-resolution atmospheric modelling to weather and climate variability in vineyard regions. *Oeno One* 51, 99–105.

Sultan, B., & Gaetani, M. (2016). Agriculture in West Africa in the twenty-first century: Climate change and impacts scenarios, and potential for adaptation. *Frontiers in Plant Science* 7: 1262.

Tao, X., and Xin, H. (2003) *Temperature-Humidity-Velocity Index for Market-Size Broilers*. Paper No. 034037. American Society of Agricultural and Biological Engineers, St Joseph, Michigan.

Tonietto, J. 1999 *Les macroclimats viticoles mondiaux et l'influence du mésoclimat sur la typicité de la Syrah et du Muscat de Hambourg dans le sud de la France: Méthodologiede cáractérisation*. Thèse Doctorat, École Nationale Supérieure Agronomique, Montpellier.

Tonietto, J., and Carbonneau, A. (2004). A multicriteria climatic classification system for grape-growing regions worldwide. *Agricultural and Forest Meteorology* 124: 81–97.

Toppo, P., and Raj, A. (2018). Role of agroforestry in climate change mitigation. *Journal of Pharmacognosy and Phytochemistry* 7: 241–3.

Torquebiau, E., Berry, D., Caron, P., and Grosclaude, J. Y. (2016). New research perspectives to address climate challenges facing agriculture worldwide. In: Torquebiau E. (ed.) *Climate Change and Agriculture Worldwide*. Springer, Dordrecht, pp. 337–48.

USGCRP (2009). *Global Climate Change Impacts in the United States: 2009 Report*. US Global Change Research Program, Washington, DC. https://nca2009.globalchange.gov/agriculture/index.html.

van Leeuwen, C., Schultz, H. R., Garcia de Cortazar-Atauri, I., Duchêne, E., Ollat, N., Pieri, P., Bois, B., Goutouly, J. P., Quénol, H., Touzard, J.-M., Malheiro, A. C., Bavarescok, L., and Delrot, S. (2013). Why climate change will not dramatically decrease viticultural suitability in main wine producing areas by 2050. *Proceedings of the National Academy of Sciences* 110: E3051–2.

Vautard, R., van Oldenborgh, G. J., Bonnet, R., Li, S., Robin, Y., Kew, S., Philip, S., Soubeyroux, J.-M., Dubuisson, B., Viovy, N., Reichstein, M., and Otto, F. (2023). Human influence on growing period frosts like the early April 2021 in central France. *Natural Hazards and Earth System Sciences* 23: 1045–58.

Winkler, A. J., Cook, J. A., Kliewer, W. M., and Lider, L. A. (1974). *General Viticulture*, 4th edition. University of California Press, Berkeley.

Xu, Y., Castel, T., Richard, Y., Cuccia, C., and Bois, B. (2012). Burgundy regional climate change and its potential impact on grapevines. *Climate Dynamics* 39: 1613–26.

Yohannes, H. (2016). A review on the relationship between climate change and agriculture. *Journal of Earth Science and Climate Change* 7: 335.

CHAPTER SIX

Natural Ecosystems

LEARNING OUTCOMES

Having read this chapter, you should be able to:

- describe the complex relationship between climate change and natural ecosystems

- discuss the approaches to and difficulties of assessing the impacts of climate change on natural ecosystems

- contrast and compare climate change impacts on forest and grassland ecosystems at the global to regional scale

- evaluate possible impacts of climate change on freshwater, coastal, and marine ecosystems

- identify the key threats to mountain, alpine, and polar ecosystems posed by climate change

- explain the likely impact of climate change on arid and semi-arid ecosystems

- outline possible options to help natural ecosystems respond to climate change and problems that may arise

6.1 Introduction: climate change and natural ecosystems

From a human perspective, **natural ecosystems** provide a range of benefits, including clean air and water, a source of food and materials (e.g. through hunting, fishing, and the gathering of wood and vegetation), and recreation and cultural identity. However, it has long been recognized that climate has a fundamental control on the distribution of natural ecosystems on planet Earth through its influence on key environmental processes, although it should be acknowledged at the outset that climate change is only one factor currently having a detrimental effect on natural ecosystems. Other factors include expansion of agricultural land to feed an ever-growing global population, and increasing pollution and disposal of waste into both terrestrial and aquatic ecosystems (Maxwell et al. 2016).

Climate influences both the thermal and moisture regimes of ecosystems, which affect their structure and function. The increased ambient carbon dioxide (CO_2) concentrations resulting from fossil-fuel emissions are also considered to have potential impacts on a range of organisms, with different species responding in different ways to elevated CO_2 concentrations. Evidence suggests that natural ecosystems can adapt to small and gradual changes in climate, but can be significantly disrupted by larger and more rapid changes. However, the complexity of ecosystem processes makes it difficult to predict accurately the effects of current and future climate change on specific ecosystems and biological communities at regional and local scales.

As with other parts of the global environment described in earlier chapters, climate change can have significant impacts on terrestrial, marine, and freshwater ecosystems (Figure 6.1), although, as mentioned above, the nature of its effect is often complex and difficult to identify. The shifting range of different organisms is one of the most recognized impacts of global warming and about 50% of species have been affected over recent decades. 'With current pledges, corresponding to ~3.2°C warming, climatically determined geographic range losses of >50% are projected in ~49% of insects, 44% of plants, and 26% of vertebrates' (Warren et al. 2018, Abstract, lines 3–5). This effect involves changes in the spatial distribution of animal, plant, and insect species, resulting in movement of land-based organisms to higher latitude and altitude under a warming climate. There is some evidence of poleward movement across North America, as well as altitude shifts in the major mountain regions of the world, such as the Andes and the Himalayas. For example, Roberts et al. (2019) identified a northward shift in bird communities of between 250 and 500 km across the North American Great Plains region based on almost 50 years of observations, although climate change was considered to be only one of several anthropogenic causes.

However, plants are not able to move as quickly as animals, creating a time–space phase lag that can cause a disconnect between different parts of the ecosystem, leading to significant stress. For instance, grazing animals could move relatively quickly to cooler regions in response to a warming climate, but their food source may take a much longer time to move, resulting in a lack of food and potential starvation for the animals unless they can adapt to a different food source. There is also the problem created when organisms reach barriers or limits to their range—for example, when migrating animals reach the edges of islands and continents or the tops of mountains. Similarly, warming of enclosed water bodies and river systems can leave some freshwater fish unable to survive, as they have limited options to migrate. It should also be noted that some species can survive in a much wider range of climate conditions (e.g. temperature and moisture) than others, so that they are less affected by changes in climate.

Range shifts can be made more complicated by other processes such as changes in wildfire regimes, particularly an increase in the frequency and intensity of fires, which

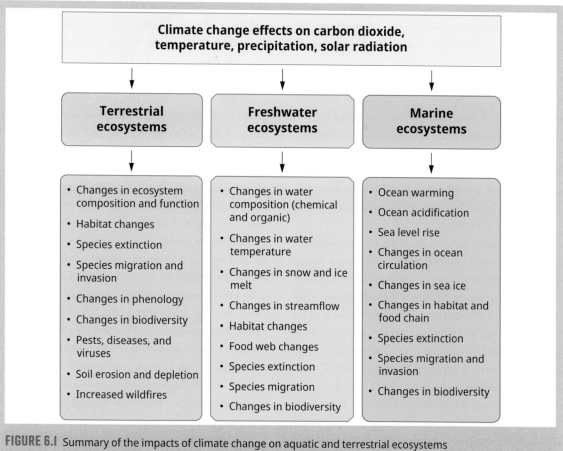

FIGURE 6.1 Summary of the impacts of climate change on aquatic and terrestrial ecosystems

Source: adapted from Häder, D.-P. and Barnes, P. W. (2019). Comparing the impacts of climate change on the responses and linkages between terrestrial and aquatic ecosystems. *Science of the Total Environment* 682: 239–46

can have devastating effects on both flora and fauna. Recent examples have occurred in North America, Australia, and Russia, while it is estimated that a global increase in wildfire frequency of around 30% by 2100 could be possible. In addition to their role in contributing to carbon loss from vegetation into the atmosphere, wildfires have dual impacts on animal species, first through animal mortality, and second through their effect on food supply.

It is also evident that changes in the timing of key phenological phases or seasonal cycles can occur in response to the global warming trend, with advances in spring timing of many species being noticed. As mentioned in Chapter 5, phenology is the study of plant or animal responses to environmental stimuli, including the seasonal cycles of germination, budburst, flowering, and fruit ripening of plants; and the migration, mating, nesting, and reproduction of insects, animals, and birds, and spawning of fish. The chilling requirements of specific plants may not be met in a warming climate, which can affect the timing of plant development as well as fruit production and future viability of particular plants. Recent evidence suggests that for some species range shifts have allowed them to adapt successfully to a changing climate, while phenological changes of other species in some regions have allowed them to adapt to a warmer climate without the need for moving to a new location. Many of the impacts of a changing climate are therefore quite subtle and regionally variable, such as minor changes in the timing of seasonal life cycle events. However, synchronicity of the timing of events between different organisms may also change in response to climate change, resulting in food web disruptions caused by changes in ecosystem composition and function, thereby impacting on the composition of biological communities (i.e. their **biodiversity**), including the possible creation of completely new ones. Such changes may be significant and affect the resilience of ecosystems to change, but there is general agreement that any genetic changes within ecosystems are unlikely to prevent a given species becoming extinct because of the slowness of the processes involved.

Climate change-induced increases in the occurrence of extreme weather events are thought to have a greater impact on natural ecosystems than more gradual climate change, although it is ultimately a combination of the two trends that is important. This is particularly so for the main marine, terrestrial, and freshwater ecosystems. There may also be threshold effects, such as the impact of tipping points—a tipping point being reached when an ecosystem is disturbed so much by changing environmental conditions that it abruptly changes irreversibly to a new ecological state (e.g. changing from savannah grassland to desert, or through eutrophication or drying up of lakes) (see Chapter 1 for a full definition). In such situations, biodiversity and **ecosystem services** can be severely impacted, resulting in widespread species extinctions.

Indirect effects of a warming climate are also evident, such as changes in the range of specific pests and diseases, including insect vectors, parasites, and pathogens. For example, warmer temperatures are thought to have caused increased infestation of forests by pests such as beetles and moths that can cause substantial damage to trees, while human and animal disease vectors such as mosquitoes appear to be moving into new areas. Not only has there been a shift of such pests into previously cooler areas, but also a longer growing season is thought to have exacerbated their impact. There is also the risk of climate change causing biodiversity decline with consequent effects on the development of viruses (e.g. Ebola, SARS, avian flu, and COVID-19). For example, climate change has contributed to the shift to higher altitudes and latitudes of ticks that are a vector of Lyme borreliosis and tick-borne encephalitis. The same phenomenon is observed in Europe with the expansion of vectors that transmit diseases such as Zika, dengue, and Chikungunya (Semenza and Suk 2018).

Clearly, environmental processes are complex, which makes it difficult to predict exactly how any given ecosystem will respond to climate change. Negative feedback effects may be able to maintain natural ecosystems in a relatively steady state, but significant climate change can result in irreversible change if a tipping point is reached. If this occurs, the biodiversity of ecosystems can be severely affected and extinction rates could be high for species that are unable to adapt or move quickly enough to other regions with a more suitable climate (Radchuk et al. 2019). Figure 6.2 illustrates the combined effect of long-term climate variability resulting from such periodic processes as sunspot cycles, short-term weather variability that is more random, and the global warming trend on the future viability of species within a natural ecosystem. In this example, the impact of the weather experienced on the population size of a single species is considered to reflect effects on the health of the entire ecosystem.

It is increasingly apparent that potential effects of climate change on biodiversity and the extinction of plants and animals vary significantly between different species in different natural ecosystems. Figure 6.3 provides an indication of the threat of extinction faced by a selection of species, although this threat is not just from a changing climate. It is also evident that there is considerable uncertainty regarding the current status of many species and their risk of extinction, as the environmental processes involved are not fully understood and it is often difficult to separate effects of climate change from other non-climate factors, such as the introduction of **exotic** predator or competing species, land-use change associated with population pressure, and over-exploitation of natural resources. The effect of climate change on predator–prey relationships in relation to other ecosystem processes is similarly complex and difficult to predict. Mammalian predators tend to be less affected by temperature change than by change in food supply, although warmer winters help to extend the breeding season of some species.

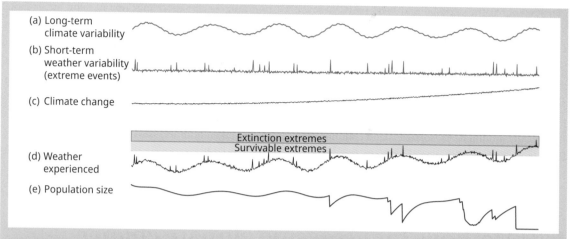

FIGURE 6.2 A schematic illustration of the combined effect of (a) long-term climate variability, (b) short-term extreme weather events, and (c) a global warming trend on (d) the weather experienced, and (e) its impact on the population of a single species within a natural ecosystem

Source: Harris et al. (2018). Biological responses to the press and pulse of climate trends and extreme events. *Nature Climate Change* 8: 579–87

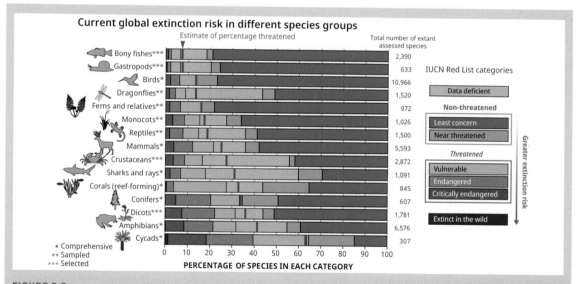

FIGURE 6.3 Selective assessment of the likelihood of extinction of a variety of species from a range of natural ecosystems

Source: IPBES (2019). *Summary for Policymakers of the Global Assessment Report on Biodiversity and Ecosystem Services of the Intergovernmental Science-Policy Platform on Biodiversity and Ecosystem Services.* Díaz, S., Settele, J., Brondízio E. S., Ngo, H. T., Guèze, M., Agard, J., Arneth, A., Balvanera, P., Brauman, K. A., Butchart, S. H. M., Chan, K. M. A., Garibaldi, L. A., Ichii, K., Liu, J., Subramanian, S. M., Midgley, G. F., Miloslavich, P., Molnár, Z., Obura, D., Pfaff, A., Polasky, S., Purvis, A., Razzaque, J., Reyers, B., Roy Chowdhury, R., Shin, Y. J., Visseren-Hamakers, I. J., Willis, K. J., and Zayas, C. N. (eds). IPBES Secretariat, Bonn

It should also be recognized that climate change will affect different parts of the world at varying rates, with more oceanic areas responding more slowly to the global warming trend. Ecosystems located in such regions will therefore have more time to adapt compared to the more rapid response needed in continental regions.

As with other components of the global environment described in earlier chapters, climate change can have significant impacts on biodiversity that vary considerably at the regional and local scales because of the complexity of the Earth's surface characteristics, including the location of major water bodies and the terrain. The fragmentation of natural ecosystems also creates problems in relation to future climate change, as they become cut off from similar areas often by landscapes that have been strongly anthropogenically modified. As isolated island communities, there is no pathway for species to move to new areas (Macinnis-Ng et al. 2021). Development of strategies to minimize climate change impacts and help adaptation of the natural environment must therefore consider the unique characteristics of specific ecosystems (e.g. coral reef systems, temperate forest and grassland communities, alpine and polar regions, or subtropical rainforest) as well as the people who rely on them. The following sections describe approaches that can be taken both to assess impacts of climate change and to establish response strategies, using major natural ecosystem types as case studies.

6.2 Methods for assessing climate change effects on natural ecosystems

Assessing the impacts of future changes on biodiversity is complex because it requires an approach that takes into account the interaction of spatial and temporal scales, but above all allows for the integration of factors other than climate, such as changes in land use related to different human activities. One of the major difficulties is to be able to assess the contribution of climate impacts relative to other disturbing factors.

On a large scale, climate zones are characterized by specific ecosystems. A classification of global ecosystem characteristics is described in Keith et al. (2022), including the main **biomes** discussed in this chapter. Studies based on the analysis of long series of past data (e.g. pollen deposition and tree rings) highlight the close connection between climate and ecosystems. Global climate modelling shows that climate change will have significant impacts on the distribution of ecosystems over a large part of the planet (Cramer and Leemans 1993; Pauly and Christensen 1995). Large-scale predictions of future climate involve the coupling of global climate change models, representing the effects of varying CO_2 levels, with large-scale ecosystem models. This work, first carried out in the early 2000s, made it possible to assess the impact of climate change on ecosystems over large areas, but without taking into account the spatial and temporal variability of land use at finer scales.

Assessment of impacts of future climate change on ecosystems requires a multimodel approach (e.g. involving both climate and species distribution models) that includes effects of a range of environmental parameters (Leemans and Eickhout 2004). Recent increases in computing capacity have improved the quality and resolution of models for assessing the effects of climate change on natural ecosystems.

In order to model the impact of future climate on species and whole ecosystems, a preliminary step is to acquire observed data sets. The objective of evolutionary observation methods is to analyse the spatial and temporal evolution of species in response to climatic parameters. Figure 6.4 illustrates the shift of plants to higher latitudes and altitudes in France in response to the observed increase in temperature. Lenoir et al. (2008) conducted a study comparing the altitudinal distribution of 171 forest plant species between the periods 1905–1985 and 1986–2005 in western Europe. The results showed 'that climate warming has resulted in a significant upward shift in species optimum elevation averaging 29 meters per decade' (Lenoir et al. 2008, p. 1768). Wiens (2016) analysed the impacts of a range shift associated with climate change on 976 plant and animal species. Figure 6.5 shows the theoretical shift of species associated with climate change.

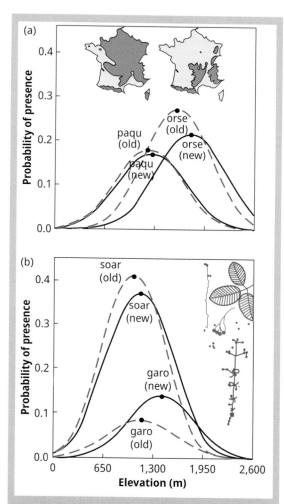

FIGURE 6.4 Examples of western European plant distributions that have shifted upwards. Elevational response curves were derived using logistic regression models for the periods 1905–1985 (dashed lines) and 1986–2005 (solid lines) for: (a) two species according to geographic distribution patterns—of ubiquitous *P. quadrifolia* (paqu—left map) and mountainous *O. secunda* (orse—right map), and (b) two species according to life form—grassy *G. rotundifolium* (garo) and woody *S. aria* (soar)

Source: Lenoir et al. (2008). A significant upward shift in plant species optimum elevation during the 20th century. *Science* 320(5884): 1768–71

The red dots correspond to locations just outside of the 'warm' limit of the species' range and thus exposed to the possibility of local extinction of the original species. The results showed that recent local extinctions linked to climate change have already occurred for many species around the world: 47% of the species studied have experienced local extinctions. These extinctions are present in all climate zones and habitats, but are greatest in tropical regions, for animal species, and in freshwater habitats (Figure 6.6).

Evolutionary observations are essential to build up biological response databases and are the basis of models of the distribution of species in relation to climatic parameters. However, it is difficult to differentiate precisely the climatic influence from other factors (e.g. changes in land use and environmental pollution). The biases are especially important as the timescales are long and the spatial scales are fine. Using a similar approach, but incorporating land-use change analysis, Bodin et al. (2013) showed that changes in forest structure masked the altitude shift response to climate change. In conclusion, their study recommended that forest dynamics, one of several causes of vegetation change, should be better accounted for in evolutionary observation methods in order to deduce more accurately the effects of climate parameters. This type of approach would allow species distribution models to be constructed based on both landscape elements and climate factors. Coupled with different future climate-modelled scenarios, these species models could then be used to improve simulation of the impact of climate change on biodiversity. For example, Miranda et al. (2019) combined avian species data with regionalized climate change projections to simulate impacts on the Amazon rainforest. These simulations considered several parameters such as 'range shifts, species loss, vulnerability of ecosystem functioning, future effectiveness of current protected areas and potential climatically stable areas for conservation actions'. At the study site, the authors estimated that between 4 and 19% of species will not find suitable habitat and that the loss of species could be more than 70%. These results showed a high spatial variability of impacts on different species depending on land-use and climate change scenarios. This approach and the information provided are essential for planning adaptation actions (Figure 6.7).

Specific experiments (*in situ* and *ex situ*) using experimental ecology research infrastructure can be carried out to understand precisely the processes affecting the

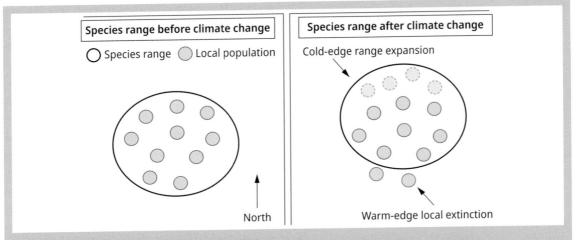

FIGURE 6.5 Theoretical impact of a northward range shift of species associated with climate change

Source: Wiens, J. J. (2016). Climate-related local extinctions are already widespread among plant and animal species. *PLOS biology* 14(12): e2001104

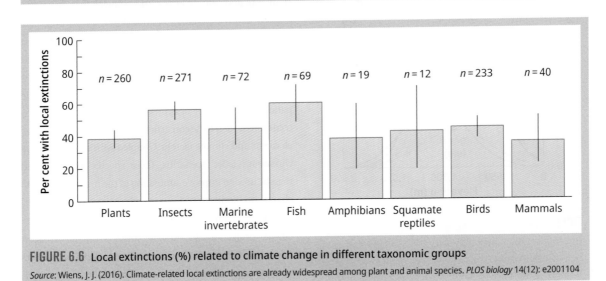

FIGURE 6.6 Local extinctions (%) related to climate change in different taxonomic groups

Source: Wiens, J. J. (2016). Climate-related local extinctions are already widespread among plant and animal species. *PLOS biology* 14(12): e2001104

relationship between climate parameters and ecosystems. In order to improve the response of ecosystems to climate change, **Free-Air Carbon dioxide Enrichment (FACE)** systems involve carrying out experiments in real conditions. The aim of the Birmingham Institute of Forest Research Free-Air Carbon dioxide Enrichment (BIFoR FACE) system is to improve the understanding of how forest plantations respond to the increase in atmospheric CO_2. The installation of measurement devices provides the opportunity to conduct experiments in real conditions in order to improve understanding of

the effect of climate projections and to estimate risks to forest ecosystems (Hart et al. 2020) (Figure 6.8). Other experimental devices, such as the **Ecotron**, aim to reproduce the environment of natural ecosystems. The Ecotron enclosures are equipped with devices to measure and model the functioning of ecosystems in response to environmental forcing. This type of experimentation in the laboratory or in the field improves understanding of the mechanisms and representation of biological processes in the models and thus improves the quality of climate change scenarios.

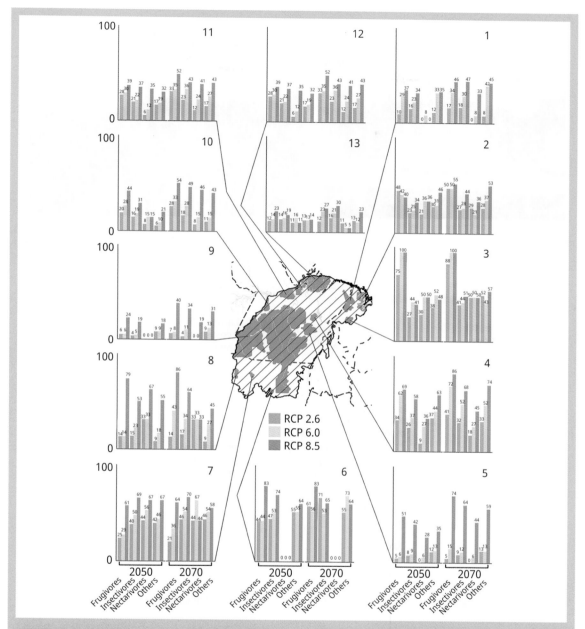

FIGURE 6.7 Percentage of bird species extinction predicted under climate change scenarios in south-eastern Amazonia

Source: Miranda et al. (2019). Climate change impact on ecosystem functions provided by birds in southeastern Amazonia. *PLOS One* 14(4): e0215229

The complexity of research into the impact of climate change on biodiversity therefore requires a multidisciplinary framework based on observation, experimentation, and modelling to allow a more accurate assessment that takes into account the interaction between climatic, environmental, and ecological parameters at overlapping spatial and temporal scales (Figure 6.9).

FIGURE 6.8 Experimental ecology research infrastructures: (a) an enclosed ecosystem platform and (b) a FACE facility

Source: Dolfilms/Alamy Stock Photo. John Keates/Alamy Stock Photo

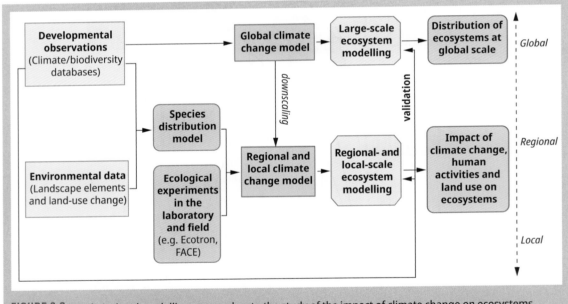

FIGURE 6.9 Analytical and modelling approaches to the study of the impact of climate change on ecosystems

As with the other themes covered in this book, this approach, which takes into account the interacting scales from global to local, is very important for modelling the impact of future climate change on biodiversity. Several studies have shown that taking local factors into account in future modelling can produce very different results.

'These studies suggest that habitat heterogeneity resulting from topographic diversity may be essential for persistence of biota in a future changing climate' (Willis and Bhagwat 2009, p. 806). For example, Randin et al. (2009) showed the contribution of improved spatial resolution in bioclimatic models for investigating habitat loss of alpine plant species in the Swiss Alps. While modelling with a spatial resolution of 16 km simulated a loss of all suitable habitats during the twenty-first century, model output of local parameters (with a spatial resolution of 25 m) predicted habitat persistence for 100% of plant species. 'The authors attributed these differences to the failure of the coarser spatial-scale model to capture local topographic diversity, as well as the complexity of spatial patterns in climate driven by topography' (Willis and Bhagwat 2009, p. 806).

6.3 Forests and grasslands

In 2000, global natural forest cover was of the order of 3.86 Gha, with plantation forest around 137 Mha (https://www.globalforestwatch.org/, accessed Jan. 2020). Extensive deforestation, mostly in tropical regions, has resulted in an ongoing net loss of forest cover globally over recent decades. Forest expansion, particularly in areas outside the tropics, is only enough to offset about a quarter of the annual forest loss (http://www.fao.org/forestry/fra/86627/en/, accessed Jan. 2020). Forest therefore covers about 7.6% of the Earth's surface, or about 30% of global land area (FAO 2018). The main types of forest are tropical and sub-tropical rainforest, and temperate and boreal forest (Figure 6.10).

In contrast, grassland ecosystems cover about 40% of the land area of the Earth's surface (Blair et al. 2014; Dlamini et al. 2016), depending on the definition of grassland (in this case, we include savannah, closed shrubland, and tundra). Temperate grassland alone is said to cover about 8% of the Earth's surface, mostly in the Northern Hemisphere (https://portals.iucn.org/

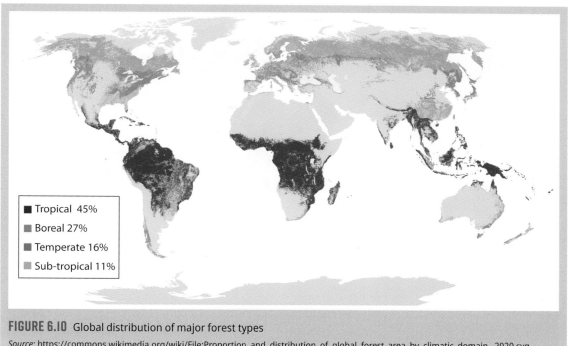

Tropical 45%
Boreal 27%
Temperate 16%
Sub-tropical 11%

FIGURE 6.10 Global distribution of major forest types
Source: https://commons.wikimedia.org/wiki/File:Proportion_and_distribution_of_global_forest_area_by_climatic_domain,_2020.svg

library/sites/library/files/documents/2020-037-En.pdf, accessed Jan. 2020). However, there are many different definitions of grassland type (as described by Dixon et al. 2014), as open grassland often transitions into shrubland, open forest, and scrub, making it difficult to define exactly where boundaries lie. Broad categories of grassland include tropical (e.g. savannah), temperate (e.g. steppes, pampas, and prairies), Mediterranean, boreal/alpine, and semi-desert, as shown in Figure 6.11. These natural ecosystems support a variety of flora and fauna, and have traditionally been grazed and/or managed by fire by indigenous inhabitants. In fact, deforestation and conversion to grazing pasture by human activity has allowed temperate grassland to expand into areas that were originally covered in forest, and which would revert to forest if abandoned. A key characteristic of grassland soils is that they have a high carbon content compared to other ecosystems.

IMPACTS ON FOREST ECOSYSTEMS

Forests represent a major global sink for CO_2, but annual growth rates can vary significantly with different forest types, as shown for the United States in Figure 6.12. It is therefore obvious that environmental change in relatively small areas of forest could have a major impact on regional carbon budgets. Alongside increasing temperatures, rising CO_2 concentrations are thought to enhance vegetation growth, so that all forest types may gain from higher anthropogenic emissions, although the wider effects of climate change may counter such benefits. For example, a range of factors may cause disturbance of the forest ecosystem, including increased wildfires, spread of pests and diseases, competing invasive species, droughts, extreme winds and rainfall, and high temperatures.

Attempts have been made to simulate the possible change in distribution of forest species under scenarios of future climate and land-use change. For example,

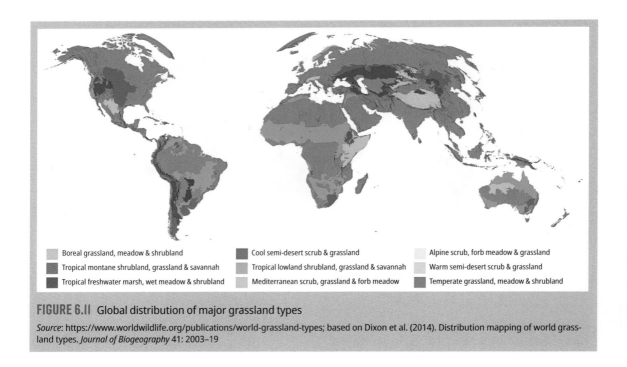

Boreal grassland, meadow & shrubland	Cool semi-desert scrub & grassland	Alpine scrub, forb meadow & grassland
Tropical montane shrubland, grassland & savannah	Tropical lowland shrubland, grassland & savannah	Warm semi-desert scrub & grassland
Tropical freshwater marsh, wet meadow & shrubland	Mediterranean scrub, grassland & forb meadow	Temperate grassland, meadow & shrubland

FIGURE 6.11 Global distribution of major grassland types

Source: https://www.worldwildlife.org/publications/world-grassland-types; based on Dixon et al. (2014). Distribution mapping of world grassland types. *Journal of Biogeography* 41: 2003–19

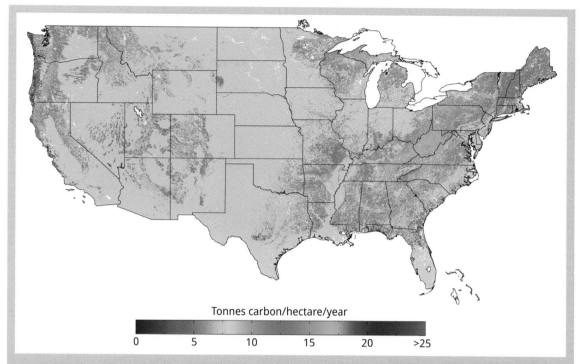

FIGURE 6.12 Spatial variation in the uptake of carbon by forests (in tonnes of carbon/hectare/year) across the United States over the period 2000–2006

Source: Joyce et al. (2014). Forests. In: Melillo, J. M., Richmond, T. C., and Yohe, G. W. (eds), *Climate Change Impacts in the United States: The Third National Climate Assessment*, US Global Change Research Program, Washington, DC, pp. 175–94

Saltré et al. (2015) used a habitat suitability model incorporating moderate climate (A1Fi scenario) and land-use change to simulate the future distribution of beech forest over western Europe (Figure 6.13). They showed that areas to the south of the region and at lower altitude are expected to become unsuitable for beech forest by 2100, while areas to the north-east and at higher altitude would provide opportunity for beech forest expansion. Figure 6.13 shows significant regional- and local-scale variability in suitability for beech forest across parts of Europe, which would need to be incorporated in any strategies designed to manage the effects of climate change.

Similarly, Figure 6.14 shows the expected rate of movement over France of thermal patterns of relevance to forest species, emphasizing the need for more continuous forest cover to allow easier movement of forest organisms than under the present fragmented pattern of forest across the country. The black dots indicate locations of forest reserves and national parks, showing that the western parts of the country have a much less dense network than to the east, making it more difficult for forest plants and animals to move in response to climate change.

Forest ecosystem health is also dependent on climate change effects on a wide range of pests and diseases, such as the spruce budworm and the pine processionary moth. It is evident that the relationship between such insect communities and climate is complex, with global warming generally favouring expansion of populations to high latitudes and altitudes, but also negatively impacting them under extreme temperature or moisture conditions (Pureswaran et al. 2018).

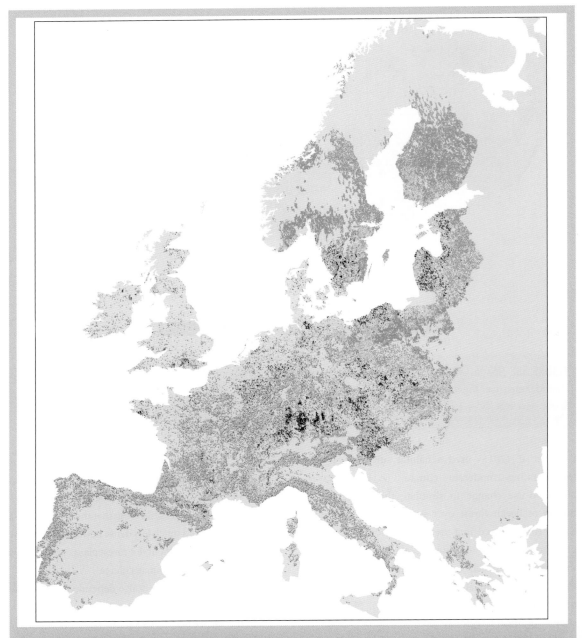

FIGURE 6.13 Simulated change in beech forest (*Fagus sylvatica*) distribution over Western Europe between 1981–2000 and 2081–2100 under moderate future climate and land-use scenarios. Red: extinction of the species; yellow: decrease in population density, green: increase in population density; black: new colonization of suitable areas; blue: suitable areas but not yet colonized

Source: Saltré et al. (2015). How climate, migration ability and habitat fragmentation affect the projected future distribution of European beech. *Global Change Biology* 21: 897–910

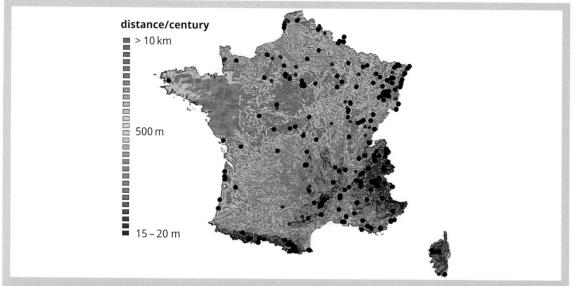

FIGURE 6.14 Expected rate of movement of the thermal niches of forest species under moderate climate change during the twenty-first century, and location of forest reserves and national parks (black dots)

Source: Dupouey, J.-L. (2017). Gestion des forêts tempérées, changement climatique et biodiversité. In: Lavorel, S., Lebreton, J.-D., and Le Maho, Y. (eds), *Les mécanismes d'adaptation de la biodiversité aux changements climatiques et leurs limites*. Académie des Sciences, Institut de France, Paris, pp. 139–42

Global warming is likely to have a range of effects on forest ecosystems (USGCRP 2017), including increased areas burnt by wildfires and a longer fire season, increased impact of drought and insect pests (bark/wood borers and defoliators), and changes to the hydrological regime. These latter changes include a reduced snowpack contribution, higher winter stream flows, increased intense rainfall throughout the year, lower summer stream flows, and increased stream water temperatures.

IMPACTS ON GRASSLAND ECOSYSTEMS

Tropical grasslands tend to be dominated by taller C_4 grass species, while temperate grasslands consist mostly of C_3 grasses. The current increasing levels of CO_2 concentration in the atmosphere are thought to favour C_3 grasses as they become more photosynthetically efficient. Changes in temperature and rainfall will also influence the viability of grassland ecosystems because of their significant role in ecosystem health, but the impact can be quite complicated. For example,

changes in the mean values of temperature and rainfall have a different impact on grassland ecosystems than changes in extreme events, such as drought, heatwaves, and severe storms. Different species of grass and herb within the ecosystem are likely to respond in a different way to extreme events such as drought, so that the overall structure and functioning of the ecosystem may change. For example, any changes in nutritional quality of grassland vegetation will impact on the health of grazing animals.

Bioclimatic envelope models have been used to try and predict the range of different grassland species based on the relationship between observed species occurrence and specific climate variables (Jones 2019). However, these models need to represent the full range of responses that grassland plants and animals can have to climate change. For example, the adaptive capacity of different species can vary significantly, with some species able to adapt their life cycles in order to survive under varying heat and moisture regimes without having to move (through a property called **phenotypic plasticity**). Grassland ecosystems occur within many different climate zones, which suggests that grass-land species generally exhibit significant phenotypic plasticity.

These grassland ecosystem response models also need to include response to the invasion by new species, that can cause changes to the structure and functioning of grassland communities. However, such models are currently limited by the lack of complete understanding of the response of species to changing climate variables (both average and extreme conditions). Three main weaknesses of current understanding appear to be in the interaction between: (1) different processes that operate within natural ecosystems, (2) intrinsic ecosystem processes and external processes associated with anthropogenic land-use change, and (3) ecosystem and climate processes.

Many grassland areas are predicted to be affected by increasing average temperatures, more frequent extreme high temperatures, fewer frosts, increased summer drought, and decreased winter rainfall, as well as more frequent extremes (such as heatwaves, floods, droughts, and wildfires). These climate factors have resulted in changes in phenology and species composition, but there has been significant regional variability of impacts. Other anthropogenic effects, such as through land-use change, habitat loss, and invasive species, are also expected to complicate things.

OVERVIEW

Global warming is resulting in the poleward movement of temperate grassland species, made up particularly of shrubs and C_3 grasses, as well as poleward movement of deciduous trees in the tropics and current temperate zones, taking over current grassland areas. The main mechanism for increased trees and shrubs is CO_2 fertilization, which is greater in the tropics than temperate regions, but there is great uncertainty regarding future changes due to poor predictability of precipitation. There is high diversity of drought tolerance within grassland communities, so it is considered that they should be resilient in the face of drought conditions, and that drought-tolerant species should dominate.

The ability for forest and grassland communities to adapt to climate change is largely a function of the capacity of species to adjust their biological processes to suit changing temperature and precipitation patterns. Where there is variation in this capacity among plant and animal species, ecosystem structure is likely to change as some species move while others stay and adapt. Changes in phenology may be all that is needed for some species to adapt to a changing climate. However, the complexity of ecosystem processes can result in the occurrence of tipping points and non-linearity in response among different species, with changes in the rate of transition between biome types. For example, changing climatic conditions may allow invasive species to affect both forest and grassland communities, especially where the invasive species are better adapted to the new climate. The movement or dispersal of species into new areas may itself be affected by changing climate through shifts in atmospheric circulation, which can cause species dispersion in different directions.

It should be noted that forest and grassland ecosystems will be impacted by changes in both average or background climate conditions and the frequency and magnitude of extremes (e.g. of temperature, precipitation, and wind speed). Interactions with other human effects, such as land-use change and environmental pollution, will make ecosystem response more unpredictable, while fragmented landscapes with pockets of more natural environments surrounded by heavily modified areas make it difficult for ecosystems to adapt/respond, due to effects on migration of plant and animal species.

In spite of the significant uncertainties mentioned above, recent research has attempted to indicate likely ecosystem changes resulting from future climate change. Figure 6.15 provides an example of possible pathways of change for major vegetation types over the African continent.

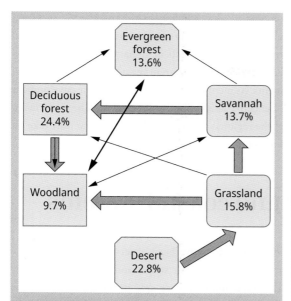

FIGURE 6.15 Possible pathways of change between major vegetation types over the African continent. The percentage values represent the amount of the surface of the African continent that is expected to be in each vegetation state by the year 2100. The width of the arrows reflects the magnitude of vegetation transitions that are expected to have occurred between 1850 and 2100

Source: Jones, M. B. (2019). Projected climate change and the global distribution of grasslands. In Gibson, D., and Newman, J. (eds), *Grasslands and Climate Change*. Cambridge University Press, Cambridge, pp. 67–81

6.4 Rivers and lakes

Rivers and lakes have been impacted severely by human activity over thousands of years, causing declines in both water quality and quantity. Freshwater ecosystems have therefore been adversely affected, causing reduced habitat for many organisms with extinctions or declines in the population of freshwater species. Climate change is expected to exacerbate other effects of human activity through changing thermal regimes, as well as precipitation and river flows. Increased air

temperatures and reduced cloud cover have a significant effect on increasing the temperatures experienced by organisms in shallow streams and rivers, while deeper-water bodies are less affected. Any reduction in precipitation and runoff leads to reduced flows and therefore higher water temperatures and loss of habitat for many species. This can be made worse by extraction of water for human use. Changes in temperature can also change the flow regimes of major river systems in alpine regions fed by snow and ice melt, so that winter runoff is increased while warmer winter conditions result in less water stored until late spring and summer to replenish water levels in rivers and lakes. In these circumstances, freshwater species need to be able to adapt to greater extremes to survive. For example, trout and salmon are cold-water fish that have an upper water temperature lethal limit of around 25 °C, with an optimal range of around 12–19 °C (Morrow and Fischenich 2000). When river flows drop, the reduced volume of water can be heated up rapidly by solar radiation and warm air temperatures, causing fish to die unless they are able to find micro-habitats within deeper pools in the river system where temperatures may remain lower. They may also be able to move to more suitable conditions if they are diadromous, meaning that they are able to migrate to new, cooler river systems by being able to travel via the sea. Santiago et al. (2016) concluded that brown trout thermal habit loss in the Duero River basin in Spain of more than 50% would occur by 2100 under the most extreme climate change scenario (RCP8.5). In New Zealand, it is thought that indigenous fish species would be less impacted by climate change than introduced species such as trout, as they are less affected by such environmental stressors as floods, low flows, and associated temperature changes (McGlone and Walker 2011). Changes in the thermal stratification of lakes due to the warming trend are also thought to have increased eutrophication and nutrient loss.

The complex nature of river and lake ecosystems makes it difficult to predict accurately the effects of global warming on the health of such freshwater systems. There is some evidence of the movement of species and the earlier timing of phenological phases, such as the spawning of fish and the length of the growing season. In addition to the major fish predators, there are many other organisms (such as algae and invertebrates) that are part of the freshwater food web, and these can respond negatively or positively to changing temperature regimes. Human activity through deforestation or reforestation of catchments can have a significant effect on both the flow and temperature regimes of rivers and water bodies, so there is potential for human action to counter negative effects of global warming through increased planting of riparian vegetation in affected catchments. As mentioned in other sections, the development of effective adaptation strategies should be undertaken at the regional and local scales in order to fully take on board the unique characteristics of each region.

6.5 Marine environment and coastal systems

The emission of greenhouse gases into the atmosphere through human activity and the resulting increased air temperatures appear to have resulted in both warming and acidification of ocean waters (Figure 6.16). In addition, increased sea surface temperatures have been associated with rising sea levels resulting from both the melting of land-based ice and thermal expansion of the oceans. Changing patterns of other atmospheric and oceanic processes (e.g. those affecting temperature, precipitation, and ocean and atmospheric circulation) are also considered to be the result of climate change. Many of these changes are occurring at the regional and local scales, so that impacts often vary geographically with some regions more adversely affected than others. Impacts on sea surface temperatures, salinity, and sea ice distribution have been observed, including downstream effects on fish stocks and marine ecosystems. The reduction of sea ice area in the Arctic has major impacts on the regional ecosystem, including reduced habitat for polar bears and seals. Sea level rise is a climate change impact of great concern in low-lying regions of the world that are often densely populated, due to increased erosion, saltwater intrusion, and flooding of coastal areas. The combination of increasing water temperature and rising sea level can also have biological effects such as the encroachment of mangroves and other organisms into newly flooded areas. However, as in other environments, it is often difficult to separate out climate change effects from other human-derived factors such as land-use change and coastal development.

6.6 Mountain and alpine regions

Mountain and alpine regions are highly sensitive to climate change and human activities because they concentrate a very high variation of biodiversity in small areas. Mountains cover just over 10% of the Earth's surface but are host to a significant share of biodiversity with about half of the world's biodiversity hotspots such as tropical forests and endemic alpine grasslands (Dimitrov et al. 2012; Engler et al. 2011). The mountain environment perfectly reflects the need to assess the impact of climate change at fine scales, taking into account the strong local climate variability caused by topographical factors (altitude, slope, exposure). Large altitudinal gradients cause high variability in climate, land use, and biodiversity over small horizontal areas. All species of plants and animals are impacted and the margins for adaptation are very limited. In contrast to the plains, where species movement is possible, mountain ecosystems are subject to the altitudinal limit. Species that are already close to mountain tops without the possibility of escaping upwards have a higher risk of extinction (Dullinger et al. 2012; Theurillat et Guisan 2001).

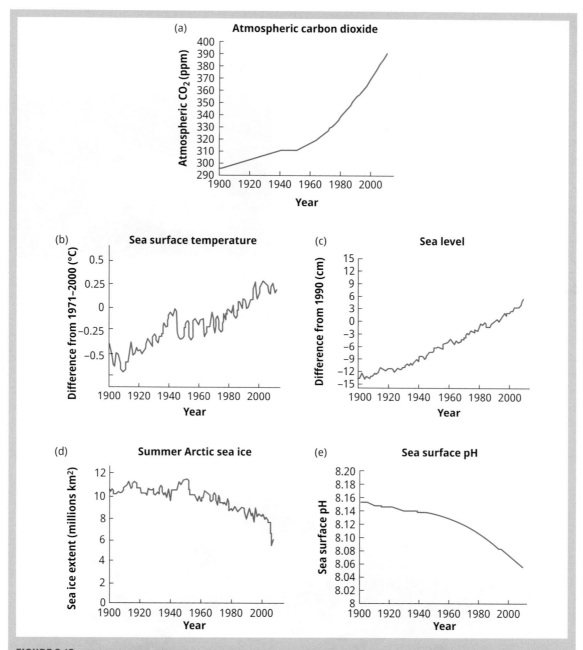

FIGURE 6.16 Recent global trends in ocean characteristics and their relationship with carbon dioxide concentrations: (a) carbon dioxide concentration, (b) sea surface temperature, (c) sea level, (d) summer Arctic sea ice extent, and (e) sea surface acidity/pH

Source: Melillo et al. (2014). *Climate Change Impacts in the United States: The Third National Climate Assessment*. US Global Change Research Program, Washington, DC

Mountains are climate-sensitive areas and are already being highly impacted by climate change. The increase in temperature and the decrease in precipitation in some parts of the world are manifested by a significant decrease in snow cover in mountain ranges, with a rise in altitude of snow-covered areas but also a reduction

CASE STUDY 6.1
Climate change and coral reefs

Rising ocean temperatures and acidification resulting from global warming are said to be two main factors having a detrimental effect on coral reefs (Ateweberhan et al. 2013), although it is increasingly evident that many other factors impact on the health of coral reef systems in different parts of the world (McClanahan et al. 2019). For example, local chemical and biological pollution from mostly land-based activities, together with dredging and over-fishing, often using destructive techniques, have had a significant impact on coral reef communities in some parts of the world. Coral bleaching is said to occur following anomalously high water temperatures that exceed the thermal limit of certain coral species, initially causing them to expel colourful algae with which they have a symbiotic relationship. This can lead to death of the coral itself, and there is evidence of increasing numbers of such events occurring over recent decades (Figure 6.17). However, it has been shown that coral bleaching is often not solely explained by high ocean temperatures, but also results from the interaction of a range of factors (McClanahan et al. 2019). These factors include periods of extreme warm and cold temperatures leading up to the bleaching event and the geographic location of the reef

FIGURE 6.17 Coral bleaching on the Keppel Islands, Great Barrier Reef, 22 August 2011
Source: Acropora/Wikimedia Commons (CC BY 3.0)

(reflecting regional and local environmental conditions). Figure 6.18 shows that there can be significant regional variability in coral bleaching intensity resulting from a single El Niño event. It is also evident that the resilience of specific coral communities and their ability to recover from environmental disruption can vary significantly depending on their location and the biological structure of

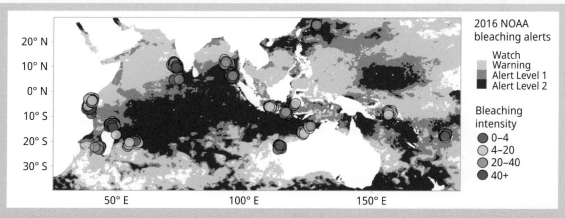

FIGURE 6.18 Observed severity of coral bleaching during the 2016 El Niño across the Indian Ocean and western Pacific region

Source: McClanahan et al. (2019). Temperature patterns and mechanisms influencing coral bleaching during the 2016 El Niño. *Nature Climate Change* 9: 845–51

the coral reef community, as well as the past history of temperature variations.

Concern with effects of ocean warming on coral reef communities is exacerbated by possible effects of the observed increasing acidification of ocean water (shown in Figure 6.16 as a decline in pH). An increase in the acidification of seawater is thought to reduce the ability of some oceanic organisms such as coral to grow through calcification. However, it is increasingly evident that the relationship between coral growth and both the temperature and acidity of seawater is complex. For example, coral reefs in some locations have been seen to grow more rapidly at higher water temperatures, as long as the lethal limit is not reached, in spite of increased acidity (Ateweberhan et al. 2013).

An overview of the range of climate factors that represent threats to coral reefs is shown in Figure 6.19. It is evident that these factors are likely to affect coral reefs over coming decades in addition to ocean temperatures and acidification. They include sea level rise, and changes in atmospheric circulation that can affect storm and precipitation patterns as well as ocean currents. For example, rising sea level would create a deeper layer of water above coral reefs, which is likely to reduce the temperatures experienced by corals during extreme events (because of the greater volume of water being heated up). This beneficial effect may be offset over the longer term by the effect on the coral community of changing environmental conditions as sea levels continue to rise, as experienced during post-glacial sea level rise over the past 18,000 years. It is also expected that changes in atmospheric circulation across a range of scales from global to local will result from global warming. It is therefore anticipated that changes in storm tracks and intensity, in combination with sea level rise, may cause increased coastal inundation in some parts of the world. Similarly, changes in precipitation regime may also cause increased freshwater, or sediment and pollutants

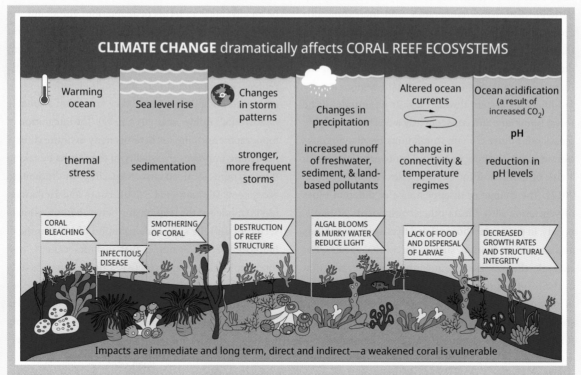

FIGURE 6.19 Climate change effects on the future viability of coral reef ecosystems

Source: adapted from https://www.noaa.gov/multimedia/infographic/infographic-how-does-climate-change-affect-coral-reefs

entering coral reef ecosystems, or increased drought and water shortages (Figure 6.19). Such circulation changes are also likely to impact on cloud cover, which has been seen to be an important factor affecting water temperature variations experienced by coral (McGowan et al. 2019). Clearly, regional variations in the impact of global warming on different coral reef communities and the range of factors that can be involved make it important that research be conducted into the unique character of each location in order to develop strategies designed to minimize local effects of climate change.

in the period with snow cover (Choi et al. 2010). The impact of contemporary climate change is also reflected in the retreat of most of the world's glaciers, especially in tropical areas.

All components of mountain biodiversity have already been impacted by climate change. This is reflected in changes to habitats, species movements, and the appearance of invasive species. Many mountain species are already reacting to the effects of ongoing global warming and these trends are expected to intensify in the future (Lenoir et al. 2008). The relationship between decreasing temperature and increasing altitude in mountain regions has long been recognized as a major factor shaping the biodiversity of plant communities and ecosystem dynamics (Mayor et al. 2017). The increase in temperature in mountain regions totally modifies this system through a shift in altitude of the forest boundary and consequently a decrease in alpine grassland. Future climate simulations predict a reduction in plant diversity in high-altitude grasslands with a risk of extinction for some species (Dullinger et al. 2012). The change or disappearance of different types of vegetation also affects other components of biodiversity, in particular those related to changes in habitats and access to nutrition, such as for animal species. For example, the increase in temperature and the reduction of the length of the cold season modify the behaviour of mammals. The distribution of several species has shifted to higher altitudes and the hibernation season for animals such as marmots has been significantly reduced. Change in phenology also has an influence on the diet of animal species. The biodiversity of mountain rivers and lakes is being altered by melting snow/ice and glaciers and rising temperatures (Brown et al.

2007), with changes in water composition threatening many freshwater species. Moreover, while glaciers are recognized as a habitat for microbial communities, their retreat will have a strong impact on the microbial ecology of rivers (Wilhelm et al. 2013). The range of impacts of current and future climate change on different plant and animal species in the mountains is illustrated in Figure 6.20.

However, although mountain ecosystems are particularly sensitive to the impacts of climate change, the high heterogeneity of climate, topography, and land use can be an advantage in terms of adaptation. The significant heterogeneity of topography causes high spatial temperature variability and provides many micro-habitats over short distances. 'This provides space for "climatic refuges" or stepping stones, and high-elevation organisms need not always migrate very far to find a suitable new habitat' (Kohler et al. 2014, p. 79). The integration of topographic and climatic heterogeneity in future climate modelling improves the quality of the results by taking into account local adaptive capacities for mountain ecosystems (Randin et al. 2009). Luoto and Heikkinen (2008) modelled the relationship between future climate scenarios and the species distribution of 100 European butterfly species. A model that includes climatic and topographical heterogeneity (e.g. altitude) predicts only half the species losses in mountainous areas for the period 2051–2080 compared to a uniform climate model. These results suggest that habitat heterogeneity resulting from topographic diversity may be essential for the persistence of biota in a changing future climate (Willis and Bhagwat 2009).

Assessing the impact of climate change on mountain ecosystems requires observation and modelling methods

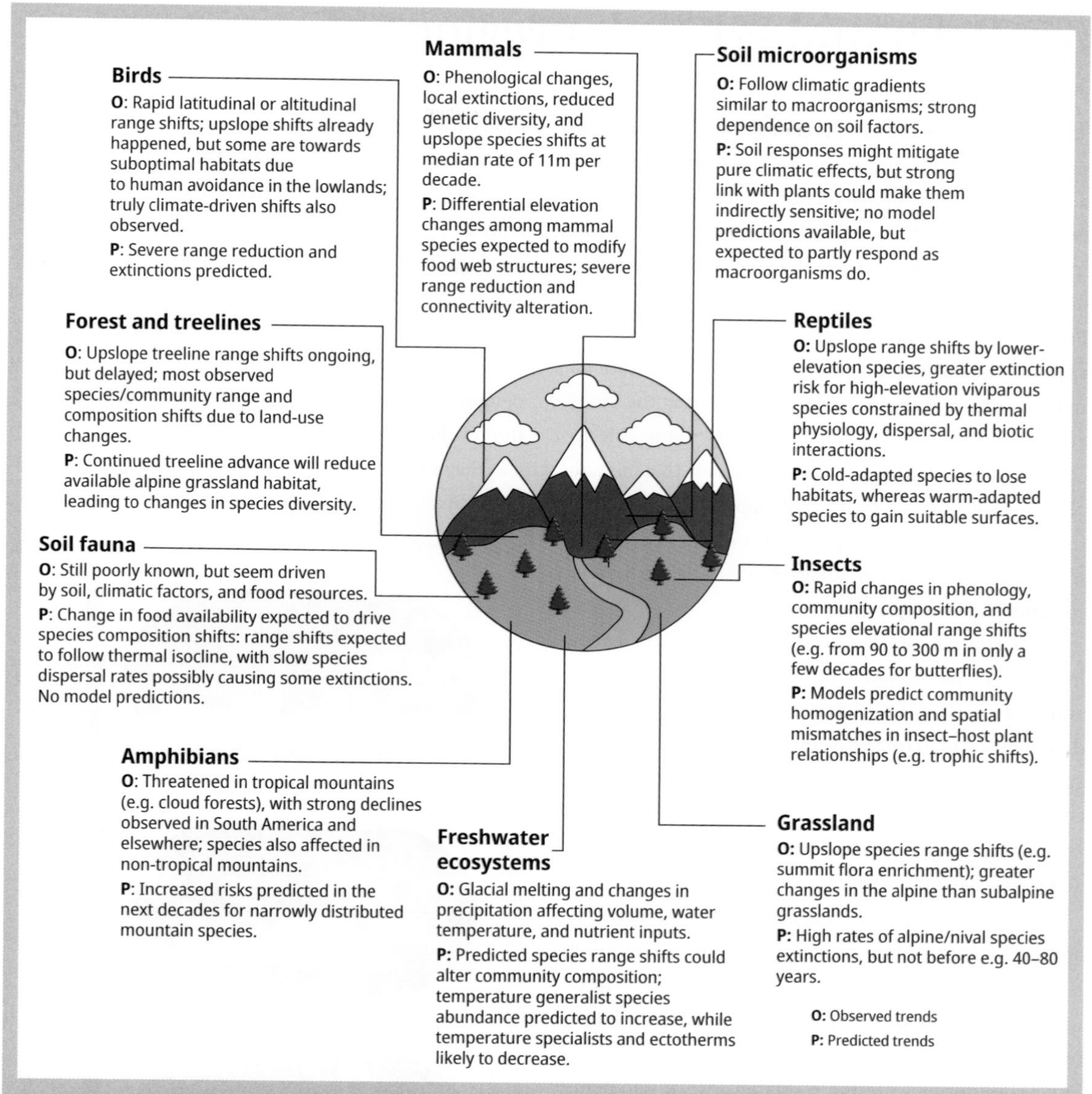

Birds

O: Rapid latitudinal or altitudinal range shifts; upslope shifts already happened, but some are towards suboptimal habitats due to human avoidance in the lowlands; truly climate-driven shifts also observed.

P: Severe range reduction and extinctions predicted.

Mammals

O: Phenological changes, local extinctions, reduced genetic diversity, and upslope species shifts at median rate of 11m per decade.

P: Differential elevation changes among mammal species expected to modify food web structures; severe range reduction and connectivity alteration.

Soil microorganisms

O: Follow climatic gradients similar to macroorganisms; strong dependence on soil factors.

P: Soil responses might mitigate pure climatic effects, but strong link with plants could make them indirectly sensitive; no model predictions available, but expected to partly respond as macroorganisms do.

Forest and treelines

O: Upslope treeline range shifts ongoing, but delayed; most observed species/community range and composition shifts due to land-use changes.

P: Continued treeline advance will reduce available alpine grassland habitat, leading to changes in species diversity.

Soil fauna

O: Still poorly known, but seem driven by soil, climatic factors, and food resources.

P: Change in food availability expected to drive species composition shifts: range shifts expected to follow thermal isocline, with slow species dispersal rates possibly causing some extinctions. No model predictions.

Reptiles

O: Upslope range shifts by lower-elevation species, greater extinction risk for high-elevation viviparous species constrained by thermal physiology, dispersal, and biotic interactions.

P: Cold-adapted species to lose habitats, whereas warm-adapted species to gain suitable surfaces.

Insects

O: Rapid changes in phenology, community composition, and species elevational range shifts (e.g. from 90 to 300 m in only a few decades for butterflies).

P: Models predict community homogenization and spatial mismatches in insect–host plant relationships (e.g. trophic shifts).

Amphibians

O: Threatened in tropical mountains (e.g. cloud forests), with strong declines observed in South America and elsewhere; species also affected in non-tropical mountains.

P: Increased risks predicted in the next decades for narrowly distributed mountain species.

Freshwater ecosystems

O: Glacial melting and changes in precipitation affecting volume, water temperature, and nutrient inputs.

P: Predicted species range shifts could alter community composition; temperature generalist species abundance predicted to increase, while temperature specialists and ectotherms likely to decrease.

Grassland

O: Upslope species range shifts (e.g. summit flora enrichment); greater changes in the alpine than subalpine grasslands.

P: High rates of alpine/nival species extinctions, but not before e.g. 40–80 years.

O: Observed trends
P: Predicted trends

FIGURE 6.20 Main impacts (observed and predicted) of climate change on the different biodiversity groups in mountain areas

Source: Guisan et al. (2019). Climate change impacts on mountain biodiversity. In: Lovejoy, T. E., and Lee, H. (eds), *Biodiversity and Climate Change*. Yale University Press, New Haven, Connecticut, pp. 221–33

that take into account the strong heterogeneity of topography, land use, and climate in small areas. Various studies have highlighted the effects of climate change on almost all taxonomic groups in the mountains, although studies of the climate change impacts on certain biodiversity groups such as mountain soil microorganisms are still lacking (Guisan et al. 2019). Improving knowledge at the local scale (through experimentation and modelling) will help to limit the uncertainties in models of the impact of climate change on mountain biodiversity.

6.7 Polar and sub-polar regions

The polar regions are the parts of the world where the impacts of climate change are the most pronounced as a result of a much higher increase in temperature. Future climate simulations predict an increase of 4–7°C in these regions by 2100, which exceeds global average temperature change by 1–2°C (Stocker et al. 2013). Polar ecosystems are composed of plant and animal species that survive in some of the coldest conditions in the world, and these conditions mean that the polar ecosystems are unique, but also highly vulnerable to climate change. Future projections suggest that climate change could have a significant impact on, including the extinction of, many species in marine and terrestrial ecosystems, thereby adversely affecting the human societies in these regions.

Polar and sub-polar ecosystems are already heavily impacted by global warming due to increased temperatures (air and water), changing precipitation patterns, deterioration of permafrost, and melting glaciers and ice caps (Djoghlaf 2008). Impacts on terrestrial and marine ecosystems are demonstrated by changes in vegetation zones, species diversity, and the distribution of marine and terrestrial animal species.

There is a clear link between marine biodiversity and ocean temperature change, where species richness is impacted by warming. Figure 6.21 shows the projection of marine biodiversity distribution patterns based on a 2°C increase in sea surface temperature (SST). Polar communities are the most sensitive to temperature increases with a more than 20% predicted change in biodiversity. The loss of local species is lower than in tropical systems, but polar areas are exposed to greater species invasion. Species turnover, which reflects the number of both invasive and locally extinct species, is expected to be highest in the Arctic and the sub-polar Southern Ocean region (Cheung et al. 2009). Simulations of the trend of polar marine biodiversity under future climate change scenarios show similar but more extreme trends with significant species turnover and

thus strong community restructuring (Beaugrand et al. 2015; Pinsky et al. 2013; Lenoir et al. 2020).

Reduction in the extent of sea ice has an impact on animal species, including marine mammals and birds that require sea ice as a habitat, for feeding and breeding. According to the RCP8.5 scenario, the average annual extent of Antarctic sea ice could decrease by almost 50%, which would lead to a very large decrease in emperor penguin colonies by 2100 and ultimately to the extinction of the species (Figure 6.22). 'Sea ice conditions affect the survival and reproduction of emperor penguins both directly (e.g. early sea ice breakup can jeopardize

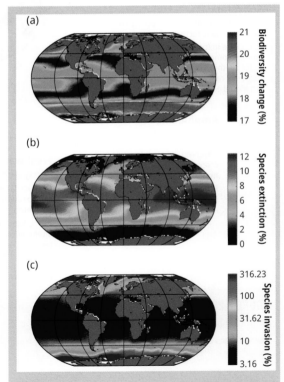

FIGURE 6.21 Predicted change in marine (a) biodiversity, (b) species extinction, and (c) species invasion in response to a 2°C increase in sea surface temperature

Source: Beaugrand et al. (2015). Future vulnerability of marine biodiversity compared with contemporary and past changes. *Nature Climate Change* 5: 695–701

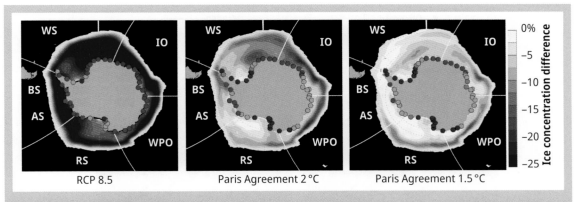

FIGURE 6.22 Population status of emperor penguins at various Antarctic sites by 2100 and model-predicted mean change of annual sea ice concentration for three climate change scenarios between 1920–2000 and the twenty-first century. Dot colours indicate likely population decline by: <30% – blue; >30% – green (vulnerable); >50% – yellow (endangered); >90% – red (quasi-extinct). AS, Amundsen Sea; BS, Bellingshausen Sea; IO, Indian Ocean; RS, Ross Sea; WPO, Western Pacific Ocean; WS, Weddell Sea

Source: Jenouvrier et al. (2020). The Paris Agreement objectives will likely halt future declines of emperor penguins. *Global Change Biology* 26: 1170–84

chick survival) and indirectly through the food web' (Jenouvrier et al. 2020, p. 1171).

The reduction in length of the season with ice has completely changed the behaviour and diet of polar bears. Several studies have shown a statistical relationship between the reduction in the length of the sea ice season and average polar bear weight (Molnár et al. 2011). These conditions require the bears to modify their feeding behaviour, particularly by finding other terrestrial sources of food. Prop et al. (2015) showed that earlier land appearance of polar bears coincided with a trend towards shorter sea ice seasons. The reduction of the sea ice season appears to change the hunting behaviour of polar bears, strongly affecting terrestrial animal communities. For example, a study conducted in Spitsbergen and Greenland showed that polar bears have seriously affected the reproduction of birds like barnacle geese, common eiders, and glaucous gulls. The reduction in sea ice extent and the increase in ocean temperature are also having a strong influence on krill populations, and with the significant importance of krill in various food chains, the entire marine food web is likely to be negatively affected (Flores et al. 2012; Atkinson et al. 2019).

Global warming causes a latitudinal shift in the vegetation growth limit, while rising temperatures and melting permafrost disturb the vegetation in polar and sub-polar regions. The poleward movement of different plant species into new regions modifies their ecosystems, with range extension for some species and reduction for others. The risk of extinction is increased for species in ecosystems that shrink, and in general, the distribution of low and sparse vegetation communities is expected to decline as forests expand their range. As a result, forests could replace a significant part of the current tundra in Arctic regions, with the tundra vegetation shifting poleward. As the permafrost melts, the tundra could become large swamps (Berner et al. 2013; Pearson et al. 2013). Figure 6.23 provides a regional case study of potential changes in Arctic vegetation based on future climate scenarios. It is evident that the predicted rapid warming of the Arctic region will have a dramatic impact on plant species distribution that is also likely to be reflected in migration of animal species.

The rapidity of climate change and the vulnerability of ecosystems are already having a very significant impact on biodiversity in polar and sub-polar regions. Future climate scenarios suggest significant impacts on

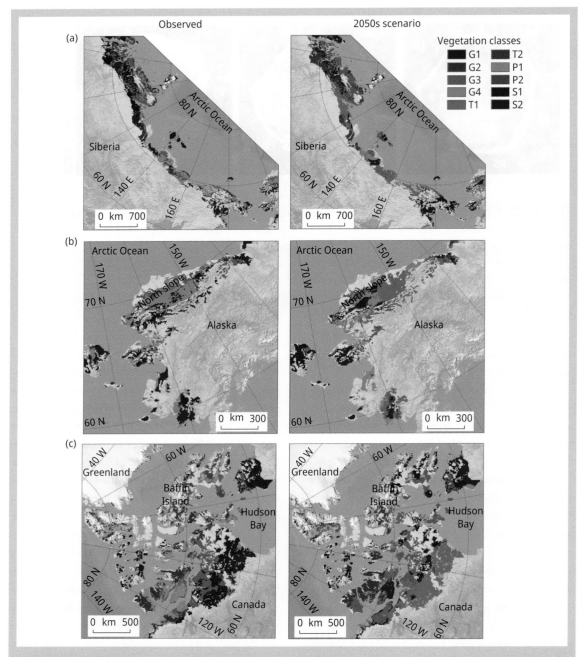

FIGURE 6.23 Distribution of vegetation in Arctic regions under current conditions (left) and under a future 2050s climate scenario (right): (a) Siberia, (b) Alaska, and (c) Canada. Predicted distributions for the 2050s based on the Random Forest Model, the HadCM3 climate model, and A2a emissions scenario. **G1**: Rush/grass, forb, cryptogam tundra; **G2**: Graminoid, prostrate dwarf-shrub, forb tundra; **G3**: Non-tussock-sedge, dwarf-shrub, moss tundra; **G4**: Tussock-sedge, dwarf-shrub, moss tundra; **P1**: Prostrate dwarf-shrub, herb tundra; **P2**: Prostrate/semiprostrate dwarf-shrub tundra; **S1**: Erect dwarf-shrub tundra; **S2**: Low-shrub tundra; **T1**: Tree-cover mosaic; **T2**: Tree cover

Source: Pearson et al. (2013). Shifts in Arctic vegetation and associated feedbacks under climate change. *Nature Climate Change* 3: 673–7

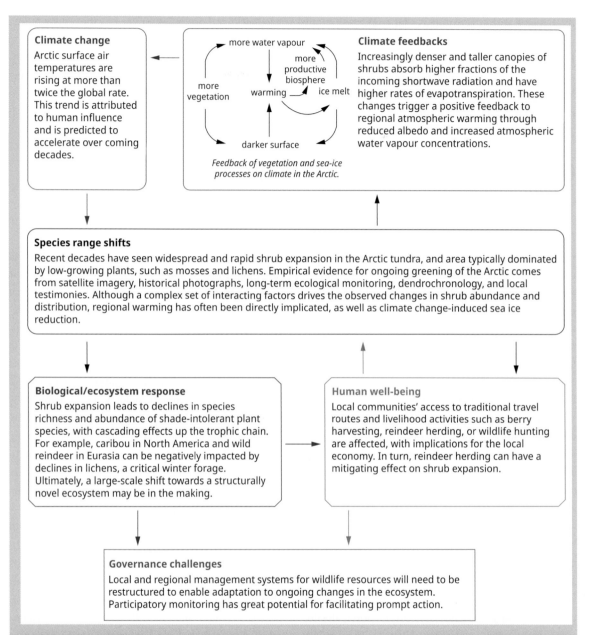

Climate change

Arctic surface air temperatures are rising at more than twice the global rate. This trend is attributed to human influence and is predicted to accelerate over coming decades.

more water vapour

more productive biosphere

more vegetation

warming

ice melt

darker surface

Feedback of vegetation and sea-ice processes on climate in the Arctic.

Climate feedbacks

Increasingly denser and taller canopies of shrubs absorb higher fractions of the incoming shortwave radiation and have higher rates of evapotranspiration. These changes trigger a positive feedback to regional atmospheric warming through reduced albedo and increased atmospheric water vapour concentrations.

Species range shifts

Recent decades have seen widespread and rapid shrub expansion in the Arctic tundra, and area typically dominated by low-growing plants, such as mosses and lichens. Empirical evidence for ongoing greening of the Arctic comes from satellite imagery, historical photographs, long-term ecological monitoring, dendrochronology, and local testimonies. Although a complex set of interacting factors drives the observed changes in shrub abundance and distribution, regional warming has often been directly implicated, as well as climate change-induced sea ice reduction.

Biological/ecosystem response

Shrub expansion leads to declines in species richness and abundance of shade-intolerant plant species, with cascading effects up the trophic chain. For example, caribou in North America and wild reindeer in Eurasia can be negatively impacted by declines in lichens, a critical winter forage. Ultimately, a large-scale shift towards a structurally novel ecosystem may be in the making.

Human well-being

Local communities' access to traditional travel routes and livelihood activities such as berry harvesting, reindeer herding, or wildlife hunting are affected, with implications for the local economy. In turn, reindeer herding can have a mitigating effect on shrub expansion.

Governance challenges

Local and regional management systems for wildlife resources will need to be restructured to enable adaptation to ongoing changes in the ecosystem. Participatory monitoring has great potential for facilitating prompt action.

FIGURE 6.24 Climate change, species movement, and the greening of the Arctic. Changes in species distribution can lead to climate feedbacks, changes in ecosystem services, and impacts on human societies, with feedbacks and linkages between each of these elements, illustrated here through climate-driven changes in Arctic vegetation

Source: Pecl et al. (2017). Biodiversity redistribution under climate change: Impacts on ecosystems and human well-being. *Science* 355(6332)

the balance within ecosystems that could potentially lead to the disappearance of plant and animal species (Figure 6.23). Biodiversity is essential for the sustainability of many ecosystem services and therefore has a significant impact on human societies in these regions. Figure 6.24 illustrates the various climate feedbacks and processes induced by the redistribution of plant species in the Arctic and the potential impacts on human activities and well-being. It is therefore essential to take into account the effects of such changes in biodiversity in the development of appropriate adaptation strategies.

6.8 Arid and semi-arid regions

Arid and semi-arid deserts account for nearly 20% of the Earth's surface (https://www.un.org/en/events/desertification_decade/whynow.shtml). As in polar and sub-polar regions, ecosystems in arid and semi-arid regions are exposed to extreme climatic conditions. These extreme conditions also make their biodiversity unique and threatened because the physiological limits of plant and animal species can be reached relatively quickly. Slight changes in temperature or precipitation regimes could therefore significantly alter the ecosystems of these regions (Archer and Predick 2008).

Climate change scenarios predict a significant increase in aridity in some parts of the world, accentuating the water deficit in current dryland areas and significantly expanding drylands globally. This increasing aridity will impact ecosystem functioning by altering the abundance and composition of species (e.g. an increase in invasive species), as well as their distribution. This will cause degradation of ecosystems with a decrease in soil fertility and biomass production, in addition to increased erosion. For example, Berdugo et al. (2020) defined aridity thresholds for ecosystems based on 20 variables (including precipitation, albedo, plant effects on soil, and photosynthesis). Their results showed that the response of drylands to aridity can be organized in three phases characterized by structural and functional changes in ecosystems: from a first threshold corresponding to the 'vegetation decline phase' to the final 'ecosystem breakdown' phase characterized by an extreme reduction in vegetation cover (Figure 6.25(a)). According to RCP8.5 climate projections, more than 20% of the world's land area could exceed one or more thresholds by 2100 as a result of climate change (Figure 6.25(b)).

Climate change-related intensification of aridity and the fragmentation and loss of habitats in drylands are also responsible for the loss of animal biodiversity that could potentially cause the extinction of vulnerable species (Vale and Brito 2015). Species distribution modelling of 107 endemic mammal species in Afro-Arab regions was carried out in order to assess the potential impact of climate change. The results showed that about 17% of endemic mammals could disappear before 2050 according to the RCP8.5 scenarios (Soultan et al. 2019). However, endemic mammals in these regions are among the most adapted to extreme environmental conditions, although the intensity of change means that even these species cannot remain sustainable in the face of the current rate of climate change (Vale et al. 2016).

The impact of climate change on biodiversity in arid and semi-arid regions depends on the evolution of climatic parameters, particularly precipitation. Analysis of rainfall in the semi-arid regions of the world reveals that the highest expansion of arid land has occurred in semi-arid regions since the 1960s. However, the dynamics of climate change has a completely different impact on the intensification or reduction of aridity in different regions of the world. For example, more humid conditions on the American continent have resulted in the displacement of arid to semi-arid regions. In contrast, in the dry regions of East Asia, the expansion of semi-arid regions has replaced sub-humid/humid regions, where the climate has become drier due to a weakened Asian summer monsoon (Huang et al. 2016).

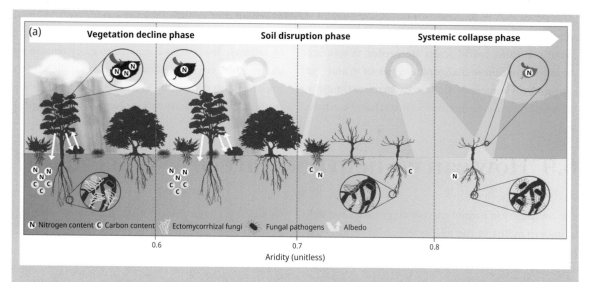

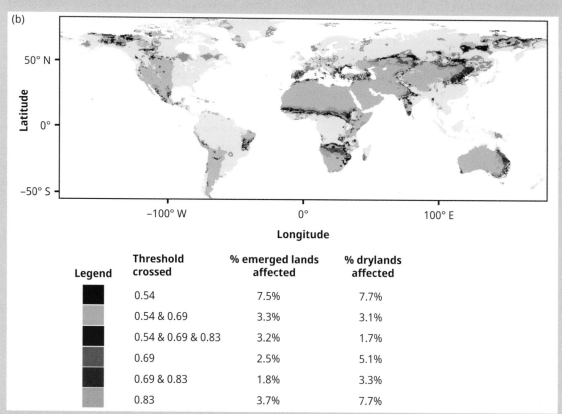

FIGURE 6.25 (a) The sequence of abrupt responses to climate change in global drylands as aridity increases and (b) a map of climate change vulnerability in global drylands

Source: Berdugo, M., Delgado-Baquerizo, M., Soliveres, S., Hernández-Clemente, R., Zhao, Y., Gaitán, J. J., Gross, N., Saiz, H., Maire, V., Lehmann, A., Rillig, M. C., Solé, R. V., and Maestre, F. T. (2020). Global ecosystem thresholds driven by aridity. *Science* 367: 787–90

It is clear that environmental processes are complex and that accurate climate simulations that take into account interacting spatial scales are needed to estimate the impacts of climate change on ecosystems in arid and semi-arid environments. These ecosystems are initially very sensitive and even moderate climate change can have a strong impact on their structure and function. With extreme climatic conditions, arid regions are characterized by relatively few species compared to ecosystems in regions with more precipitation. This makes it all the more important that dryland biodiversity is given higher priority through the implementation of adaptation strategies.

6.9 How can we help natural ecosystems adapt?

The complexity of natural ecosystem processes and lack of understanding of the relative effects of climate and non-climate factors make it difficult to develop effective adaptation strategies for such environments. This situation is made more complicated by regional variations in the extent and nature of climate change, as well as variations in the robustness of different natural ecosystems. In line with the theme of this text, it is clear that adaptation strategies need to be developed at the regional and local scales based on improved understanding of how ecosystems work in specific areas, particularly the key components of those systems and the major processes that drive them. It is anticipated that the resilience of ecosystems in different areas will vary considerably, with some environments much more sensitive to change than others. It is also evident that some plant and animal communities will be unable to change as rapidly as the projected changes in climate, and will therefore be unable to adapt (Jezkova and Wiens 2016). The development of predictive models for ecosystem response to climate change is in its infancy. It is possible to use evidence of the effects of past climates to provide some sort of indication of the impact of future climate changes, but the relationships are not simple and there are many external factors (e.g. land-use change and changing CO_2 concentrations) that need to be considered.

Human intervention to assist in adaptation of natural environments to climate change is at an early stage of development. It is a difficult matter because the processes that operate in the many different natural ecosystems are very complex and not fully understood.

In addition, natural ecosystems have been adversely affected by a range of anthropogenic factors, of which climate change is only one. These other factors include such things as land-use change to plantation forest, agriculture and urban development, mineral exploitation, over-fishing, and pollution. For example, increased demands have been placed on grassland regions to expand global food production, especially milk and meat production from ruminant animals (Gibson and Newman 2019). Adaptive responses should therefore develop a 'whole-of-ecosystem' approach to management of natural ecosystems in order to account for the multiple stress factors involved. Management of natural ecosystems with the aim of reducing impacts of climate change must go hand in hand with addressing the impacts of many other factors on the environment.

Mitigation of the effects of climate change through reduction in greenhouse gas emissions is the only genuine solution to the impacts of global warming on natural ecosystems on planet Earth, leaving limited options available for effective human intervention to aid adaptation. However, a number of adaptation strategies have been suggested for terrestrial ecosystems, including prescribed burning to reduce the effects of wildfires, controlling invasive species through eradication programmes, establishing managed reserves for specific species under threat, and developing new, better-adapted species through genetic manipulation (USGCRP 2018). However, there is a limit to the effectiveness of such approaches. For example, establishment of isolated reserves where natural ecosystems are surrounded by heavily modified land use would be susceptible to catastrophic collapse when increasing temperatures exceed the viability threshold for most species, as there is no way in which they can easily migrate to another more suitable environment. Ideally, networks or connected pathways would be needed to allow plant and animal species to move to more favourable locations, but where this is not possible plants and animals may need to be transplanted or physically moved.

A HOLISTIC ECOSYSTEM-BASED APPROACH TO ADAPTATION

A **'whole-of-ecosystem' management plan** therefore needs to address multiple objectives of natural ecosystem management with a particular focus on reducing effects of climate change. It should facilitate ecological adaptation, contribute to societal adaptation through the creation of ecosystem services for adaptation, and mitigate climate change through the creation of ecosystem services for mitigation (e.g. through enhanced carbon storage). Clearly, such a broad, integrated approach should take into account ecological, social, and economic considerations, as well as actively involving partners from industry, national, regional, and local government, and civil society (Locatelli et al. 2015). Figure 6.26 shows that adaptation strategies based on sustainable ecosystems and their services can have a positive impact on long-term economic sustainability by helping to limit the negative effects of climate change.

Ecosystem-based adaptation strategies aim to increase resilience and reduce vulnerability of people and their environment to the impacts of climate change. It is important to be able to understand the response to the changing pattern of climatic hazards, such as severe storms and drought, especially in developing countries, in order to reduce exposure of people and

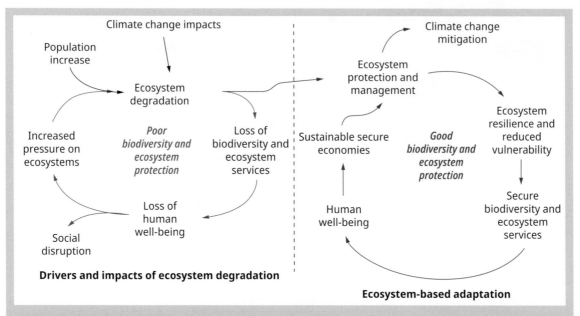

FIGURE 6.26 An illustration of the positive effects of the application of ecosystem-based adaptation in response to climate change, compared with the alternative situation

Source: Munang et al. (2013). Climate change and ecosystem-based adaptation: A new pragmatic approach to buffering climate change impacts. *Current Opinion in Environmental Sustainability* 5: 67–71

their environment to negative effects. Such strategies need to identify the benefits of biodiversity and ecosystem services (the advantages to humans provided by a healthy natural environment), and then conserve, restore, and manage ecosystems for the benefit of both the natural ecosystems and the people who live within them. Adaptation therefore needs to be applied at landscape scale, with the aim of sustaining and restoring the range of unique ecosystem functions within local areas. Examples are often focused on specific environments or aspects of them, including coastal zone restoration, integrated water resource management, and sustainable forest management. Figure 6.27 illustrates the diversity of ecosystem activities and services in a

coastal ecosystem and the complexity of developing an adaptation strategy in response to climate change and sea level rise.

Wherever possible, it is advantageous to use nature to reduce vulnerability of natural ecosystems to climate change, with the approach determined by site-specific characteristics of the natural and cultural environment, including traditional, local, and wider scientific knowledge. Any adaptation strategy should allow the maintenance of biological and cultural diversity within a region, as well as the ability of ecosystems to continue to evolve over time. Figure 6.28 illustrates an iterative approach to conservation of natural environments in response to

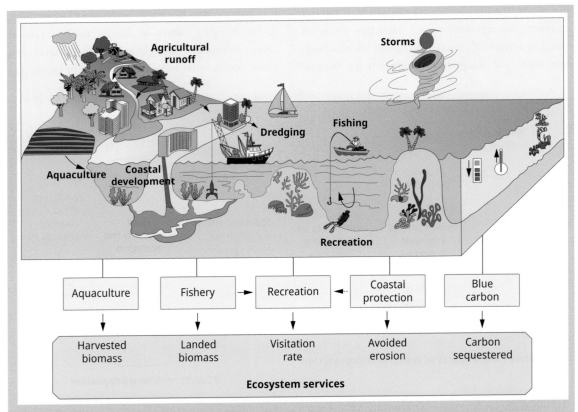

FIGURE 6.27 An illustration of the complexity of coastal ecosystem processes and factors to be considered in developing adaptation strategies

Source: Levrel, H. (2017). Adaptation des sociétés au changement climatique via la biodiversité et les services écosystémiques marins et côtiers. In Lavorel, S., Lebreton, J.-D., and Le Maho, Y. (eds), *Les mécanismes d'adaptation de la biodiversité aux changements climatiques et leurs limites*, Académie des Sciences, Institut de France, Paris, pp. 155–7

climate change that starts with identification of goals and objectives and includes reassessment and adjustment adaptation options and actions as part of the environmental management process. A key aspect of this process is monitoring the effectiveness of adaptation programmes implemented (step 7 in Figure 6.28) and then assessing possible changes. Monitoring should assess the overall health of key ecosystems in relation to changes in biotic distributions and the invasion of new species (e.g. pests and diseases), as well as the impacts of actions taken to respond to climate change. In the latter case, this includes the effects of planting exotic and native trees, the development of renewable energy sources such as hydroelectric stations and wind farms, and the construction of irrigation schemes (which can often have negative impacts on natural ecosystems). Janowiak et al. (2014) developed a comprehensive list of possible specific actions for forest management that could easily be adapted for developing climate change response strategies for other natural ecosystems (Table 6.1), particularly in steps 4, 5, and 6 of Figure 6.28.

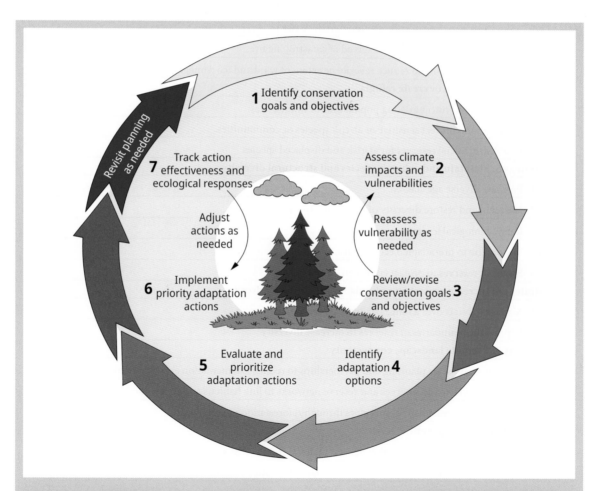

FIGURE 6.28 An iterative approach to developing and implementing adaptation strategies for natural ecosystems in response to climate change

Source: Groffman et al. (2014). Ecosystems, biodiversity, and ecosystem services. In: Melillo, J. M., Richmond, T. C., and Yohe, G. W. (eds), *Climate Change Impacts in the United States: The Third National Climate Assessment*, US Global Change Research Program, Washington, DC, pp. 195–219

TABLE 6.1 Comprehensive list of possible adaptive actions that could be applied to a range of natural ecosystems in response to climate change

Strategy 1: Sustain fundamental ecological functions
1.1 Maintain or restore soil quality and nutrient cycling.
1.2 Maintain or restore hydrology.
1.3 Maintain or restore riparian areas.
Strategy 2: Reduce the impact of existing biological stressors
2.1 Maintain or improve the ability of forests to resist pests and pathogens.
2.2 Prevent the introduction and establishment of invasive plant species and remove existing invasives.
2.3 Manage herbivory to protect or promote regeneration.
Strategy 3: Protect forests from severe fires and wind disturbance
3.1 Alter forest structure or composition to reduce risk or severity of fire.
3.2 Establish fuelbreaks to slow the spread of catastrophic fire.
3.3 Alter forest structure to reduce severity or extent of wind and ice damage.
Strategy 4: Maintain or create refugia
4.1 Prioritize and protect existing populations or unique sites.
4.2 Prioritize and protect sensitive or at-risk species or communities.
4.3 Establish artificial reserves for at-risk and displaced species.
Strategy 5: Maintain and enhance species and structural diversity
5.1 Promote diverse age classes.
5.2 Maintain and restore diversity of native tree species.
5.3 Retain biological legacies.
5.4 Restore fire to fire-adapted ecosystems.
5.5 Establish reserves to protect ecosystem diversity.
Strategy 6: Increase ecosystem redundancy across the landscape
6.1 Manage habitats over a range of sites and conditions.
6.2 Expand the boundaries of reserves to increase diversity.
Strategy 7: Promote landscape connectivity
7.1 Use landscape-scale planning and partnerships to reduce fragmentation and enhance connectivity.
7.2 Establish and expand reserves and reserve networks to link habitats and protect key communities.
7.3 Maintain and create habitat corridors through reforestation or restoration.
Strategy 8: Enhance genetic diversity
8.1 Use seeds, germplasm, and other genetic material from across a greater geographic range.
8.2 Favour existing genotypes that are better adapted to future conditions.
8.3 Increase diversity of nursery stock to provide those species or genotypes likely to succeed.
Strategy 9: Facilitate community adjustments through species transitions
9.1 Anticipate and respond to species decline.

(continued)

TABLE 6.1 (*Continued*)

9.2 Favour or restore native species that are expected to be better adapted to future conditions.
9.3 Manage for species and genotypes with wide moisture and temperature tolerances.
9.4 Emphasize drought- and heat-tolerant species and populations.
9.5 Guide species composition at early stages of stand development.
9.6 Protect future-adapted regeneration from herbivory.
9.7 Establish or encourage new mixes of native species.
9.8 Identify and move species to sites that are likely to provide future habitat.
Strategy 10: Plan for and respond to disturbance
10.1 Prepare for more frequent and more severe disturbances.
10.2 Prepare to realign significantly altered ecosystems to meet expected future environmental conditions.
10.3 Promptly revegetate sites after disturbance.
10.4 Allow for areas of natural regeneration after disturbance.
10.5 Maintain seed or nursery stock of desired species for use after severe disturbance.
10.6 Remove or prevent the establishment of invasives and other competitors after disturbance.

Source: Janowiak et al. (2014). A practical approach for translating climate change adaptation principles into forest management actions. *Journal of Forestry* 112: 424–33

Figure 6.29 provides a different approach to adaptation of ecosystems to climate change, in this case from the perspective of developing integrated **nature-based solutions** to maintaining biodiversity and human well-being. This approach includes restoration, management, and protection of the environment, as well as identification of specific issues of concern within the local area. For example, it has been shown that restoration and maintenance of coastal mangroves has the potential to reduce the impact of severe storms such as tropical cyclones on loss of life in India (Das and Vincent 2009). But some mitigation actions based on nature-based solutions can have negative effects on biodiversity, such as large-scale bioenergy or afforestation of natural grasslands (Seddon et al. 2019). There is therefore a need to better understand the complexity and benefits of nature-based solutions on human activities and biodiversity to avoid **maladaptation** (Seddon et al. 2020; Malhi et al. 2020).

Initially developed by international non-governmental organizations, adaptation to climate change based on ecosystem management is increasingly being adopted in the strategies of many countries. Knowledge of ecosystem services and factors affecting biodiversity has been increasingly used to define national climate change adaptation plans as a complement to traditional engineering-based approaches. Costa Rica is one of the first countries in Central America to take concrete measures to conserve ecosystems by adopting an ecosystem-based approach in developing its climate change adaptation plan. The country's National Climate Change Strategy involves identifying important sectors (water, energy, agriculture, fisheries, coastal zones, and biodiversity) and then assessing their vulnerability to climate change. For example, the adaptation strategy for agriculture aims to increase the resilience and adaptability of smallholder farms to climate change through adaptation technologies that take into account sustainable land use and integrated water resource management. This approach emphasizes the importance of planning climate adaptation policies and programmes for the diverse socio-economic conditions, biophysical

FIGURE 6.29 An approach to climate change adaptation using nature-based solutions to achieve benefits to biodiversity and human well-being

Source: https://www.iucn.org/commissions/commission-ecosystem-management/our-work/nature-based-solutions)

contexts, and climatic hazards faced by smallholder farmers (Harvey et al. 2018).

Ecosystem-based adaptation strategies provide a set of sustainable and cost-effective solutions to the challenges of climate change and sustainable development, particularly when used in combination with other methods and approaches (Munang et al. 2013).

BARRIERS TO ADAPTATION AND THE RISK OF MALADAPTATION

Fragmentation of natural habitats with a resulting lack of pathways for species migration impacts on their biodiversity and resilience in the face of climate change. Problems are created because it is difficult for species within specific habitats to move in response to increasing temperatures. The ability of individual species to adapt *in situ* varies, so that the species composition of these fragmented habitats is likely to change over time as less adaptable species disappear. The resulting changes in biodiversity can be destabilizing for the entire community. It is therefore important that adaptation strategies be designed around the needs of the most specialized species, and that the most sensitive ecosystems are given highest priority (Lavorel et al. 2017).

There is evidence that some adaptation practices, such as widespread forest planting in inappropriate areas, may become a threat to natural ecosystems. The risk of such maladaptation can be avoided by careful consideration of actions that may affect biodiversity and impact on ecosystem services in a given region. This requires improvements in knowledge of both climate and ecosystem processes at the regional and local scales. A holistic approach needs to consider impacts of climate change, impacts of land-use and water-use changes, and resultant changes in biodiversity and the structure of ecosystems.

Summary

- There is a strong link between climate and natural ecosystems, so that a changing climate has inevitable effects on the natural environment.

- However, direct impacts on the environment of human activity through changing land use, resource exploitation, and pollution have increasingly affected the health of both terrestrial and aquatic ecosystems.

- The relationship between ecosystem health and climate can therefore be very complex, making it difficult to predict accurately the specific effects of climate change on ecosystems at regional and local scales.

- It is recognized that a changing climate can produce changes in the spatial distribution of different species, with a warming trend resulting in shifts towards the poles and to higher altitude.

- However, there are many problems that can negatively impact on specific ecosystems, such as differences in the ability and speed with which organisms can respond, barrier effects that block migration, and the sensitivity of different species to change.

- The indirect effects of climate change on such things as pests and diseases, including insect vectors, parasites, and pathogens (such as COVID-19), are also difficult to predict, especially as it is difficult to distinguish the effects of climate change from other non-climate factors.

- Recent climate change has resulted in both latitudinal and altitudinal shifts of species, and models have been developed to predict ecosystem response at regional and local scales.

- Forest and grassland ecosystems are wide ranging, but are expected to shift poleward with continued global warming. They may also be impacted by wildfires and changing hydrological systems.

- Climate change is expected to impact on rivers and lakes through changes in temperature and precipitation causing effects on hydrological regimes. Wildlife that depends on and lives in these environments has limited options for adaptation.

- The oceans respond more slowly to climate change, although both warming and acidification of ocean waters have been observed, while sea level rise is associated with thermal expansion and the melting of land-based ice.

- The health of coral reefs responds in complex ways to climate and other factors, with effects on ocean temperatures, acidity, sea level rise, and localized pollution and environmental degradation.

- Mountain and alpine regions are particularly sensitive to climate change as they are relatively small marginal areas and have an altitude limit to species movement. The complexity of their terrain also creates a multitude of niche environments controlled by their microclimate.

- There is significant concern regarding effects of climate change on polar and sub-polar ecosystems, as these areas are experiencing some of the most rapid changes of climate, with many potential impacts on both terrestrial and marine communities.

- Latitudinal shifts in climate zones are predicted to intensify aridity in some parts of the globe with flow-on effects on the biodiversity of arid and semi-arid ecosystems. However, there is significant variability in the changes in aridity experienced regionally, making development of adaptation strategies a complex process.

- Developing adaptation strategies for natural ecosystems is made difficult because of the complex interactions between human and natural processes. Improved understanding of these processes is required in order to develop a 'whole-of-ecosystem' approach that accounts for the effects of both climate change and other anthropogenic activities (such as land-use change, pollution, and over-exploitation of resources).

- As there is so much variability in the effects of climate change on natural ecosystems, and so many other often anthropogenic factors that affect the future health of natural ecosystems, it is important to develop adaptation strategies that consider the unique characteristics of specific regions. These regions may be relatively small or very extensive, depending on their geographical characteristics, so that the environmental response should be tailored to suit the local or regional situation.

For case studies and updates, visit the online resources

 www.oup.com/he/sturman-quenol1e

References

Archer, S. R., and Predick, K. I. (2008). Climate change and ecosystems of the southwestern United States. *Rangelands* 30(3): 23–8.

Ateweberhan, M., Feary, D. A., Keshavmurthy, S., Chen, A., Schleyer, M. H., and Sheppard, C. R. C. (2013). Climate change impacts on coral reefs: Synergies with local effects, possibilities for acclimation, and management implications. *Marine Pollution Bulletin* 74: 526–39.

Atkinson, A., Hill, S. L., Pakhomov, E. A., Siegel, V., Reiss, C. S., Loeb, V. J., . . . and Sailley, S. F. (2019). Krill (*Euphausia superba*) distribution contracts southward during rapid regional warming. *Nature Climate Change* 9(2): 142–7.

Beaugrand, G., Edwards, M., Raybaud, V., Goberville, E., and Kirby, R. R. (2015). Future vulnerability of marine biodiversity compared with contemporary and past changes. *Nature Climate Change* 5: 695–701.

Berdugo, M., Delgado-Baquerizo, M., Soliveres, S., Hernández-Clemente, R., Zhao, Y., Gaitán, J. J., Gross, N., Saiz, H., Maire, V., Lehmann, A., Rillig, M. C., Solé, R. V., and Maestre, F. T. (2020). Global ecosystem thresholds driven by aridity. *Science* 367: 787–90.

Berner, L. T., Beck, P. S., Bunn, A. G., and Goetz, S. J. (2013). Plant response to climate change along the forest-tundra ecotone in northeastern Siberia. *Global Change Biology* 19(11): 3449–62.

Blair, J., Nippert, J., and Briggs, J. (2014). Grassland ecology. In: Monson, R. K. (ed.), *Ecology and the Environment*. The Plant Sciences. Springer, New York, pp. 389–423.

Bodin, J., Badeau, V., Bruno, E., Cluzeau, C., Moisselin, J. M., Walther, G. R., and Dupouey, J. L. (2013). Shifts of forest species along an elevational gradient in southeast France: Climate change or stand maturation? *Journal of Vegetation Science* 24(2): 269–83.

Brown, L. E., Hannah, D. M., and Milner, A. M. (2007). Vulnerability of alpine stream biodiversity to shrinking glaciers and snowpacks. *Global Change Biology* 13(5): 958–66.

Cheung, W. W., Lam, V. W., Sarmiento, J. L., Kearney, K., Watson, R., and Pauly, D. (2009). Projecting global marine biodiversity impacts under climate change scenarios. *Fish and Fisheries* 10(3): 235–51.

Choi, G., Robinson, D. A., and Kang, S. (2010). Changing Northern Hemisphere snow seasons. *Journal of Climate* 23: 5305–10.

Cramer, W. P., and Leemans, R. (1993). Assessing impacts of climate change on vegetation using climate classification systems. In: Solomon, A. M., and Shugart, H. H. (eds), *Vegetation Dynamics Modelling and Global Change*. Chapman-Hall, New York, pp. 190–217.

Das, Saudamini, and Vincent, J. R. (2009). Mangroves protected villages and reduced death toll during Indian Super Cyclone. *Proceedings of the National Academic of Science* 106(18): 7357–60.

Dimitrov, D., Nogués-Bravo, D., and Scharff, N. (2012). Why do tropical mountains support exceptionally high biodiversity? The Eastern Arc Mountains and the drivers of *Saintpaulia* diversity. *PLOS One* 7: e48908.

Dixon, A. P., Faber-Langendoen, D., Josse, C., Morrison, J., and Loucks, C. J. (2014). Distribution mapping of world grassland types. *Journal of Biogeography* 41: 2003–19.

Djoghlaf, A. (2008). Climate change and biodiversity in polar regions. *Sustainable Development Law and Policy* 8: 14–17.

Dlamini, P., Chivenge, P., and Chaplot, V. (2016). Overgrazing decreases soil organic carbon stocks the most under dry climates and low soil pH: A meta-analysis shows. *Agriculture, Ecosystems and Environment* 221: 258–69.

Dullinger, S., Gattringer, A., Thuiller, W., Moser, D., Zimmermann, N. E., Guisan, A., Willner, W., Plutzar, C., Leitner, M., Mang, T., Caccianiga, M., Dirnböck, T., Ertl, S., Fischer, A., Lenoir, J., Svenning, J.-C., Psomas, A., Schmatz, D. R., Silc, U., Vittoz, P., and Hülber, K. (2012). Extinction debt of high-mountain plants under twenty-first-century climate change. *Nature Climate Change* 2: 619–22.

Dupouey, J.-L. (2017). Gestion des forêts tempérées, changement climatique et biodiversité. In: Lavorel, S., Lebreton, J.-D., and Le Maho, Y. (eds), *Les mécanismes d'adaptation de la biodiversité aux changements climatiques et leurs limites*. Académie des Sciences, Institut de France, Paris, pp. 139–42.

Engler, R., Randin, C. F., Thuiller, W., Dullinger, S., Zimmermann, N. E., Araújo, M. B., Pearman, P. B., Lay, G. L., Piedallu, C., Albert, C. H., Choler, P., Coldea, G., Lamo, X. D., Dirnböck, T., Gégout, J.-C., Gómez-García, D., Grytnes, J.-A., Heegaard, E., Høistad, F., Nogués-Bravo, D., Normand, S., Puşcaş, M., Sebastià, M.-T., Stanisci, A., Theurillat, J.-P., Trivedi, M. R., Vittoz, P., and Guisan, A. (2011). 21st century climate change threatens mountain flora unequally across Europe. *Global Change Biology* 17: 2330–41.

FAO (2018). *The State of the World's Forests 2018: Forest Pathways to Sustainable Development*. Food and Agriculture Organization of the United Nations, Rome.

Flores, H., Atkinson, A., Kawaguchi, S., Krafft, B. A., and others (2012) Impact of climate change on Antarctic krill. *Marine Ecology Progress Series*, 458: 1–19.

Gibson, D. J., and Newman, J. A. (2019). Grasslands and climate change: an overview. In: Gibson, D., and Newman, J. (eds), *Grasslands and Climate Change*. Cambridge University Press, Cambridge, pp. 3–18.

Groffman, P. M., Kareiva, P., Carter, S., Grimm, N. B., Lawler, J., Mack, M., Matzek, V., and Tallis, H. (2014). Ecosystems, biodiversity, and ecosystem services. In: Melillo, J. M., Richmond, T. C., and Yohe, G. W. (eds), *Climate Change Impacts in the United States: The Third National Climate Assessment*, US Global Change Research Program, Washington, DC, pp. 195–219.

Guisan, A., Broennimann, O., Buri, A., Cianfrani, C., D'Amen, M., Di Cola, V., ... and Pradervand, J. N. (2019). Climate change impacts on mountain biodiversity. In: Lovejoy, T. E., and Lee, H. (eds), *Biodiversity and Climate Change*. Yale University Press, New Haven, Connecticut, pp. 221–33.

Häder, D.-P. and Barnes, P. W. (2019). Comparing the impacts of climate change on the responses and linkages between terrestrial and aquatic ecosystems. *Science of the Total Environment* 682: 239–46.

Harris, R. M. B., Beaumont, L. J., Vance, T. R., Tozer, C. R., Remenyi, T. A., Perkins-Kirkpatrick, S. E., Mitchell, P. J., Nicotra, A. B., McGregor, S., Andrew, N. R., Letnic, M., Kearney, M. R., Wernberg, T., Hutley, L. B., Chambers, L. E., Fletcher, M.-S., Keatley, M. R., Woodward, C. A., Williamson, G., Duke, N. C., and Bowman, D. M. J. S. (2018). Biological responses to the press and pulse of climate trends and extreme events. *Nature Climate Change* 8: 579–87.

Hart, K. M., Curioni, G., Blaen, P., Harper, N. J., Miles, P., Lewin, K. F., ... and Krause, S. (2020). Characteristics of free air carbon dioxide enrichment of a northern temperate mature forest. *Global Change Biology* 26: 1023–37.

Harvey, C. A., Saborio-Rodríguez, M., Martinez-Rodríguez, M. R., Viguera, B., Chain-Guadarrama, A., Vignola, R., and Alpizar, F. (2018). Climate change impacts and adaptation among smallholder farmers in Central America. *Agriculture and Food Security* 7: 57.

Huang, J., Ji, M., Xie, Y., Wang, S., He, Y., and Ran, J. (2016). Global semi-arid climate change over last 60 years. *Climate Dynamics* 46(3–4): 1131–50.

IPBES (2019). *Summary for Policymakers of the Global Assessment Report on Biodiversity and Ecosystem Services of the Intergovernmental Science-Policy Platform on Biodiversity and Ecosystem Services*. Díaz, S., Settele, J., Brondízio E. S., Ngo, H. T., Guèze, M., Agard, J., Arneth, A., Balvanera, P., Brauman, K. A., Butchart, S. H. M., Chan, K. M. A., Garibaldi, L. A., Ichii, K., Liu, J., Subramanian, S. M., Midgley, G. F., Miloslavich, P., Molnár, Z., Obura, D., Pfaff, A., Polasky, S., Purvis, A., Razzaque, J., Reyers, B., Roy Chowdhury, R., Shin, Y. J., Visseren-Hamakers, I. J., Willis, K. J., and Zayas, C. N. (eds). IPBES Secretariat, Bonn.

Janowiak, M. K., Swanston, C. W., Nagel, L. M., Brandt, L. A., Butler, P. R., Handler, S. D., Shannon, P. D., Iverson, L. R., Matthews, S. N., and Prasad, A. (2014). A practical approach for translating climate change adaptation principles into forest management actions. *Journal of Forestry* 112: 424–33.

Jenouvrier, S., Holland, M., Iles, D., Labrousse, S., Landrum, L., Garnier, J., ... and Barbraud, C. (2020). The Paris Agreement objectives will likely halt future declines of emperor penguins. *Global Change Biology* 26: 1170–84.

Jezkova, T., and Wiens, J. J. (2016). Rates of change in climatic niches in plant and animal populations are much slower than projected climate change. *Proceedings of the Royal Society B: Biological Sciences* 283(1843): 20162104.

Jones, M. B. (2019). Projected climate change and the global distribution of grasslands. In Gibson, D., and Newman, J. (eds), *Grasslands and Climate Change*. Cambridge University Press, Cambridge, pp. 67–81.

Joyce, L. A., Running, S. W., Breshears, D. D., Dale, V. H., Malmsheimer, R. W., Sampson, R. N., Sohngen, B., and Woodall, C. W. (2014). Forests. In: Melillo, J. M., Richmond, T. C., and Yohe, G. W. (eds), *Climate Change Impacts in the United States: The Third National Climate Assessment*, US Global Change Research Program, Washington, DC, pp. 175–94.

Keith, D. A., Ferrer-Paris, J. R., Nicholson, E., Bishop, M. J., Polidoro, B. A., Ramirez-Llodra, E., Tozer, M. G., Nel, J. L., Mac Nally, R., Gregr, E. J., Watermeyer, K. E., Essl, F., Faber-Langendoen, D., Franklin, J., Lehmann, C. E. R., Etter, A., Roux, D. J., Stark, J. S., Rowland, J. A., Brummitt, N. A., Fernandez-Arcaya, U. C., Suthers, I. M., Wiser, S. K., Donohue, I., Jackson, L. J., Pennington, R. T., Iliffe, T. M., Gerovasileiou, V., Giller, P., Robson, B. J., Pettorelli, N., Andrade, A., Lindgaard, A., Tahvanainen, T., Terauds, A., Chadwick, M. A., Murray, N. J., Moat, J., Pliscoff, P., Zager, I., and Kingsford, R. T. (2022). A function-based typology for Earth's ecosystems. *Nature* 610: 513–18.

Kohler, T., Wehrli, A., and Jurek, M. (eds) (2014). *Mountains and Climate Change: A Global Concern*. Sustainable Mountain Development Series. Centre for Development and Environment (CDE), Swiss Agency for Development and Cooperation (SDC), and Geographica Bernensia, Bern.

Lavorel, S., Lebreton, J.-D., and Le Maho, Y. (2017). *Les mécanismes d'adaptation de la biodiversité aux changements climatiques et leurs limites*. Académie des Sciences, Institut de France, Paris.

Leemans, R., and Eickhout, B. (2004). Another reason for concern: Regional and global impacts on ecosystems for different levels of climate change. *Global Environmental Change* 14(3): 219–28.

Lenoir, J., Gégout, J. C., Marquet, P. A., De Ruffray, P., and Brisse, H. (2008). A significant upward shift in plant species optimum elevation during the 20th century. *Science* 320(5884): 1768–71.

Lenoir, J., Bertrand, R., Comte, L., Bourgeaud, L., Hattab, T., Murienne, J., and Grenouillet, G. (2020). Species better track climate warming in the oceans than on land. *Nature Ecology and Evolution* 4: 1044–59.

Levrel, H. (2017). Adaptation des sociétés au changement climatique via la biodiversité et les services écosystémiques marins et côtiers. In Lavorel, S., Lebreton, J.-D., and Le Maho, Y. (eds), *Les mécanismes d'adaptation de la biodiversité aux changements climatiques et leurs limites*, Académie des Sciences, Institut de France, Paris, pp. 155–7.

Locatelli, B., Catterall, C. P., Imbach, P., Kumar, C., Lasco, R., Marín-Spiotta, E., Mercer, B., Powers, J. S., Schwartz, N., and Uriarte, M. (2015). Tropical reforestation and climate change: Beyond carbon. *Restoration Ecology* 23: 337–43.

Luoto, M., and Heikkinen, R. K. (2008). Disregarding topographical heterogeneity biases species turnover assessments based on bioclimatic models. *Global Change Biology* 14: 483–94.

McClanahan, T. R., Darling, E. S., Maina, J. M., Muthiga, N. A., 'agata, S. D., Jupiter, S. D., Arthur, R., Wilson, S. K., Mangubhai, S., Nand, Y., Ussi, A. M., Humphries, A. T., Patankar, V. J., Guillaume, M. M. M., Keith, S. A., Shedrawi, G., Julius, P., Grimsditch, G., Ndagala, J., and Leblond, J. (2019). Temperature patterns and mechanisms influencing coral bleaching during the 2016 El Niño. *Nature Climate Change* 9: 845–51.

McGlone, M., and Walker, S. (2011). *Potential Effects of Climate Change on New Zealand's Terrestrial Biodiversity and Policy Recommendations for Mitigation, Adaptation and Research*. Science for Conservation 312, Department of Conservation, Wellington.

McGowan, H., Sturman, A., Saunders, M., Theobald, A., and Wiebe, A. (2019). Insights from a decade of research on coral reef–atmosphere energetics. *Journal of Geophysical Research: Atmospheres* 124: 4269–82.

Macinnis-Ng, C., Mcintosh, A. R., Monks, J. M., Waipara, N., White, R. S., Boudjelas, S., ... and Peltzer, D. A. (2021). Climate-change impacts exacerbate conservation threats in island systems: New Zealand as a case study. *Frontiers in Ecology and the Environment* 19(4): 216–24.

Malhi, Y., Franklin, J., Seddon, N., Solan, M., Turner, M. G., Field, C. B., and Knowlton, N. (2020). Climate change and ecosystems: Threats, opportunities and solutions. *Philosophical Transactions of the Royal Society B* 375: 20190104.

Maxwell, S., Fuller, R. A., Brooks, T. M., and Watson, J. E. M. (2016). The ravages of guns, nets and bulldozers. *Nature* 536 (7615): 143–5.

Mayor, J. R., Sanders, N. J., Classen, A. T., Bardgett, R. D., Clément, J. C., Fajardo, A., . . . and Cieraad, E. (2017). Elevation alters ecosystem properties across temperate treelines globally. *Nature* 542(7639): 91–5.

Melillo, J. M., Richmond, T. C., and Yohe, G. W. (eds) (2014). *Climate Change Impacts in the United States: The Third National Climate Assessment*. US Global Change Research Program, Washington, DC.

Miranda, L. S., Imperatriz-Fonseca, V. L., and Giannini, T. C. (2019). Climate change impact on ecosystem functions provided by birds in southeastern Amazonia. *PLOS One* 14(4): e0215229.

Molnár, P. K., Derocher, A. E., Klanjscek, T., and Lewis, M. A. (2011). Predicting climate change impacts on polar bear litter size. *Nature Communications* 2(1): 1–8.

Morrow, J. V., and Fischenich, C. (2000). *Habitat Requirements for Freshwater Fishes*. Technical note ERDC TN-EMR-RP-SR-06, Ecosystem Management and Restoration Research Program (US Army Corps of Engineers). https://www.arlis.org/docs/vol1/EMRRP/47088107.pdf.

Munang, R., Thiaw, I., Alverson, K., Mumba, M., Liu, J., and Rivington, M. (2013). Climate change and ecosystem-based adaptation: A new pragmatic approach to buffering climate change impacts. *Current Opinion in Environmental Sustainability* 5: 67–71.

Pauly, D., and Christensen, V. (1995). Primary production required to sustain global fisheries. *Nature* 374: 255–7.

Pearson, R. G., Phillips, S. J., Loranty, M. M., Beck, P. S. A., Damoulas, T., Knight, S. J., and Goetz, S.J. (2013). Shifts in Arctic vegetation and associated feedbacks under climate change. *Nature Climate Change* 3: 673–7.

Pecl, G. T., Araújo, M. B., Bell, J. D., Blanchard, J., Bonebrake, T. C., Chen, I. C., . . . and Falconi, L. (2017). Biodiversity redistribution under climate change: Impacts on ecosystems and human well-being. *Science* 355(6332).

Pinsky, M. L., Worm, B., Fogarty, M. J., Sarmiento, J. L., and Levin, S. A. (2013). Marine taxa track local climate velocities. *Science* 341: 1239–42.

Prop, J., Aars, J., Bårdsen, B. J., Hanssen, S. A., Bech, C., Bourgeon, S., . . . and Oudman, T. (2015). Climate change and the increasing impact of polar bears on bird populations. *Frontiers in Ecology and Evolution* 3: 33.

Pureswaran, D. S., Roques, A., and Battisti, A. (2018). Forest insects and climate change. *Current Forestry Reports* 4: 35–50.

Radchuk, V., Reed, T., Teplitsky, C., Van De Pol, M., Charmantier, A., Hassall, C., . . . and Kramer-Schadt, S. (2019). Adaptive responses of animals to climate change are most likely insufficient. *Nature Communications* 10(1): 1–14.

Randin, C. F., Engler, R., Normand, S., Zappa, M., Zimmermann, N. E., Pearman, P. B., . . . and Guisan, A. (2009). Climate change and plant distribution: Local models predict high-elevation persistence. *Global Change Biology* 15: 1557–69.

Roberts, C. P., Allen, C. R., Angeler, D. G., and Twidwell, D. (2019). Shifting avian spatial regimes in a changing climate. *Nature Climate Change* 9: 562–6.

Saltré, F., Duputé, A., Gaucherel, C., and Chuine I. (2015). How climate, migration ability and habitat fragmentation affect the projected future distribution of European beech. *Global Change Biology* 21: 897–910.

Santiago, J. M., Jalón, D. G. de, Alonso, C., Solana, J., Ribalaygua, J., Pórtoles, J., and Monjo, R. (2016). Brown trout thermal niche and climate change: Expected changes in the distribution of cold-water fish in central Spain. *Ecohydrology* 9: 514–28.

Seddon, N., Chausson, A., Berry, P., Girardin, C. A., Smith, A., and Turner, B. (2020). Understanding the value and limits of nature-based solutions to climate change and other global challenges. *Philosophical Transactions of the Royal Society B* 375(1794): 20190120.

Seddon, N., Turner, B., Berry, P., Chausson, A., and Girardin, C. A. (2019). Grounding nature-based climate solutions in sound biodiversity science. *Nature Climate Chang* 9: 84–7.

Semenza, J. C., and Suk, J. E. (2018). Vector-borne diseases and climate change: A European perspective. *FEMS Microbiological Letters* 365(2): 244.

Soultan, A., Wikelski, M., and Safi, K. (2019). Risk of biodiversity collapse under climate change in the Afro-Arabian region. *Scientific Reports* 9(1): 1–12.

Stocker, T. F., Qin, D., Plattner, G. K., Tignor, M., Allen, S. K., Boschung, J., . . . and Midgley, P. M. (2013). Climate change 2013: The physical science basis. Contribution of Working Group I to the Fifth Assessment Report of the Intergovernmental Panel on Climate Change, 1535.

Theurillat, J. P., and Guisan, A. (2001). Potential impact of climate change on vegetation in the European Alps: A review. *Climatic Change* 50: 77–109.

USGCRP (2017). *Climate Science Special Report: Fourth National Climate Assessment*, Volume I (Wuebbles, D. J., Fahey, D. W., Hibbard, K. A., Dokken, D. J., Stewart, B. C., and Maycock, T. K. (eds)). US Global Change Research Program, Washington, DC.

USGCRP (2018). *Impacts, Risks, and Adaptation in the United States: Fourth National Climate Assessment*, Volume II (Reidmiller, D. R., Avery, C. W., Easterling, D. R., Kunkel, K. E., Lewis, K. L. M., Maycock, T. K., and Stewart, B. C. (eds)). US Global Change Research Program, Washington, DC.

Vale, C. G., and Brito, J. C. (2015). Desert-adapted species are vulnerable to climate change: Insights from the warmest region on Earth. *Global Ecology and Conservation* 4: 369–79.

Vale, C. G., Campos, J. C., Silva, T. L., Gonçalves, D. V., Sow, A. S., Martínez-Freiría, F., . . . and Brito, J. C. (2016). Biogeography and conservation of mammals from the West Sahara-Sahel: An application of ecological niche-based models and GIS. *Hystrix* 27(1). https://doi.org/10.4404/hystrix-27.1-11659.

Warren, R., Price, J., Graham, E., Forstenhaeusler, N., and VanDerWal, J. (2018). The projected effect on insects, vertebrates, and plants of limiting global warming to 1.5 C rather than 2 C. *Science* 360(6390): 791–5.

Wiens, J. J. (2016). Climate-related local extinctions are already widespread among plant and animal species. *PLOS biology* 14(12): e2001104.

Wilhelm, L., Singer, G. A., Fasching, C., Battin, T. J., and Besemer, K. (2013). Microbial biodiversity in glacier-fed streams. *The ISME Journal* 7(8): 1651–60.

Willis, K. J., and Bhagwat, S. A. (2009). Biodiversity and climate change. *Science* 326(5954): 806–7.

Zhou, G., Zhou, X., He, Y., Shao, J., Hu, Z., Liu, R., Zhou, H., and Hosseinibai, S. (2017). Grazing intensity significantly affects belowground carbon and nitrogen cycling in grassland ecosystems: A meta-analysis. *Global Change Biology* 23: 1167–79.

CHAPTER **SEVEN**

Environmental Hazards and Climate Change

LEARNING OUTCOMES

Having read this chapter, you should be able to:

- critically discuss the relationship between environmental hazards, natural disasters, and anthropogenic climate change

- explain the problem of uncertainty associated with model predictions of future trends in extreme weather events, and the difficulty of attributing extreme events to human activity

- describe a range of possible effects of climate change on the occurrence of environmental hazards and their impacts on regional and local communities

- discuss the relationship between increasing average global temperatures and heatwave occurrence, and its impact globally and on local communities

- describe the difficulties in predicting future regional flood and drought conditions based on global model predictions

- provide a critical assessment of our ability to predict future severe storm and wildland fire occurrence at the regional scale resulting from the impacts of climate change

- explore the problem of separating the effects of climate change, human modification of the landscape, and natural factors on environmental hazards and natural disasters

- outline some possible options for reducing the impact of climate change-induced environmental hazards and natural disasters on local communities

7.1 Introduction: environmental hazards and climate change

This chapter examines the possible effects of climate change on both the frequency and magnitude of environmental hazards, particularly extreme events such as severe storms, floods, drought, and wildfires. Possible effects of climate change on such events are often discussed at the global level in a range of publications from media articles to scientific reports (e.g. IPCC 2021), although their impact is often greatest at the regional and local scales. Because of the widespread interest in environmental hazards, we believe that it is important to examine separately their impact on local communities and the extent to which adaptation strategies can be applied at the community level to reduce their impact. In previous chapters, we have mentioned the impacts of climate change in relation to different areas such as agriculture, natural biodiversity, and the urban environment. Here, we focus on the impact of the increased frequency and intensity of extreme events across a range of different areas, and explore how communities can respond.

ENVIRONMENTAL HAZARDS AND NATURAL DISASTERS

A severe or extreme weather or climate event is an 'environmental hazard' that has the potential to create a '**natural disaster**' if it has a significant impact on humans. An environmental or natural hazard can therefore be defined as a 'natural process or phenomenon that may cause loss of life, injury or other health impacts, property damage, loss of livelihoods and services, social and economic disruption or environmental damage' (United Nations International Strategy for Disaster Reduction 2009, p. 20), while a disaster is a 'serious disruption of the functioning of a community or a society involving widespread human, material, economic or environmental losses and impacts, which exceeds the ability of the affected community or society

to cope using its own resources' (ibid. p. 9). That is, a hazard (e.g. a tornado) has the potential to cause a disaster, but it may not always do so (e.g. if it does not impact on a human community).

Environmental hazards are often extreme events that fall outside the normal range of variability, either extremely high or low. They may occur suddenly (e.g. a tornado) or develop slowly (e.g. a drought). Climate change can increase both the frequency and intensity of environmental hazards and their impact on the vulnerability of human populations. An environmental hazard is therefore anything, typically an event, that may threaten the natural environment and adversely affect human health. Severe storms, floods, wildfires, and droughts can be considered environmental hazards that have the capacity to cause natural disasters. However, such events on their own do not necessarily result in natural disasters (e.g. not all tropical cyclones or thunderstorms have a significant impact on humans), as the latter also require a vulnerable and poorly prepared community to be impacted. A natural disaster is effectively the result of both the impact of an environmental hazard and human exposure to it, as well as the pre-existing vulnerability and ability of communities to respond to its impact. Natural disasters are therefore often not due to natural processes alone. For example, the impact of a flooding disaster may partly result from previous modification of a natural drainage system by human activity (e.g. by deforestation), increasing community vulnerability. The risk associated with a changing climate is therefore a function of climate variability, whether natural or anthropogenic in origin, alongside community vulnerability and exposure (as shown in Figure 7.1).

It should also be noted that some natural disasters may be the result of more than one environmental hazard. For example, wildfires can result from a combination of extreme high temperatures and drought, while

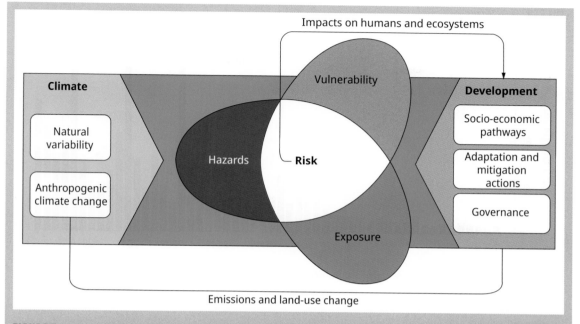

FIGURE 7.1 Risk of natural disaster as a combination of the effects of changing climate on environmental hazards and community vulnerability and exposure

Source: Intergovernmental Panel on Climate Change (2012). *Managing the Risks of Extreme Events and Disasters to Advance Climate Change Adaptation.* A Special Report of Working Groups I and II of the Intergovernmental Panel on Climate Change (Field, C. B., Barros, V., Stocker, T. F., Qin, D., Dokken, D. J., Ebi, K. L., Mastrandrea, M. D., Mach, K. J., Plattner, G.-K., Allen, S. K., Tignor, M., and Midgley, P. M. (eds)). Cambridge University Press, Cambridge and New York

coastal flooding may be caused by a combination of sea level rise and intense rainfall in inland catchments.

The increasing impact of climate-related natural disasters on insured losses shown in Figure 7.2 might, at first glance, be assumed to result from an increase in environmental hazards of atmospheric origin. However, this apparent increase in the impact of weather-related natural disasters could be due to either increased human exposure and vulnerability to insured losses, or an increased frequency of extreme weather/climate events, or both. This trend could therefore merely indicate increased wealth and insurance cover among the population, hence increasing the magnitude of any insured losses, rather than a real trend in the number of hazardous events. In fact, although rising trends have been identified in some environmental hazards, analysis of extreme weather events such as tropical cyclones has often shown no significant long-term trend (Alimonti et al. 2022; Figure 7.3). There are other problems in interpreting

past records of extreme events, including improvements in reporting of such events as a result of improved technology and increasing populations causing greater exposure. There is also much regional variability in observed trends of extreme events such as droughts and severe storms, so it is hard to identify the true trend of extreme events in any specific location. This makes it really difficult for local communities and regional governments to develop effective adaptation strategies.

The global pattern of natural disasters is strongly influenced by the distribution of global population. Not all environmental hazards cause natural disasters, but they are more likely to cause disasters where population density is higher. However, when considering the impact of climate-related events, areas experiencing the highest number of such natural disasters are not necessarily the same as those experiencing the greatest impact on human populations. For example, the Americas tend to experience the greatest economic losses due to natural

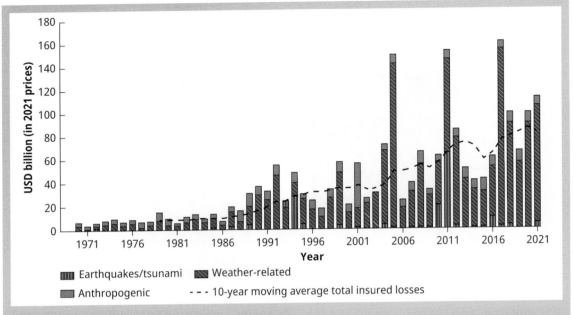

FIGURE 7.2 Global insured losses associated with natural disasters of earthquake, weather-related and anthropogenic origin (1970–2021)

Source: https://www.swissre.com/media/press-release/nr-20211214-sigma-full-year-2021-preliminary-natcat-loss-estimates.html

disasters, while those experienced in Africa are much less (Handmer et al. 2012).

UNDERSTANDING THE EFFECTS OF CLIMATE CHANGE

Predicting future trends in extreme events over different parts of the world has a low level of confidence because of the uncertainty implicit in climate models, the character of each type of extreme event, and the inability of global climate models to represent accurately the key processes that operate at the regional and local scales (see Chapter 2). One could reasonably suggest that, based on climate model studies, severe weather will increase globally over coming decades, but that is not particularly useful for local communities located in small regions whose weather/climate is strongly affected by their unique geographical situation (e.g. their terrain and land cover, and proximity to sea or mountain barriers).

Although more extreme events might be expected from a warming climate based on our understanding of atmospheric processes, it is difficult to identify specific links with either the frequency or magnitude of such events, or their spatial and temporal distribution. Recent trends in a range of severe environmental hazards have been associated with climate change, including severe storms (wind, lightning, hurricanes), intense rainfall/floods, snowstorms, extreme heat, droughts, wildfires, and coastal flooding. However, non-linearities such as tipping points make it difficult to identify current or predict future trends in extreme weather, particularly at the regional and local scales.

Improvements in climate model design and available data can help reduce this uncertainty, particularly through the development of improved downscaling techniques (as discussed in Chapter 2). There is a clear need to obtain data at a much higher spatial and temporal resolution than provided by global climate models in order to assess impacts of climate change on extreme weather experienced at community level (Dosio 2018;

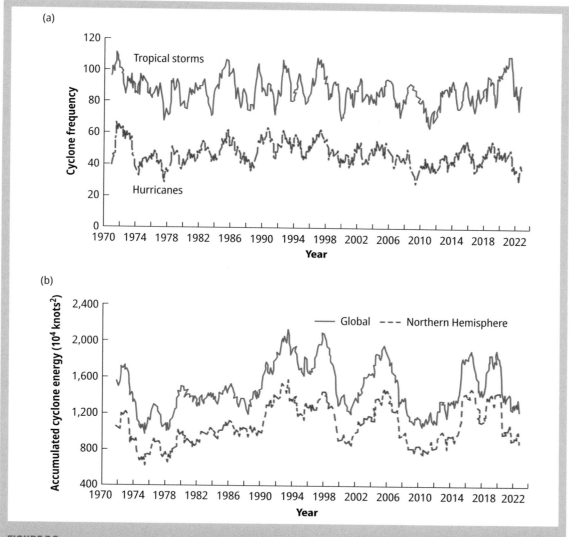

FIGURE 7.3 Recent trends in (a) global tropical cyclone frequency and (b) accumulated energy, 1971–2022, shown as 12-month running sums

Source: https://climatlas.com/tropical/

Xu 2019; Eum et al. 2016). Regional climate models allow much better resolution of the effects of small-scale features, such as variations in terrain and land use, but even they often need bias correction in order to be useful for assessing climate change impacts on extreme events and developing appropriate adaptation strategies.

CLIMATE MODEL UNCERTAINTY FOR EXTREME PREDICTIONS

Large-scale climate models are often unable to represent atmospheric processes and phenomena at the regional and local scales, particularly in regions of complex terrain. Bias in the results of global climate models may be due to a range of factors, including imperfect representation of atmospheric processes (e.g. surface–atmosphere feedbacks) and an inability to represent processes generated by the fine-scale variability of surface characteristics that is not resolved at the global scale. There is also uncertainty associated with assumptions made regarding the constancy of statistical distributions of climate factors during climate change, and this is of particular concern when attempting to predict extreme events (Flato et al. 2013). Changes in average conditions are easier to predict than extremes, which tend to be randomly chaotic and rare. It is often assumed that the statistical distribution of variables such as hourly temperature, precipitation, or wind speed will stay essentially the same, when in fact it is evident that this is often not the case (Sippel et al. 2016; Dosio 2018). This is of significant concern when dealing with extreme weather events, as suggested by Figure 7.4, in which a similar change of average temperature is predicted for two European cities (Modena in Italy and Paris in France) although the statistical distributions are quite different. The predicted increased monthly mean summer temperature range shown for Paris (Figure 7.4(b))

would increase the occurrence of heatwaves without changing the frequency of low temperatures. It is expected that changes in the frequency distributions of climate factors such as temperature and rainfall (at hourly, daily, monthly, or annual timescales) will vary spatially, resulting in both increases and decreases in extreme events such as floods, droughts, heatwaves, and frosts at the regional and local scales.

A key reason for changes in the occurrence and/or intensity of extreme weather events in a given area is that, in addition to a long-term warming trend, there are also likely to be changes in the movement and intensity of weather systems (Priestley and Catto 2022). The daily temperature range is significantly greater under anticyclonic conditions than under cyclonic weather systems. Therefore, shifts in the location of anticyclones and changes in their intensity can lead to regional changes in the frequency distribution of hourly temperatures (similar to that shown for monthly temperatures in Figure 7.4(b)) while the average daily temperature continues to increase.

It should be noted that climate change can affect not only the frequency and intensity of extreme events, but also their timing and duration (Greenough et al. 2001).

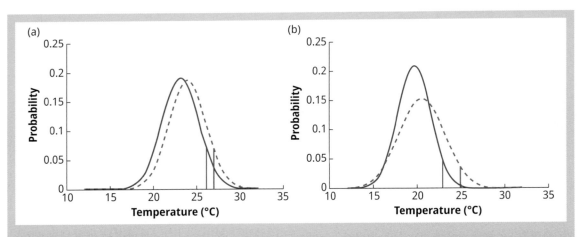

FIGURE 7.4 Frequency distribution curves of monthly mean summer temperatures obtained for two European cities, (a) Modena, Italy, and (b) Paris, France, for the past (blue line: 1971–2000) and the future (red line: 2021–2050). The 95th percentile is indicated by the vertical lines

Source: Fallmann et al. (2017). High resolution climate projections to assess the future vulnerability of European urban areas to climatological extreme events. *Theoretical and Applied Climatology* 127: 667–83

An assessment of model predictions of extreme temperatures and precipitation over the north-eastern United States and south-eastern Canada based on 13 different global climate models identified reasonable confidence in predictions of extreme cold, but significant uncertainty in predictions of extreme heat and precipitation associated with inter-model variations in the **skewness** of predictions (Vavrus et al. 2015).

It is therefore difficult to absolutely confirm links between climate change and extreme events using commonly applied statistical techniques. Consequently, a range of linear and non-linear techniques have been applied in order to develop transfer functions to correct model output (Sippel et al. 2016). For example, **quantile mapping** techniques have been used to try and correct problems with the statistical distribution of modelled extreme values. This involves correcting each **quantile** of the distribution of the predicted variable, although there is concern that this approach causes problems for climate indices based on thresholds or duration of events. It is therefore considered that climate model prediction of climate indices that involve the duration of a severe weather event, such as drought, cannot be easily bias adjusted (Viceto et al. 2019). Clearly, any climate model prediction study should acknowledge that the statistical distribution of climate variables may well change in the future, while current methods of bias correction are of limited applicability as they are statistically based and do not necessarily reflect physical processes.

Combinations of different global and regional models have been used to assess possible impacts of climate change on extreme weather at the regional scale, often resulting in significant inter-model variability (Eum et al. 2016; Fontolan et al. 2019). For example, Eum et al. (2016) identified seasonal variation in the bias of 12 different regional climate models when applied to change in temperature extremes over southern Quebec, Canada, concluding that predictions of future temperature extremes at the regional and local scales may be significantly affected by local atmospheric processes that may not be adequately represented.

Bias-correction techniques have been developed to address the inability of available models to adequately predict effects of climate change on the future occurrence and intensity of extreme weather events. However, recent research has suggested that in some cases extreme impacts can be the result of a combination of only moderate weather events (van der Wiel et al. 2020). It is therefore important not to focus on predicting just one type of extreme event (e.g. strong winds, heavy rainfall, storm surge, or high temperatures), as this could easily fail to identify the risk associated with combinations of events.

ANTHROPOGENIC ATTRIBUTION STUDIES

A number of studies have tried to evaluate the contribution of anthropogenic effects to extreme weather at the regional scale using a comparison of different models and observations (National Academies of Sciences, Engineering, and Medicine 2016; Zwiers et al. 2013). The process of attributing rare extreme events to human activity is a challenging and complex task, as it requires comparison of the actual record of occurrence of such events with a simulated record that assumes that the effect of human activity has been removed. For example, Christidis and Stott (2016) used 16 different temperature indices to assess the contribution of human activity to longer-term climate trends globally and over Europe using both observed and modelled data. A clear attribution signal was identified at this coarse scale, but it was concluded that multimodel high-resolution simulations were required to explain smaller-scale, local extreme temperature variability. Angélil et al. (2016) obtained overly strong attribution of extreme temperatures over Africa and Australia to human effects when compared with North America and Asia. The results for precipitation were much more spatially variable. There was also significant variability between models and different re-analysis data sets, suggesting that there is significant uncertainty associated with the use of such models and data sets for investigating human contributions to changes in extreme weather (Angélil et al. 2017). Similarly, it has been identified that unreliable models are prone to overestimate extreme event attribution and that careful climate model ensemble calibration needs to be conducted as part of event attribution studies (Bellprat and Doblas-Reyes 2016; Bellprat et al. 2019). However, this is difficult because of the low frequency of extreme events.

In addition, different events can combine to create an enhanced negative affect (e.g. sea level rise and increased severe storms). So, climate change can increase the level of risk of event occurrence while the magnitude of the impact of environmental hazards may also rise. Such extreme events have likely downstream effects on human health and welfare, volatility of food harvest yields, and infrastructure damage (buildings, roads, water and power supplies, etc.), and it is the poorest countries that have the least ability to cope with the increasing impact of such environmental hazards under climate change. Table 7.1 provides a list of recent examples of major natural disasters thought to be affected by the global warming trend, organized by the nature of their economic impact. The most common events appear to have been heatwaves and

TABLE 7.1 List of recent climate-related natural disasters, organized by the nature of their economic impact

IMPACTED ECONOMIC SYSTEM	AREA OF DIRECT RISK	SOCIOECONOMIC IMPACT	HOW CLIMATE CHANGE EXACERBATED HAZARD
Liveability and workability	1. 2003 European heatwave	$15 billion in losses	2× more likely
	2. 2010 Russian heatwave	~55,000 deaths attributed	3× more likely
	3. 2013–14 Australian heatwave	~$6 billion in productivity loss	Up to 3× more likely
	4. 2017 East African drought	~8 million people displaced in Somalia	2× more likely
	5. 2019 European heatwave	~1,500 deaths in France	~10× more likely in France
Food systems	6. 2015 Southern Africa drought	Agriculture outputs declined by 15%	3× more likely
	7. Ocean warming	Up to 35% decline in North Atlantic fish yields	Ocean surface temperatures have risen by 0.7 °C globally
Physical assets	8. 2012 Hurricane Sandy	$62 billion in damage	3× more likely
	9. 2016 Fort McMurray Fire, Canada	$10 billion in damage, 1.5 million acres of forest burned	1.5–6× more likely
	10. 2017 Hurricane Harvey	$125 billion in damage	8–20% more intense
Infrastructure services	11. 2017 flooding in China	$3.55 billion of direct economic loss, including severe infrastructure damage	2× more likely
Natural capital	12. 30-year record low Arctic sea ice in 2012	Reduced albedo effect, amplifying warming	70–95% attributable to human-induced climate change
	13. Decline of Himalayan glaciers	Potential reduction in water supply for more than 240 million people	~70% of global glacier mass lost in past 20 years is due to human-induced climate change

Source: Woetzel et al. (2020). *Climate Risk and Response: Physical Hazards and Socioeconomic Impacts*. McKinsey Global Institute, New York

droughts, with severe storms such as hurricanes, wild-fires, and flooding also being important. Their main impacts have been on the health and welfare of human populations, as well as on food production, physical assets, and infrastructure. It should be noted that the list reflects those events that caught global attention, while many other smaller-scale events have also had economic impacts at the regional and local scales over the past several decades.

Figure 7.5 provides a diagram summarizing the relationship between our understanding of the effects of climate on extreme events and our ability to identify effects of climate change on their future occurrence. The vertical axis indicates our ability to be able to identify the effects of climate change on extreme events, while the horizontal axis indicates our current understanding of how climate processes affect such events. It is clear that the more we understand about the effect of

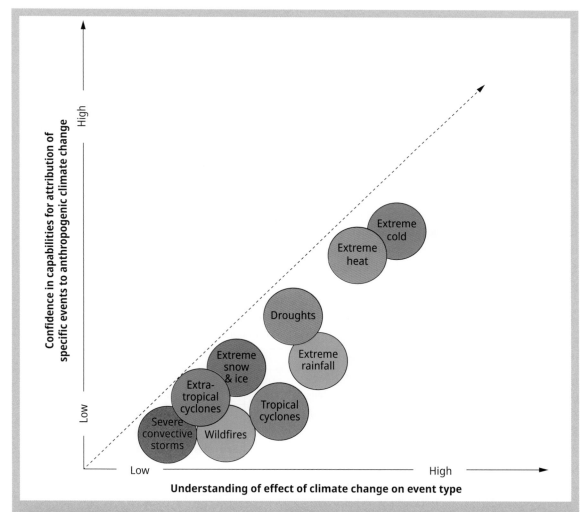

FIGURE 7.5 Schematic illustration of the relationship between knowledge of the effects of climate change processes on extreme events (horizontal axis) and our ability to attribute effects of climate change to such events (vertical axis)

Source: National Academies of Sciences, Engineering, and Medicine (2016). *Attribution of Extreme Weather Events in the Context of Climate Change*. National Academies Press, Washington, DC. https://doi.org/10.17226/21852 [available at http://www.nap.edu/21852]

climate processes on extreme events, the better we are at being able to identify and predict the impacts of climate change. Not surprisingly, attributing the occurrence of extreme hot and cold events to the effects of global warming is much easier than attributing severe local storms and wildfires. Although changes at the global and hemispheric scale are known to affect the controlling large-scale environmental conditions, spatial and temporal variability in the occurrence of severe local storms and wildfires is also strongly influenced by very localized effects, making prediction of their future occurrence and characteristics difficult.

7.2 Temperature-related events

The increasing occurrence of heatwaves can confidently be related to the global warming trend, in association with spikes in the rising trend in the weather experienced, shown in Figure 6.2 in Chapter 6. Both the rising temperature trend and any increased short-term variability will impact on the frequency of extreme high temperatures. Increasing temperatures also contribute to drought through increasing rates of evaporation, and possibly to more intense storms through the added heat energy. However, the impacts of extreme high temperatures on human well-being depend on a variety of other factors, such as whether people spend their time indoors or outdoors, what bulky protective clothing they are required to wear, their level of physical activity, and their pre-disposition to heat stress effects.

Studies based on the analysis of observed temperatures and future modelling have shown that local or regional high temperature extremes are increasing faster than the average temperature in some regions. The greater the mean global warming (according to climate change scenarios), the greater the frequency and intensity of extreme temperatures (Seneviratne et al. 2016). King et al. (2017) showed an increase of about 25% in the probability of extreme heat records in Australia if the warming was 2 °C instead of 1.5 °C (under the Paris Agreement). According to simulated CMIP5 (Coupled Model Intercomparison Project) data, a global warming of 2–3 °C could lead to a more than threefold increase in the probability of extreme events (e.g. 'hottest day', 'warmest night') in North America, Europe, East Asia, and southern South America (Diffenbaugh et al. 2018). Therefore, the assessment of 'regional hotspots' is important in order to identify the areas that will be most exposed to the intensification of extreme temperatures. Table 7.2 and Figure 7.6 illustrate the extreme hotspots expected following a global mean warming of 1.5–2 °C (Lewis et al. 2019).

The risk associated with heatwave impacts depends on the intensity of climatic events and the level of human vulnerability. The summer 2003 heatwaves in western Europe highlighted the high vulnerability of temperate regions. In France, a high excess mortality

TABLE 7.2 Summary of hotspots of warming for maximum and minimum temperature following 1.5 °C and 2 °C of warming (where regional extremes increase more rapidly than land surface mean temperatures) and extremes (where the tails of the temperature distributions expand under future warming)

		HOTSPOT REGIONS
Tmax	1.5	CAS; EAS; NAS; SAS; WAS; CEU; MED; NAU
	2	EAS; SAS; CAS; CEU; MED; NAU; CNA; ENA
	Extremes	CEU; NAS; WNA; ENA
Tmin	1.5	CEU; WAS; NAS; WNA; CNA
	2	CEU; CAS; SAS; NAS; CNA; ENA
	Extremes	CAS; WAS; EAS; NAS; ENA

CAS = Central Asia; CEU = Central Europe; CNA = Central North America; EAS = East Asia; ENA = Eastern North America; MED = Mediterranean; NAS = North Asia; NAU = North Australia; SAS = South Asia; WAS = West Asia; WNA = Western North America
Source: Lewis et al. (2019). Regional hotspots of temperature extremes under 1.5 °C and 2 °C of global mean warming. *Weather and Climate Extremes* 26: 100233. https://doi.org/10.1016/j.wace.2019.100233

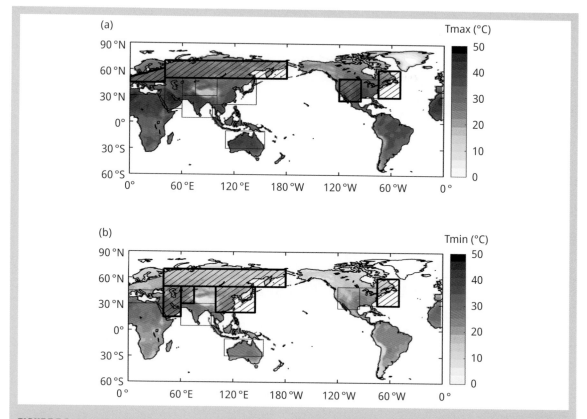

FIGURE 7.6 Hotspots of predicted future warming of (a) maximum and (b) minimum temperature (Tmax and Tmin) superimposed on maps of observed extreme high values of maximum and minimum temperatures. Hatched areas are regions where the greatest warming effect is expected

Source: Lewis et al. (2019). Regional hotspots of temperature extremes under 1.5 °C and 2 °C of global mean warming. *Weather and Climate Extremes* 26: 100233. https://doi.org/10.1016/j.wace.2019.100233

rate was recorded, particularly for older people living at home or in retirement institutions. Figure 7.7 shows the relationship between the number of deaths and daily temperatures, particularly in the period with maximum temperatures >30 °C and minimum temperatures >20 °C. Geographical variations in mortality have shown a clear relationship between high excess mortality and highly urbanized and densely populated areas. The highest excess mortality was observed in Paris and its suburbs (+142%) while the least populated and more rural regions recorded an excess mortality of around 20%. Although the heatwave was very intense in the Mediterranean regions, excess mortality rates were significantly lower than in the Paris region. Mediterranean populations are more accustomed to extreme summer temperatures, and dwellings are also better adapted with air conditioning, cooling building designs, etc. (Fouillet et al. 2006).

The combination of high temperatures and humidity also has an impact on human well-being. The risk of human illness and mortality increases in hot and humid weather associated with heatwaves. The most significant human impacts related to these climate extremes could potentially be those in developing countries due to the vulnerability of their populations. Based on high spatial resolution simulations of

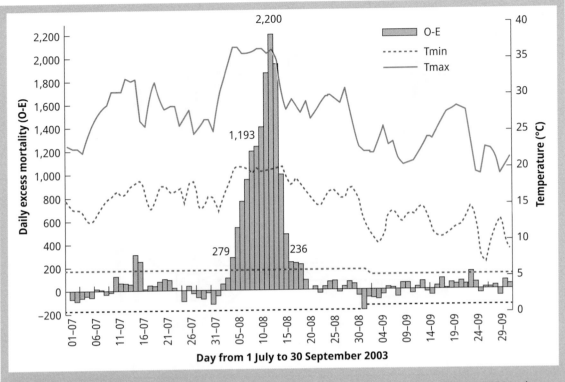

FIGURE 7.7 Number of excess deaths observed during the French heatwave from July to September 2003 and average daily maximum (Tmax) and minimum (Tmin) temperatures recorded during the period. O-E represents observed minus expected

Source: Fouillet et al. (2006). Excess mortality related to the August 2003 heat wave in France. *International Archives of Occupational and Environmental Health* 80: 16–24

climate change and the RCP8.5 scenario ('business-as-usual' leading to highest greenhouse gas emissions), Im et al. (2017) predicted that heatwaves exceeding a critical wet-bulb temperature threshold (>35 °C) for human well-being would occur before the end of the twenty-first century in many densely populated areas of South Asia (Figure 7.8). A trend of increasing frequency of deadly heatwaves has already been observed in these regions over recent decades (Dash et al. 2007).

7.3 Water-related events

Water is essential for survival of biological organisms, but it can also be a hazard when there is either too much or too little of it. Climate change can affect the frequency of both floods and droughts at a range of spatial scales, especially from the regional to the local scale. However, both of these hazards can have highly variable impacts on humans and their environment.

HEAVY PRECIPITATION AND FLOODING

Both models and observations suggest that the frequency and rainfall intensity of short-term (1-day to 5-day) events appears to be increasing globally, but the exact processes responsible for this trend are poorly understood. In particular, spatial variability and its causes

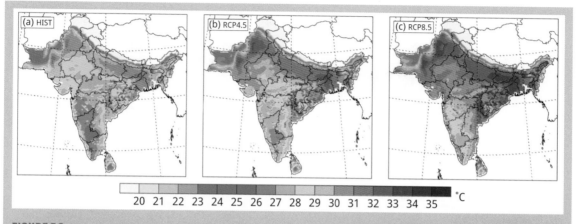

FIGURE 7.8 Spatial modelling of wet-bulb temperature in South Asia according to climate change scenarios: (a) the recent past (1976–2005), (b) RCP4.5 (2071–2100), and (c) RCP8.5 (2071–2100). RCP = Representative Concentration Pathway

Source: Im et al. (2017). Deadly heat waves projected in the densely populated agricultural regions of South Asia. *Science Advances* 3: e1603322

are not fully understood, so it is difficult to predict likely future changes in regional- and local-scale heavy precipitation patterns. There is some suggestion that tropical, mid-latitude, and high-latitude regions may experience more extreme precipitation while sub-tropical regions may experience little change (Pfahl et al. 2017; Donat et al. 2019). It is well known that extreme precipitation requires rapid ascent of air, and this often varies regionally and locally as a result of the complex nature of Earth's surface characteristics (both land cover and orography).

There is a range of different causes of flooding including snowmelt and rain-on-snow events, ice-jams and glacial lake outbursts, localized thunderstorms, and coastal storms in association with sea level rise. However, it is difficult to associate global warming and flood events with any certainty. The reasons for increasing occurrence of flood events may not be just climatic, but may include changing land-use patterns and human activity causing changes in catchment hydrology. Certainly, global warming should induce changes in snowmelt flood regimes because of changes in the timing of the seasonal snowmelt cycle. Earlier spring snowmelt, or the elimination of spring snowmelt altogether, could occur.

It is also known that there is large uncertainty in predicting future regional and local flood conditions, as they depend on both regional atmospheric circulation and catchment characteristics, both of which may undergo change over time. For example, severe flooding can occur as a result of both more intense and slower-moving weather systems. Changes in seasonality of extreme precipitation and flooding may occur in association with the current warming trend, while recent research also suggests that flood risk may increase in some areas. For example, Alfieri et al. (2017) applied a multimodel approach under different climate change scenarios with a spatial resolution of 1 km with the aim of estimating population exposure to river flooding on a global scale. River-flow simulations were analysed to assess the frequency and magnitude of river floods and their impacts according to scenarios corresponding to global warming of 1.5 °C, 2 °C, and 4 °C. The largest increases in flood risk appear to occur in Asia, the United States, and Europe (Figure 7.9).

With a very high spatial resolution approach, Figure 7.10 shows the estimated area of floods resulting from extreme precipitation events in different catchments under the RCP8.5 scenario over the

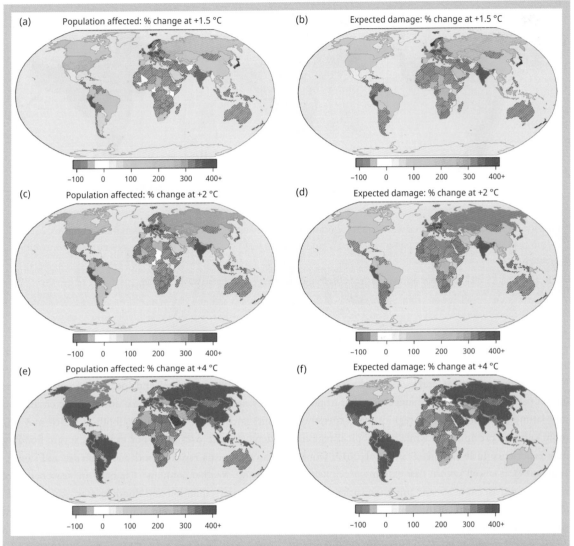

FIGURE 7.9 Predicted regional changes in global flood risk, as reflected by average change in population affected (a, c, e) and expected damage (b, d, f) per country based on the level of warming. Hatching indicates countries where the confidence level of the average change is less than 90%

Source: Alfieri et al. (2017). Global projections of river flood risk in a warmer world. *Earth's Future* 5: 171–82

period 2050–2079. The combination of a climate model large ensemble and a high-resolution hydro-dynamic flood model has allowed determination of the level of exposure of the local populations as a function of the intensity of heavy precipitation events (Swain et al. 2020).

These two case studies show the potential impact of heavy rainfall on flooding and population exposure. There appears to be a contrast in the response of different types of flooding to global warming, with flash flooding more likely to increase than large-scale flooding (Anderson and Bausch 2006). This more intense

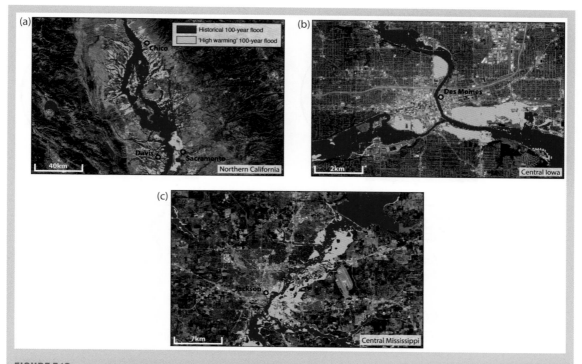

FIGURE 7.10 Change in flood derived from a hydrodynamic model describing the estimated flood extent resulting from an extreme precipitation episode with a recurrence interval of 100 years following the historical period (1995–2005, dark violet shading) and the future period (RCP 8.5, 2050–2079, light violet shading) in (a) the Sacramento Valley in northern California, including the Sacramento River, (b) the confluence of the Des Moines River and Raccoon River near Des Moines in central Iowa, and (c) the Pearl River near Jackson, Mississippi. RCP = Representative Concentration Pathway

Source: Swain et al. (2020). Increased flood exposure due to climate change and population growth in the United States. *Earth's Future* 8: e2020EF001778

localized rainfall and flooding may create other environmental hazards, such as landslides as the soil and substrate becomes quickly saturated.

DROUGHT

Both increasing temperature and declining precipitation can be responsible for increasing the frequency and intensity of droughts. Drought is one of the major threats to food security and the environment (Markonis et al. 2021). In recent decades, many parts of the world have experienced very intense droughts that have caused significant damage. Increased summer droughts in Europe

(e.g. events in 2003) have had a strong economic impact, particularly on agricultural productivity (Ciais et al. 2005) and ecosystems (Mastrotheodoros et al. 2020). However, the succession of droughts, even of moderate intensity, also poses a significant risk due to the decrease in resistance to subsequent droughts (Udall and Overpeck 2017). An assessment on a regional scale of the frequency and intensity of future droughts is essential to develop an adaptation strategy at the socio-economic level and to limit the impacts on ecosystems.

Current research indicates that many drought-affected regions are likely to face an increased risk of drought due to global warming. Regionalized modelling (0.35° resolution) of the Standardized Precipitation–

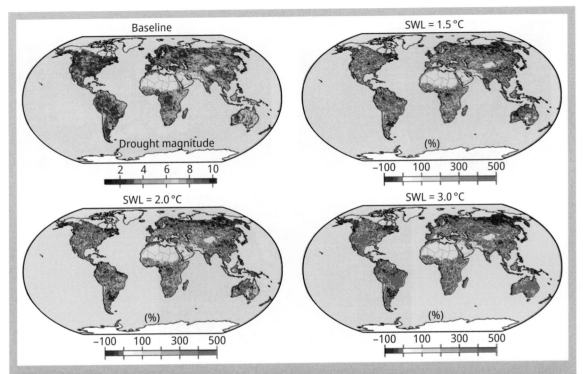

FIGURE 7.11 Drought magnitude and relative change (%) in drought magnitude with respect to a baseline for the three specific warming levels (SWL = 1.5, 2.0, and 3.0°C). Territories excluded from the analysis are masked in grey

Source: Naumann et al. (2018). Global changes in drought conditions under different levels of warming. *Geophysical Research Letters* 45: 3285–96

Evapotranspiration Index (SPEI) has shown that with a global temperature increase of 3°C, the magnitude of drought could increase fivefold over wide areas of the world (Naumann et al. 2018; Figure 7.11). The results of future simulations reveal that the risk of drought would increase significantly in most areas with a global warming of more than +2°C, while an increase in global warming of only +1.5°C could result in little change in drought risk compared to the current period in some regions (e.g. parts of western Australia and South America). In other regions, such as the Mediterranean and central Europe, the risk of drought could increase considerably under a 1.5°C warming scenario (Lehner et al. 2017).

However, future projections of drought are subject to significant biases related to the difficulties in modelling the intensity and frequency of extreme events. Droughts are defined by a combination of several climatic factors (precipitation and temperature) and their impact varies according to their intensity, frequency, and duration. Knowledge of the past and future evolution of droughts is an essential issue for adaptation. The study of past droughts through the analysis of observed data is complicated because long rainfall series are rare, which causes analysis difficulties, particularly for the risks of multi-decadal droughts (Coats and Mankin 2016). These difficulties are accentuated by the fact that there are several types of drought (e.g. meteorological, agricultural, hydrological) requiring specific indicators (e.g. the SPEI and the Palmer drought severity index) as there is no universal drought indicator. Multiplying the parameters used to calculate these drought indicators increases the probability of bias in addition to the biases inherent in climate change models.

7.4 Severe storms

Climate change has the potential to increase the frequency and intensity of both synoptic-scale (e.g. tropical cyclones or mid-latitude low-pressure systems) and sub-synoptic-scale (e.g. local thunderstorms) weather systems as a result of the additional heat provided by global warming.

TROPICAL CYCLONES

Tropical cyclones (or hurricanes) obtain their energy in the form of sensible and latent heat from the high air and ocean temperatures in the tropics. Rising sea surface temperatures therefore provide more energy for storm intensification, allowing them to maintain their energy over wider areas (Bruyère et al. 2019). It has not been possible to identify clearly the effect of climate change on the timing and location of tropical

cyclone formation, but both models and observations suggest that their maximum wind speed is likely to increase by about 5% for each degree Celsius rise of sea surface temperature (Bruyère et al. 2019). Predictions from different climate models are not consistent, though, making future predictions of tropical cyclone characteristics uncertain. Results of recent research shown in Figure 7.12 suggest that the intensity of wind and rainfall in tropical cyclones is likely to increase, while their frequency of occurrence should decline, although the number of more intense tropical cyclones should increase in most regions. This is largely consistent with observations, although both increasing and decreasing trends in tropical cyclone occurrence and intensity have occurred in different parts of the world (Banholzer et al. 2014; Knutson et al. 2020). However, in contrast to the future trend shown in Figure 7.12, Holmes (2020) concluded that category

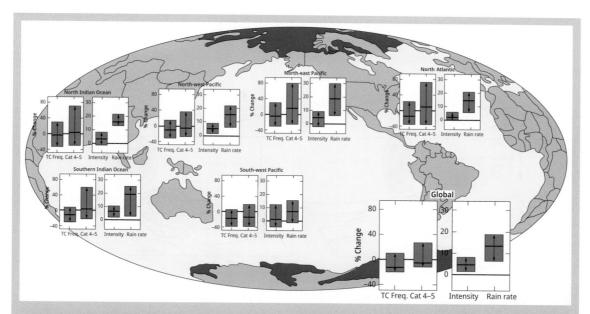

FIGURE 7.12 Future prediction of tropical cyclone characteristics (frequency, intensity, and rainfall rate) in different parts of the world under a 2°C global warming scenario

Source: Knutson et al. (2020). Tropical cyclones and climate change assessment: Part II. Projected response to anthropogenic warming. *Bulletin of the American Meteorological Society* 101: E303–22

4 and 5 tropical cyclones appear to have increased in the South-west Pacific since the 1970s. Clearly, there is still significant uncertainty in predictions of likely future patterns of tropical cyclones at the regional and local scales.

In summary, it seems that tropical cyclones may not be more frequent but should be more intense as a result of the global warming trend, and they should increasingly impact on areas further from the equator. Individual tropical cyclones may also expand to cover larger areas, although understanding the causes of changes in cyclone tracks, which may be random or caused by shifts in atmospheric circulation, needs to be improved before it is possible to predict future paths of tropical cyclones resulting from climate change and therefore regional variations in tropical cyclone activity. Some studies suggest that reductions in atmospheric pollution due to increased air pollution controls in many countries have resulted in increased tropical cyclone activity in some parts of the world, such as the North Atlantic, as a result of increased solar radiation receipt at the Earth's surface (Banholzer et al. 2014).

EXTRA-TROPICAL LOW-PRESSURE SYSTEMS

There is a general consensus that changes are likely to occur in the frequency of occurrence, preferred location, and general characteristics of extra-tropical low-pressure systems in response to the global warming trend, although there are significant uncertainties involved because of the non-linearity of the processes involved. Possible future changes in extra-tropical weather systems in the Northern Hemisphere are summarized in Figure 7.13 (Catto et al. 2019). It is expected that the horizontal temperature gradient in the upper troposphere should increase, while in the lower troposphere it should decrease. An increase in atmospheric stability would be associated with these changes in temperature. Warmer air temperatures should also result in an increase in latent heat released into the atmosphere, which would also be linked to increased precipitation intensity and greater moisture transport, leading to greater chances of flooding (Catto et al. 2019). Possible future changes in the dimensions of extra-tropical low-pressure systems and the intensity of the winds

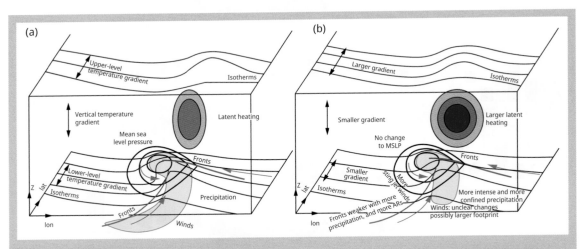

FIGURE 7.13 Schematic representation of likely effects of future climate change on extra-tropical cyclonic (ETC) weather systems in the Northern Hemisphere, with (a) present-day ETCs and (b) future ETCs. MSLP = mean sea level pressure, ARs = atmospheric rivers, lat = latitude, lon = longitude

Source: Catto et al. (2019). The future of midlatitude cyclones. *Current Climate Change Report* 5: 407–20

associated with them are less certain, although an increase in storm surge activity could be expected in association with rising sea levels.

LOCAL CONVECTIVE STORMS

Growth in available computer resources and continued development of atmospheric models have improved the simulation of local convective storms through better resolving of atmospheric processes at higher spatial and temporal resolutions (Bruyère et al. 2019). The improved representation of surface–atmosphere interaction in models at such fine scales suggests that high-intensity precipitation at an hourly timescale will increase under a warming climate. Peak hourly precipitation resulting from mesoscale convective weather systems such as thunderstorms or squall lines is predicted to increase by about 7% for 1 °C of warming (Prein et al. 2017), while storm frequency is likely to increase significantly. Predicting the spatial variability of such extreme events at the regional and local scales is a difficult task, due to the random nature of convective systems. However, although there is still significant uncertainty, it is evident that the impact of severe local storms is likely to increase in a warmer world and local communities need to factor this into their adaptation strategies.

Changes in the occurrence of high wind hazards in response to the global warming trend are more difficult to predict as the causes of strong winds at the regional and local scales are often complex. For example, strong winds result not only from local severe convective storms but also from effects of terrain on airflow, such as severe downslope winds or topographic channelling. So, increases in wind velocity, including both stronger average winds and wind gusts, could result from stronger local convective storms, increased pressure gradients leading to stronger flow over complex terrain, or local impacts of synoptic-scale weather systems such as tropical cyclones and mid-latitude low-pressure systems. Very little research has been conducted on this

topic, making it difficult to develop response strategies. However, regions where convective activity is likely to increase, mountain regions where increased pressure gradients are predicted, and areas likely to be affected by more intense, larger-scale synoptic weather systems should prepare for stronger winds. The incidence of wind-driven rain is also likely to increase in such areas and should be considered in any changes to building codes.

There is considerable uncertainty over possible future changes in the occurrence and nature of hail under a warmer climate because of its intermittent occurrence and lack of field data. The general understanding that climate change will result in a greater likelihood of extreme convective storms suggests that hail may increase in size but be less frequent (Bruyère et al. 2019). However, the warming trend within the sub-tropical troposphere may also result in fewer hailstones in these regions because of increased melting. A case study of possible future hailstorm occurrence in the Sydney area in Australia concluded that high-resolution models are required to be able to model hailstorm occurrence adequately over local areas in order to resolve the effects of local topography (Leslie et al. 2008). Although it was concluded that an increasing trend in the occurrence of severe hailstorms was likely up to 2050, the intermittency of hailstorms and the complex effects of terrain and land–sea boundaries on convective storm development make it difficult to provide reliable predictions of future hailstorm regimes for such small areas. In order to estimate future impacts of climate change and develop adaptation strategies, it is important to understand and predict possible changes in the key weather patterns that provide the environment within which hailstorms develop. These include mid-latitude weather systems, squall lines, intense local convection, sea breeze circulations, and **orographic effects**. Figure 7.14 provides an overview of expected changes in the occurrence of hail associated with severe thunderstorms over Australia as a result of a 3 °C temperature increase. There is a clear regional difference between southern

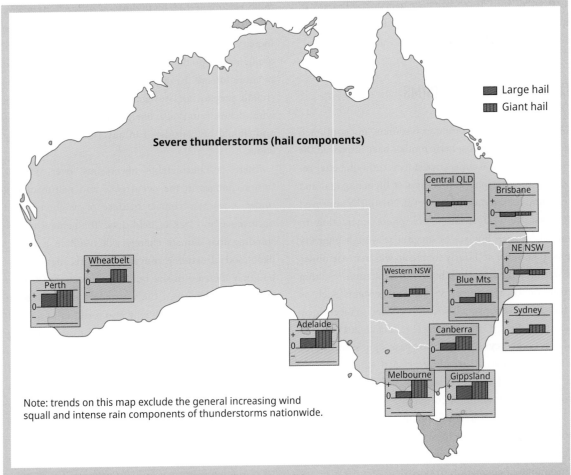

FIGURE 7.14 Relative change in the frequency of thunderstorms producing large and giant hail associated with a global warming of +3°C in Australia. QLD = Queensland, NSW = New South Wales

Source: Bruyère et al. (2019). *Severe Weather in a Changing Climate*. Insurance Australia Group and National Center for Atmospheric Research, USA. https://www.iag.com.au/severe-weather-changing-climate

(mid-latitude) regions of increased large and giant hail and northern (sub-tropical) regions showing a decline (Bruyère et al. 2019).

It is difficult to predict the effects of climate change on future regional and local trends in tornadoes because of both the spatial and temporal scale at which they occur and the lack of knowledge of the relationship between climate change processes and tornado characteristics. As shown earlier in Figure 7.5 and mentioned by a number of researchers, it is not easy to identify any clear relationship between climate change and local severe

convective storms of any sort (Greenough et al. 2001; Handmer et al. 2012; National Academies of Sciences, Engineering, and Medicine 2016). In regard to tornadoes, one of the key reasons is that the observational record is unreliable, as it has depended on reports by amateur observers, so that spatially and temporally consistent records of tornadoes are not available for most regions. For example, assessment of both the occurrence and intensity of tornadoes depends on observers being in the right place at the right time, and is also based on subjective assessment of the damage produced. More modern observation techniques using weather radar have not been available long enough to be able to conduct more soundly based climatic research.

It should be noted at the outset that the global occurrence of tornadoes tends to be concentrated in the United States. Figure 7.15 provides a summary of trends of observed tornado days (in green) and of the number of days with many tornadoes (>30, in purple) in the United States since the 1950s (Brooks et al. 2014). The impression given is that there is an overall decline in the number of days per annum on which F1 tornadoes have been observed, but also an increase in the number of days with more than 30 F1 tornadoes. The tornado regime therefore appears to be changing. However, other researchers present a more complex picture with regional shifts in tornado activity across different parts of the United States, including an eastward shift in tornado occurrence, especially in summer (Moore and

DeBoer 2019). Figure 7.16 provides an overview of tornado occurrence in the United States, while Figure 7.17 indicates a sudden change in the pattern of F1 tornado occurrence in the early 1990s when the proportion occurring within the South-east and Lower Midwest region seems to have experienced an increasing trend with a corresponding decline particularly in the Great Plains region. It also seems that there is an increased number of days with many F1 tornadoes, particularly in autumn and winter (Moore and DeBoer 2019).

Due to the difficulties of downscaling global climate model predictions to simulate local severe storms, prediction of the effects of climate change on tornado occurrence and characteristics needs to rely on knowledge of the general environmental conditions that are favourable for local severe storm formation. The key contributing factors are: warm, moist air near the ground surface and cooler air aloft; an unstable atmosphere allowing

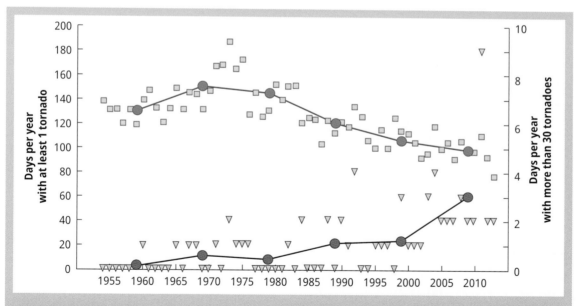

FIGURE 7.15 Trends in annual tornado occurrence over the United States from 1955 to 2013, showing the number of days with at least one F1 tornado (green line, with squares showing annual totals and circles showing decadal averages) and the number of days with more than 30 F1 tornadoes (purple line, with triangles showing annual totals and circles showing decadal averages). F1 represents the second step on the **Fujita tornado intensity scale**, representing wind speeds of 117–180 km/h and moderate damage

Source: Brooks et al. (2014). Increased variability of tornado occurrence in the United States. *Science* 346(6207): 349–52

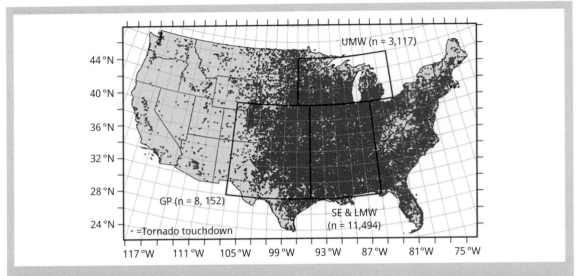

FIGURE 7.16 Annual counts of tornadoes of F1 or greater (see Figure 7.15) in the United States between 1954 and 2017, showing three main regions (UMW = Upper Midwest, GP = Great Plains, and SE & LMW = Southeast and Lower Midwest)

Source: Moore, T. W., and DeBoer, T. A. (2019). A review and analysis of possible changes to the climatology of tornadoes in the United States. *Progress in Physical Geography* 43: 365–90

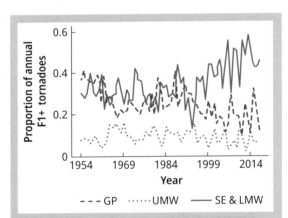

FIGURE 7.17 Trends in occurrence of tornadoes F1 or greater based on the proportion recorded within each region (see Figure 7.16 for definitions)

Source: Moore, T. W., and DeBoer, T. A. (2019). A review and analysis of possible changes to the climatology of tornadoes in the United States. *Progress in Physical Geography* 43: 365–90

speeds, allowing large convective storms to develop. So, a useful approach is to try and downscale global climate predictions of such conditions to the regional level. For example, Lee (2012) applied this concept using a synoptic climatological approach to analyse the broad conditions within which tornadoes have occurred in the past, and used climate model predictions to assess likely trends in intense tornado occurrence through to 2050 and 2090. He concluded that, in spite of the difficulties outlined above, a 4–13% increase in more intense tornadoes might be expected over the United States due to predicted climate change. It was also suggested that both the seasonal timing and geographical distribution would be likely to change, as has been observed above and as suggested in Figure 7.18.

However, the trends in total observed number of tornadoes over the last century are generally attributed to improvements in observation techniques rather than actual changes in frequency, as the environmental conditions within which tornadoes develop have shown no major increasing trend (National Academies of Sciences, Engineering, and Medicine 2016). Irrespective

development of strong updrafts and downdrafts; wind shear in the vertical, with wind at different levels occurring from different directions and/or at different

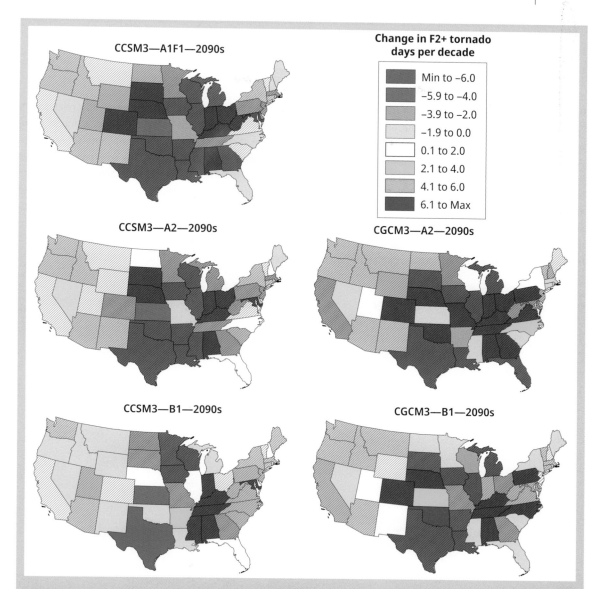

FIGURE 7.18 Difference from twentieth-century model predictions of days of tornadoes of F2 or greater intensity for different climate change scenarios and two different climate change models (Community Climate Simulation Model 3—CCSM3, and Coupled Global Climate Model 3—CGCM3). Differences that are statistically significant at the 0.05 level are indicated by hatching. F2 represents the third step on the Fujita tornado intensity scale, representing wind speeds of 181–253 km/h and significant damage

Source: Lee, C. (2012). Utilizing synoptic climatological methods to assess the impacts of climate change on future tornadofavorable environments. *Natural Hazards* 62: 325–43

of whether climate change is having an effect on trends in tornado occurrence in different parts of the world, as with other types of severe local weather (strong winds, intense precipitation, lightning, etc.), more stringent building codes, public education, and improved early warning systems are the three main factors that should be addressed in any response strategy to reduce impacts on human mortality and property damage.

CASE STUDY 7.1
Climate change and wildland fires

Wildland fires are generated through the interaction of weather, climate, and vegetation, but are also affected by human activity through land management practices. Wildfire occurrence in any year or season is strongly affected by longer-term climate variations that influence the build-up of inflammable material, while fire behaviour is affected by short-term weather processes, including variations in temperature and wind. It is generally considered that the current global warming trend should lead to more frequent and possibly more intense wildfires, primarily due to higher temperatures. However, the relationship between wildfires and climate change is made more complex through changes in regional atmospheric circulation, leading to spatial variability of expected changes in wildfire occurrence. For example, some global climate model simulations suggest that although large parts of the globe are likely to experience increased fire risk, tropical and sub-tropical areas may experience a decrease (Figure 7.19), but there is significant uncertainty associated with this conclusion (Bruyère et al. 2019).

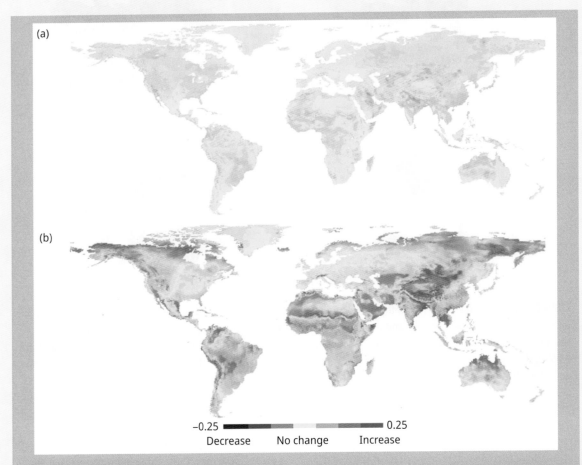

FIGURE 7.19 Average predicted mean change in fire probability derived from an ensemble of 16 GCMs (global climate models) for the periods (a) 2010–2039 and (b) 2070–2099 compared to a baseline period of 1971–2000

Source: Moritz et al. (2012). Climate change and disruptions to global fire activity. *Ecosphere* 3: 1–22

Various indices have been used to assess fire risk in different parts of the world. These indices are based on the atmospheric conditions, such as a combination of high temperatures, low humidity, and strong winds, that typically lead to wildfire occurrence and severity in a given area. It is important to understand the relationship between global changes of climate and the specific conditions that increase fire risk in given regions in order to evaluate the effects of climate change on future patterns of wildfire occurrence. Recent trends in the **Forest Fire Danger Index (FFDI)** over Australia have been assessed in relation to changes in regional atmospheric circulation, as shown in Figure 7.20 (Bruyère et al. 2019).

There is significant regional variability in the occurrence of wildland fires, as is evident in the comparison between the top 10 countries affected by wildland fires shown in Figure 7.21 (Dowdy et al. 2022). It is also clear that the inter-annual variation of fires differs a lot between different regions, often as a result of the dominant climate regime. For example, wildland fires tend to

be a regular annual occurrence in savannah and tropical regions (e.g. in parts of Africa—Figure 7.21), while there is much greater inter-annual variability in Australia where El Niño Southern Oscillation effects have an impact on temperature and rainfall patterns. An analysis of global fire occurrence between 2003 and 2016 based on satellite data showed that 77% of wildland fires occurred in savannah regions, with only 13% associated with agriculture, 7% with deforestation, and 2% and 1% occurring in boreal and temperate forest, respectively (Dowdy et al. 2022). Major fire events tend to be associated with heatwaves and droughts, but may also be affected by human activity through such activities as land clearance and inappropriate fire management policies. Clearly, fire is a natural environmental hazard that has increasingly become a natural disaster where it impacts on humans. Human activity is a major factor in changing fire regimes, causing an increased frequency of fires in tropical rainforest due to deforestation and changes in both wildfire occurrence and intensity in mid-latitude

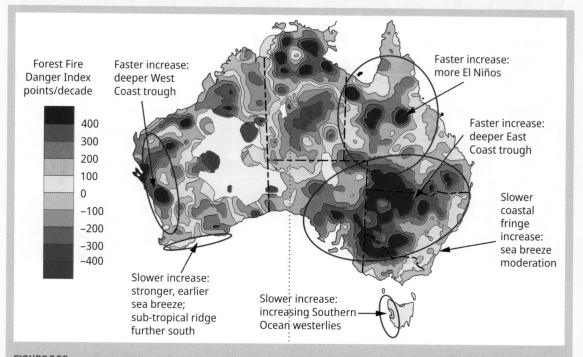

FIGURE 7.20 The pattern of changes in the daily FFDI (Forest Fire Danger Index) between 1978 and 2017 with annotations indicating regional changes in atmospheric circulation that appear to be influencing these changes in wildfire risk
Source: Bruyère et al. 2012

forests because of changes to plant species and application of fire-control policies (Dowdy et al. 2022).

It is evident that significant regional- and local-scale variability can occur in response to large-scale changes in climate, so that future predictions of the risk and likely impacts of wildfires under future climates are difficult to make. It is therefore very important that regional authorities and local communities develop adaptation strategies that are based on a thorough understanding of the wildfire characteristics and risk unique to their own regions.

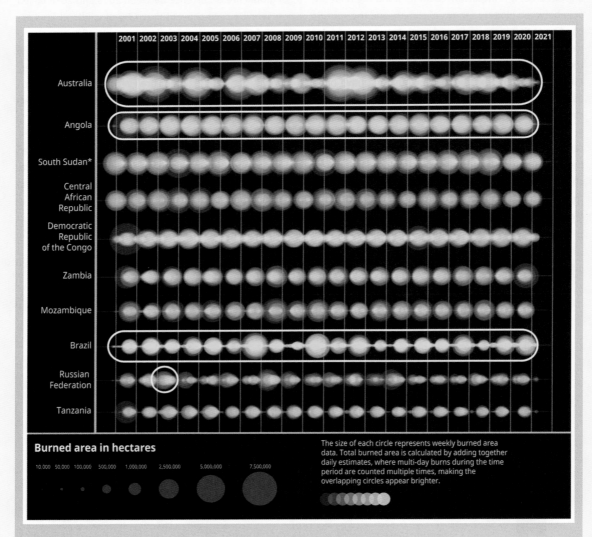

FIGURE 7.21 Variation in wildland fire occurrence in the top ten affected countries

Source: Dowdy et al. (2022). Wildfires under climate change A burning issue. In: *Frontiers 2022: Noise, Blazes and Mismatches—Emerging Issues of Environmental Concern*. United Nations Environment Programme, Nairobi, pp. 23–59

Severe storms are obviously linked to other environmental hazards, as their impact on coastal erosion through storm surge events is expected to increase due to rising sea level, and they are often associated with significant flooding and landslides in inland areas. They may also contribute to lightning and strong winds, which together can have significant impacts on infrastructure such as buildings, power lines, and transport networks (e.g. shipping, road, rail, and air traffic).

7.5 How can we adapt to extreme events?

Understanding the nature and causes of the increased occurrence and intensity of environmental hazards provides the basis for developing effective adaptation strategies. To that end, some research has been conducted into identifying the contribution of different factors to individual extreme events, such as floods or droughts. This is called 'event attribution', which often has the focus of trying to identify what proportion of a specific event is likely to have been caused by human activity, and what by natural causes. Event attribution is a difficult task. It is often expressed in probabilistic terms, but should be based on solid knowledge of the physical processes involved.

It is better to develop a well-thought-out adaptation strategy that aims to limit the impacts of extreme events than merely to set up infrastructure such as civil defence to respond to events after they have happened. It is also important to avoid maladaptation, which often occurs when well-meaning actions are taken based on a confused understanding of the processes involved.

Referring back to Figure 7.1, reducing vulnerability through administrative action (e.g. improved building codes), developing engineering solutions (e.g. coastal and fluvial flood defences), and encouraging changes in personal behaviour can form a major component of any adaptation strategy. Early warning systems need to be developed to reduce the impact of extreme events on the community, while evacuation plans and post-disaster relief efforts should also be put in place. Recent research has suggested that global vulnerability to climate-related hazards has declined, particularly for wealthier areas (Formetta and Feyen 2019). Increased protection from the impacts of climate-related hazards therefore appears to have been effective in wealthier countries, while poorer countries are still vulnerable to such hazards as drought, inland flooding, coastal flooding, and strong winds.

It is important to identify the key aims of adaptation (Woetzel et al. 2020) at the outset. These include protecting people and assets (emergency response and engineering), building resilience (management and technology, supply chains, etc.), and reducing exposure by making tough decisions about allocation of resources. The design of any adaptation strategy should therefore consider climate change effects on human life and welfare, food and water resources, and property and economic activities, as well as the impact of the adaptation strategy itself on these three areas.

Examples of actions that can be taken include:

- Heatwaves—establishment of alerts for advanced warnings and awareness campaigns; creation of a register of susceptible people; and establishment of action protocols for healthcare services.

- Flooding—planning aimed at reducing vulnerability (e.g. land-use controls); engineering to reduce flood impacts; establishment of alerts and awareness campaigns; creation of a register of people in areas susceptible to flooding; establishment of action protocols for emergency services; and establishment of a post-flooding relief and recovery plan (Anderson and Bausch 2006).

- Severe thunderstorms and tornadoes—establishment of alerts for advanced warnings and awareness campaigns; creation of a register of people in areas susceptible to tornadoes; establishment of action protocols for emergency services; and establishment of a post-storm relief and recovery plan.

A number of key elements of a response programme have been identified (UNISDR 2008). These include establishment of a disaster risk-reduction strategy which would set up the infrastructure required to organize a response. It is also important to monitor and assess disaster risk in order to provide early warning, and develop knowledge that strengthens the robustness and resilience of the local community. Exposure to hazards can also be reduced by decreasing underlying risk through appropriate environmental planning and engineering, and by establishing a strong disaster-preparedness programme.

Summary

- Environmental hazards provide a challenge to the development of effective adaptation strategies in response to climate change because of the often localized and random nature of their occurrence.

- An 'environmental hazard', such as a severe or extreme weather or climate event, has the potential to create a 'natural disaster' if it has a significant impact on humans. The aim of developing adaptation strategies is to minimize the negative impact of such 'disasters'.

- Climate change can result in changes in either the frequency of occurrence or intensity of environmental hazards, or both, resulting in negative impacts on human populations that we need to prepare for.

- Environmental hazards, such as wildfires, may be the result of climate change impacts on more than one variable—for example, extremely high temperatures and drought.

- Global climate models have difficulty in predicting changes in environmental hazards that are driven by atmospheric processes affected by fine-scale variations in surface characteristics, such as localized convection and wind channelling, making it difficult to apply global climate model predictions successfully.

- Such models can only provide a generalized view of the future occurrence of specific types of environmental hazard, so that it may be possible to say that severe storms may increase in occurrence and intensity globally, but it may not be possible to indicate exactly where this is likely to happen or what its impact may be.

- It should be remembered that climate change does not only affect mean values of temperature and other climate variables; it can also affect their statistical distribution, causing extreme values to be more or less frequent.

- Uncertainty over the impact of climate change on the statistical distributions of specific variables makes predicting effects on extreme events at the regional and local scales very difficult, making adaptation a difficult process.

- Trends in extreme temperatures are unlikely to be uniform across the globe, with some regions experiencing greater increases in extreme high temperatures than in average temperatures, leading to regional hotspots.

- Extreme high temperatures can combine with high levels of humidity to worsen impacts on human health. It is therefore important to try and predict the future combination of climate conditions in order to develop appropriate adaptation strategies.

- Uncertainty in the spatial and temporal occurrence of intense precipitation is high because of the complexity of the atmospheric processes involved. Reasonable prediction of likely changes in precipitation can only be provided at a broad scale, making it difficult to develop effective localized adaptation strategies.

- Drought has a different time frame from other hydrometeorological events such as floods, and involves a combination of both high temperatures (leading to high evaporation) and low precipitation over often extended periods. As a result, it can vary in intensity, frequency, and duration, characteristics that need to be considered when designing an appropriate response strategy.

- Severe storms occur across a range from very local (a few kilometres) to synoptic scale (hundreds of kilometres), and changes in the impact of very localized storms are the most difficult to predict, often because of interaction between the Earth's surface and overlying atmosphere. As with many other atmospheric hazards, future changes in their characteristics resulting from climate change are really predictable only at the larger scale, making detailed preparation of adaptation strategies for regional- and local-scale response challenging.

- Wildland fires are affected by both long-term climate variability that affects the build-up of vegetation available for burning, and short-term weather processes that affect the likelihood and behaviour of fires over the short term. Predicting the impact of wildfires and developing response strategies therefore requires ongoing monitoring of a range of different climate parameters, including temperature, precipitation, wind, and relative humidity.

- Adaptation to the effects of climate change on the occurrence and intensity of environmental hazards requires detailed knowledge of the underlying processes responsible for their occurrence. Attempts have been made to identify the contribution of different factors, both human and natural, to the frequency and intensity of such severe events as flooding and drought.

- Responses to predicted changes in risk due to climate change can involve a range of actions, from careful design of infrastructure and development of early warning systems in order to reduce exposure to harm to actions taken during and after events in order to reduce loss of life and to help the recovery of local communities.

For case studies and updates, visit the online resources
www.oup.com/he/sturman-quenol1e

References

Alfieri, L., Bisselink, B., Dottori, F., Naumann, G., de Roo, A., Salamon, P., Wyser, K., and Feyen, L. (2017). Global projections of river flood risk in a warmer world. *Earth's Future* 5: 171–82.

Alimonti, G., Mariani, L., Prodi, F., and Ricci, R. A. (2022). A critical assessment of extreme events trends in times of global warming. *The European Physical Journal Plus* 137(112). https://doi.org/10.1140/epjp/s13360-021-02243-9.

Anderson, J., and Bausch, C. (2006). *Climate Change and Natural Disasters: Scientific Evidence of a Possible Relation between Recent Natural Disasters and Climate Change*. Briefing Note IP/A/ENVI/FWC/2006_19, Policy Department Economy and Science, European Parliament.

Angélil, O., Perkins-Kirkpatrick, S., Alexander, L. V., Stone, D., Donat, M. G., Wehner, M., Shiogama, H., Ciavarella, A., and Christidis, N. (2016). Comparing regional precipitation and temperature extremes in climate model and reanalysis products. *Weather and Climate Extremes* 13: 35–43.

Angélil, O., Stone, D., Wehner, M., Paciorek, C. J., Krishnan, H., and Collins, W. (2017). An independent assessment of anthropogenic attribution statements for recent extreme temperature and rainfall events. *Journal of Climate* 30: 5–16.

Banholzer, S., Kossin, J., and Donner, S. (2014). The impact of climate change on natural disasters. In: Zommers, Z., and Singh, A. (eds), *Reducing Disaster: Early Warning Systems for Climate Change*. Springer Science + Business Media, Dordrecht, pp. 21–49.

Bellprat, O., and Doblas-Reyes, F. (2016). Attribution of extreme weather and climate events overestimated by unreliable climate simulations. *Geophysical Research Letters* 43: 2158–64.

Bellprat, O., Guemas, V., Doblas-Reyes, F., and Donat, M. G. (2019). Towards reliable extreme weather and climate event attribution. *Nature Communications* 10: 1732. https://doi.org/10.1038/s41467-019-09729-2.

Brooks, H. E., Carbin, G. W., and Marsh, P. T. (2014). Increased variability of tornado occurrence in the United States. *Science* 346(6207): 349–52.

Bruyère, C., Holland, G. J., Prein, A., Done, J., Buckley, B., Chan, P., Leplastrier, M., and Dyer, A. (2019). *Severe Weather in a Changing Climate*. Insurance Australia Group and National Center for Atmospheric Research, USA. https://www.iag.com.au/severe-weather-changing-climate

Catto, J. L., Ackerley, D., Booth, J. F., Champion, A. J., Colle, B. A., Pfahl, S., Pinto, J. G., Quinting, J. F., and Seiler, C. (2019). The future of midlatitude cyclones. *Current Climate Change Report* 5: 407–20.

Christidis, N., and Stott, P. A. (2016). Attribution analyses of temperature extremes using a set of 16 indices. *Weather and Climate Extremes* 14: 24–35.

Ciais, P., Reichstein, M., Viovy, N., Granier, A., Ogée, J., Allard, V., Aubinet, M., Buchmann, N., Bernhofer, C., Carrara, A., Chevallier, F., De Noblet, N., Friend, A. D., Friedlingstein, P., Grünwald, Heinesch, T. B., Keronen, P., Knohl, A., Krinner, G., Loustau, D., Manca, G., Matteucci, G., Miglietta, F., Ourcival, J. M., Papale, D., Pilegaard, K., Rambal, S., Seufert, G., Soussana, J. F., Sanz, M. J., Schulze, E. D. Vesala, T., and Valentini, R. (2005). Europe-wide reduction in primary productivity caused by the heat and drought in 2003. *Nature* 437: 529–33.

Coats, S., and Mankin, J. S. (2016). The challenge of accurately quantifying future megadrought risk in the American Southwest. *Geophysical Research Letters* 43: 9225–33.

Dash, S. K., Jenamani, R. K., Kalsi, S. R., and Panda, S. K. (2007). Some evidence of climate change in twentieth-century India. *Climatic Change* 85: 299–321.

Diffenbaugh, N. S., Singh, D., and Mankin, J. S. (2018). Unprecedented climate events: Historical changes, aspirational targets, and national commitments. *Science Advances* 4: eaao3354. https://doi.org/10.1126/sciadv.aao3354.

Donat, M. G., Angélil, O., and Ukkola, A. M. (2019). Intensification of precipitation extremes in the world's humid and water-limited regions. *Environmental Research Letters* 14: 065003. https://doi.org/10.1088/1748-9326/ab1c8e.

Dosio, A. (2018). *PESETA III—Task 1: Climate Change Projections, Bias-Adjustment, and Selection of Model Runs*. Technical Report EUR 29444-EN, Joint Research Centre, European Commission, Brussels. https://doi.org/10.2760/44883.

Dowdy, A., Purcell, L., Boulter, S., and Carvalho Moura, L. (2022). Wildfires under climate change A burning issue. In: *Frontiers 2022: Noise, Blazes and Mismatches—Emerging Issues of Environmental Concern*. United Nations Environment Programme, Nairobi, pp. 23–59.

Eum, H.-I., Gachon, P., and Laprise, R. (2016). Impacts of model bias on the climate change signal and effects of weighted ensembles of regional climate model simulations: A case study over Southern Québec, Canada. *Advances in Meteorology*, Article ID 1478514. https://doi.org/10.1155/2016/1478514.

Fallmann, J., Wagner, S., and Emeis, S. (2017). High resolution climate projections to assess the future vulnerability of European urban areas to climatological extreme events. *Theoretical and Applied Climatology* 127: 667–83.

Flato, G., Marotzke, J., Abiodun, B., Braconnot, P., Chou, S. C., Collins, W., Cox, P., Driouech, F., Emori, S., Eyring, V., Forest, C., Gleckler, P., Guilyardi, E., Jakob, C., Kattsov, V., Reason, C., and Rummukainen, M. (2013). Evaluation of climate models. In: Stocker, T. F., Qin, D., Plattner, G.-K., Tignor, M., Allen, S. K., Boschung, J., Nauels, A., Xia, Y., Bex, V., and Midgley, P. M. (eds), *Climate Change 2013: The Physical Science Basis*. Contribution of Working Group I to the Fifth Assessment Report of the Intergovernmental Panel on Climate Change. Cambridge University Press, Cambridge and New York, pp. 741–866.

Fontolan, M., Freitas Xavier, A. C., Ramos Pereira, H., and Blain, G. C. (2019). Using climate change models to assess the probability of weather extremes events: A local scale study based on the generalized extreme value distribution. *Bragantia, Campinas* 78: 146–57.

Formetta, G., and Feyen, L. (2019). Empirical evidence of declining global vulnerability to climate-related hazards. *Global Environmental Change* 57: 101920. https://doi.org/10.1016/j.gloenvcha.2019.05.004.

Fouillet, A., Rey, G., Laurent, F., Pavillon, G., Bellec, S., Guihenneuc-Jouyaux, C., Clavel, J., Jougla, E., and Hémon, D. (2006). Excess mortality related to the August 2003 heat wave in France. *International Archives of Occupational and Environmental Health* 80: 16–24.

Greenough, G., McGeehin, M., Bernard, S. M., Trtanj, J., Riad, R., and Engelberg, D. (2001). The potential impacts of climate variability and change on health impacts of extreme weather events in the United States. *Environmental Health Perspective* 109 (suppl. 2): 191–8.

Handmer, J., Honda, Y., Kundzewicz, Z. W., Arnell, N., Benito, G., Hatfield, J., Mohamed, I. F., Peduzzi, P., Wu, S., Sherstyukov, B., Takahashi, K., and Yan, Z. (2012). Changes in impacts of climate extremes: human systems and ecosystems. In: Field, C. B., Barros, V., Stocker, T. F., Qin, D., Dokken, D. J., Ebi, K. L., Mastrandrea, M. D., Mach, K. J., Plattner, G.-K., Allen, S. K., Tignor, M., and Midgley, P. M. (eds), *Managing the Risks of Extreme Events and Disasters to Advance Climate Change Adaptation*. A Special Report of Working Groups I and II of the Intergovernmental Panel on Climate Change (IPCC). Cambridge University Press, Cambridge and New York, pp. 231–90.

Holmes, J. D. (2020). Land-falling tropical cyclones on the Queensland coast and implications of climate change for wind loads. *Australian Journal of Structural Engineering* 21: 135–42.

Im, E. S., Pal, J. S., and Eltahir, E. A. (2017). Deadly heat waves projected in the densely populated agricultural regions of South Asia. *Science Advances* 3: e1603322.

IPCC (2012). *Managing the Risks of Extreme Events and Disasters to Advance Climate Change Adaptation*. A Special Report of Working Groups I and II of the Intergovernmental Panel on Climate Change (Field, C. B., Barros, V., Stocker, T. F., Qin, D., Dokken, D. J., Ebi, K. L., Mastrandrea, M. D., Mach, K. J., Plattner, G.-K., Allen, S. K., Tignor, M., and Midgley, P. M. (eds)). Cambridge University Press, Cambridge and New York.

IPCC (2021). Summary for policymakers. In: Masson-Delmotte, V., Zhai, P., Pirani, A., Connors, S. L., Péan, C., Berger, S., Caud, N., Chen, Y., Goldfarb, L., Gomis, M. I., Huang, M., Leitzell, K., Lonnoy, E., Matthews, J. B. R., Maycock, T. K., Waterfield, T., Yelekçi, O., Yu, R., and Zhou, B. (eds), *Climate Change 2021: The Physical Science Basis*. Contribution of Working Group I to the Sixth Assessment Report of the Intergovernmental Panel on Climate Change. Cambridge University Press, Cambridge and New York, pp. 3–32.

King, A. D., Karoly, D. J., and Henley, B. J. (2017). Australian climate extremes at 1.5 °C and 2 °C of global warming. *Nature Climate Change* 7: 412–16.

Knutson, T. R., Camargo, S. J., Chan, J. C. L., Emanuel, K., Ho, C.-H., Kossin, J., Mohapatra, M., Satoh, M., Sugi, M., Walsh, K., and Wu, L. (2020). Tropical cyclones and climate change assessment: Part II. Projected response to anthropogenic warming. *Bulletin of the American Meteorological Society* 101: E303–22.

Lee, C. (2012). Utilizing synoptic climatological methods to assess the impacts of climate change on future tornado-favorable environments. *Natural Hazards* 62: 325–43.

Lehner, F., Coats, S., Stocker, T. F., Pendergrass, A. G., Sanderson, B. M., Raible, C. C., and Smerdon, J. E. (2017). Projected drought risk in 1.5 °C and 2 °C warmer climates. *Geophysical Research Letters* 44: 7419–28.

Leslie, L. M., Leplastrier, M., and Buckley, B. W. (2008). Estimating future trends in severe hailstorms over the Sydney Basin: A climate modelling study. *Atmospheric Research* 87: 37–51.

Lewis, S. C., King, A. D., Perkins-Kirkpatrick, S. E., and Mitchell, D. M. (2019). Regional hotspots of temperature extremes under 1.5 °C and 2 °C of global mean warming. *Weather and Climate Extremes* 26: 100233. https://doi.org/10.1016/j.wace.2019.100233.

Markonis, Y., Kumar, R., Hanel, M., Rakovec, O., Máca, P., and AghaKouchak, A. (2021). The rise of compound warm-season droughts in Europe. *Science Advances* 7: eabb9668. https://doi.org/10.1126/sciadv.abb9668.

Mastrotheodoros, T., Pappas, C., Molnar, P., Burlando, P., Manoli, G., Parajka, J., Riccardo Rigon, R., Szeles, B., Bottazzi, M., Hadjidoukas, P., and Fatichi, S. (2020). More green and less blue water in the Alps during warmer summers. *Nature Climate Change* 10: 155–61.

Moore, T. W., and DeBoer, T. A. (2019). A review and analysis of possible changes to the climatology of tornadoes in the United States. *Progress in Physical Geography* 43: 365–90.

Moritz, M. A., Parisien, M. A., Batllori, E., Krawchuk, M. A., Van Dorn, J., Ganz, D. J., and Hayhoe, K. (2012). Climate change and disruptions to global fire activity. *Ecosphere* 3: 1–22.

National Academies of Sciences, Engineering, and Medicine (2016). *Attribution of Extreme Weather Events in the Context of Climate Change*. National Academies Press, Washington, DC. https://doi.org/10.17226/21852 [available at http://www.nap.edu/21852].

Naumann, G., Alfieri, L., Wyser, K., Mentaschi, L., Betts, R. A., Carrao, H., Spinoni, J., Vogt, J., and Feyen, L. (2018). Global changes in drought conditions under different levels of warming. *Geophysical Research Letters* 45: 3285–96.

Pfahl, S., O'Gorman, P. A., and Fischer, E. M. (2017). Understanding the regional pattern of projected future changes in extreme precipitation. *Nature Climate Change* 7: 423–7.

Prein, A. F., Liu, C., Ikeda, K., Trier, S. B., Rasmussen, R. M., Holland, G. J., and Clark, M. P. (2017). Increased rainfall volume from future convective storms in the US. *Nature Climate Change* 7: 880–4.

Priestley, M. D. K., and Catto, J. L. (2022). Future changes in the extratropical storm tracks and cyclone intensity, wind speed, and structure. *Weather and Climate Dynamics* 3: 337–60.

Seneviratne, S. I., Donat, M. G., Pitman, A. J., Knutti, R., and Wilby, R. L. (2016). Allowable CO_2 emissions based on regional and impact-related climate targets. *Nature* 529: 477–83.

Sippel, S., Otto, F. E. L., Forkel, M., Allen, M. R., Guillod, B. P., Heimann, M., Reichstein, M., Seneviratne, S. I., Thonicke, K., and Mahecha, M. D. (2016). A novel bias correction methodology for climate impact simulations. *Earth System Dynamics* 7: 71–88.

Swain, D. L., Wing, O. E. J., Bates, P. D., Done, J. M., Johnson, K. A., and Cameron, D. R. (2020). Increased flood exposure due to climate change and population growth in the United States. *Earth's Future* 8: e2020EF001778.

Udall, B., and Overpeck, J. (2017). The 21st century Colorado River hot drought and implications for the future. *Water Resources Research* 53: 2404–18.

UNISDR (2008). *Climate Change and Disaster Risk Reduction*. Briefing note 01, United Nations International Strategy for Disaster Reduction, Geneva.

UNISDR (2009). *2009 UNISDR terminology on disaster risk reduction*. United Nations International Strategy for Disaster Reduction, Geneva.

US Global Climate Research Program (2017). *Climate Science Special Report: Fourth National Climate Assessment*, Volume I (Wuebbles, D. J., Fahey, D. W. Hibbard, K. A., Dokken, D. J., Stewart, B. C., and Maycock, T. K. (eds)). US Global Change Research Program, Washington, DC.

van der Wiel, K., Selten, F. M., Bintanja, R., Blackport, R. and Screen, J. A. (2020). Ensemble climate-impact modelling: Extreme impacts from moderate meteorological conditions. *Environmental Research Letters* 15: 034050. https://doi.org/10.1088/1748-9326/ab7668.

Vavrus, S. J., Notaro, M., and Lorenz, D. J. (2015). Interpreting climate model projections of extreme weather events. *Weather and Climate Extremes* 10: 10–28.

Viceto, C., Cardoso Pereira, S., and Rocha, A. (2019). Climate change projections of extreme temperatures for the Iberian Peninsula. *Atmosphere* 10: 229. https://doi.org/10.3390/atmos10050229.

Woetzel, J., Pinner, D., Samandari, H., Engel, H., Krishnan, M., Boland, B., and Powis, C. (2020). *Climate Risk and Response: Physical Hazards and Socioeconomic Impacts*. McKinsey Global Institute, New York.

Xu, Y. (2019). Estimates of changes in surface wind and temperature extremes in southwestern Norway using dynamical downscaling method under future climate. *Weather and Climate Extremes* 26: 100234.

Zwiers, F. W., Alexander, L. V., Hegerl, G. C., Knutson, T. R., Kossin, J. P., Naveau, P., Nicholls, N., Schär, C., Seneviratne, S. I., and Zhang, X. (2013). Climate extremes: Challenges in estimating and understanding recent changes in the frequency and intensity of extreme climate and weather events. In: Asrar, G. R., and Hurrell, J. W. (eds), *Climate Science for Serving Society: Research, Modeling and Prediction Priorities*, Springer Science + Business Media, Dordrecht, pp. 339–89.

CHAPTER **EIGHT**

Developing Appropriate Adaptation Strategies

LEARNING OUTCOMES

Having read this chapter, you should be able to:

- explain the factors that contribute to local vulnerability to climate change

- describe the importance of assessing both the costs and benefits of climate change when developing climate change adaptation strategies at the community level

- explain why we should identify key sectors within a region that are sensitive to climate change when planning the community-level response to future climate change

- discuss the importance of combining accurate downscaling of global climate model predictions with knowledge of the local environment in order to develop useful adaptation strategies

- assess the need for responsive and dynamic adaptation strategies, as well as the need for ongoing monitoring of their effectiveness

- use examples to critically evaluate different logical approaches to the development of regional and local adaptation strategies in response to climate change

8.1 Introduction: climate change adaptation

The current global warming trend appears to be associated with a range of environmental impacts, such as intense storms (e.g. tornadoes and tropical cyclones), heatwaves, wildfires, floods, and droughts, and there is significant interest in developing adaptation strategies that are appropriate for individual regions and environments. Different parts of the world are impacted by their own unique combination of meteorological and climatological events, which means that effective adaptation strategies need to be developed with the involvement of the local community. Similarly, managing the response in different sectors of activity, such as human health, urban environments, energy generation, and agriculture, needs to be customized in order to address the range of impacts experienced in each sector.

Earlier chapters have used selected case studies to identify impacts of climate change and show how climate change adaptation strategies can be developed in different sectors (urban, air pollution, and health; energy and infrastructure; agriculture and forestry; natural ecosystems; and environmental hazards). The importance of downscaling climate predictions from the global to the regional and local scales has been discussed along with the need to address uncertainty associated with model-based predictions. It is also clear that adaptation strategies should reflect the complex interaction of a variety of environmental factors across a range of spatial and temporal scales, as well as a multitude of socioeconomic factors specific to a region.

It is interesting to note that in many areas of activity, a lot more publications have been devoted to climate change impacts than to adaptation strategies. For example, Keenan (2015) surveyed the literature on climate change impacts and adaptation for forests from 1985 to 2013 and discovered that only 12.6% of the publications found addressed the topic of adaptation.

A key objective of this book is therefore to provide a practical approach to climate change adaptation based on both analytical and modelling techniques applied at much smaller scales than has often been the case. It does not aim to be comprehensive, but is focused more on the scientific and analytical techniques that can be applied to ensure that adaptation strategies are fit for purpose, thereby bridging the gap between climate change science and adaptation policy. It is expected that this approach will be of interest to both students and practitioners concerned with effective decision-making at the community level. This final chapter examines possible approaches to the development of comprehensive adaptation strategies that could be applied at the regional and local scales across a range of environments and sectors of human activity.

CONSIDERATIONS OF CLIMATE CHANGE ADAPTATION STRATEGIES

It should be acknowledged that while much of the world will be negatively affected by climate change, some regions and sectors might actually benefit. It is also difficult to estimate the benefits and costs associated with climate change, as there are many different sectors of society and the economy that are sensitive to a range of different climate factors (e.g. temperature, humidity, wind, and rainfall), and the degree of sensitivity varies significantly. For example, costs associated with floods and droughts are frequently estimated and publicly released, while those associated with sea level rise, extreme winds, hail, and wildfires may make fewer headlines because either their impact is difficult to assess or the events generally occur more rarely. It is clear that weather and climate have always had an impact on the supply and use of energy, as well as on the complex infrastructure that supports human communities. However, clearly identifying the effects of the current global warming trend, as distinct from 'normal' weather events, can be extremely complicated.

As discussed in Chapter 7 in relation to environmental hazards, the impacts and costs of climate change on communities and national infrastructure vary significantly across the globe, with poorer countries generally being potentially more negatively impacted. Regional differences in governance, administration, and political environments may enhance or hinder successful implementation of adaptation strategies at the regional and local levels. The ability of regional or local communities to develop adaptation strategies tailored to their needs can therefore depend on the social, cultural, economic, and political environment within which they are located. Policy development at international and national levels provides only the broad framework for responding to climate change at community level, being generally based on large-scale (global) modelling and analysis. It lacks the precision to provide local communities with a customized plan to address their specific problems related to climate change, such as sea level rise or floods and droughts. A new approach is therefore needed that combines the downscaling of global climate predictions with knowledge of the local environment to provide the basis for effective adaptation.

The main aim of adaptation is to reduce the damage to a community, or in some cases to exploit any benefit that accrues, from climate change. It is clear that the most effective approaches to developing adaptation strategies will be based on a good understanding of the natural and human processes that affect the environment at the local scale. Such approaches should also be dynamic and responsive to improvements in knowledge, as well as being customized to different geographical situations (e.g. mid-latitude, tropical, continental, and oceanic at the broadest scale). New adaptive tools, such as dynamic adaptive policy pathways (Lawrence et al. 2020; Haasnoot et al. 2015), allow adaptation strategies to be responsive to the vagaries of climate change, as a successful adaptation strategy needs to be dynamic and able to be continually updated, given that the role of different factors will change over time.

It is also important to monitor both the impacts of climate change and the effectiveness of actions taken to respond to them, leaving options open to allow adaptation strategies to be flexible and to recognize triggers that could necessitate a change in response. Changes in the level of risk to the local community should be continually evaluated in order to ensure that current actions are appropriate and sufficient. Adaptation strategies therefore need to be responsive to changes in both climate and the environmental response to those changes, as well as changes in socio-economic conditions. There may be various thresholds, and tipping and turning points, affecting sustainability under climate change that require the efficacy of adaptation strategies to be continually evaluated (Werners et al. 2013). In addition, significant uncertainty associated with predictions of climate change at the regional and local scales may make it difficult to identify appropriate actions to take. This uncertainty requires an adaptation strategy to be flexible and capable of modification as new knowledge becomes available and climate change predictions are updated.

Before developing an appropriate adaptation strategy for a specific sector and region, it is important to examine the sector's level of exposure to climate risk, its sensitivity to variations in climate, and the adaptive capacity of the community (van Noordwijk et al. 2011). The vulnerability of the community depends on both its sensitivity to climate variation and its adaptive capacity, while the adaptive capacity of different communities may vary, depending on social, cultural, economic, and political factors. For example, an effective adaptation strategy might be impossible to implement because a region is too poor, so that the strategy is overridden by economic factors such as the welfare and livelihoods of local inhabitants. However, in some cases, prioritizing adaptation to climate change may have wider benefits to the community and provide opportunities for economic development. Similarly, if mitigation and adaptation programmes are carefully integrated into a common strategy, there may be some synergistic benefits.

The ultimate aim is to build resilience for both society and the environment, and this can be achieved by integrating adaptation into the day-to-day governance of local communities, from the development of policy through to practical actions. This would require engagement with the community (e.g. its inhabitants) and relevant stakeholders (e.g. universities, research institutes, engineers, and water and waste companies).

8.2 Generic practical steps

In this section, some generic practical steps are suggested as a guide to developing a climate change adaptation strategy at regional and local scales. A key aim of this chapter is to provide guidance for national and/or regional authorities responsible for developing climate change adaptation strategies for specific regions, at the same time as providing students with a fundamental understanding of the issues involved in developing adaptation strategies that can be applied effectively to a range of different regions and sectors.

STEP 1: IDENTIFY KEY SECTORS AND THEIR OBSERVED CLIMATE SENSITIVITY

The most important sectors need to be identified for each region, recognizing that they will have their own unique combination of sectors or environments that need to be considered (urban, coastal, energy/infrastructure, natural ecosystems, agriculture/rural, forestry, etc.). Some sectors are more important than others and need to be weighted accordingly. This assessment process should involve the skills and experience of local environmental managers and policy-makers, as well as external (national or international) experts, working together in a consultative manner with affected communities. Community engagement in the adaptation decision-making process is vitally important in order to make use of local knowledge and opinions as to what actions are appropriate for the region.

It is also important to evaluate the sensitivity of each sector (e.g. urban areas, renewable energy, transport, agriculture, fisheries, and natural ecosystems) to current climate conditions and their variation, including sensitivity to both mean climate and its variability. Key questions include:

- In which sectors does climate/weather have its greatest impact in the region?
- Based on a comprehensive analysis of recent climate effects, what is the relationship between current climate and each of the key sectors in a given area?

- What climate factors are the most important to each specific sector, and why?
- What is the sensitivity of each sector to variation of those climate factors?
- What time/space scales are most important in relation to climate impacts on each sector?

STEP 2: EVALUATE FUTURE CLIMATE PREDICTIONS AND THEIR LIKELY IMPACT

Predictions of future climate for a given region need to be assessed in relation to their possible impact at regional and local scales. Some critical questions need to be addressed, including:

- How is climate predicted to change within the region under consideration?
- Which critical climate factors will be affected, and in what way?
- Over what time and space scales are changes in climate likely to occur, and what interactions of scale are important (from the hemispheric to the synoptic, regional, and local scales)?
- What is the level of uncertainty associated with global climate predictions and their downscaling to given regions, and what are the implications for decision-making at regional and local scales?

It is important to evaluate the uncertainty associated with scenarios/predictions of change in both mean climate conditions and their spatial and temporal variability, in relation to a range of different climate variables (e.g. temperature, rainfall, wind, and solar radiation). This is likely to require advice from specialized experts who can evaluate uncertainty associated with the downscaled climate model predictions for the region, using current knowledge of regional and local atmospheric processes relevant to each sector.

For each sector identified in Step 1, it is important to provide a detailed assessment of the likely impacts of predicted future climate change. Different sectors (e.g. renewable energy generation or agriculture) will have their own sensitivity to future climate change, often involving different climate parameters, and any evaluation of impacts is likely to require sector-based expertise. The analysis completed in Step 1 provides the basis for evaluating the most likely impacts of climate change in the key sectors within regions under consideration, although future climate conditions may result in new climate–sector relationships being established that differ from those identified in the past.

This analysis of climate–sector relationships should consider the time and space scales most relevant to the selected sector and region, and should consider both positive and negative impacts of future climate change. In some sectors, inter-regional impacts may be relevant, so it may also be important to evaluate future climate impacts on other regions. For example, agricultural industries in different regions may experience opposing impacts, depending on the specific climate conditions and their change within those regions, resulting in market advantages for some regions over others. Similarly, climate-induced ecosystem change in one region may impact on such things as bird migrations affecting other regions, while there may also be effects on fish migration between regions.

STEP 3: DEVELOP BOTH SECTOR-BASED AND OVER-ARCHING ADAPTATION STRATEGIES

Adaptation strategies developed for each sector (e.g. transport or tourism) should be based on their own unique relationship with both current and predicted future climate. Each sector-based adaptation strategy needs to be fine-tuned to the unique role that the sector plays within the region. Some key questions are:

- What steps can be taken to reduce negative impacts of climate change on the selected sector in a given region?

- What positive effects can be exploited by given sectors within the region?

- How are the impacts of climate change on different sectors likely to affect other sectors within the region?

- What adaptive actions can a region take to become more resilient to climate change across all sectors?

Responses can be wide ranging, including changes in infrastructure (e.g. development of water management systems, coastal zone management, changes in infrastructure, and renewable energy generation), but they can also involve fine-scale interventions at the local level that allow specific activities to adapt to the particular issues that affect them. For example, in agriculture new crop types or varieties can be chosen and different techniques used as part of the response to change (e.g. changes in irrigation and spraying regimes, and crop canopy management).

Based on existing knowledge, the key climate-related factors likely to affect each sector are fairly obvious:

- Agriculture (drought, heat, humidity, sunshine, wind, flood)

- Urban issues (drought, heat, flood, air pollution)

- Infrastructure/energy/water (drought, heat, flood, storminess, wind, sunshine)

- Hazards (storminess, wind, hail, snow, floods, drought, fire)

- Natural environments (drought, heat, flood, snow, wind, fire)

Adaptation strategies for each sector should be designed to reflect the space and timescales of most importance to specific activities and regions, as well as the administrative and/or governance structure in place. All the individual sector-based adaptation strategies need to be integrated into a single, comprehensive, over-arching strategy that reflects the linkages between each sector, as well as their relationship with climate. It is evident that some proposed actions in adaptation strategies developed for individual sectors may negatively or positively impact on other sectors within a region, making ultimate outcomes sometimes difficult to predict. Commonalities and differences therefore need to be identified in order to benefit from coordinated actions where possible, and to reduce incompatibility between sector strategies. A coordinated schedule of actions needs to be organized over specific time frames, including monitoring, and identification of trigger points and thresholds, to ensure that the over-arching strategy can be dynamically responsive to changing circumstances, as suggested by Haasnoot et al. (2015) and Lawrence et al. (2020).

STEP 4: REVIEW OUTCOMES OF ADAPTATION ACTIONS AND THE SIGNIFICANCE OF NEW KNOWLEDGE

Ongoing monitoring and reviews should be undertaken of the effectiveness of the adaptation strategies developed for a region and its most important sectors. These reviews should include both the effectiveness of the actions taken as part of a coordinated over-arching strategy, and changes in the scientific knowledge that underpin strategy design. The outcomes of these reviews should be used to modify the design of adaption strategies for each sector, as well as the comprehensive regional adaptation strategy. It is evident that such climate change adaptation strategies need to be dynamic, allowing changes in and fine-tuning of the range of actions taken in response to observed changes in climate as a result of ongoing evaluation of the effectiveness of such actions. It is therefore important to monitor both climate and the effectiveness

of the adaptation actions taken, and to provide feedback into the decision-making process.

GENERAL IMPLICATIONS

The above steps need to be applied specifically to the unique combination of sectors of importance in a given region, as the climate change impacts, the most important climate and other variables, and the space and timescales involved can be quite different for different sectors (e.g. agriculture, urban, energy and infrastructure, hazards, and natural ecosystems).

It may be found that future climate change may have positive effects in one sector, but negative effects in another, so the comprehensive integrated plan prepared for a region should be developed recognizing that it may be necessary to shift priority from one sector to another. Major change may therefore occur in the weighting of the key sectors identified at the outset as a result of climate change and the implementation of a region's adaptation strategy, so that one industry or sector replaces another in importance (e.g. there could be a shift between forestry and agriculture, or between pastoral farming and horticulture). In some cases, completely new sectors may appear, although this is unlikely over the medium term. It should also be remembered that there are often relationships between adaptation and mitigation approaches, so any adaptation strategy should allow for complementarity between these two objectives.

8.3 Climate change adaptation strategies in practice

Some approaches to the development of adaptation strategies for specific applications and regions have provided useful general guidance that can be applied in a range of sectors or environments. The following three case studies provide selected examples of the way in which some of the principles discussed in earlier sections can be applied in a practical way to development of sound climate change adaptation strategies.

CASE STUDY 8.I
Climate change adaptation in forestry

Janowiak et al. (2014) identified a gap between the growing scientific knowledge of climate change and its significance for a variety of activities and the integration of this knowledge into management practices in forestry. This appears to be the result of the range of different management goals, ecosystems, ownership types, and spatial scales in the forestry industry (Janowiak et al. 2014). A generalized approach was therefore described for the forest sector to help development of practical climate change adaptation strategies, as shown in Figure 8.1. They recognized the need to identify potential effects of climate change on forestry, taking on board the uncertainty associated with climate predictions and their likely impacts, as well as the importance of integrating adaptation into the forest management process. This example incorporates feedback through ongoing monitoring of effectiveness, as well as new knowledge of climate change impacts and adaptation approaches. The five-step approach illustrated in Figure 8.1 is generic enough to be applicable to a range of different situations and sectors.

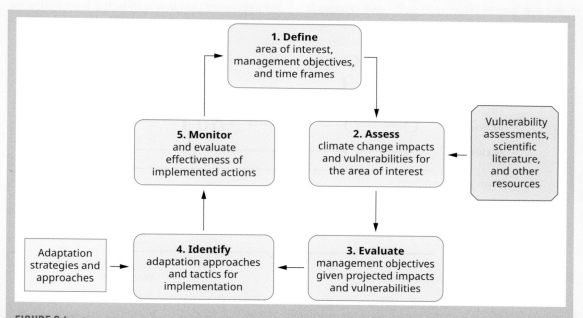

FIGURE 8.I A five-step approach to developing a climate change adaptation strategy for the forestry sector

Source: Janowiak et al. (2014). A practical approach for translating climate change adaptation principles into forest management actions. *Journal of Forestry* 112: 424–33

CASE STUDY 8.2
Dynamic adaptive pathways for responding to climate change

Haasnoot et al. (2015) suggested that climate change adaptation strategies need to be based on time-dependent climate scenarios, thereby emphasizing the dynamic nature of climate change adaptation. They demonstrated the need to apply transient scenarios that are continually updated as new knowledge is generated about possible future climate conditions and once the effect of actions taken as part of adaptation strategies can be assessed. That is, they recommended that static scenarios with fixed targets should be avoided. This approach has led to the concept of Dynamic Adaptive Policy Pathways (DAPP), which allows a climate change adaptation strategy to evolve over time in response to both actual changes in

climate and evaluation of the effectiveness of specific actions (Haasnoot et al. 2019). Adaptation tipping points and triggers can be established within such a dynamic framework in order to allow an adaptation strategy to be reviewed and/or updated over time, thereby taking into account the significant uncertainty inherent in future predictions of the climate–environment system. A range of different decision pathways can therefore eventuate, depending on the action taken, the ongoing review process, and various trigger points, tipping points, and adaptation signals, leading to different outcomes.

Figure 8.2 illustrates this concept graphically, with the passage of time indicated by the black horizontal

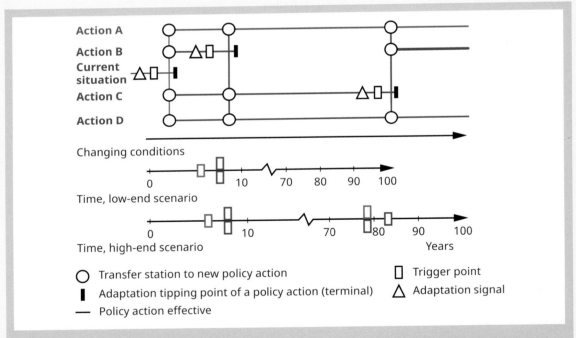

FIGURE 8.2 Schematic illustration of action pathways within a dynamic adaptive climate change adaptation strategy. The circles represent points in time when a decision can be made relating to a specific action, resulting in a continuation or change in action. Triangles and rectangles indicate the timing of signals (warnings) and decision points before a terminal end point is reached (indicated by the vertical bar)

Source: Haasnoot et al. (2019). *Dynamic Adaptive Policy Pathways (DAPP) BT*. In: Marchau, V. A. W. J., et al. (eds), *Decision Making under Deep Uncertainty: From Theory to Practice*. Springer, Berlin, pp. 71–92

lines with arrowheads (in this case, two different scenarios of change), and separate action pathways represented by the different-coloured lines in the top part of the diagram. The actions A to D represent different responses that a community can make in order to adapt to the changing conditions. So, in response to a specific climate change-induced problem such as rising sea level, a community could respond by building protective walls, establishing a beach renourishment programme, removing vulnerable buildings and structures from the coastal area, and/or placing restrictions on future development near the coast. The time frame over which each of these actions might be effective would vary as a result of the nature of the actions, as well as the rate at which sea level rises. The actions are therefore affected by adaptation signals, trigger points, and tipping points (or thresholds) as indicated in Figure 8.2. Adaptation signals in this case could reflect indicators in the coastal environment as to whether the adaptation action is working or not, such as the rate of coastal erosion. In this example, adaptation signals can be monitored through regular observations of the state of the coast. Trigger points represent previously defined events, such as cliff or beach erosion reaching a specific distance inland, signifying that a timely response is needed before a tipping point is reached. When an action reaches a tipping point or threshold, it becomes obvious that the

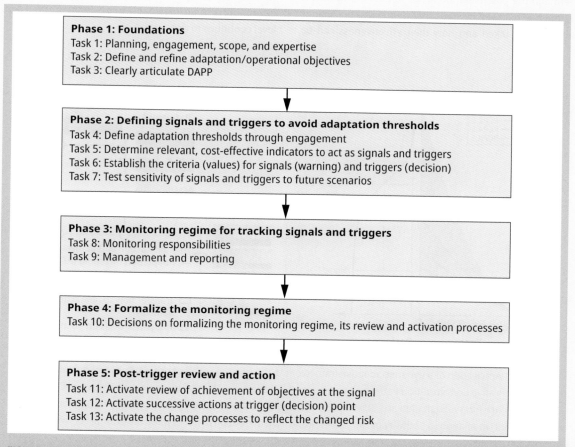

Phase 1: Foundations
Task 1: Planning, engagement, scope, and expertise
Task 2: Define and refine adaptation/operational objectives
Task 3: Clearly articulate DAPP

Phase 2: Defining signals and triggers to avoid adaptation thresholds
Task 4: Define adaptation thresholds through engagement
Task 5: Determine relevant, cost-effective indicators to act as signals and triggers
Task 6: Establish the criteria (values) for signals (warning) and triggers (decision)
Task 7: Test sensitivity of signals and triggers to future scenarios

Phase 3: Monitoring regime for tracking signals and triggers
Task 8: Monitoring responsibilities
Task 9: Management and reporting

Phase 4: Formalize the monitoring regime
Task 10: Decisions on formalizing the monitoring regime, its review and activation processes

Phase 5: Post-trigger review and action
Task 11: Activate review of achievement of objectives at the signal
Task 12: Activate successive actions at trigger (decision) point
Task 13: Activate the change processes to reflect the changed risk

FIGURE 8.3 Generic scheme for deriving signals, triggers, and adaptation thresholds within a dynamic adaptive framework

Source: Lawrence et al. (2020). *Supporting Decision Making through Adaptive Tools in a Changing Climate: Practice Guidance on Signals and Triggers*. Deep South Challenge, Wellington. https://deepsouthchallenge.co.nz/wp-content/uploads/2021/01/Supporting-decisionmaking-through-adaptive-tools-in-a-changing-climate-.pdf

specific action is no longer an effective response strategy, and should therefore be terminated (as indicated with actions B and C in Figure 8.2).

Lawrence et al. (2020) developed this concept and applied it to sea level rise and river flooding under a changing climate in New Zealand. They focused particularly on practical approaches to the development of signals, triggers, and thresholds within a dynamic adaptive framework, including the role of community engagement. Figure 8.3 provides a generic framework guiding the establishment of a dynamic adaptive framework including these key components.

As described earlier, Lawrence et al. (2020) indicated that the first step is to define the dimensions of the problem and the possible approaches to addressing it. This should be followed by steps that clearly identify actions that can be taken and how their effectiveness can be

assessed, including monitoring and report processes, as well as how decisions will be made as actions are implemented and found to be effective or not. As with Case study 8.1, the generic scheme shown in Figure 8.3 could be applied to a range of different sectors or environments.

Figure 8.4 illustrates the application of this approach to adaptation of a coastal region to the issue of sea level rise, with each pathway representing alternative actions or responses to the problem (see Chapter 2 for a detailed explanation of the Representative Concentration Pathway scenarios). Clearly, taking no action is unsustainable in relation to limiting damage to the environment and infrastructure in the coastal region, while constructing barriers may be effective to a certain extent, but also unsustainable in the longer term if sea level continues to rise.

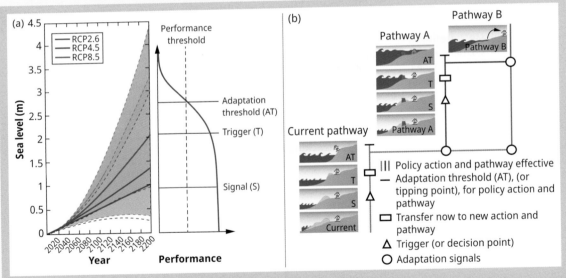

FIGURE 8.4 Application of a dynamic adaptive framework to the issue of sea level rise. (a) Sea level rise projections for Representative Concentration Pathway 2.6, 4.5, and 8.5 scenarios, with median projection (coloured lines) and 95% confidence intervals (shaded areas), as well as the signal, trigger/decision points, and adaptation threshold (tipping point) in relation to pathway performance. (b) A dynamic adaptive policy pathway example comparing the options: current pathway (no action), pathway A (seawall construction), and pathway B (managed retreat). See Chapter 2 for a detailed explanation of the RCP scenarios

Source: Lawrence et al. (2020). *Supporting Decision Making through Adaptive Tools in a Changing Climate: Practice Guidance on Signals and Triggers*. Deep South Challenge, Wellington. https://deepsouthchallenge.co.nz/wp-content/uploads/2021/01/Supporting-decisionmaking-through-adaptive-tools-in-a-changing-climate-.pdf

CASE STUDY 8.3

Climate change adaptation strategy for the Quebec region

The Quebec region of Canada has followed a systematic approach by producing a guide providing basic guidelines for the development of a 'tailor-made' strategy for the various municipalities in the region. This adaptation strategy takes into account the uniqueness of local or regional characteristics such as the geographical, socio-economic, environmental, and administrative attributes of each municipality. Figure 8.5 shows the different steps involved in developing a climate change adaptation plan in this case. It is a long-term, progressive plan in a context where it

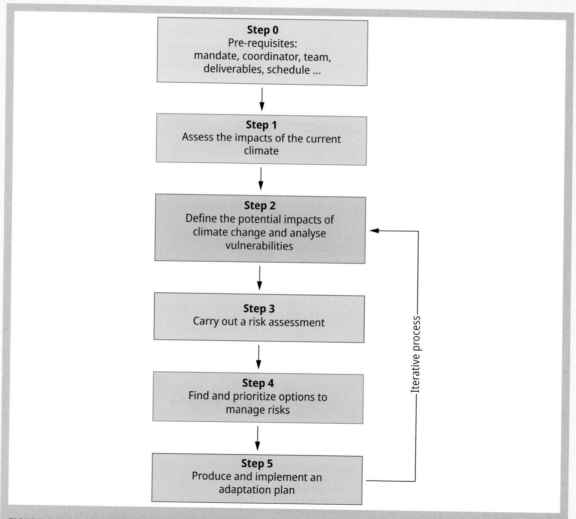

FIGURE 8.5 Key stages in the development of a climate change adaptation plan for municipalities in Quebec, Canada

Source: Larrivée, C. (2010). *Élaborer un plan d'adaptation aux changements climatiques: Guide destiné au milieu municipal québécois. Ouranos*, Montreal

is anticipated that the level of risk will change over time. Monitoring mechanisms aim to allow adjustments to the adaptation strategy as climate risks evolve and knowledge about climate change and associated risks improves. Decisions about which risks are considered most important and which adaptation measures should be applied are to be re-evaluated based on lessons learned from the initial implementation of adaptation measures and new information, as it becomes available. This 'step-by-step' approach aims to develop a long-term strategy, while establishing short- and medium-term adaptation actions.

As suggested earlier, an important preliminary step in this case was to identify key sectors and their sensitivity to climate risks. Analysis of the outputs of regionalized climate change models allows assessment of the short-, medium-, and long-term climate risks for the various sectors managed by Quebec municipalities. The same climatic event will have different impacts on different sectors, requiring an adaptation strategy that takes into account the inter-relationships between all sectors. Figure 8.6 identifies the sectors that would be impacted by a decrease in the water level of the Great Lakes–St Lawrence Basin, for example. This decrease in water level would have economic, social, and environmental effects that municipalities must integrate into climate change adaptation plans. The interaction of adaptation measures requires a multidisciplinary strategy across different municipal services. The objective of this approach is to ensure that an adaptation measure in one sector does not increase the vulnerability and risks for other sectors.

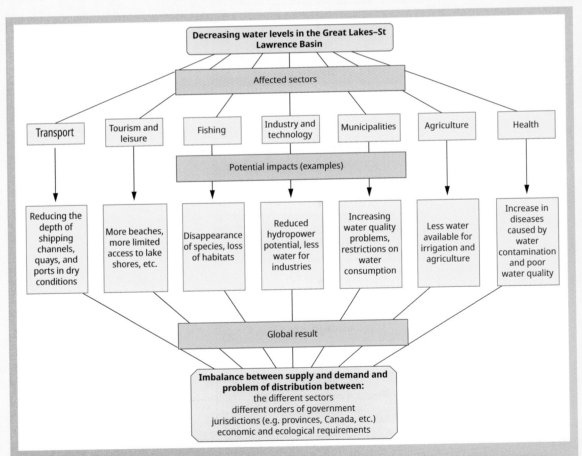

FIGURE 8.6 An example of inter-related climate change issues: impacts of a decrease in water levels on different sectors in the Great Lakes–St Lawrence Basin, Canada

Source: Larrivée, C. (2010). *Élaborer un plan d'adaptation aux changements climatiques: Guide destiné au milieu municipal québécois*. Ouranos, Montreal

8.4 Concluding comments

There is significant interest in developing climate change adaptation strategies at the regional and local levels, both from regional authorities and from other stakeholders. However, there is a general lack of practical guidance as to how local communities should go about designing a comprehensive strategy that suits their unique needs. In spite of this, the case studies above indicate that various sectors and communities have made a start, and have drafted strategies that include actions that reflect the unique characteristics of their region (e.g. urban environments, natural environments, specific regions, and specific sectors). However, many of these attempts lack a comprehensive focus and address only one or two aspects of a specific region, such as the viticulture sector or the impacts of sea level rise (see case studies above). Ideally, an effective adaptation strategy should reflect the complexity of the region that it is applied to, including consideration of the various human activity sectors and the importance of the region's physical, social, cultural, political, and economic environment. Such strategies should also be dynamic and flexible tools that can be continuously updated to ensure that they continue to maintain the sustainability of the local community and its environment. It is hoped that the general guidance provided here can provide a useful starting point for regional and local communities in their quest to develop a climate change adaptation strategy that is appropriate to their needs.

Summary

- Climate change adaptation strategies should be based on a multisectoral approach and consider different spatial (from global to local and vice versa) and temporal scales (short, medium, and long term).

- The general development and structure of climate change adaptation plans are often defined at international and national levels. However, they need to provide regional and local communities with a framework for developing their own individual adaptation strategies that reflect their unique physical, social, cultural, economic, and political conditions.

- A practical approach is therefore needed to strategy development that can be applied at regional and local scales, across a range of environments and sectors of human activity.

- The sensitivity of different sectors of society and the economy to a changing climate can be very variable and difficult to quantify, making cost–benefit analysis difficult to perform.

- Adaptation strategies need to be flexible and dynamic so that they can be modified in response to improving knowledge of climate change projections, environmental and sectoral response to climate change impacts at the regional and local level, and ongoing monitoring of the effects of implementing adaptive actions.

- Regional- and local-scale adaptation strategies should be based on good knowledge of the level of exposure of each sector or activity to climate risk, its sensitivity to variations in climate, and the adaptive capacity of the community in order to build resilience for both society and the environment.

- Operational adaptation strategies for specific regions should be composed of several sequential steps, such as: (1) identifying key sectors and their observed climate sensitivity; (2) evaluating future climate predictions and their likely impact; (3) developing both sector-based and over-arching adaptation strategies; (4) reviewing outcomes of adaptation actions and the significance of new knowledge, making changes to adaptation actions in response to ongoing reviews and improvements in knowledge.

- A strategy for adapting to climate change should evolve over time based both on observed climate change and on continual ongoing assessment of the effectiveness of specific actions. This may involve the application of triggers and tipping points to stimulate specific responses, including changes of direction.

- The effectiveness of climate change adaptation plans for specific regions strongly depends not only on the vulnerability of different sectors to climate risks but also on the quality of governance from the national to the local level. The poorest countries are often the most exposed to the impacts of climate change, and the political and economic situations in these countries do not always enable the implementation of an effective adaptation strategy.

- Well-thought-out, dynamic, and ecosystem-based adaptation strategies should provide communities with a set of sustainable and cost-effective solutions to the challenges of climate change and sustainable development at regional and local scales.

For case studies and updates, visit the online resources

www.oup.com/he/sturman-quenol1e

References

Haasnoot, M., Schellekens, J., Beersma, J. J., Middelkoop, H., and Kwadijk, J. C. J. (2015). Transient scenarios for robust climate change adaptation illustrated for water management in the Netherlands. *Environmental Research Letters* 10: 105008. https://doi.org/10.1088/1748-9326/10/10/105008.

Haasnoot, M., Warren, A., and Kwakkel, J. H. (2019). *Dynamic Adaptive Policy Pathways (DAPP) BT*. In: Marchau, V. A. W. J., et al. (eds), *Decision Making under Deep Uncertainty: From Theory to Practice*. Springer, Berlin, pp. 71–92.

Janowiak, M. K., Swanston, C. W., Nagel, L. M., Brandt, L. A., Butler, P., Handler, S., Shannon, D., Iverson, L. R., Matthews, S. N., Prasad, A., and Peters, M. P. (2014). A practical approach for translating climate change adaptation principles into forest management actions. *Journal of Forestry* 112: 424–33.

Keenan, R. J. (2015). Climate change impacts and adaptation in forest management: A review. *Annals of Forest Science* 72: 145–67.

Larrivée, C. (2010). *Élaborer un plan d'adaptation aux changements climatiques: Guide destiné au milieu municipal québécois*. Ouranos, Montreal.

Lawrence, J., Bell, R., Blackett, P., Stephens, S., Collins, D., Cradock-Henry, N., and Hardcastle, M. (2020). *Supporting Decision Making through Adaptive Tools in a Changing Climate: Practice Guidance on Signals and Triggers*. Deep South Challenge, Wellington. https://deepsouthchallenge.co.nz/wp-content/uploads/2021/01/Supporting-decision-making-through-adaptive-tools-in-a-changing-climate-.pdf.

van Noordwijk, M., Hoang, M. H., Neufeldt, H., Öborn, I., and Yatich, T. (eds) (2011). *How Trees and People Can Co-adapt to Climate Change: Reducing Vulnerability through Multifunctional Agroforestry Landscapes*. World Agroforestry Centre, Nairobi.

Werners, S. E., Pfenninger, S., van Slobbe, E., Haasnoot, M., Kwakkel, J. H., and Swart, R. J. (2013). Thresholds, tipping and turning points for sustainability under climate change. *Current Opinion in Environmental Sustainability* 5: 334–40.

Glossary

acidification of ocean water the long-term decrease in the pH of ocean waters that is thought to be caused by increasing absorption of carbon dioxide resulting from elevated levels of greenhouse gases in the atmosphere

adaptation strategies action plans that aim to reduce the impacts of climate change in order to limit negative consequences and enhance positive benefits for the natural environment and human life

aerosol a suspension of very small droplets or particles in the atmosphere

aerosol optical depth a measure of the aerosol content of the atmosphere through a vertical column between the ground surface and the top of the atmosphere

agroforestry agricultural practices integrating the growth of trees with crops or livestock in order to preserve biodiversity and improve management of natural resources

air pollution a modification of atmospheric constituents that harmfully affects plants, animals (including humans), or materials

Aladin-Climat model Aire Limitée Adaptation dynamique Développement InterNational—a limited area (regional) climate model used by the French National Centre of Meteorological Research

albedo the proportion of solar radiation that is reflected back from different surfaces to the atmosphere and outer space

algorithm a set of logical steps in calculations applied to the solution of particular problems (often in the form of a computer program or script)

analytical a practical approach taken to solving problems through logical analysis or reasoning

anomaly the deviation from an expected value, which is often the long-term mean or average

anthropogenic originating as the result of human activity

atmospheric absorption spectrum typically illustrated by a graph showing the sections of the electromagnetic radiation spectrum that are absorbed by atmospheric gaseous composition

atmospheric boundary layer the lowest layer of the atmosphere that is most affected by contact with the underlying ground surface

atmospheric stability the ability of the atmosphere to resist vertical motion—a stable atmosphere resists forces (e.g. mountains) that may try to move the air vertically, while an unstable atmosphere enhances vertical motion

bias the difference or error between a predicted and an observed value

bioclimatic indices indices that are generally based on the link between climate parameters (especially temperature) and plant or animal response

biodiversity indicated by the range of plants and animals within a specific habitat—it is assumed that the greater the variety, the healthier the environment

biofuel a fuel that has been derived by processing living matter

biogenic volatile organic compounds organic chemical compounds emitted by plants, often having high vapour pressure and low boiling point (e.g. formaldehyde, acetone, ethylene, isoprene)

biomass total weight of biological matter in a given area or volume

biome type an area defined by the combination of different environmental components that occur within it, such as its characteristic climate, soil, plants, and animals (e.g. grassland, forest, tundra, marine, freshwater, desert)

biosphere the part of the Earth–atmosphere system occupied by biological organisms

boundary conditions (in climate models) specific values or formulae to be applied at the edge of a spatial field or domain within a climate model

budburst the first phase of plant response that occurs at the start of the vegetative season (i.e. spring) as the buds begin to open

carbon budget an annual assessment of the balance between carbon emissions and carbon uptake in the Earth–atmosphere system. It can be assessed globally or locally

cardinal temperatures the key temperatures that influence the growth of an organism, including the absolute minimum and maximum temperatures below/above which it will not survive, and the optimum temperature at which growth is most rapid

climate the integrated weather experienced by a site or region over a period of many years

climate change long-term change or trends in climate

climate modelling the use of computer programs to simulate changes in climate over long periods of time (from decades to centuries)

climate projection a description of the future state of the climate often based on climate modelling and assumptions about possible effects of human activity on atmospheric processes (scenarios)

climate system a complex system resulting from the interaction of several key components—the atmosphere, hydrosphere, cryosphere, lithosphere, and biosphere

cloud fraction the proportion of the sky covered by cloud, often measured in eighths, tenths, or as a percentage

CMIP Coupled Model Intercomparison Project—an international project comparing future climate predictions obtained from a range of different global climate models

complex models models that attempt to simulate the effects of many interacting components on the future state of a specific environment

condensation nuclei small particles acting as nuclei onto which condensation occurs during the formation of individual ice crystals or droplets in cloud or fog

cryosphere the part of the Earth's environment that is composed of frozen water, in the form of ice or snow

daily temperature range the difference in temperature between the maximum and minimum values recorded during a day

deterministic a philosophical concept in which particular occurrences are caused by preceding events or processes—that is, they are the direct result of previous actions and not the result of random chance (i.e. **stochastic**).

downscaling the application of a procedure to derive higher-resolution spatial information from low-resolution data (e.g. deriving local patterns of climate data from global climate model output)

dynamical downscaling the use of physics-based numerical models to increase the spatial resolution of larger-scale (often global) climate information

dynamical model a model used to represent atmospheric processes based on the solution of physical equations (in contrast to a statistical model)

Earth–atmosphere system all of the components of the Earth's environment from the Earth's surface through to the outer edge of the Earth's atmosphere

Earth's energy budget the balance between the energy receipt of planet Earth and the energy that is returned to space from the Earth–atmosphere system

Earth-system models computer models that attempt to simulate the complex environment of the Earth–atmosphere system, as influenced by a range of chemical, physical, biological, and dynamical processes

ecosystem a biological community in which organisms interact with their physical environment

ecosystem services advantages to humans provided by a healthy natural environment, including providing sustenance (food and water), regulation limiting adverse effects such as pollution and enhancing resilience, cultural services based on human spiritual and recreational interaction with the environment, and the support provided by natural processes such as nutrient cycles and oxygen production

ecotron one or more enclosures used to conduct controlled environmental experiments investigating ecosystem processes

El Niño Southern Oscillation (ENSO) the name given to variations in the intensity of the Walker circulation in the southern Pacific Ocean. This circulation describes the relationship between winds and ocean currents that causes cyclical changes in the movement of ocean water between the eastern and western sides of the ocean

emission scenarios possible pathways that human society might take that influence the future emissions of greenhouse gases into the atmosphere

empirical based on actual observations (i.e. not theoretical)

energy balance the balance between energy gain and loss in a system

environmental hazards physical, chemical, biological, or related events that have the potential to impact on humans and their environment

evapotranspiration the combined process of evaporation and transpiration (water loss from plants during photosynthesis)

exotic species introduced, alien, or non-indigenous organisms found in a given environment

extreme event an event that produces conditions that exceed subjectively derived upper or lower thresholds, such as droughts, floods, winds, and heatwaves

feedback the process by which change introduced into a system either enhances (positive feedback) or reduces (negative feedback) the change

forcing the application of energy to cause change in a system

Forest Fire Danger Index (FFDI) a measure of the risk of wildfire outbreak in a particular location or area

fossil fuel solid fuel found in the Earth's crust created by the decomposition and compression of plants and animals over long periods of time

Free-Air Carbon Dioxide Enrichment (FACE) experimentation involving the modification of the environment of growing plants by increasing carbon dioxide concentrations

Fujita tornado intensity scale a measure of tornado intensity based on the damage inflicted on natural and artificial structures in the environment

geographic information system (GIS) a computer-based set of tools for creating, manipulating, and analysing mapped data

global climate model (GCM) a mathematical representation of the Earth–atmosphere system expressed in computer code that is used to simulate possible changes in global climate over time

greenhouse effect the natural contribution to tropospheric temperatures due to the atmosphere's transparency to solar radiation and partial opaqueness to terrestrial radiation

greenhouse gases trace gases in the atmosphere that selectively absorb outgoing terrestrial radiation, resulting in the greenhouse effect

growing degree-day a measure of the heat accumulation during the growing season based on the daily exceedance of a threshold mean daily temperature that can be used to relate to plant response (e.g. budburst, flowering, maturity, and harvest)

growing season the period of time during which plants or crops grow successfully—it varies between different types of plant or crop

hydrography the science of measuring and describing water bodies of different types (e.g. oceans, lakes, and rivers)

impact model a model representing the range of natural and human factors that contribute to impacts on a particular system

infrastructure the underlying structures, such as roads, bridges, dams, power supply networks, transport systems, and waste and sewage systems, that support economic and related human activity

Intergovernmental Panel on Climate Change (IPCC) the United Nations body responsible for evaluating and communicating science related to climate change

isotopes different forms of the same chemical element differentiated by the number of neutrons (e.g. carbon has 15 known isotopes)

jet stream a relatively narrow and shallow stream of fast-flowing air, usually located in the middle and high troposphere

latent heat the heat given out when gases and liquids change phase to liquids and solids, respectively, and that is absorbed when solids change to liquids and liquids evaporate

linear a process by which there is a proportional change in two related variables—an incremental change in one variable is associated with a proportional change in another variable

Little Ice Age a period of cold winters that affected particularly the North Atlantic region between the fourteenth and nineteenth centuries, especially around 1650, 1770, and 1850

maladaptation a failure to adapt adequately to changing environmental conditions, often resulting in increased vulnerability to climate variability and change

Maunder Minimum a period of minimal sunspot activity between about 1645 and 1715, during the Little Ice Age

mesoscale climate model a physics-based atmospheric numerical model that is used to investigate climate variability at the mesoscale—that is, focused on spatial variations of climate between 10 and 1,000 km resolution

microphysics/microphysical processes physical processes active on the scale of individual cloud and precipitation droplets and particles

Milankovitch cycle/mechanisms periodic changes in the Earth's orbital parameters that are considered to influence long-term climate variations

mitigation actions taken to combat and possibly reverse negative impacts, such as in relation to climate change

model ensemble a group of different climate models, or copies of the same model run with different settings, used to assess the likely variability across a range of possible outcomes

model uncertainty uncertainty in model predictions derived from a range of different sources, such as imperfect representation of all the process involved, errors in input data, and random chaos inherent in the operation of atmospheric processes

morphology study of the size, shape, and structure of different features or organisms

multiscale models the simultaneous application of models at different scales to investigate processes within a complex system

natural disaster the negative impact of an environmental hazard on humans and their environment, resulting from a combination of both natural (e.g. severe storms) and human (e.g. poor environmental management) processes

natural ecosystem a community of natural physical, chemical, and biological components that interact through complex processes, dominated by natural processes rather than human activity

nature-based solutions application of sustainable management and natural processes to tackle socio-environmental challenges such as climate change

neural network model a computer model that attempts to replicate the behaviour of neurons in the brain by creating artificial neural networks that describe links between different types of data in order to address particular complex problems

non-linear/non-linearities a situation in which the value of a variable is not directly proportional to a change in another variable. The relationship between the two variables cannot therefore be described by a simple straight line—it is therefore non-linear.

orographic effects the effects of large-scale mountain ranges on the atmosphere

parameterization simplification of the representation of a process in an atmospheric model when the process is of too small a scale or too complex to be described by a simple physical equation

particulate material (airborne particulates) a mixture of solid particles and/or liquid droplets (aerosols) that are suspended in the atmosphere

periodicities the regularly varying characteristics exhibited by some environmental variables (e.g. the daily and seasonal variations in temperature)

permafrost soil or substrate where the temperature is below 0 °C for more than two consecutive years, typically occurring in high latitudes of the Northern Hemisphere

phenology study of the evolution of the different growth phases (e.g. from budburst to flowering and maturity) that define the biological cycle of living things (plants and animals)

phenotypic plasticity the ability of different species to change their form in order to adapt to different environmental conditions

photochemical smog air pollution created by the effect of light on chemical reactions in the atmosphere

photoperiodic a variation in physiological response in natural organisms in response to the daily cycle of illumination by solar radiation

photosynthesis the process by which green plants and other organisms use sunlight to synthesize nutrients from carbon dioxide and water

photovoltaic converting light into electricity using semiconductor materials

precipitation products created by the condensation of water vapour into liquid or solid form in the atmosphere, such as rain, ice particles, snow, hail, sleet, and graupel

predictand the predicted value of some variable

primary biological industry an industry involved with the conversion of raw materials of biological origin into consumer products (e.g. agriculture, fishing, and forestry)

primary pollutants pollutants in unmodified form that are directly emitted from a source

proxy data physical characteristics indicative of past environments that are used in place of instrumental measurements in order to study changes in past climates

quantile break points in a frequency distribution that divide it into equal parts (e.g. quartiles divide distributions into four equal parts while percentiles divide them into 100 parts)

quantile mapping a technique used to correct for bias in model predictions based on the quantiles of the frequency distribution of climate data rather than just the mean and variance

quartile see 'quantile' above

regional and local scales regional scale can be defined as an overall spatial dimension of around 1,000 by 1,000 km with a resolution down to about 10 km, while local scale refers to those smaller than around 100 by 100 km with a resolution down to about 50 m

regional climate model (RCM) a model that covers a limited area of the globe using a much finer spatial resolution than a global climate model (i.e. using a grid spacing of 1 to 30 km as opposed to 100 km or more)

relative humidity a measure of the water vapour content of the atmosphere expressed in terms of the percentage of the amount required for the air to be saturated

renewable energy sources energy derived from natural sources that are continually being replenished (e.g. wind, hydro, and solar power)

Representative Concentration Pathways (RCPs) future greenhouse gas concentration trajectories adopted by the IPCC that are based on assumptions of the effects of human activity on future emissions. Four main pathways were used in the IPCC fifth assessment to assess the possible impacts of different emissions scenarios on atmospheric composition and future climate. They replaced an earlier set of scenarios established by the Special Report on Emissions Scenarios (see below)

resilience the ability to recover from the impact of negative events respiration a biological process involving the intake of oxygen and output of carbon dioxide during development of living organisms

runoff the movement of water over the surface of the ground associated with precipitation events

satellite thermography the use of satellite imagery to map temperature patterns at the Earth's surface

scattering deviation of beams of light resulting from interaction with atmospheric particles

scenario a scientifically based future climate projection based on assumptions about possible changes in the factors that influence climate change

secondary pollutants pollutants that are created in the environment as a result of chemical reactions that take place between primary pollutants (defined above) and natural gases or materials

sensible heat heat energy that can be felt or sensed, and that can change the temperature of a solid or gas and can therefore be directly measured

Shared Socioeconomic Pathways (SSPs) five different ways in which society might develop over coming decades that are used by the IPCC to assess the range of possible impacts on future climate change (replacing RCPs—defined above). They include: SSP1—Sustainability (Taking the Green Road); SSP2—Middle of the Road; SSP3—Regional Rivalry (A Rocky Road); SSP4—Inequality (A Road Divided); SSP5—Fossil-fueled Development (Taking the Highway)

skewness a measure of the asymmetry of a statistical distribution that causes it to deviate from the symmetrical shape (the bell curve) of a 'normal' distribution

smart agriculture the use of advanced technology to improve the management of food production

solar radiation electromagnetic radiation emitted by the Sun

Special Report on Emissions Scenarios (SRES) trajectories of future greenhouse gas concentrations defined by the IPCC in its 4th Assessment to evaluate the possible impacts of different emission scenarios on atmospheric composition and future climate. Four main scenarios were defined to assess the possible impacts of future climate change: A1 (rapid economic growth), B1 (global environmental sustainability), A2 (regionally oriented economic development), and B2 (local environmental sustainability)

specific humidity a measure of water vapour content of the atmosphere expressed as the mass of water per kilogram of air

spectral intensity curves graphs indicating the strength of radiation emission at different wavelengths across the radiation spectrum

speleotherm/speleothem laminated deposits in limestone caves that are used to provide proxy data (see definition above) about past climate changes (especially temperature variations)

statistical downscaling the application of statistical techniques based on observed relationships between climate and other variables to map global climate model predictions at much higher spatial resolution

statistical model a model based on statistical relationships between variables

stochastic the result of random or chaotic processes (see **deterministic**)

stratosphere a layer in the atmosphere located above the **troposphere** occurring between approximately 10 and 50 km in altitude in mid-latitudes, with its lower boundary varying between about 7 km at the poles and 20 km at the equator

sub-grid-scale processes processes that operate at scales finer than the grid used in an atmospheric (weather/climate) model

sunspots temporary dark areas that appear on the surface of the Sun, typically associated with increases in solar energy output

sustainability the capacity to support or maintain environmental quality indefinitely into the future

taxonomic referring to the naming and classification of organisms into groups within a system

teleconnection links in weather and climate anomalies between widely separated parts of the globe

temperature anomaly a negative or positive deviation of temperature from some base temperature (typically the mean value)

terrestrial radiation electromagnetic radiation emitted from the Earth's surface or overlying atmosphere

thermal conductivity the rate at which heat can move through a material

thermal forcing the addition or transfer of energy resulting from the application of heat

thermal imagery maps of temperature patterns based on the emission of infrared radiation from different surfaces

tipping point the point at which relatively small changes can lead to major shifts in the status of an environmental system

trace gases gases that occur in small concentrations in the atmosphere

tree rings concentric rings that form inside the trunk of a tree, with each ring representing one year's growth

troposphere the lowest layer of the Earth's atmosphere, occurring between the ground surface and the bottom of the stratosphere (defined above), with a depth varying between about 7 and 20 km

urban air quality an indicator of how clean the air is within an urban area

urban heat island (UHI) an urban area that is significantly warmer than the surrounding rural land as a result of its artificial surface characteristics

variable resolution global climate model (VRGCM) a global climate model whose grid can be modified to improve spatial resolution over a specific study region

vector-borne diseases infections carried by biting insects, such as mosquitoes, ticks, and fleas (vectors)

vernalization the cooling of a plant seed during winter required to stimulate flowering later in the growing season

vulnerability the degree of exposure to harm from specific events or environmental conditions

water vapour the water contained in the atmosphere in gaseous form

weather the instantaneous state of the atmosphere at a given place and/or time (i.e. relating to the occurrence of sunshine, cloud, temperature, rainfall, snow, wind, etc.)

weather forecasting model a numerical model that simulates atmospheric processes in order to predict the weather

Weather Research and Forecasting (WRF) model a community-based atmospheric numerical model used to simulate meteorological processes and phenomena at the regional to local scale (i.e. at spatial grid resolutions of less than about 10 km)

weather typing a process used to classify, in generalized form, the dominant weather patterns experienced over a given area

'whole-of-ecosystem' management plan an approach to environmental management involving the integration of a wide range of ecosystem and human processes

Index

Tables and figures are indicated by an italic *t* and *f* following the page number